V.B. Rose

Volume 1

Banri Hidaka

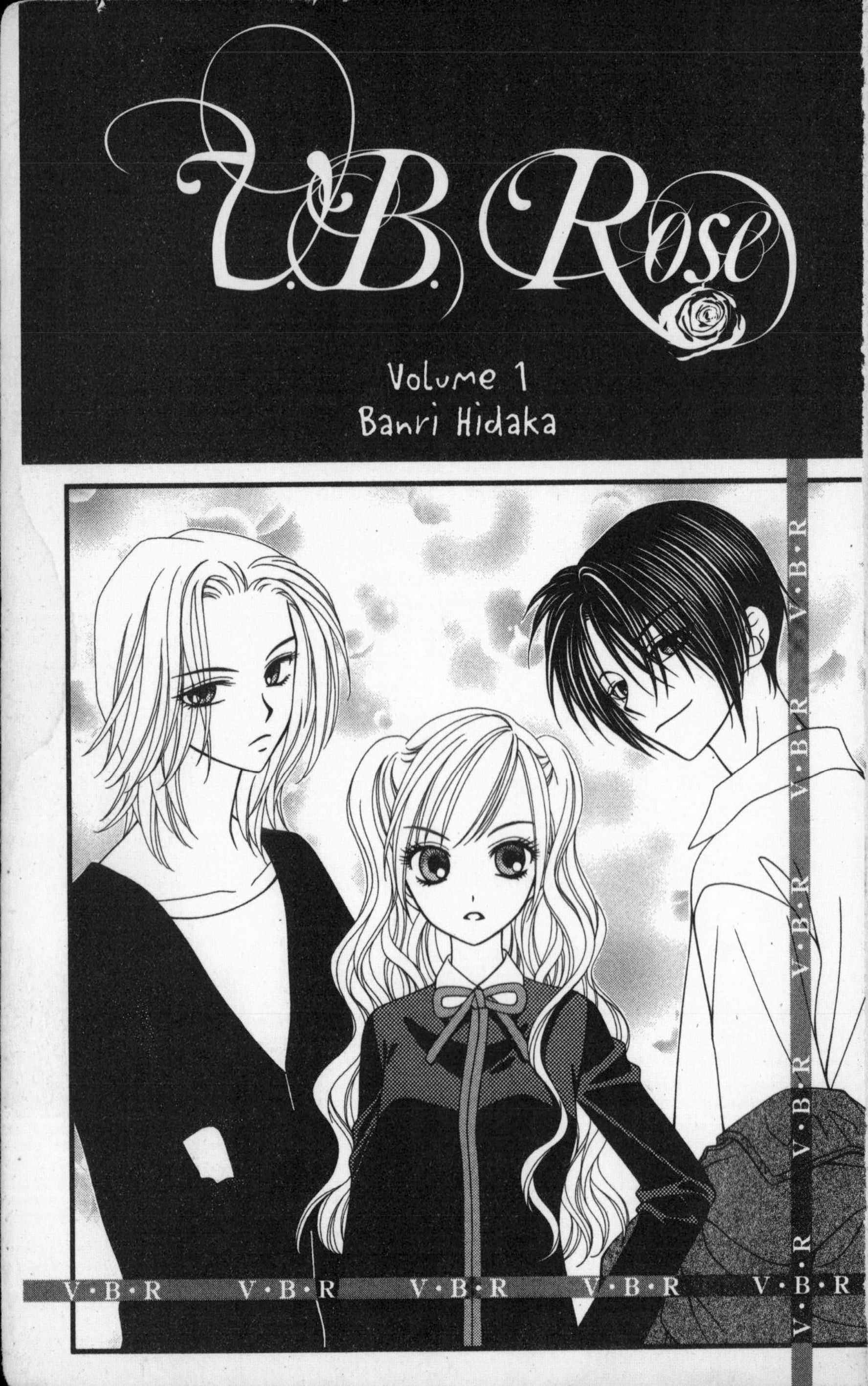

V.B. Rose Volume 1
Created by Banri Hidaka

Translation - Yuya Otake
English Adaptation - Rachel Brown
Associate Editor - Stephanie Duchin
Retouch and Lettering - Star Print Brokers
Production Artist - Michael Paolilli
Graphic Designer - James Lee

Editor - Lillian Diaz-Przybyl
Digital Imaging Manager - Chris Buford
Pre-Production Supervisor - Erika Terriquez
Production Manager - Elisabeth Brizzi
Managing Editor - Vy Nguyen
Creative Director - Anne Marie Horne
Editor-in-Chief - Rob Tokar
Publisher - Mike Kiley
President and C.O.O. - John Parker
C.E.O. and Chief Creative Officer - Stuart Levy

A 🐾 TOKYOPOP Manga

TOKYOPOP and 🐾 are trademarks or registered trademarks of TOKYOPOP Inc.

TOKYOPOP Inc.
5900 Wilshire Blvd. Suite 2000
Los Angeles, CA 90036

E-mail: info@TOKYOPOP.com
Come visit us online at www.TOKYOPOP.com

V. B. ROSE by Banri Hidaka © 2004 Banri Hidaka
All rights reserved. First published in Japan in 2004 by
HAKUSENSHA, INC., Tokyo English language translation
rights in the United States of America and Canada arranged
with HAKUSENSHA, INC., Tokyo through Tuttle-Mori Agency
Inc., Tokyo
English text copyright © 2008 TOKYOPOP Inc.

All rights reserved. No portion of this book may be
reproduced or transmitted in any form or by any means
without written permission from the copyright holders.
This manga is a work of fiction. Any resemblance to
actual events or locales or persons, living or dead, is
entirely coincidental.

ISBN: 978-1-4278-0330-6

First TOKYOPOP printing: January 2008
10 9 8 7 6 5 4 3 2 1
Printed in the USA

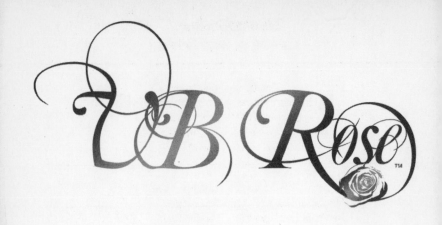

Volume 1

By Banri Hidaka

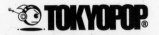

HAMBURG // LONDON // LOS ANGELES // TOKYO

Contents

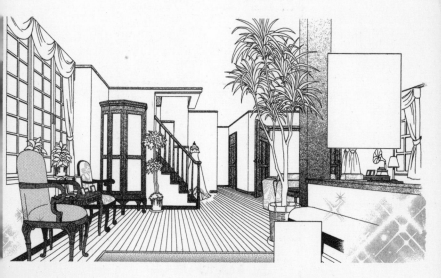

Instructions to velvet V. ①

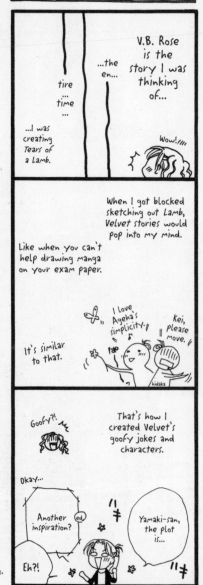

V.B. Rose is the story I was thinking of...
...the en...
tire ... time ...
...I was creating Tears of a Lamb.
Wow!
When I got blocked sketching out Lamb, Velvet stories would pop into my mind.
Like when you can't help drawing manga on your exam paper.
Kei, please move.
I love Ageha's simplicity.
It's similar to that.
hidaka
Is this an escape?
That's how I created Velvet's goofy jokes and characters.
Goofy?!
Yamaki-san, the plot is...
Another inspiration? (ed.)
Okay...
Eh?!
I guess this is an escape.

*Yamaki is the editor.

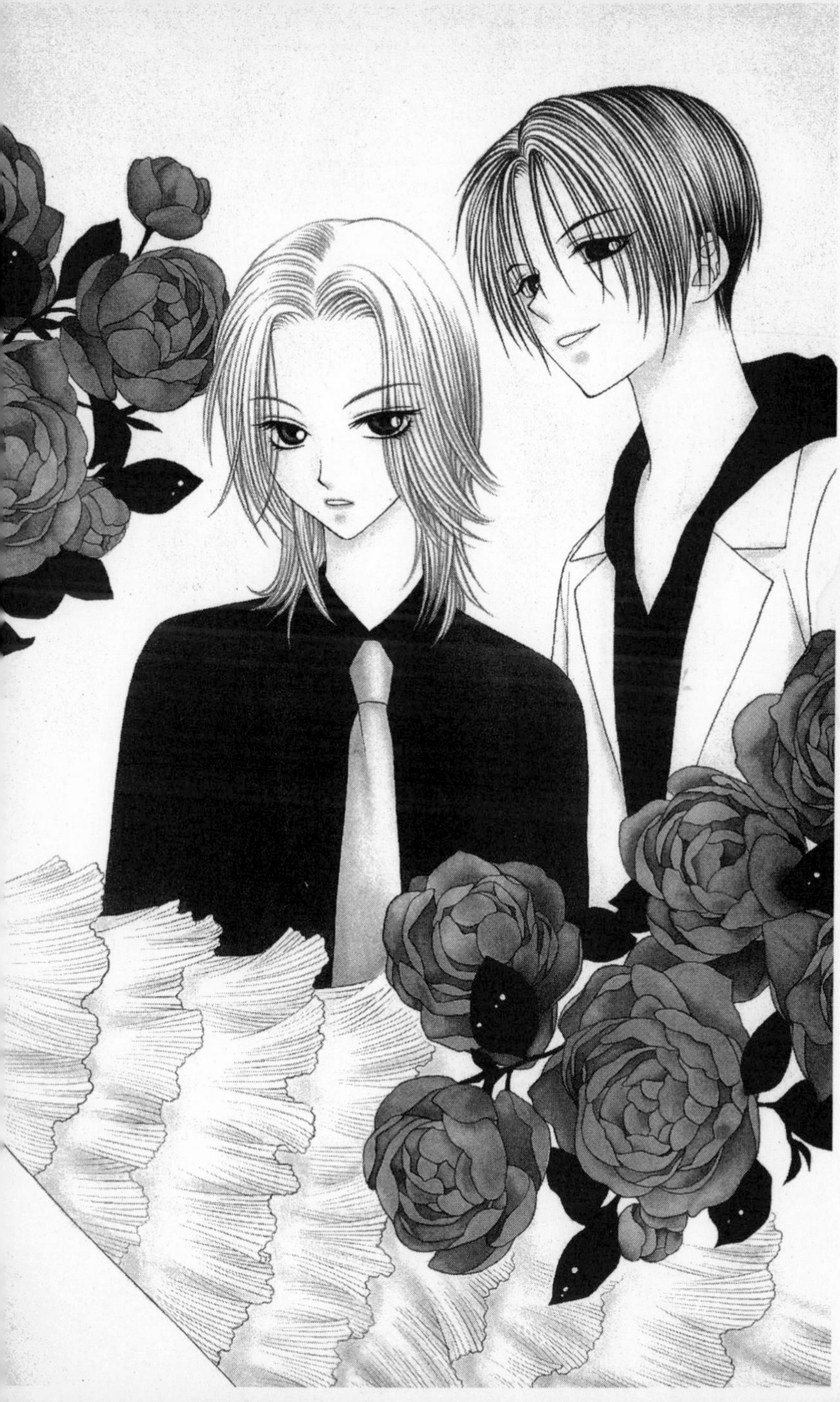

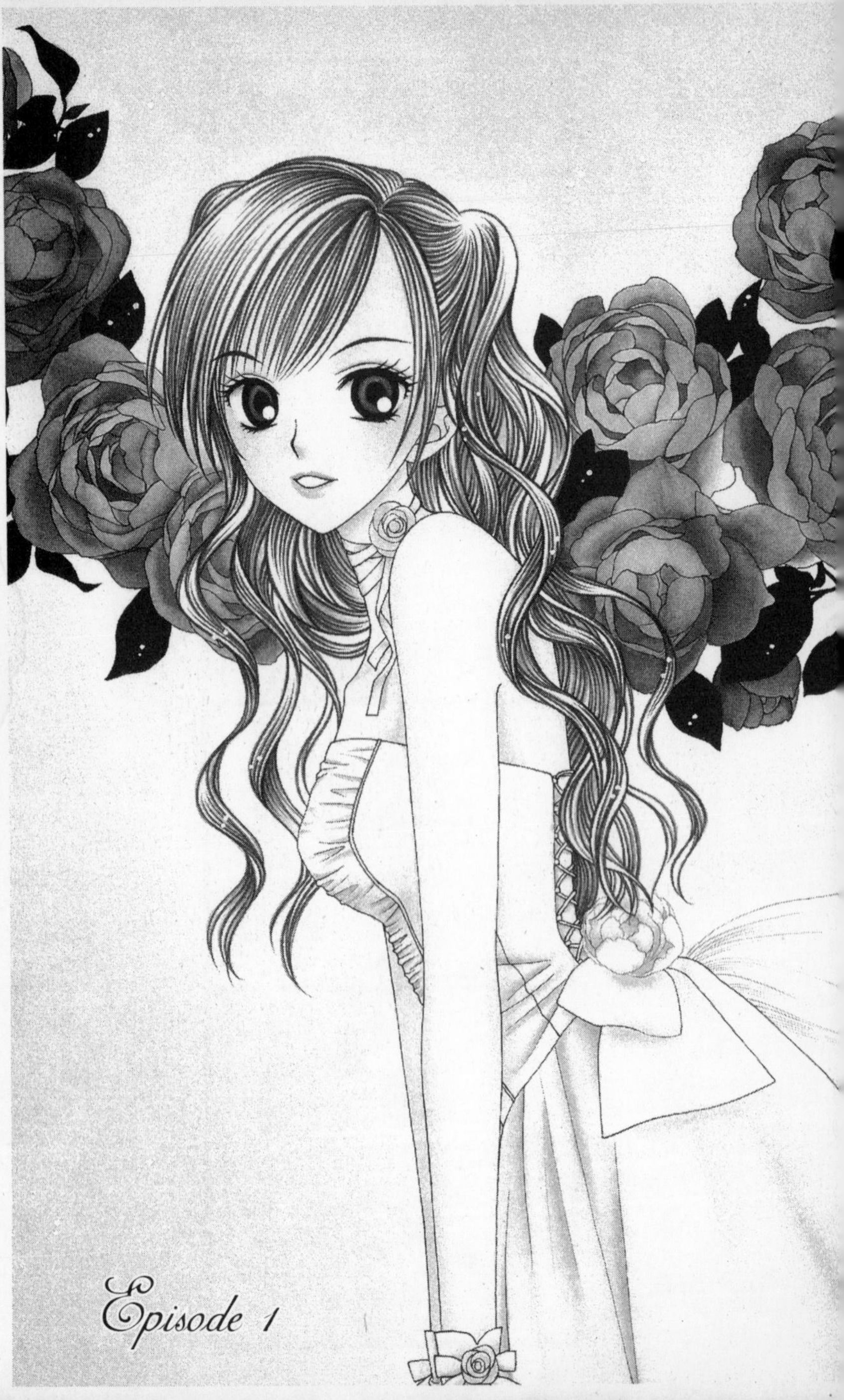
Episode 1

Instructions to velvet V. ②

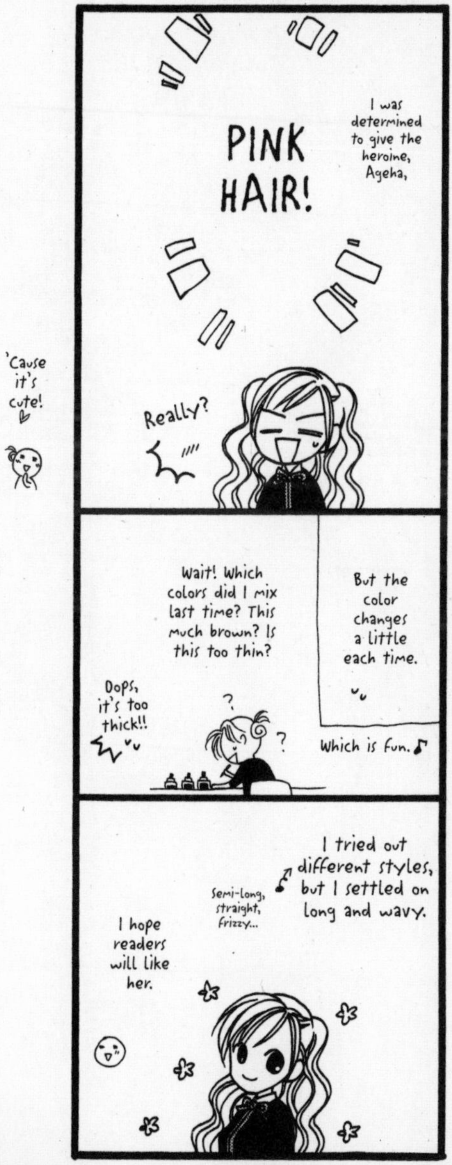
I was determined to give the heroine, Ageha,
PINK HAIR!
Really?
'Cause it's cute! ♥
But the color changes a little each time.
Which is fun. ♪
Wait! Which colors did I mix last time? This much brown? Is this too thin?
Oops, it's too thick!!
I tried out different styles, but I settled on long and wavy.
Semi-long, straight, frizzy...
I hope readers will like her.

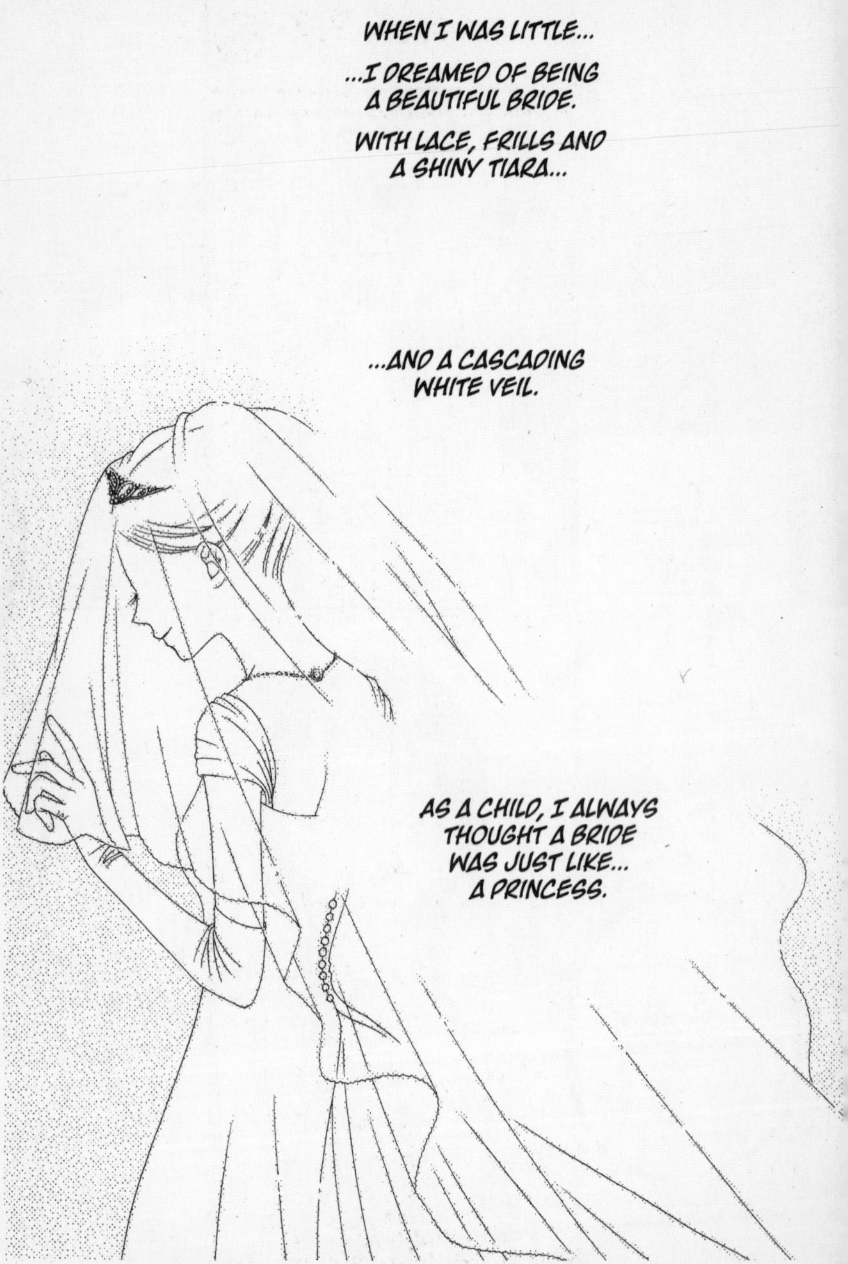
WHEN I WAS LITTLE...
...I DREAMED OF BEING A BEAUTIFUL BRIDE.
WITH LACE, FRILLS AND A SHINY TIARA...
...AND A CASCADING WHITE VEIL.
AS A CHILD, I ALWAYS THOUGHT A BRIDE WAS JUST LIKE... A PRINCESS.

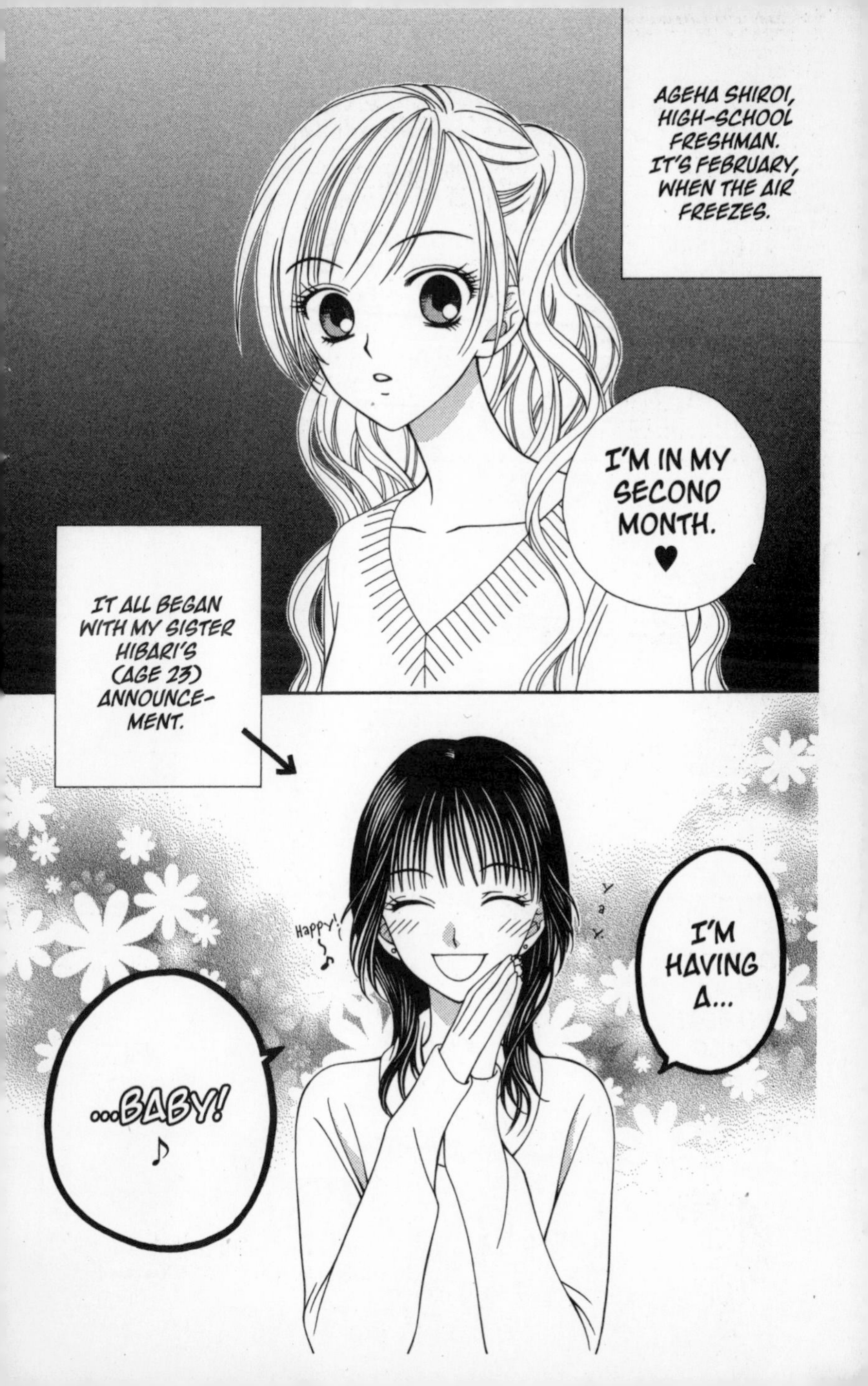
AGEHA SHIROI, HIGH-SCHOOL FRESHMAN. IT'S FEBRUARY, WHEN THE AIR FREEZES.
I'M IN MY SECOND MONTH. ♥
IT ALL BEGAN WITH MY SISTER HIBARI'S (AGE 23) ANNOUNCE-MENT.
I'M HAVING A...
yay
Happy!
...BABY! ♪

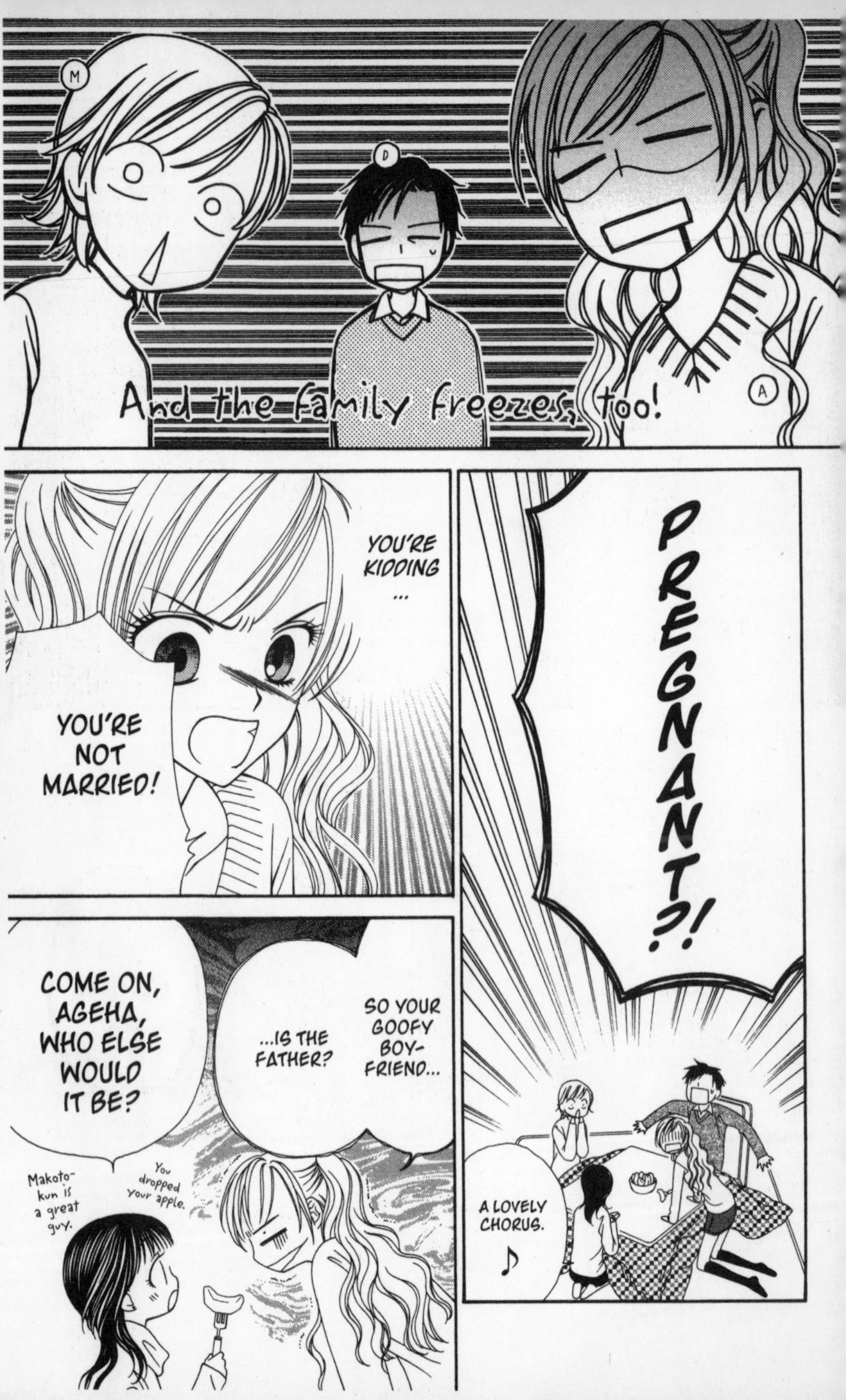
M
D
A
And the family freezes, too!
PREGNANT?!
A LOVELY CHORUS. ♪
YOU'RE KIDDING ...
YOU'RE NOT MARRIED!
SO YOUR GOOFY BOY-FRIEND...
...IS THE FATHER?
COME ON, AGEHA, WHO ELSE WOULD IT BE?
You dropped your apple.
Makoto-kun is a great guy.

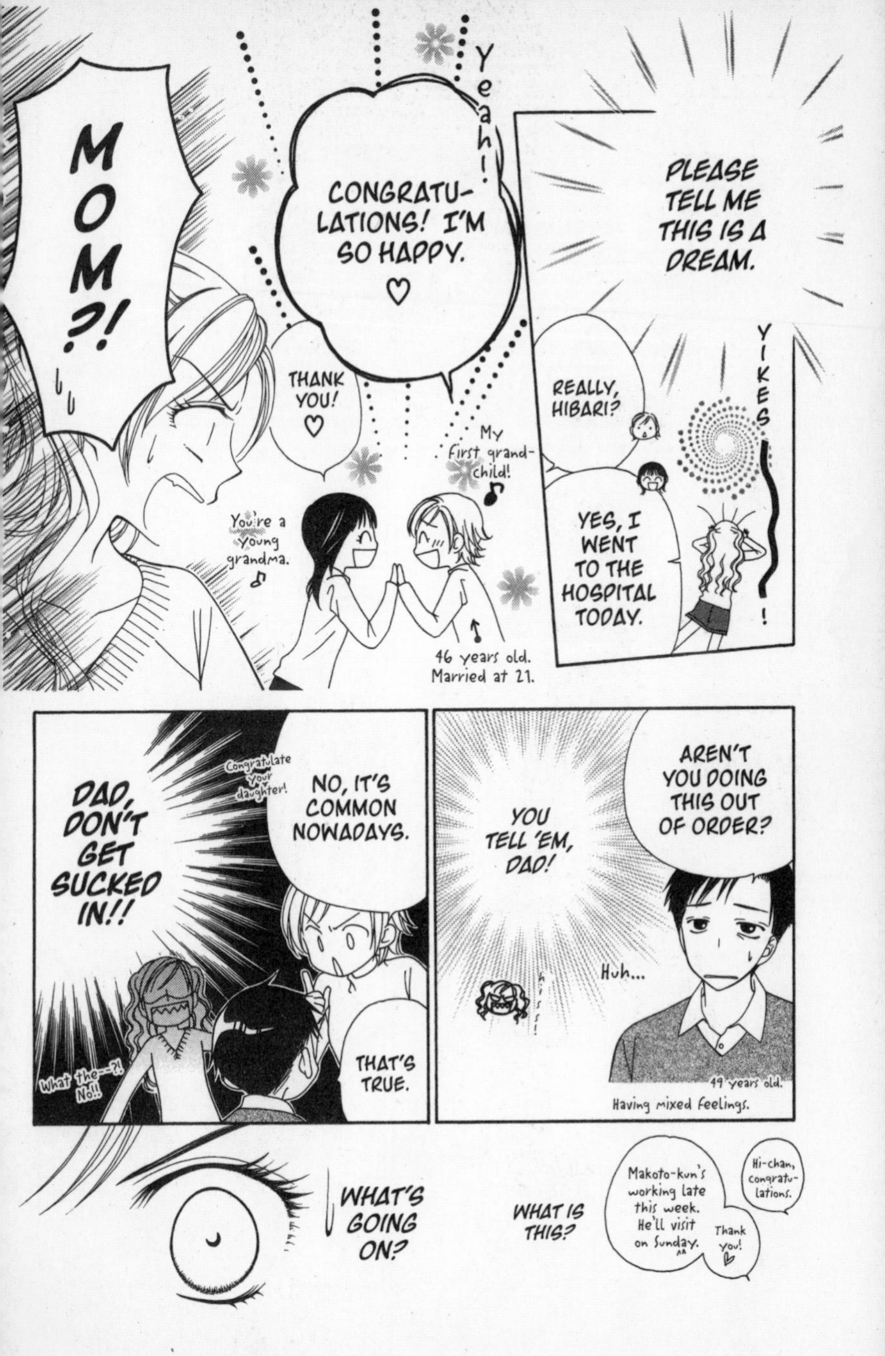
PLEASE TELL ME THIS IS A DREAM.
YIKES!
REALLY, HIBARI?
YES, I WENT TO THE HOSPITAL TODAY.
Yeah!
CONGRATULATIONS! I'M SO HAPPY. ♡
My first grandchild! ♪
THANK YOU! ♡
46 years old. Married at 21.
You're a young grandma. ♪
MOM?!
AREN'T YOU DOING THIS OUT OF ORDER?
YOU TELL 'EM, DAD!
hiss!
Huh...
49 years old. Having mixed feelings.
NO, IT'S COMMON NOWADAYS.
Congratulate your daughter!
DAD, DON'T GET SUCKED IN!!
THAT'S TRUE.
What the--?! No!!
Hi-chan, congratulations.
Makoto-kun's working late this week. He'll visit on Sunday. ^^
Thank you! ♡
WHAT IS THIS?
WHAT'S GOING ON?

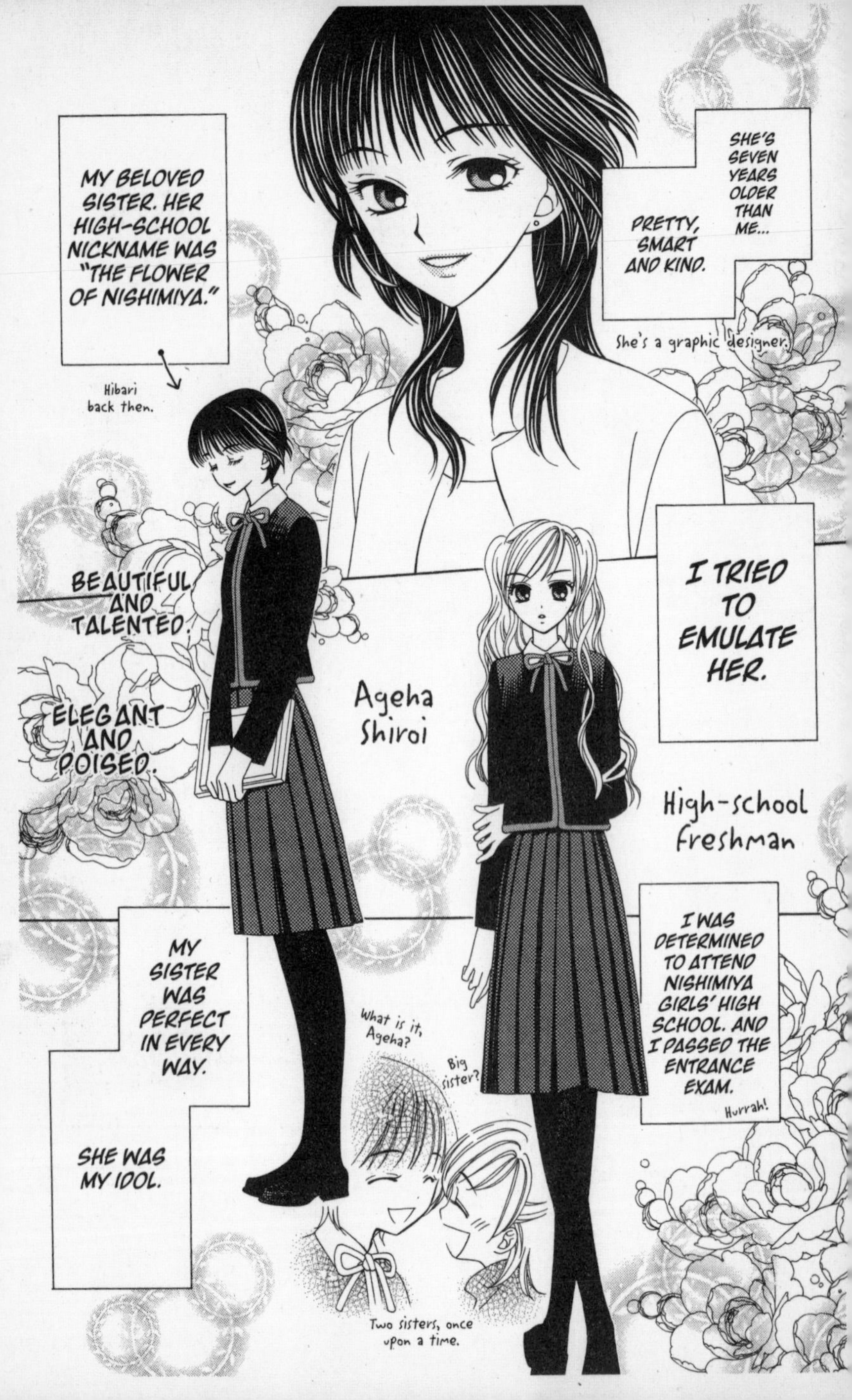
SHE'S SEVEN YEARS OLDER THAN ME...
PRETTY, SMART AND KIND.
She's a graphic designer.
MY BELOVED SISTER. HER HIGH-SCHOOL NICKNAME WAS "THE FLOWER OF NISHIMIYA."
Hibari back then.
I TRIED TO EMULATE HER.
High-school Freshman
Ageha Shiroi
BEAUTIFUL AND TALENTED.
ELEGANT AND POISED.
I WAS DETERMINED TO ATTEND NISHIMIYA GIRLS' HIGH SCHOOL. AND I PASSED THE ENTRANCE EXAM.
Hurrah!
Big sister?
What is it, Ageha?
Two sisters, once upon a time.
MY SISTER WAS PERFECT IN EVERY WAY.
SHE WAS MY IDOL.

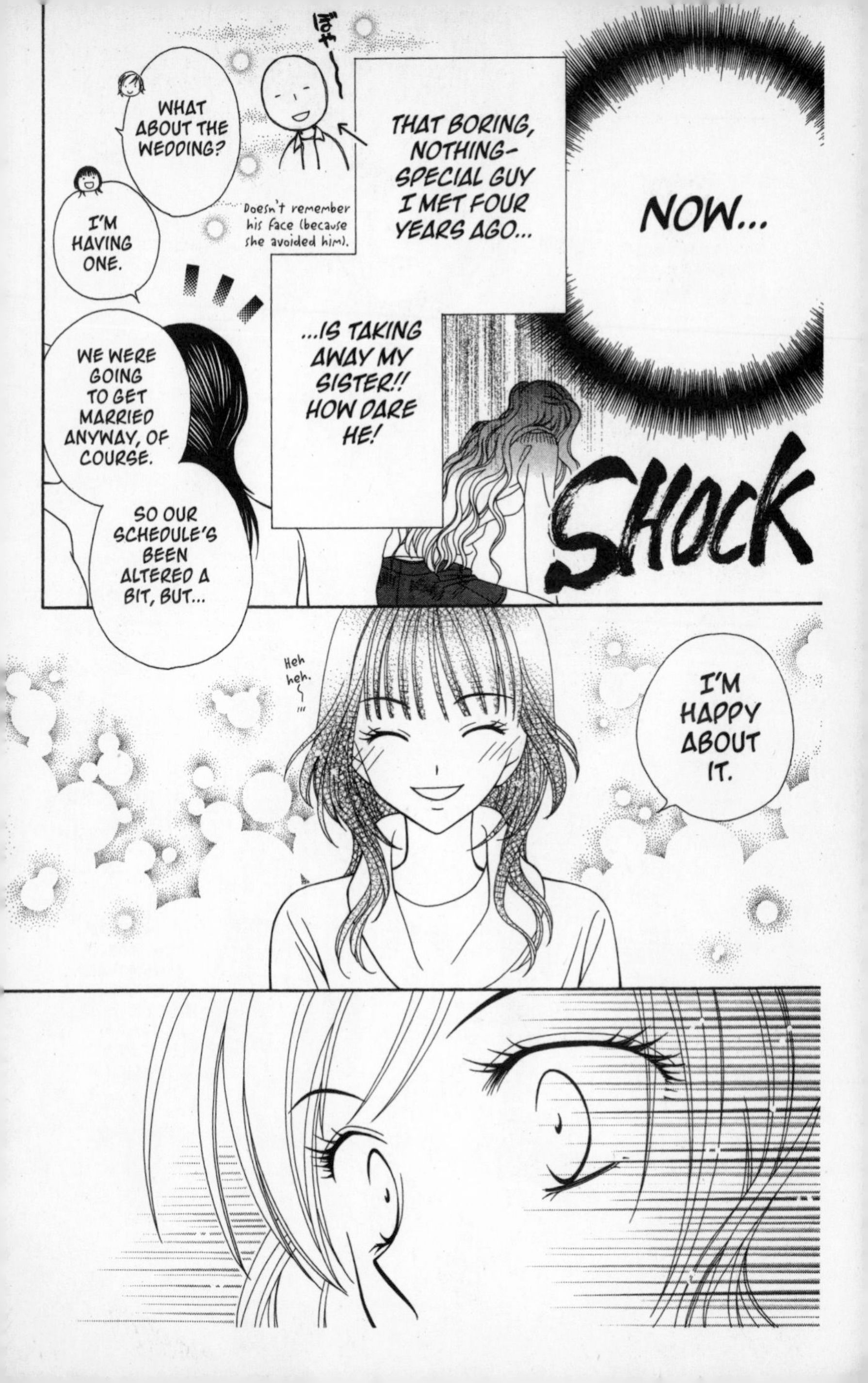
NOW...
THAT BORING, NOTHING-SPECIAL GUY I MET FOUR YEARS AGO...
...IS TAKING AWAY MY SISTER!! HOW DARE HE!
SHOCK
WHAT ABOUT THE WEDDING?
I'M HAVING ONE.
Doesn't remember his face (because she avoided him).
ぼや～
WE WERE GOING TO GET MARRIED ANYWAY, OF COURSE.
SO OUR SCHEDULE'S BEEN ALTERED A BIT, BUT...
I'M HAPPY ABOUT IT.
Heh heh.

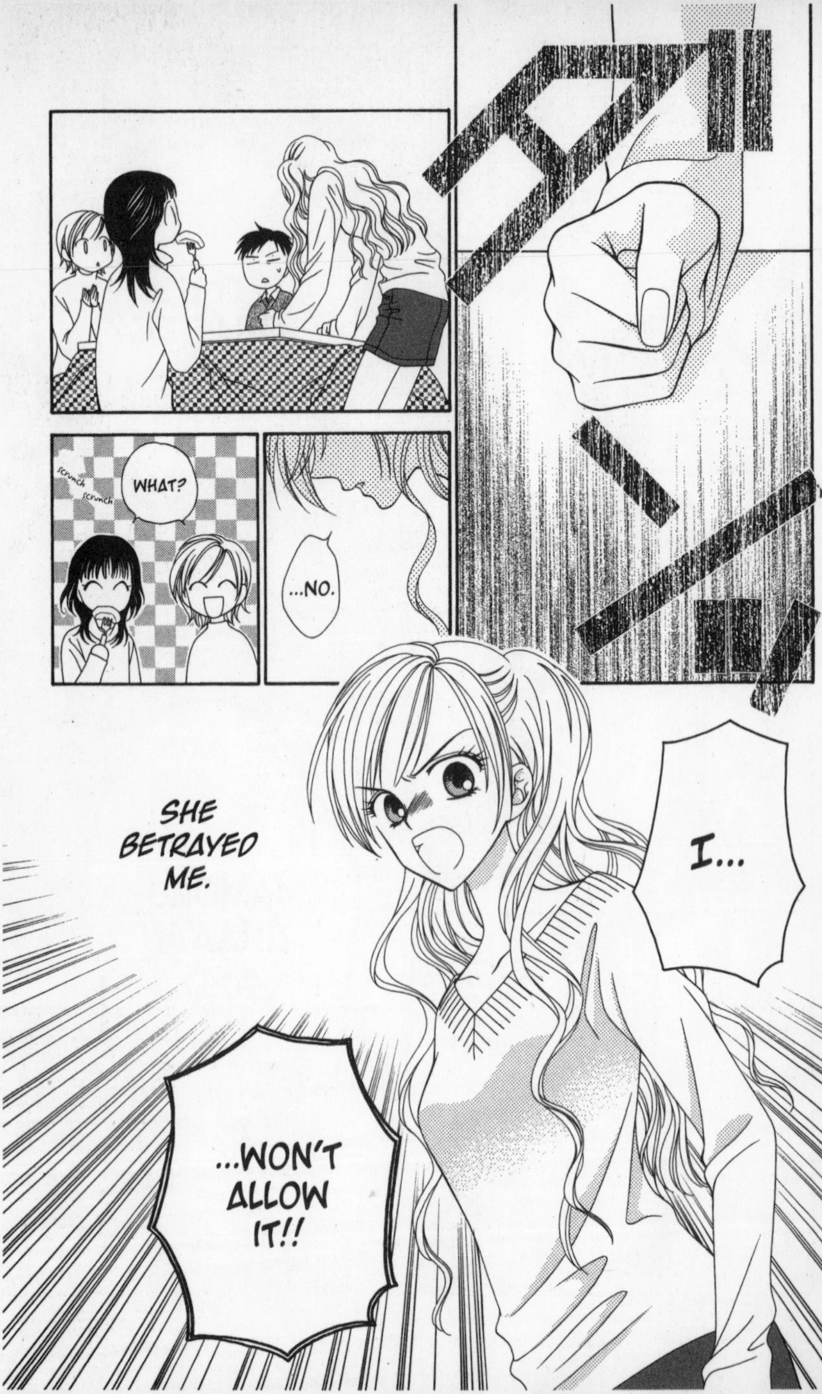
...NO.
WHAT?
scrunch
scrunch
I...
SHE BETRAYED ME.
...WON'T ALLOW IT!!

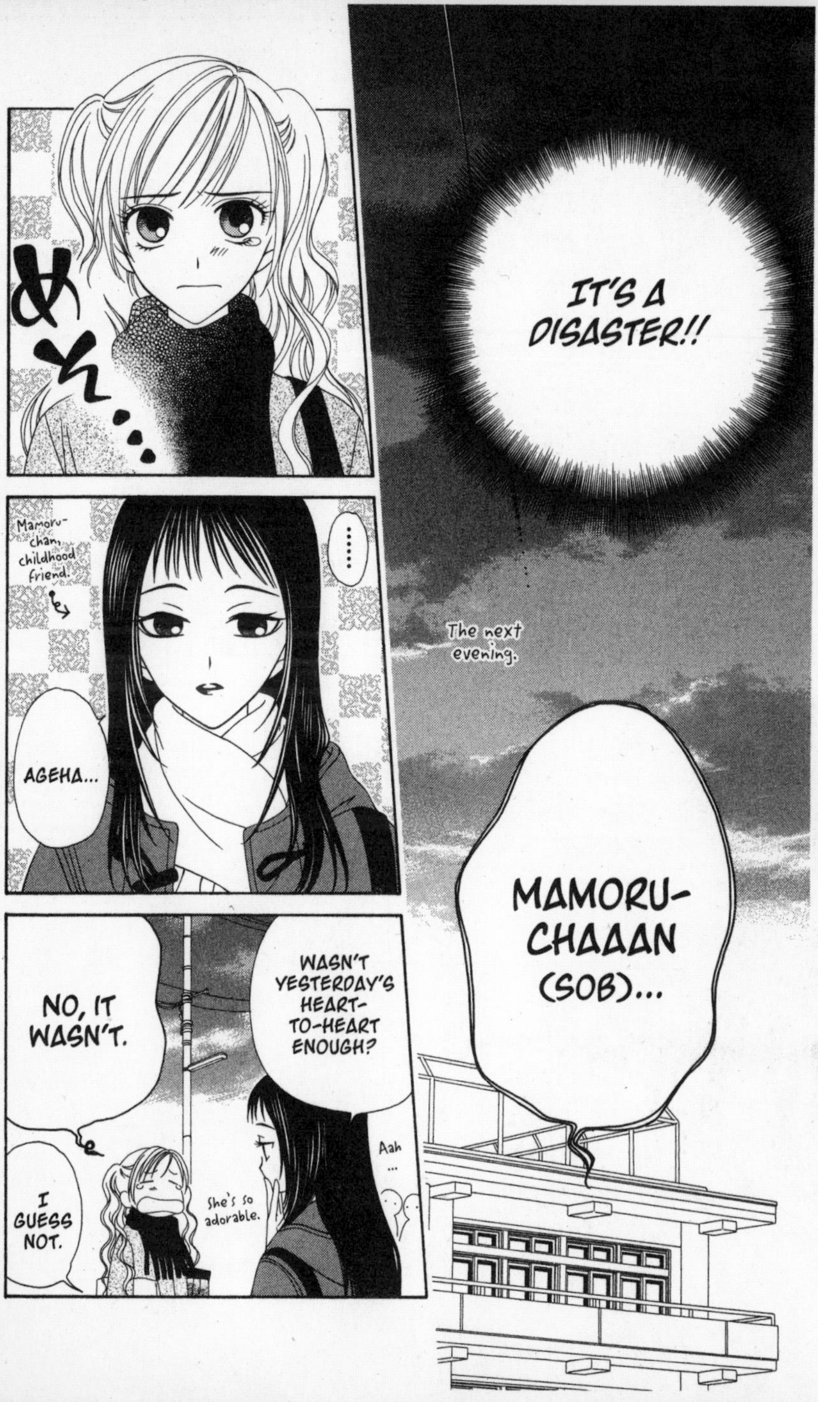
IT'S A DISASTER!!
The next evening.
MAMORU-CHAAAN (SOB)...
めそ...
Mamoru-chan, childhood friend.
......
AGEHA...
WASN'T YESTERDAY'S HEART-TO-HEART ENOUGH?
NO, IT WASN'T.
I GUESS NOT.
Aah...
She's so adorable.

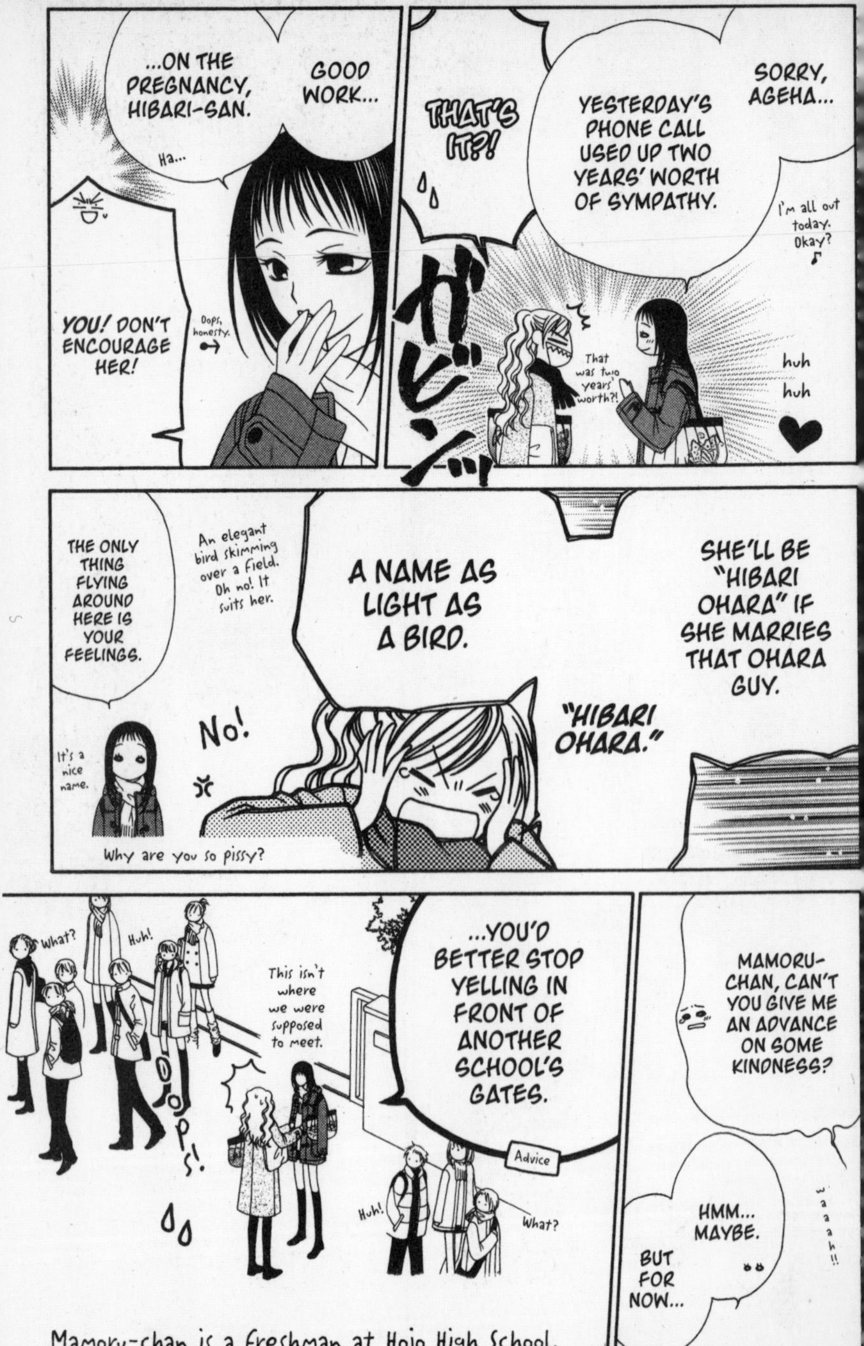
SORRY, AGEHA...
YESTERDAY'S PHONE CALL USED UP TWO YEARS' WORTH OF SYMPATHY.
I'm all out today. Okay? ♪
huh huh
THAT'S IT?!
That was two years' worth?!
GOOD WORK...
...ON THE PREGNANCY, HIBARI-SAN.
Ha...
Oops, honesty.
YOU! DON'T ENCOURAGE HER!
SHE'LL BE "HIBARI OHARA" IF SHE MARRIES THAT OHARA GUY.
A NAME AS LIGHT AS A BIRD.
"HIBARI OHARA."
An elegant bird skimming over a field. Oh no! It suits her.
THE ONLY THING FLYING AROUND HERE IS YOUR FEELINGS.
No!
It's a nice name.
Why are you so pissy?
MAMORU-CHAN, CAN'T YOU GIVE ME AN ADVANCE ON SOME KINDNESS?
HMM... MAYBE.
BUT FOR NOW...
waaah!!
...YOU'D BETTER STOP YELLING IN FRONT OF ANOTHER SCHOOL'S GATES.
Advice
This isn't where we were supposed to meet.
What?
Huh!
OOPS!
Huh!
What?
Mamoru-chan is a freshman at Hojo High School.

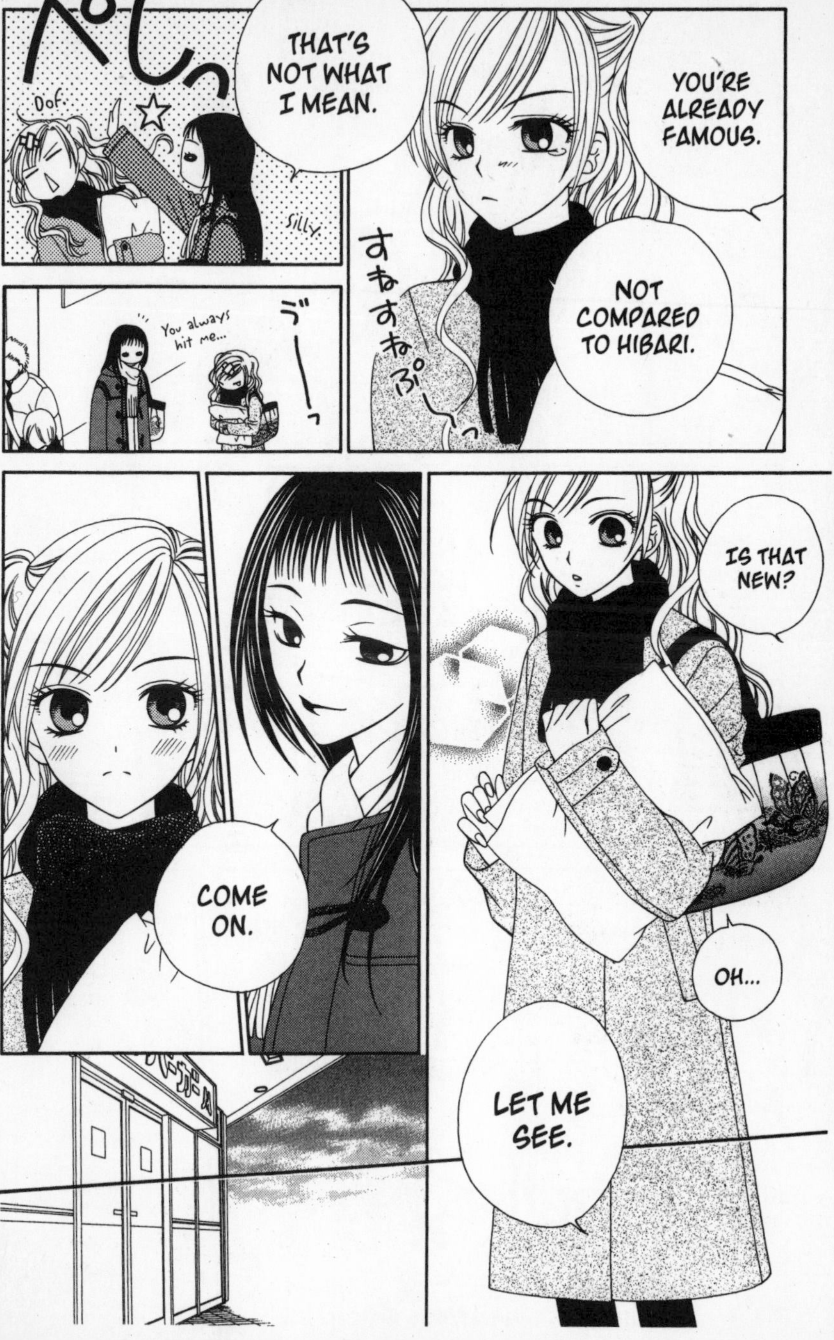
YOU'RE ALREADY FAMOUS.
NOT COMPARED TO HIBARI.
すねすねぷーっ
THAT'S NOT WHAT I MEAN.
ぺしっ
Oof.
Silly.
You always hit me...
IS THAT NEW?
OH...
LET ME SEE.
COME ON.

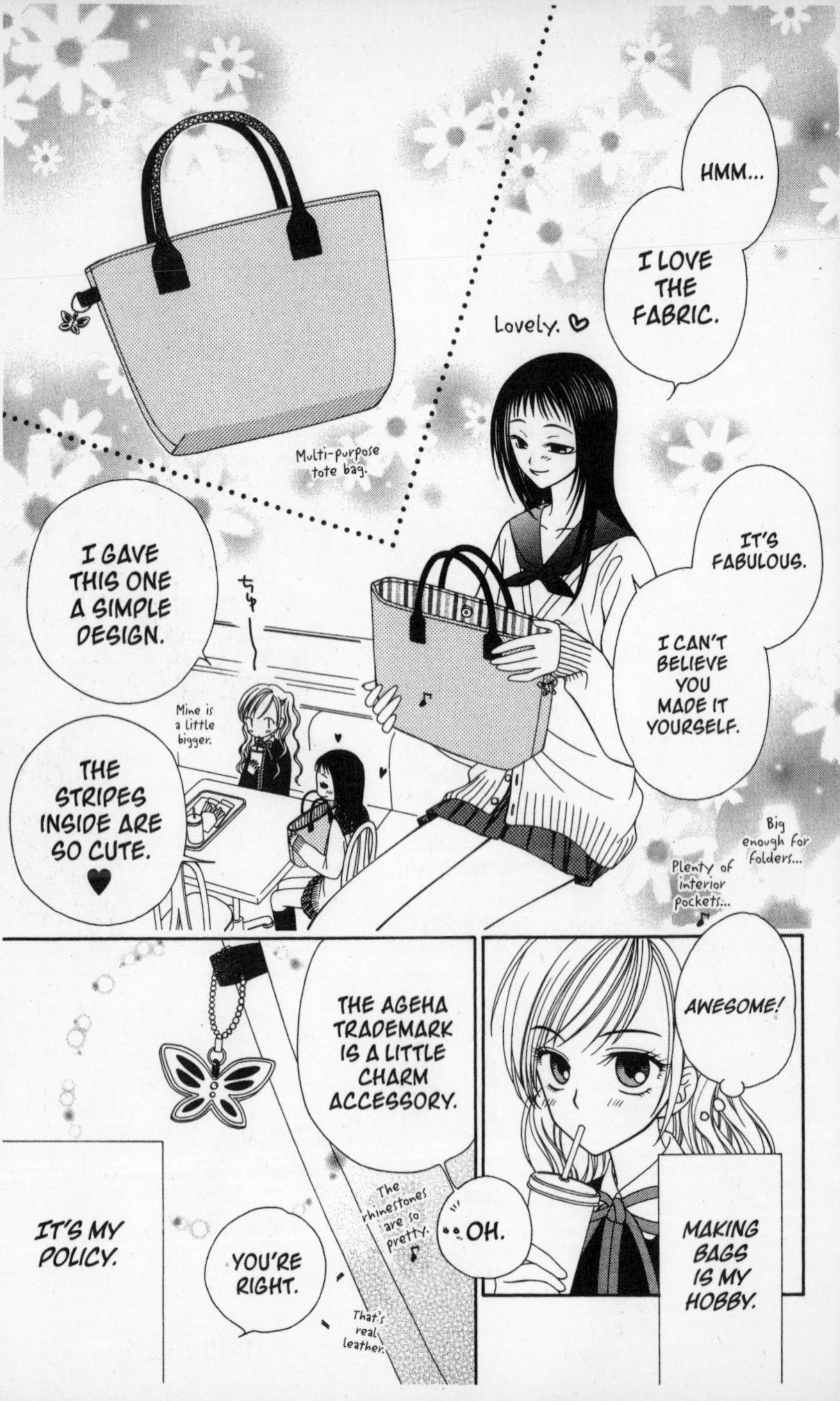
HMM...
I LOVE THE FABRIC.
Lovely.
IT'S FABULOUS.
I CAN'T BELIEVE YOU MADE IT YOURSELF.
Big enough for folders...
Plenty of interior pockets...
Multi-purpose tote bag.
I GAVE THIS ONE A SIMPLE DESIGN.
Mine is a little bigger.
THE STRIPES INSIDE ARE SO CUTE.
AWESOME!
MAKING BAGS IS MY HOBBY.
OH.
THE AGEHA TRADEMARK IS A LITTLE CHARM ACCESSORY.
The rhinestones are so pretty.
YOU'RE RIGHT.
That's real leather.
IT'S MY POLICY.

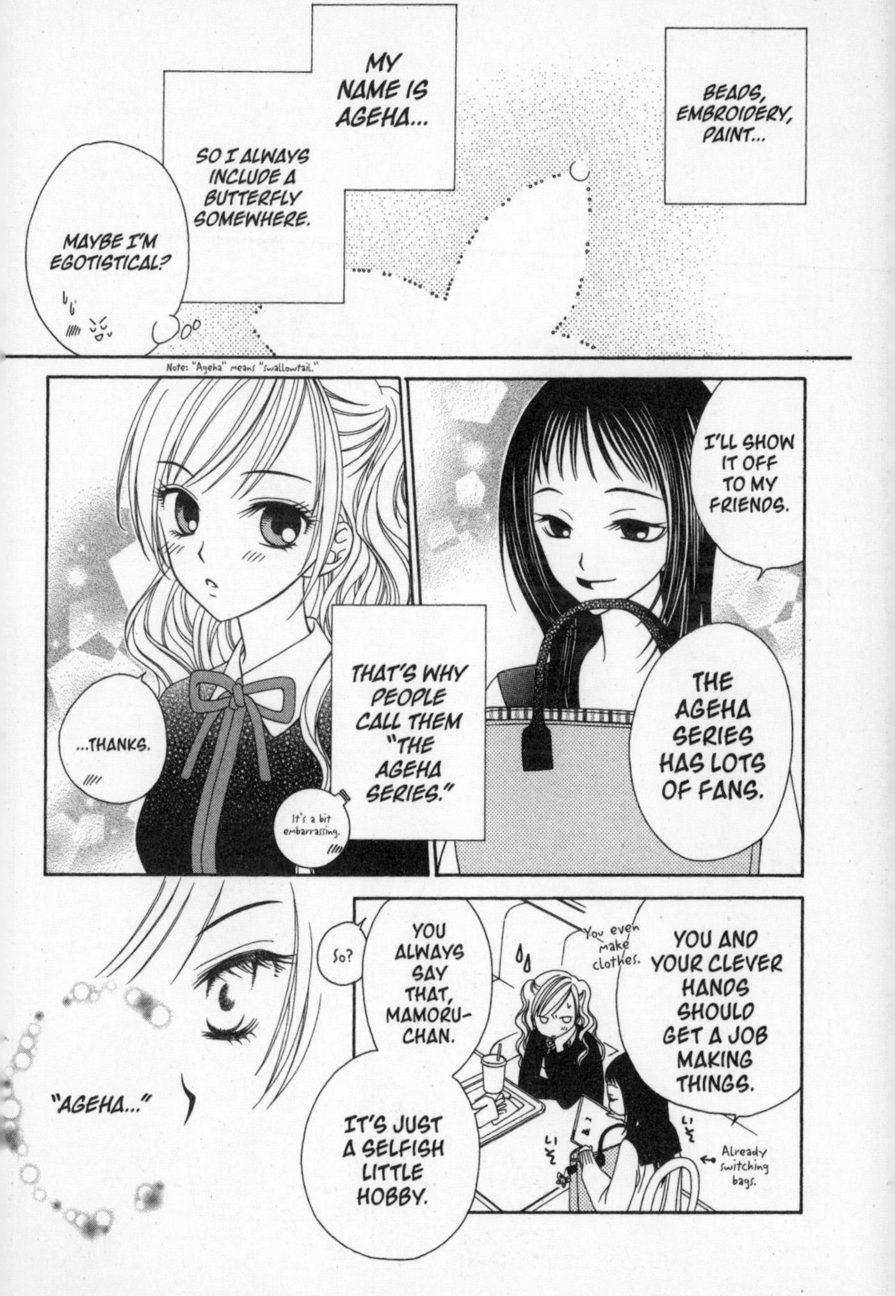
BEADS, EMBROIDERY, PAINT...
MY NAME IS AGEHA...
SO I ALWAYS INCLUDE A BUTTERFLY SOMEWHERE.
MAYBE I'M EGOTISTICAL?
Note: "Ageha" means "swallowtail."
I'LL SHOW IT OFF TO MY FRIENDS.
THE AGEHA SERIES HAS LOTS OF FANS.
THAT'S WHY PEOPLE CALL THEM "THE AGEHA SERIES."
It's a bit embarrassing.
...THANKS.
YOU AND YOUR CLEVER HANDS SHOULD GET A JOB MAKING THINGS.
You even make clothes.
Already switching bags.
YOU ALWAYS SAY THAT, MAMORU-CHAN.
So?
IT'S JUST A SELFISH LITTLE HOBBY.
"AGEHA..."

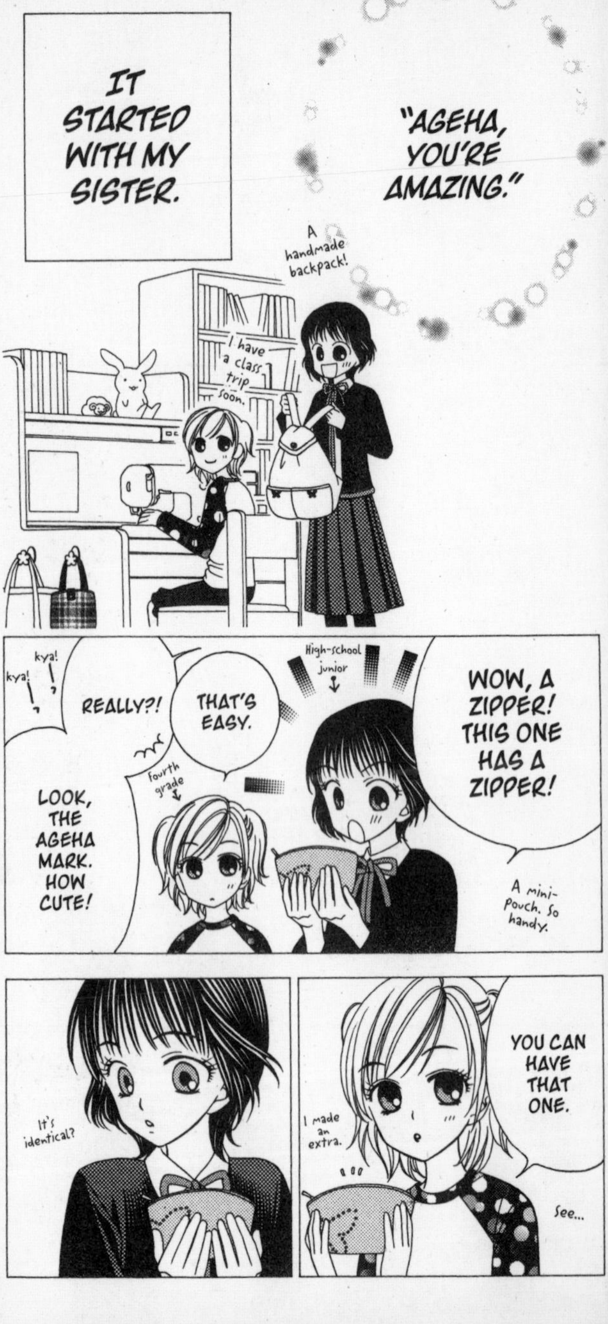
"AGEHA, YOU'RE AMAZING."
IT STARTED WITH MY SISTER.
A handmade backpack!
I have a class trip soon.
WOW, A ZIPPER! THIS ONE HAS A ZIPPER!
A mini-pouch. So handy.
High-school junior
THAT'S EASY.
REALLY?!
kya! kya!
Fourth grade
LOOK, THE AGEHA MARK. HOW CUTE!
YOU CAN HAVE THAT ONE.
I made an extra.
See...
It's identical?

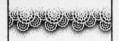

Hello! I'm pleased to meet you all, or to see you again! My name is Banri Hidaka.

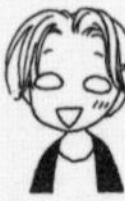
Now-adays I scrunch up my hair...
...and pin it with a clip.

This new series is...what should I say...? Why does my head always spin when I begin a new series? (Sorry, there's no way answer this question right.)

I hope you enjoy my 27th manga, V.B. Rose volume 1.

I throw my away my used pens and blades into an empty can of XYLITOL gum. It has a lid, and it's very useful! But the other day I mistook it for a full can and stuck my hand in to get some gum.

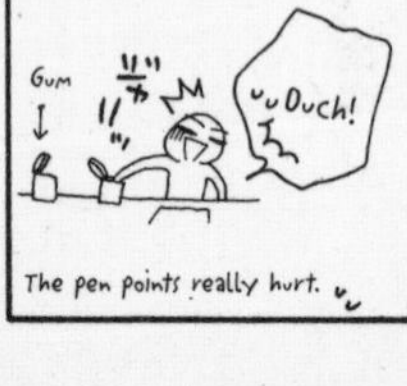
Gum
Ouch!

The pen points really hurt.

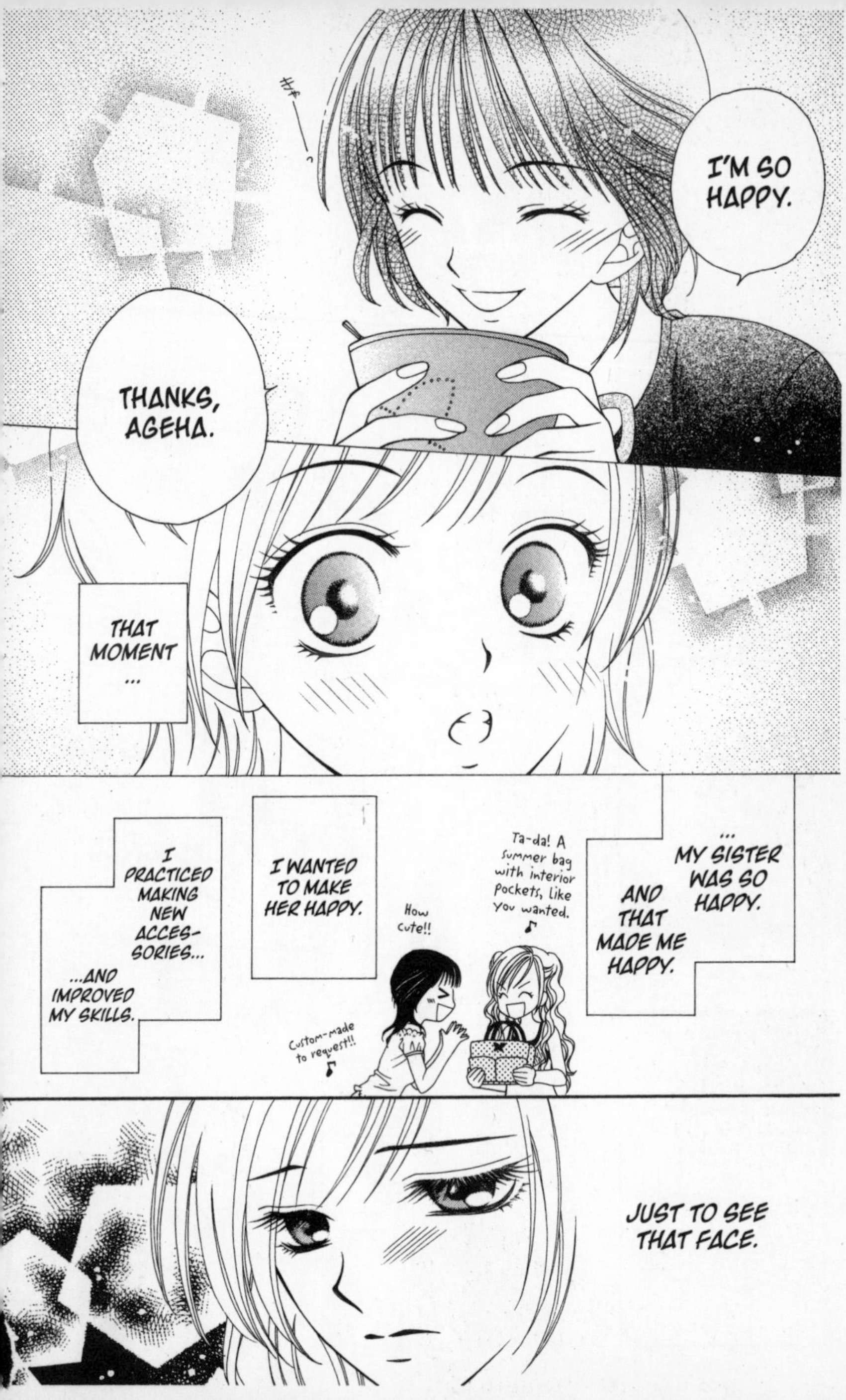
I'M SO HAPPY.
THANKS, AGEHA.
THAT MOMENT...
...MY SISTER WAS SO HAPPY.
AND THAT MADE ME HAPPY.
Ta-da! A summer bag with interior pockets, like you wanted.
How cute!!
Custom-made to request!!
I WANTED TO MAKE HER HAPPY.
I PRACTICED MAKING NEW ACCES-SORIES...
...AND IMPROVED MY SKILLS.
JUST TO SEE THAT FACE.

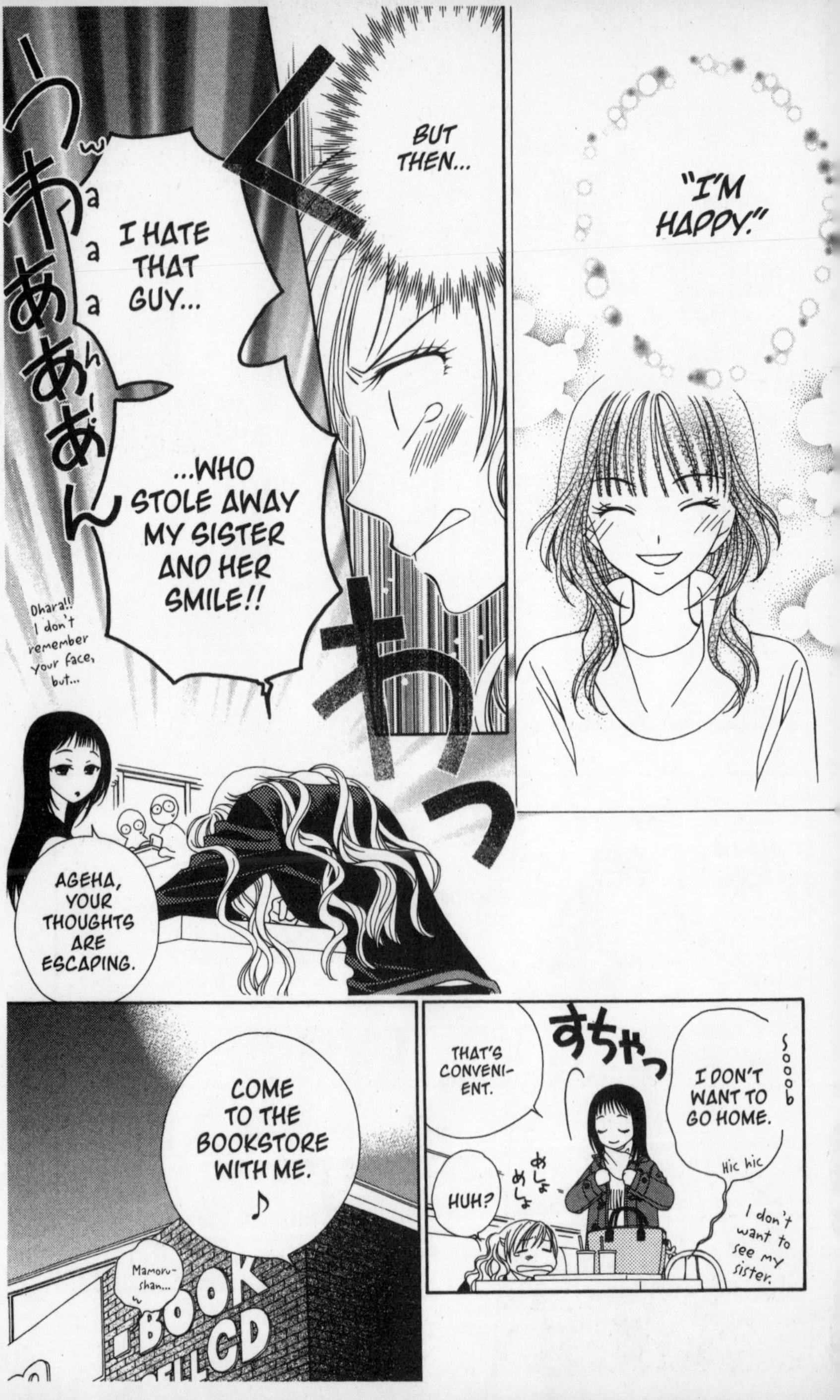
"I'M HAPPY."
BUT THEN...
I HATE THAT GUY...
...WHO STOLE AWAY MY SISTER AND HER SMILE!!
うわぁぁぁぁん
Ohara!! I don't remember your face, but...
わっ
AGEHA, YOUR THOUGHTS ARE ESCAPING.
Sooob
I DON'T WANT TO GO HOME.
Hic hic
I don't want to see my sister.
すちゃっ
THAT'S CONVENI-ENT.
HUH?
めしょめしょ
COME TO THE BOOKSTORE WITH ME. ♪
Mamoru-shan...
BOOK
CD

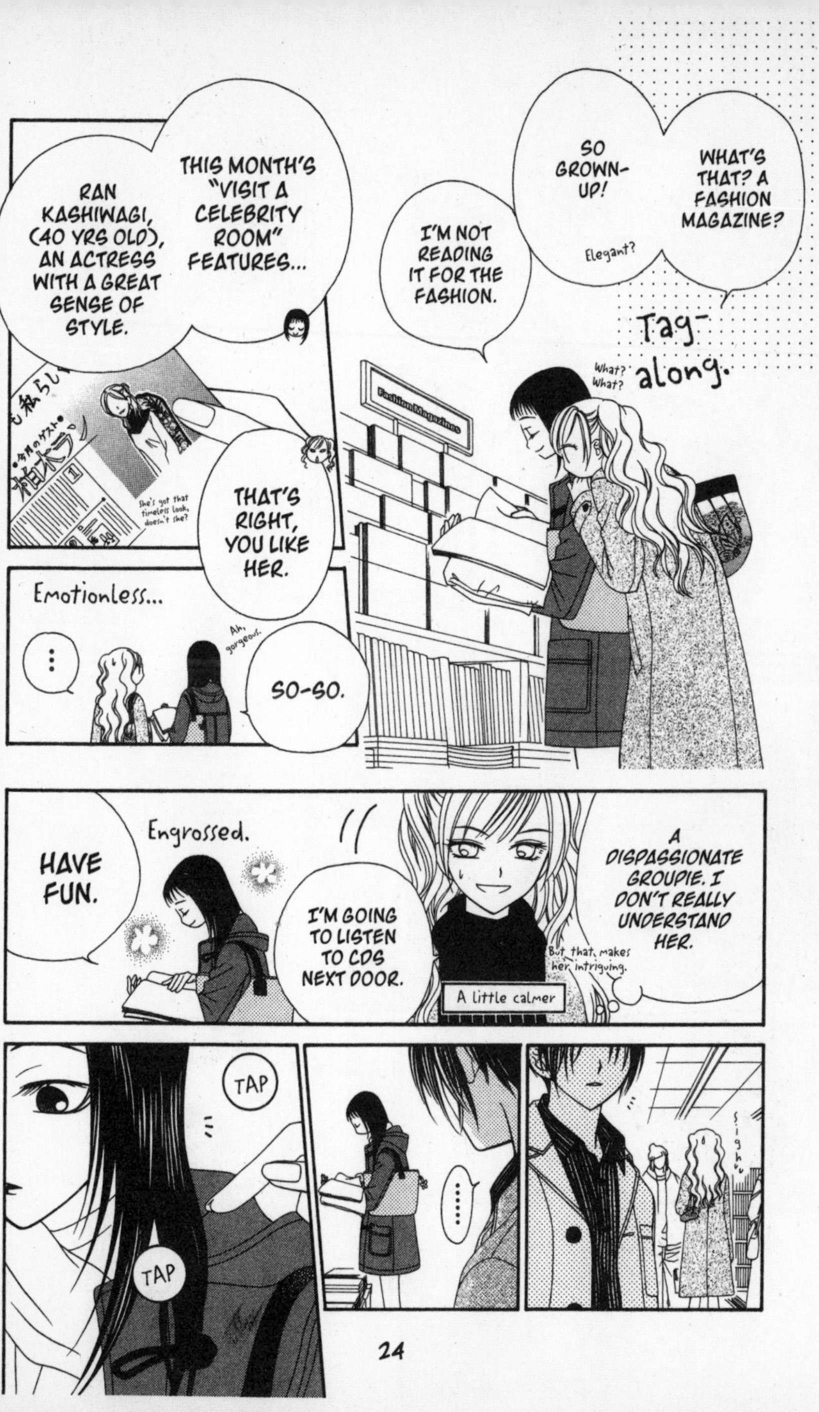
WHAT'S THAT? A FASHION MAGAZINE?
SO GROWN-UP!
Elegant?
I'M NOT READING IT FOR THE FASHION.
Tag-along.
What? What?
Fashion Magazines
THIS MONTH'S "VISIT A CELEBRITY ROOM" FEATURES...
RAN KASHIWAGI, (40 YRS OLD), AN ACTRESS WITH A GREAT SENSE OF STYLE.
She's got that timeless look, doesn't she?
THAT'S RIGHT, YOU LIKE HER.
Emotionless...
Ah, gorgeous.
SO-SO.
A DISPASSIONATE GROUPIE. I DON'T REALLY UNDERSTAND HER.
But that makes her intriguing.
A little calmer
I'M GOING TO LISTEN TO CDS NEXT DOOR.
Engrossed.
HAVE FUN.
sigh
TAP
TAP

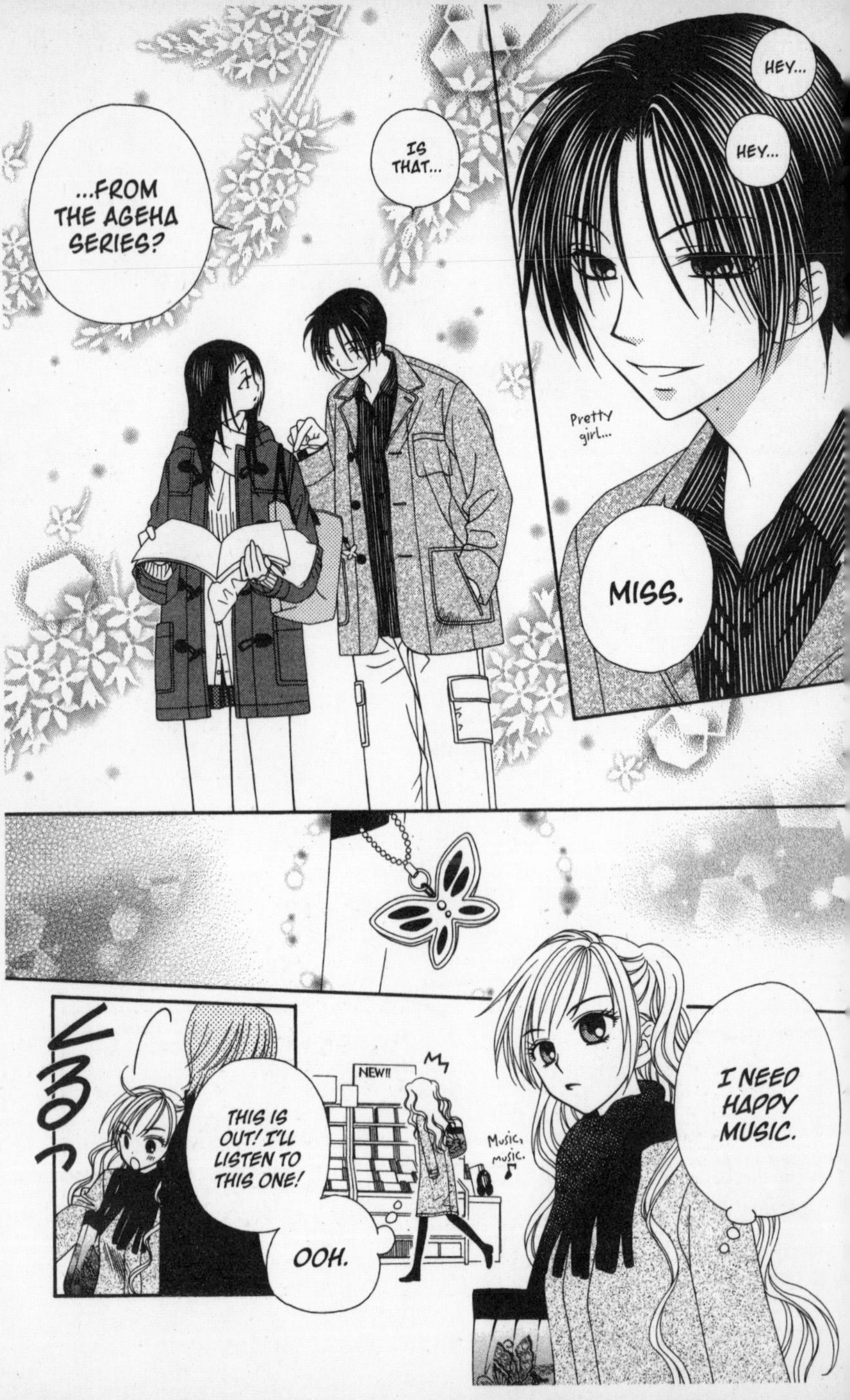
HEY...
HEY...
Pretty girl...
MISS.
IS THAT...
...FROM THE AGEHA SERIES?
I NEED HAPPY MUSIC.
Music, music.
NEW!!
THIS IS OUT! I'LL LISTEN TO THIS ONE!
OOH.
くるっ

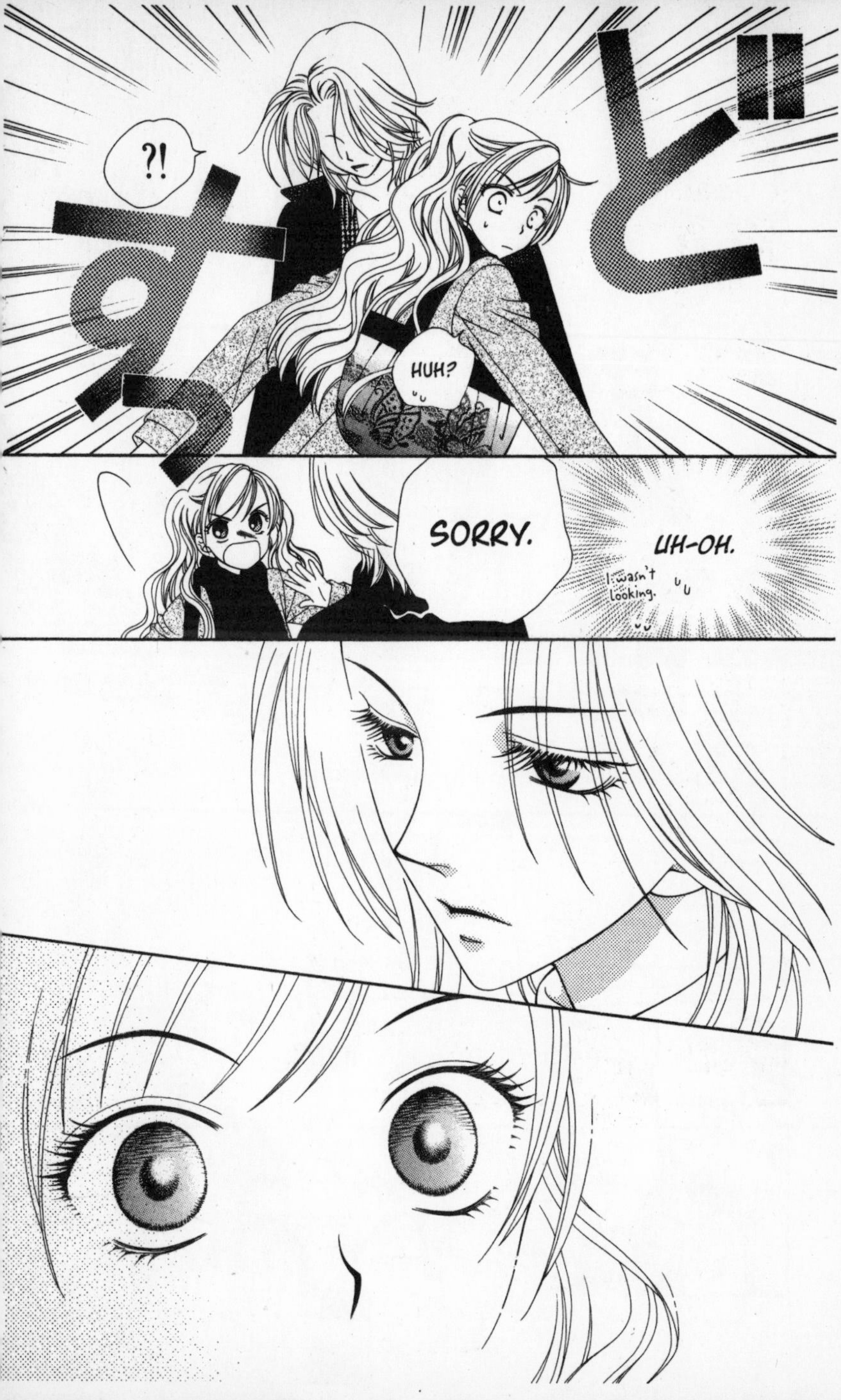
ど
?!
HUH?
すっ
UH-OH.
I wasn't looking.
SORRY.

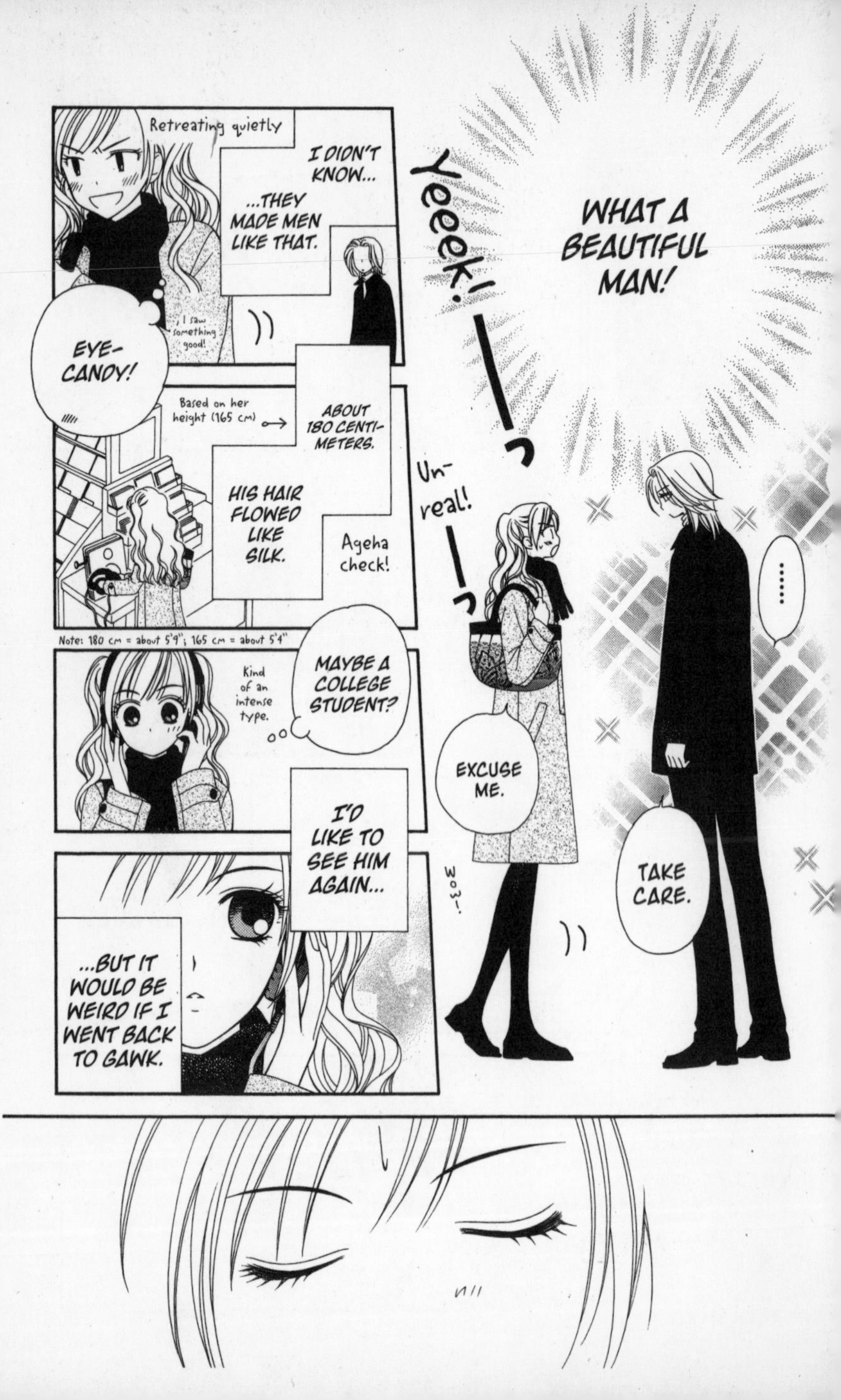
WHAT A BEAUTIFUL MAN!
Yeeek!
......
Un-real!
TAKE CARE.
EXCUSE ME.
wow-!
I DIDN'T KNOW...
Retreating quietly
...THEY MADE MEN LIKE THAT.
EYE-CANDY!
I saw something good!
ABOUT 180 CENTIMETERS.
Based on her height (165 cm)
HIS HAIR FLOWED LIKE SILK.
Ageha check!
Note: 180 cm = about 5'9"; 165 cm = about 5'4"
MAYBE A COLLEGE STUDENT?
Kind of an intense type.
I'D LIKE TO SEE HIM AGAIN...
...BUT IT WOULD BE WEIRD IF I WENT BACK TO GAWK.

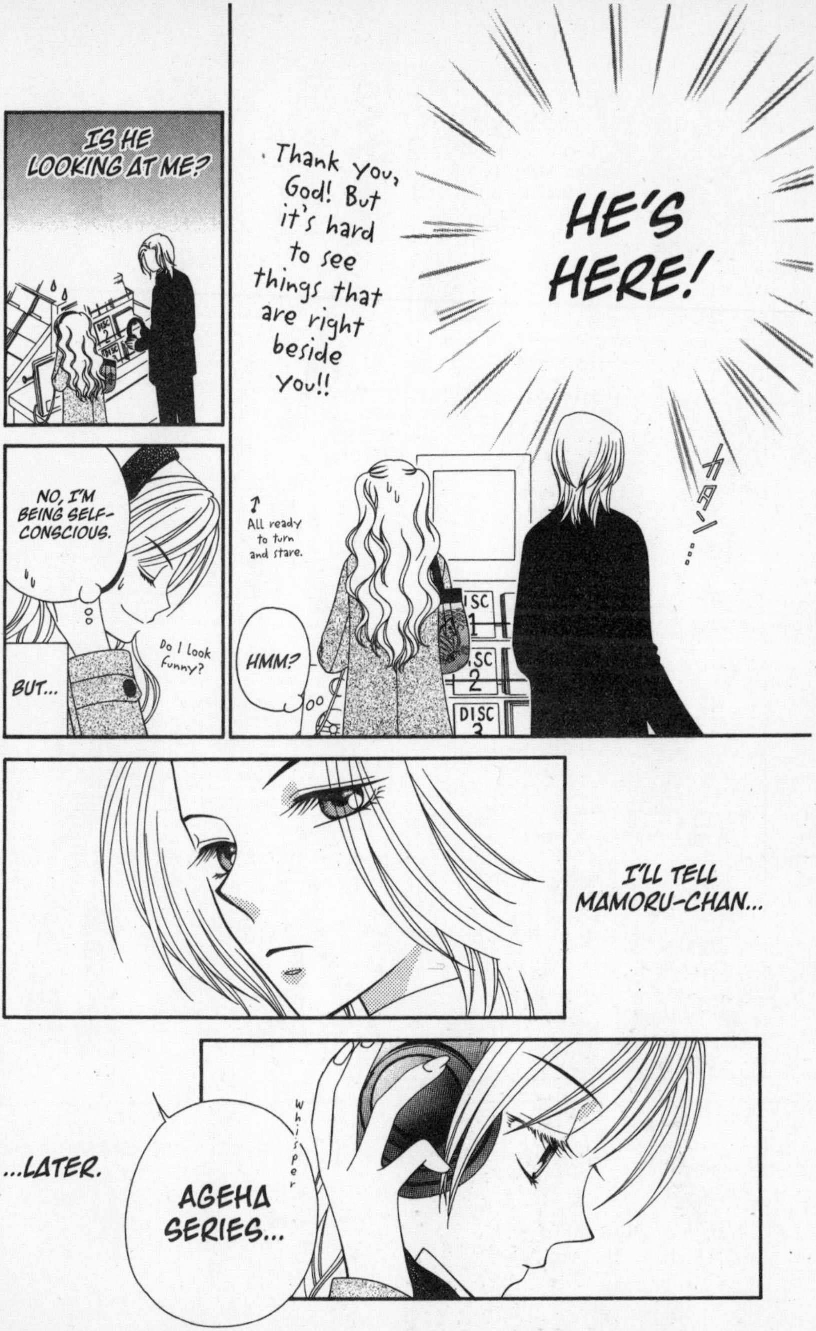
HE'S HERE!
Thank you, God! But it's hard to see things that are right beside you!!
All ready to turn and stare.
HMM?
IS HE LOOKING AT ME?
NO, I'M BEING SELF-CONSCIOUS.
Do I look funny?
BUT...
I'LL TELL MAMORU-CHAN...
...LATER.
Whisper
AGEHA SERIES...

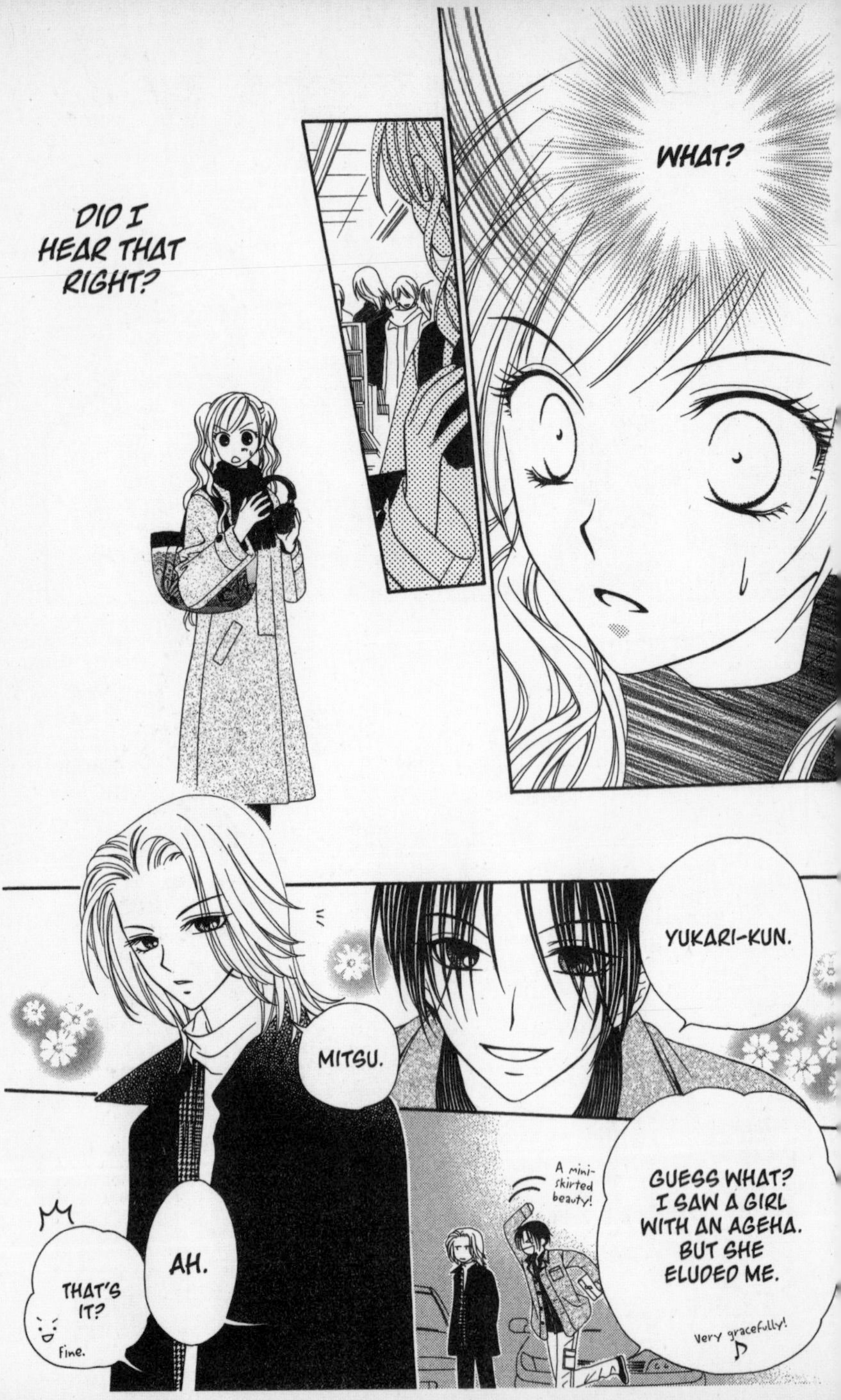
WHAT?
DID I HEAR THAT RIGHT?
YUKARI-KUN.
MITSU.
GUESS WHAT? I SAW A GIRL WITH AN AGEHA. BUT SHE ELUDED ME.
Very gracefully!
A mini-skirted beauty!
AH.
THAT'S IT?
Fine.

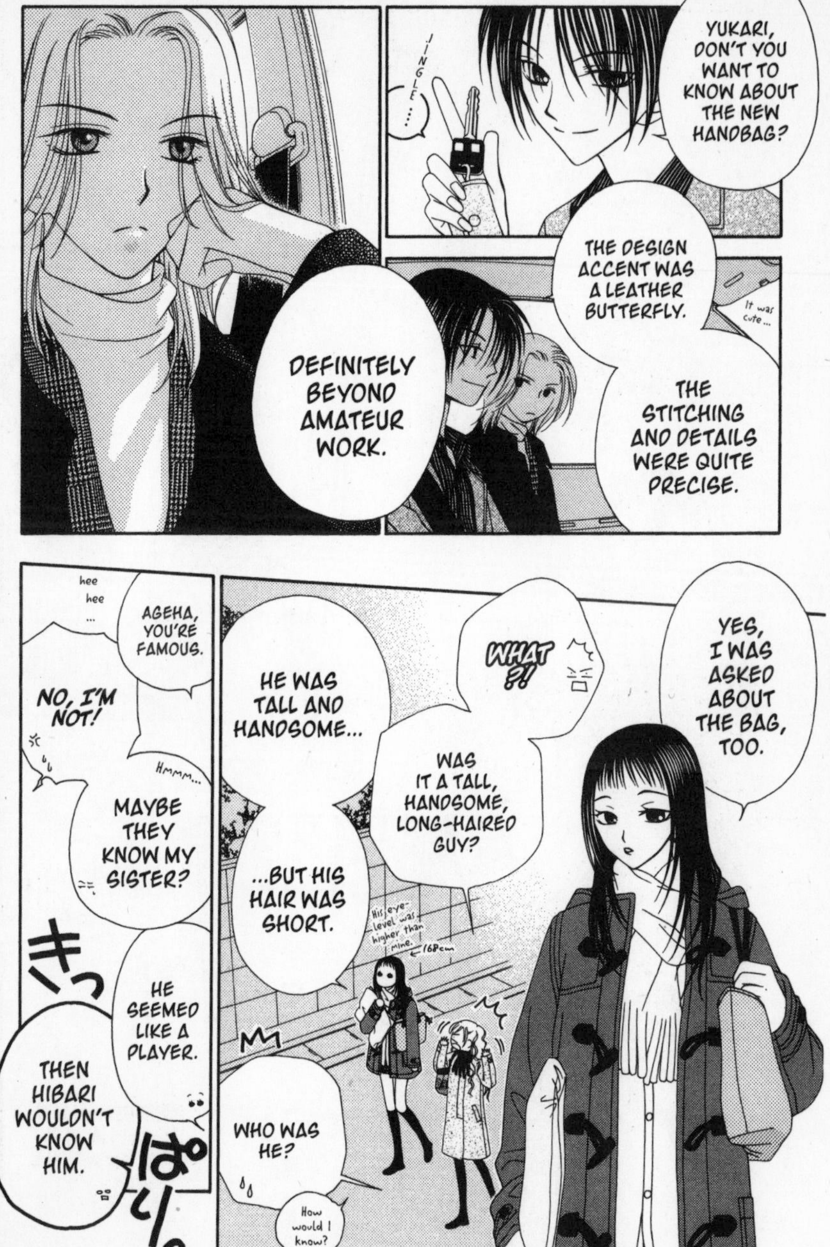
JINGLE...
YUKARI, DON'T YOU WANT TO KNOW ABOUT THE NEW HANDBAG?
THE DESIGN ACCENT WAS A LEATHER BUTTERFLY.
It was cute...
THE STITCHING AND DETAILS WERE QUITE PRECISE.
DEFINITELY BEYOND AMATEUR WORK.
YES, I WAS ASKED ABOUT THE BAG, TOO.
WHAT?!
WAS IT A TALL, HANDSOME, LONG-HAIRED GUY?
HE WAS TALL AND HANDSOME...
...BUT HIS HAIR WAS SHORT.
His eye-level was higher than mine.
←168cm
WHO WAS HE?
How would I know?
hee hee ...
AGEHA, YOU'RE FAMOUS.
NO, I'M NOT!
Hmmm...
MAYBE THEY KNOW MY SISTER?
きっ
HE SEEMED LIKE A PLAYER.
THEN HIBARI WOULDN'T KNOW HIM.
ぱり。

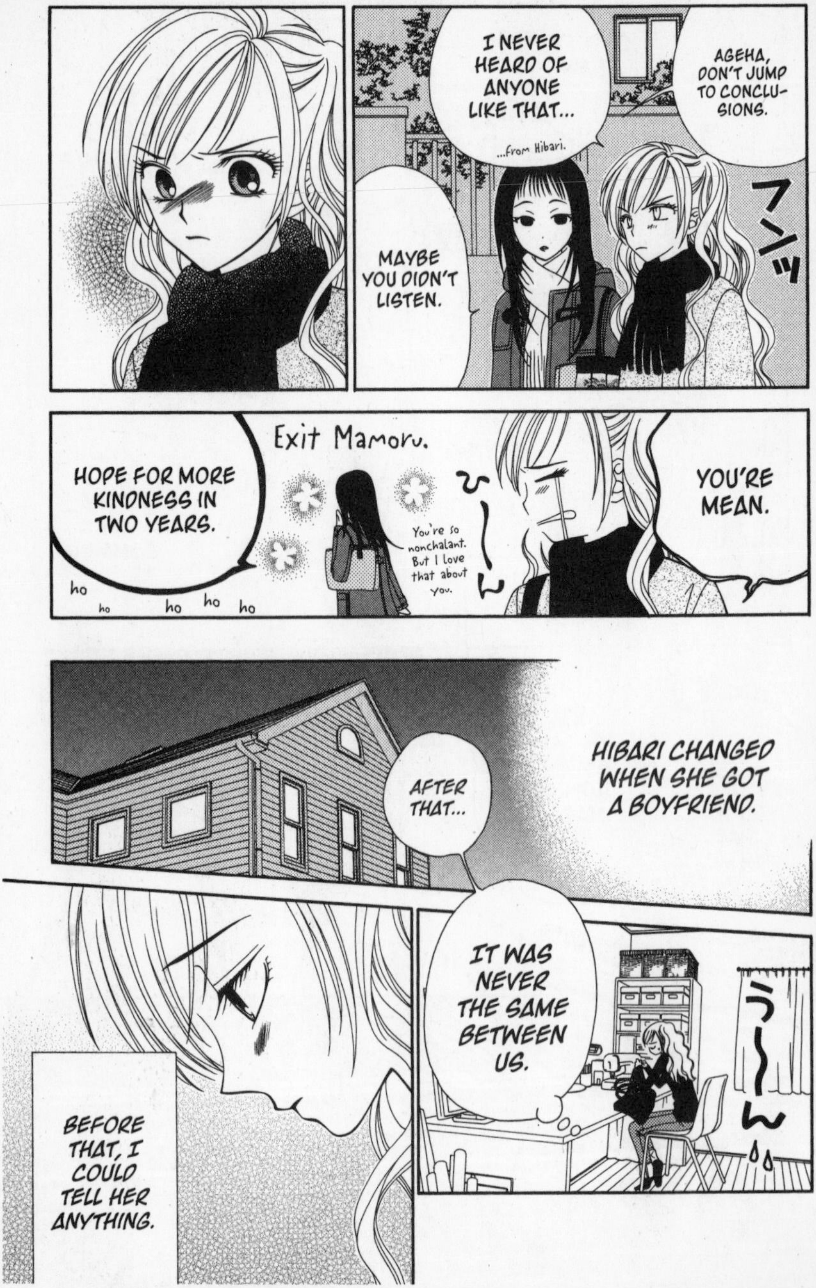
AGEHA, DON'T JUMP TO CONCLUSIONS.
I NEVER HEARD OF ANYONE LIKE THAT...
...from Hibari.
MAYBE YOU DIDN'T LISTEN.
フンッ
YOU'RE MEAN.
ひ～ん
You're so nonchalant. But I love that about you.
Exit Mamoru.
HOPE FOR MORE KINDNESS IN TWO YEARS.
ho ho ho ho ho
HIBARI CHANGED WHEN SHE GOT A BOYFRIEND.
AFTER THAT...
IT WAS NEVER THE SAME BETWEEN US.
う～ん
BEFORE THAT, I COULD TELL HER ANYTHING.

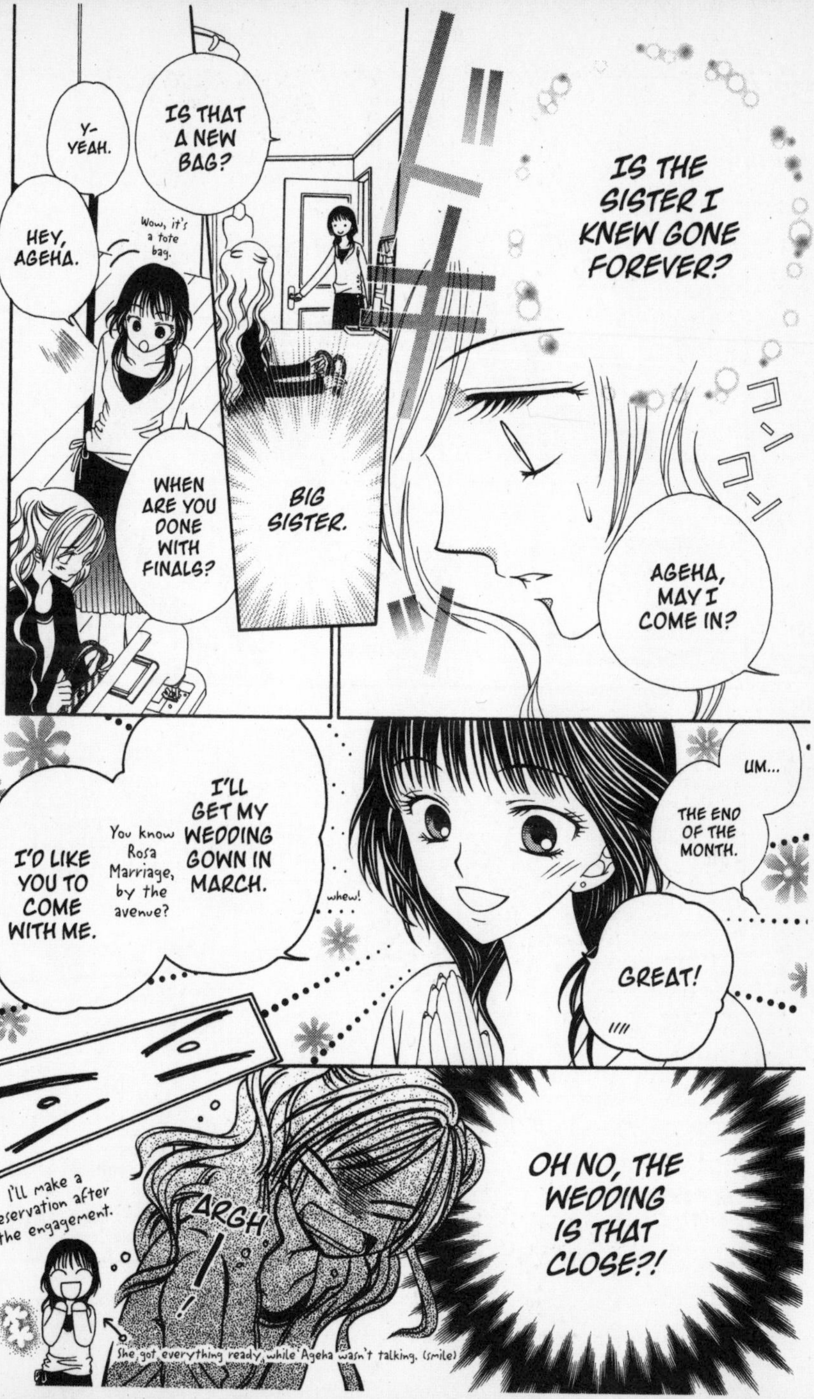

IS THE SISTER I KNEW GONE FOREVER?
AGEHA, MAY I COME IN?
BIG SISTER.
IS THAT A NEW BAG?
Y-YEAH.
Wow, it's a tote bag.
HEY, AGEHA.
WHEN ARE YOU DONE WITH FINALS?
UM...
THE END OF THE MONTH.
GREAT!
whew!
I'LL GET MY WEDDING GOWN IN MARCH.
You know Rosa Marriage, by the avenue?
I'D LIKE YOU TO COME WITH ME.
OH NO, THE WEDDING IS THAT CLOSE?!
ARGH
I'll make a reservation after the engagement.
She got everything ready, while Ageha wasn't talking. (smile)

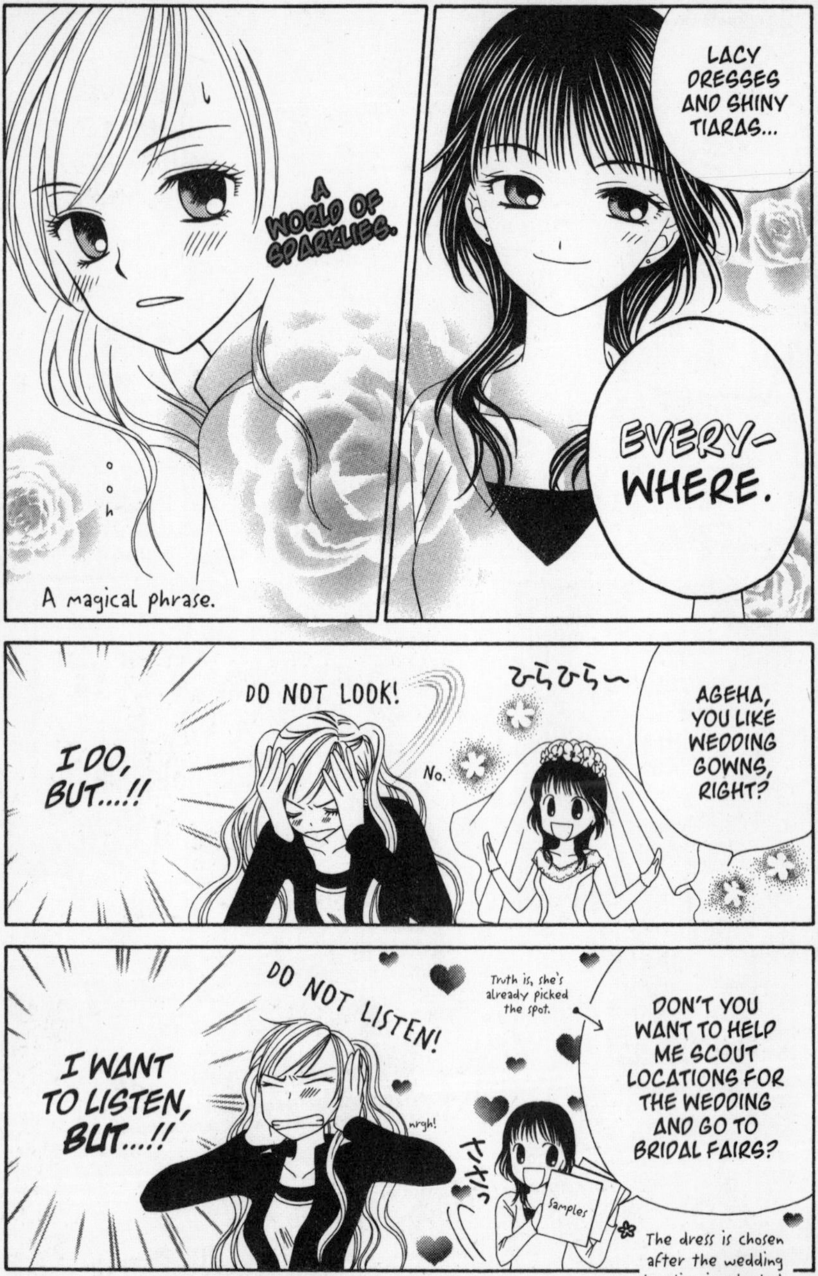
LACY DRESSES AND SHINY TIARAS...
EVERY-WHERE.
A WORLD OF SPARKLIES.
ooh
A magical phrase.
ひらひら〜
AGEHA, YOU LIKE WEDDING GOWNS, RIGHT?
No.
DO NOT LOOK!
I DO, BUT...!!
DON'T YOU WANT TO HELP ME SCOUT LOCATIONS FOR THE WEDDING AND GO TO BRIDAL FAIRS?
Truth is, she's already picked the spot.
Samples
ささっ
nrgh!
DO NOT LISTEN!
I WANT TO LISTEN, BUT...!!
The dress is chosen after the wedding location is selected.

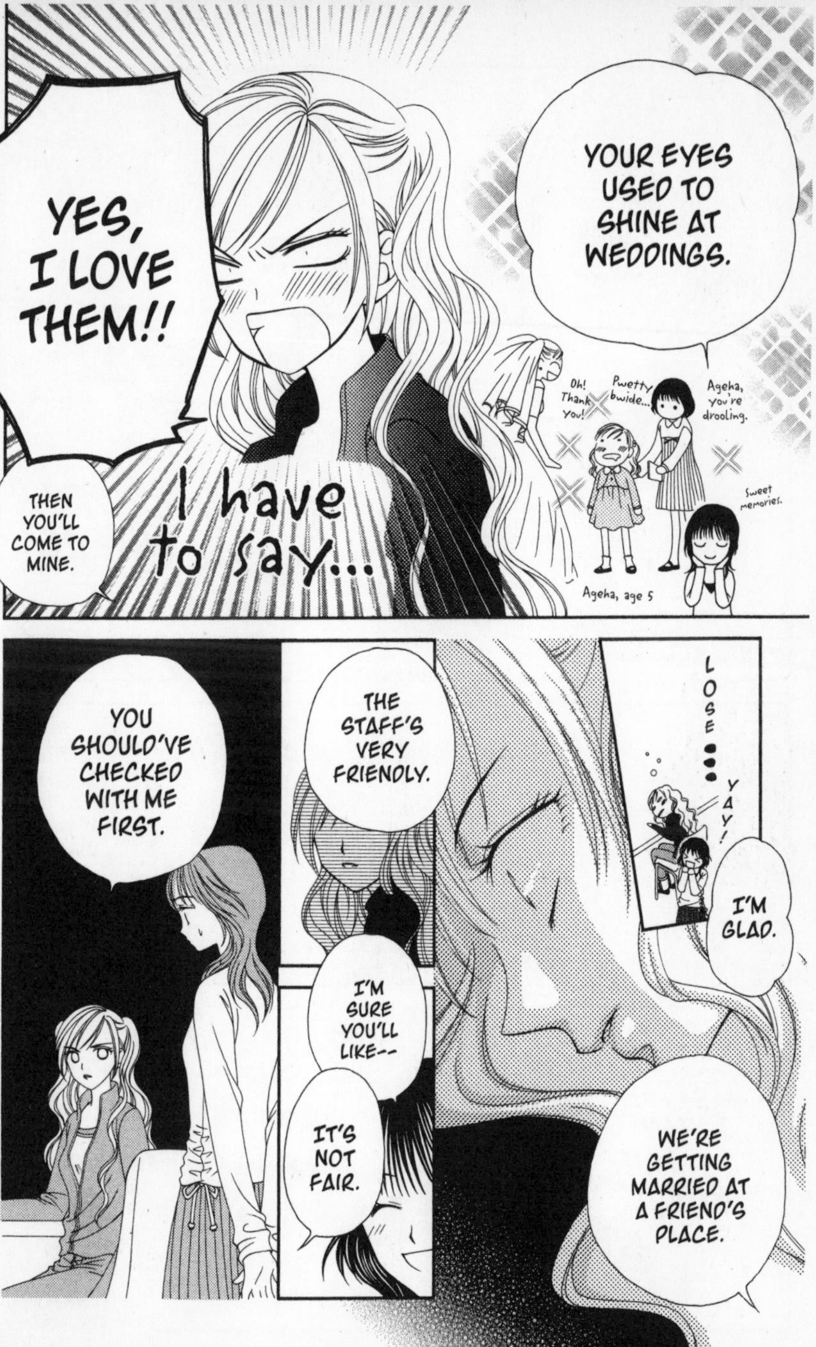
YOUR EYES USED TO SHINE AT WEDDINGS.
Ageha, you're drooling.
Pwetty bwide...
Oh! Thank you!
Sweet memories.
Ageha, age 5
YES, I LOVE THEM!!
I have to say...
THEN YOU'LL COME TO MINE.
LOSE...
YAY!
I'M GLAD.
WE'RE GETTING MARRIED AT A FRIEND'S PLACE.
THE STAFF'S VERY FRIENDLY.
I'M SURE YOU'LL LIKE--
IT'S NOT FAIR.
YOU SHOULD'VE CHECKED WITH ME FIRST.

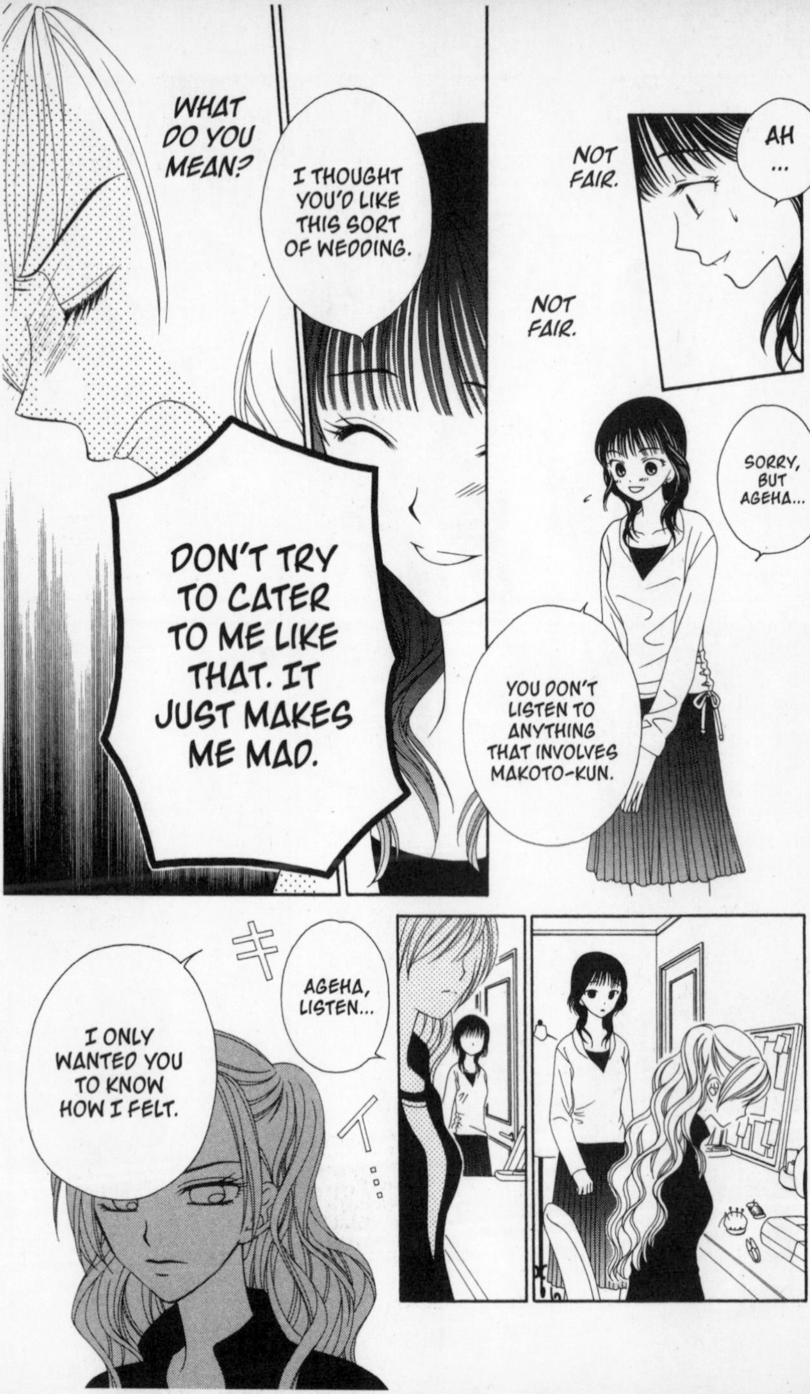
AH ...
NOT FAIR.
NOT FAIR.
SORRY, BUT AGEHA...
YOU DON'T LISTEN TO ANYTHING THAT INVOLVES MAKOTO-KUN.
I THOUGHT YOU'D LIKE THIS SORT OF WEDDING.
WHAT DO YOU MEAN?
DON'T TRY TO CATER TO ME LIKE THAT. IT JUST MAKES ME MAD.
AGEHA, LISTEN...
キ
イ...
I ONLY WANTED YOU TO KNOW HOW I FELT.

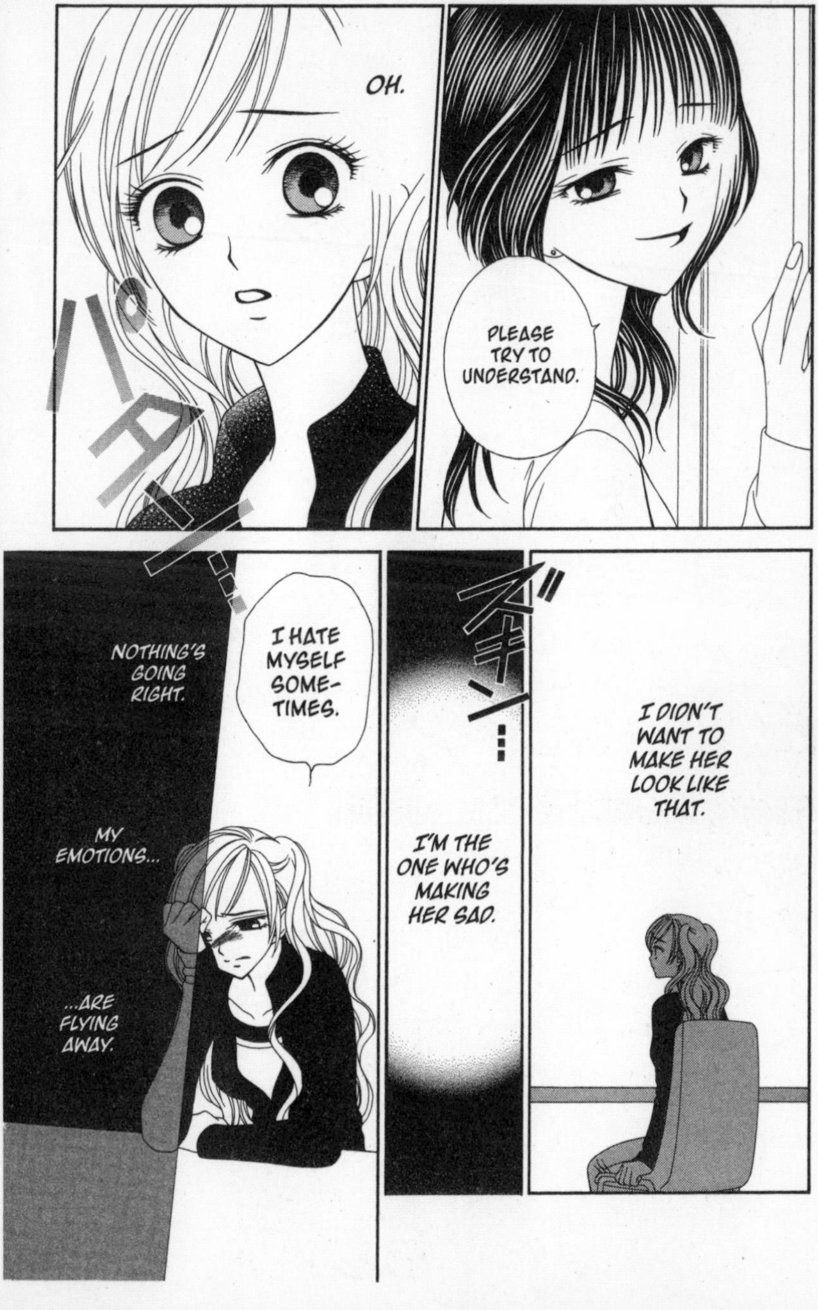
PLEASE TRY TO UNDERSTAND.
OH.
パタン…
I DIDN'T WANT TO MAKE HER LOOK LIKE THAT.
ズキン…
I'M THE ONE WHO'S MAKING HER SAD.
I HATE MYSELF SOME-TIMES.
NOTHING'S GOING RIGHT.
MY EMOTIONS...
...ARE FLYING AWAY.

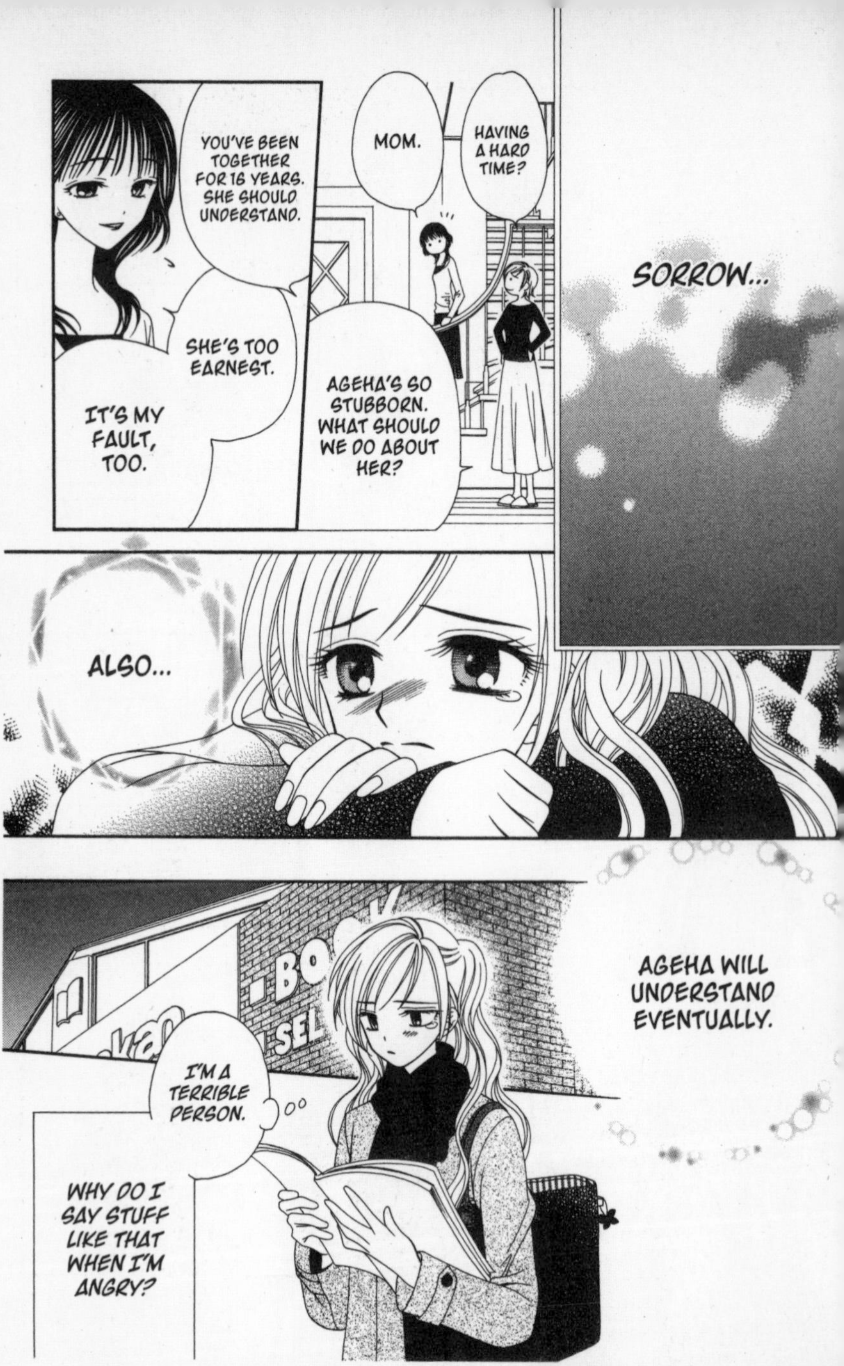
SORROW...
HAVING A HARD TIME?
MOM.
AGEHA'S SO STUBBORN. WHAT SHOULD WE DO ABOUT HER?
YOU'VE BEEN TOGETHER FOR 16 YEARS. SHE SHOULD UNDERSTAND.
SHE'S TOO EARNEST.
IT'S MY FAULT, TOO.
ALSO...
AGEHA WILL UNDERSTAND EVENTUALLY.
I'M A TERRIBLE PERSON.
WHY DO I SAY STUFF LIKE THAT WHEN I'M ANGRY?

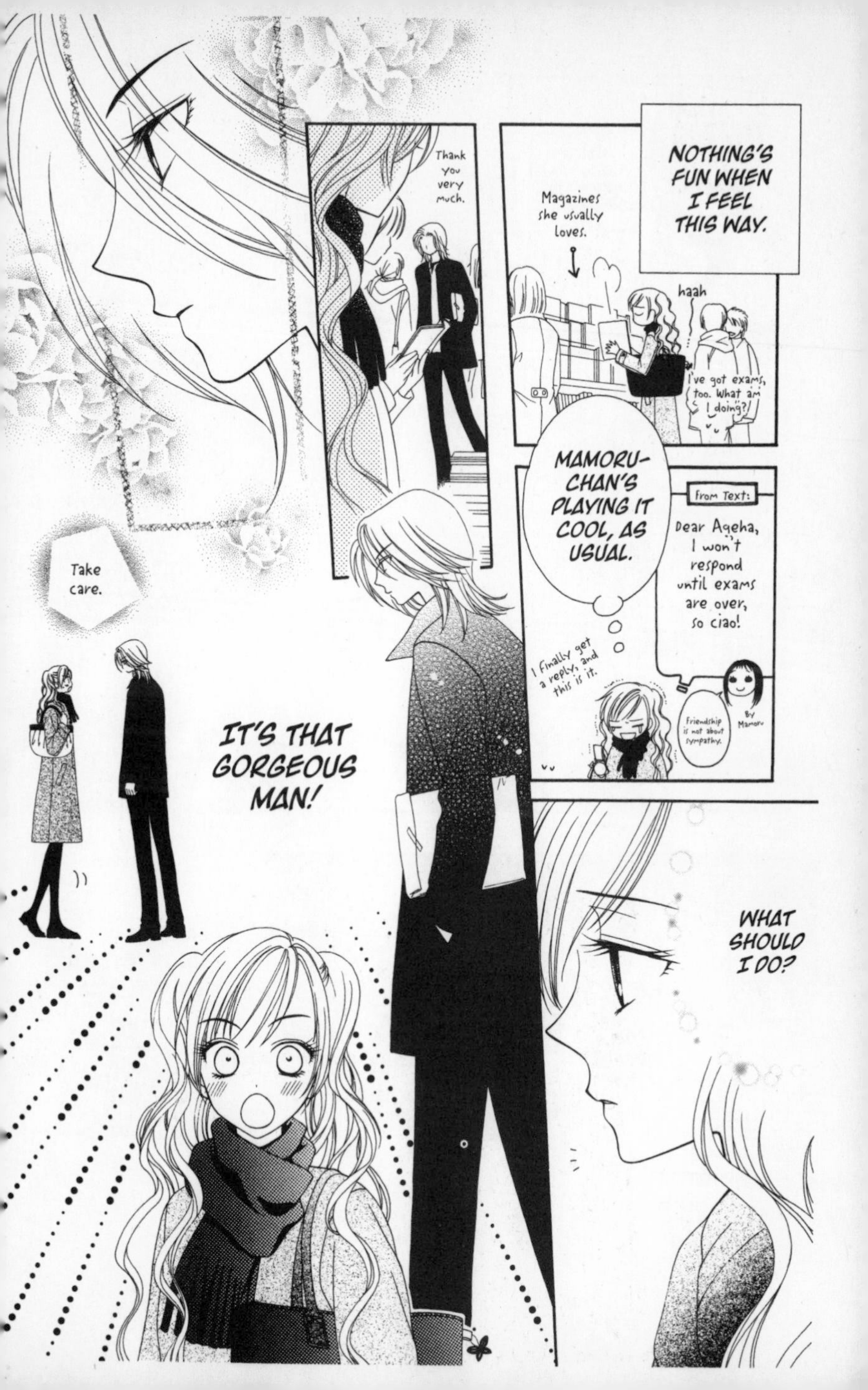
NOTHING'S FUN WHEN I FEEL THIS WAY.
Magazines she usually loves.
haah
I've got exams, too. What am I doing?
MAMORU-CHAN'S PLAYING IT COOL, AS USUAL.
From Text:
Dear Ageha, I won't respond until exams are over, so ciao!
By Mamoru
Friendship is not about sympathy.
I finally get a reply, and this is it.
Thank you very much.
WHAT SHOULD I DO?
IT'S THAT GORGEOUS MAN!
Take care.

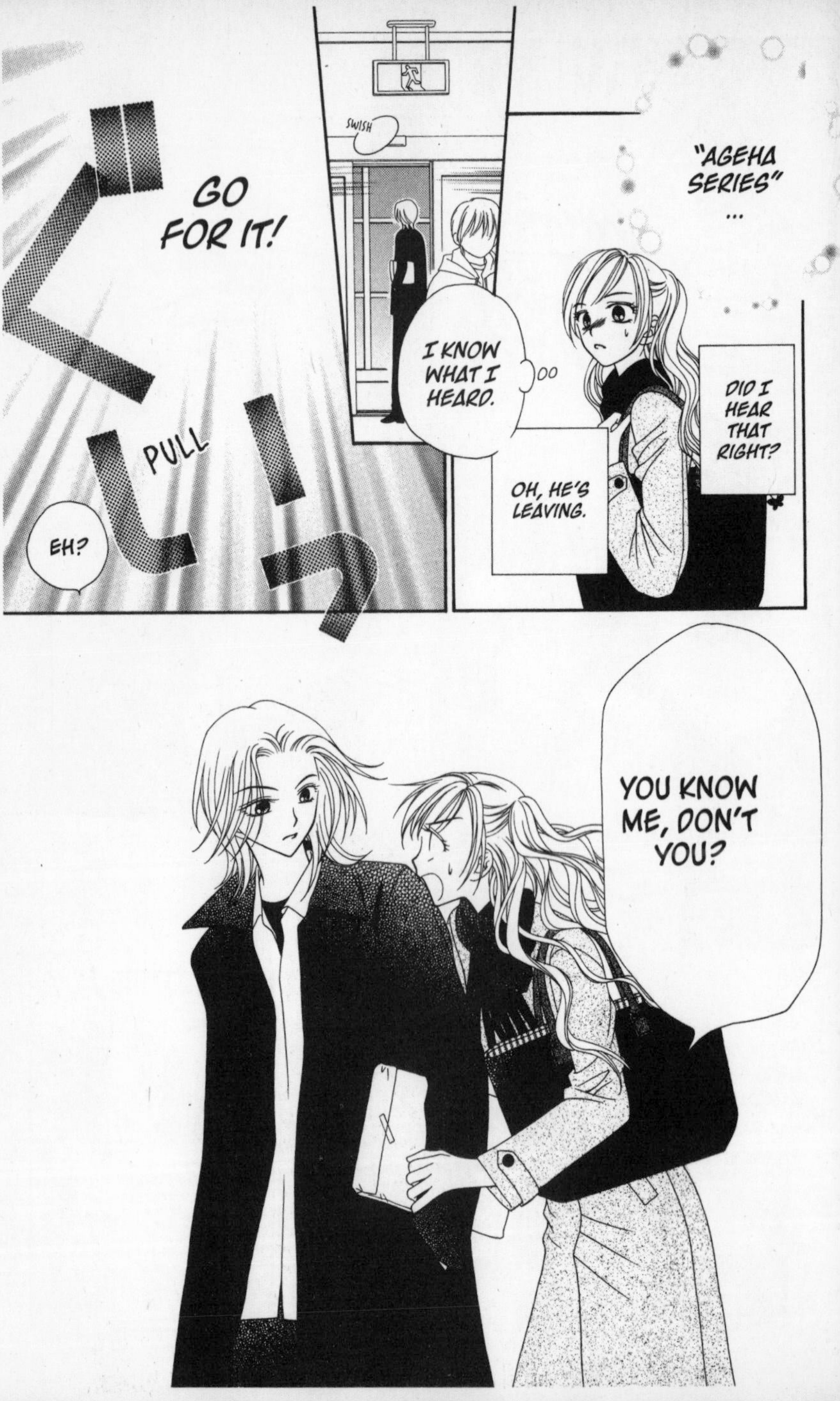
"AGEHA SERIES" ...
DID I HEAR THAT RIGHT?
OH, HE'S LEAVING.
SWISH
I KNOW WHAT I HEARD.
GO FOR IT!
PULL
EH?
YOU KNOW ME, DON'T YOU?

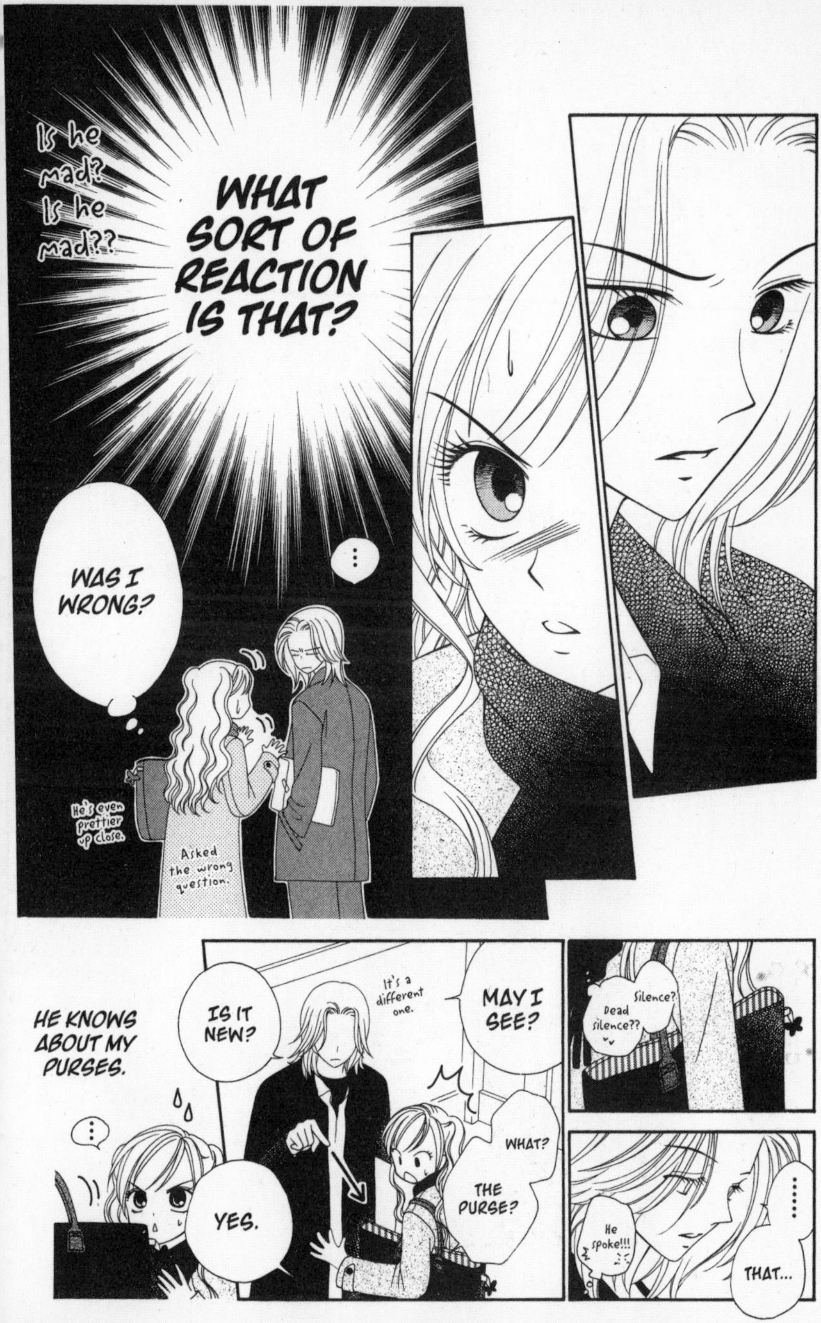
WHAT SORT OF REACTION IS THAT?
Is he mad? Is he mad??
...
WAS I WRONG?
Asked the wrong question.
He's even prettier up close.
Silence? Dead silence??
......
He spoke!!!
THAT...
MAY I SEE?
It's a different one.
IS IT NEW?
WHAT? THE PURSE?
HE KNOWS ABOUT MY PURSES.
...
YES.

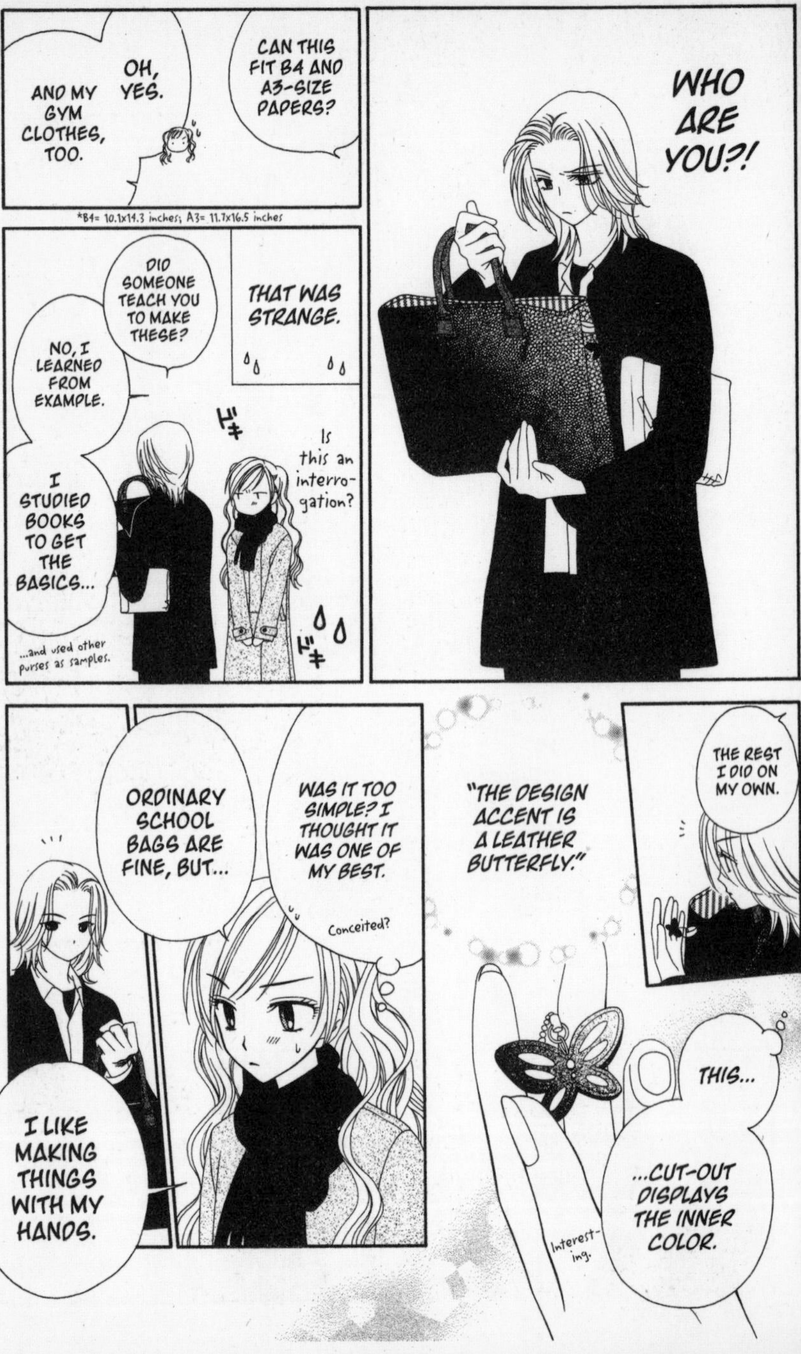
WHO ARE YOU?!
CAN THIS FIT B4 AND A3-SIZE PAPERS?
OH, YES.
AND MY GYM CLOTHES, TOO.
*B4= 10.1x14.3 inches; A3= 11.7x16.5 inches
THAT WAS STRANGE.
DID SOMEONE TEACH YOU TO MAKE THESE?
NO, I LEARNED FROM EXAMPLE.
I STUDIED BOOKS TO GET THE BASICS...
Is this an interrogation?
...and used other purses as samples.
THE REST I DID ON MY OWN.
"THE DESIGN ACCENT IS A LEATHER BUTTERFLY."
THIS...
...CUT-OUT DISPLAYS THE INNER COLOR.
Interesting.
WAS IT TOO SIMPLE? I THOUGHT IT WAS ONE OF MY BEST.
Conceited?
ORDINARY SCHOOL BAGS ARE FINE, BUT...
I LIKE MAKING THINGS WITH MY HANDS.

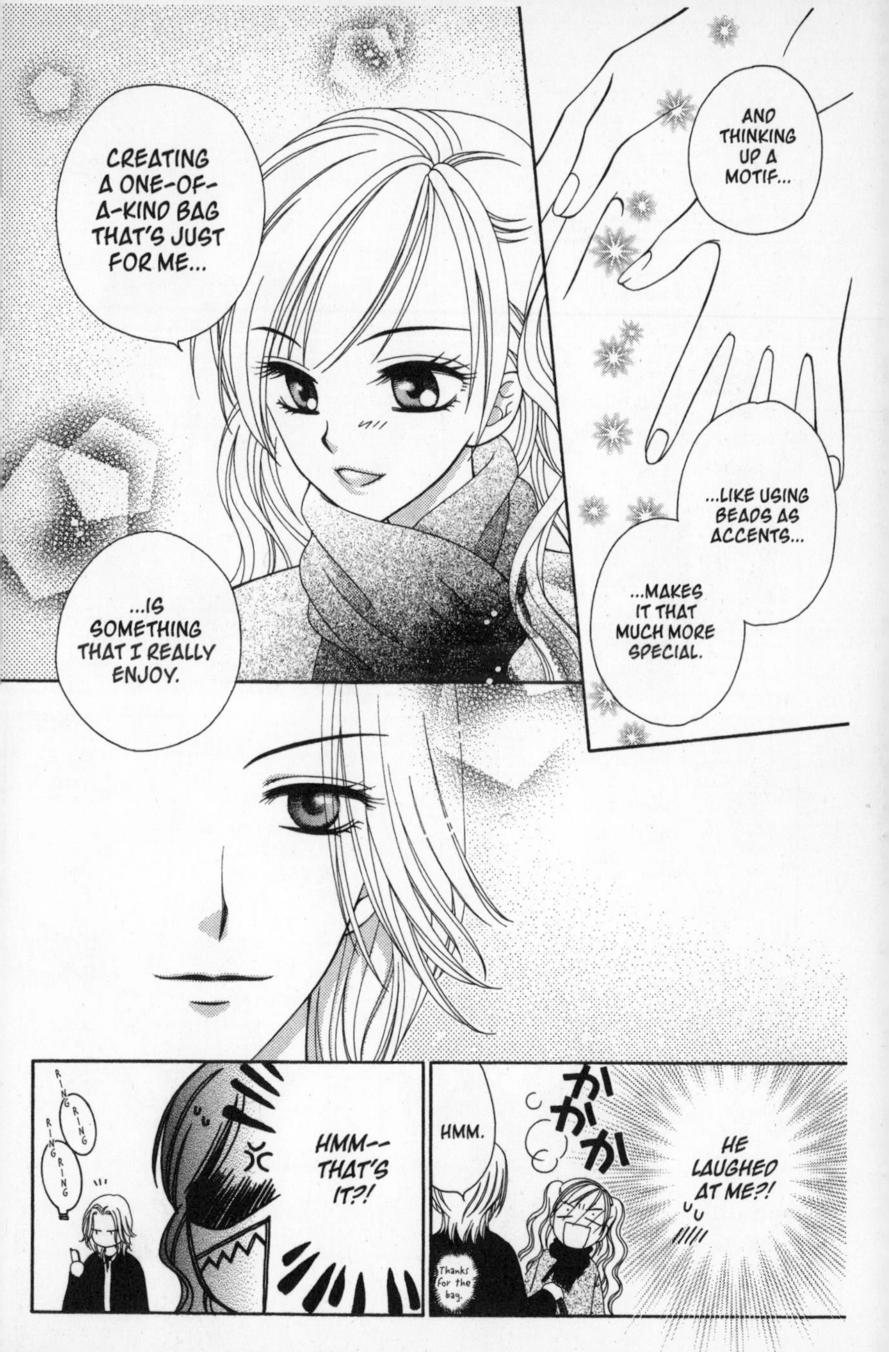
CREATING A ONE-OF-A-KIND BAG THAT'S JUST FOR ME...
...IS SOMETHING THAT I REALLY ENJOY.
AND THINKING UP A MOTIF...
...LIKE USING BEADS AS ACCENTS...
...MAKES IT THAT MUCH MORE SPECIAL.
かかか
HMM.
Thanks for the bag.
HE LAUGHED AT ME?!
HMM-- THAT'S IT?!
RING RING
RING RING

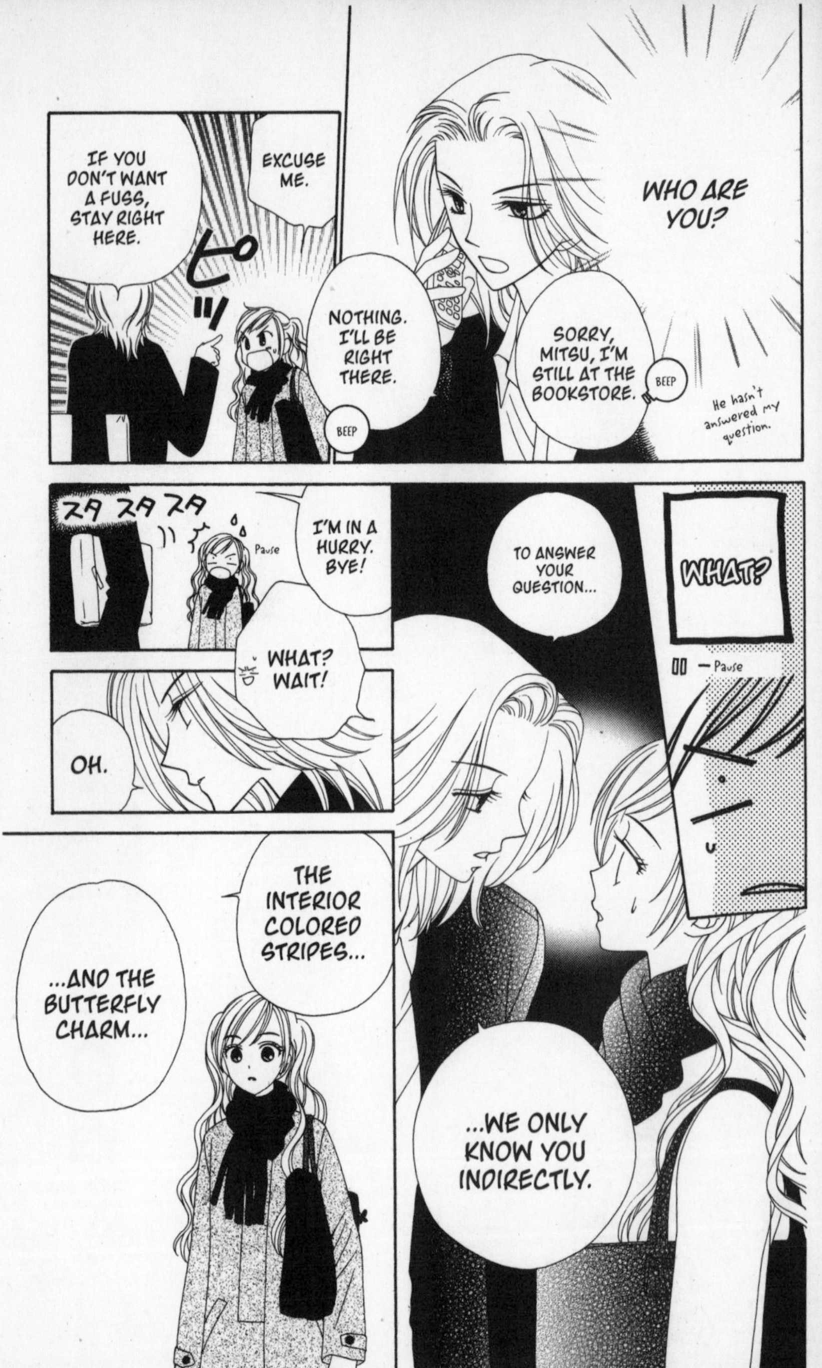
WHO ARE YOU?
SORRY, MITSU, I'M STILL AT THE BOOKSTORE.
BEEP
He hasn't answered my question.
NOTHING. I'LL BE RIGHT THERE.
BEEP
EXCUSE ME.
IF YOU DON'T WANT A FUSS, STAY RIGHT HERE.
ピッ
スタ スタ スタ
I'M IN A HURRY. BYE!
Pause
WHAT? WAIT!
OH.
TO ANSWER YOUR QUESTION...
THE INTERIOR COLORED STRIPES...
...AND THE BUTTERFLY CHARM...
...WE ONLY KNOW YOU INDIRECTLY.
WHAT?
Pause

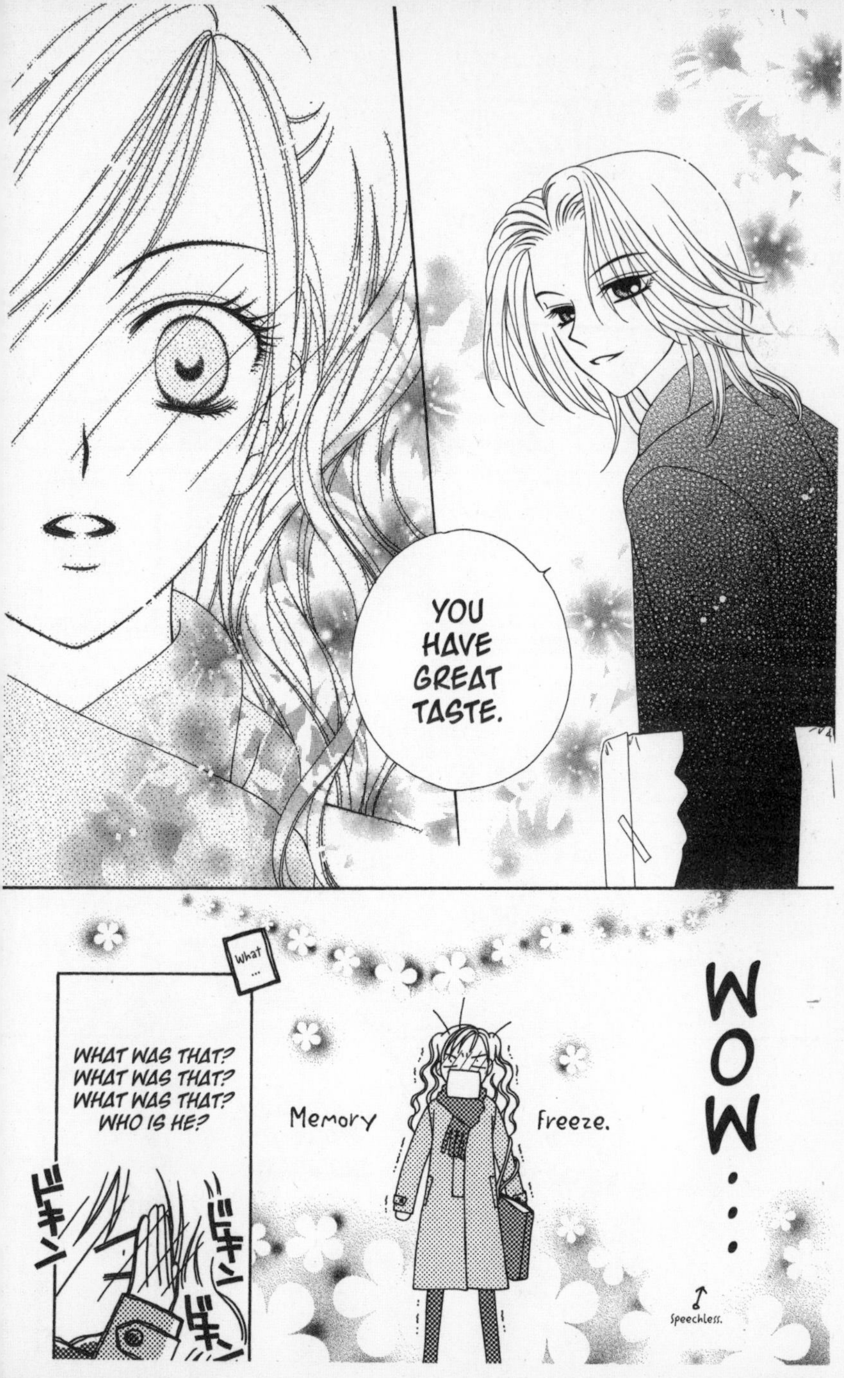
YOU HAVE GREAT TASTE.
WOW...
Speechless.
Memory freeze.
What...
WHAT WAS THAT? WHAT WAS THAT? WHAT WAS THAT? WHO IS HE?
ドキン
ドキン
ドキン

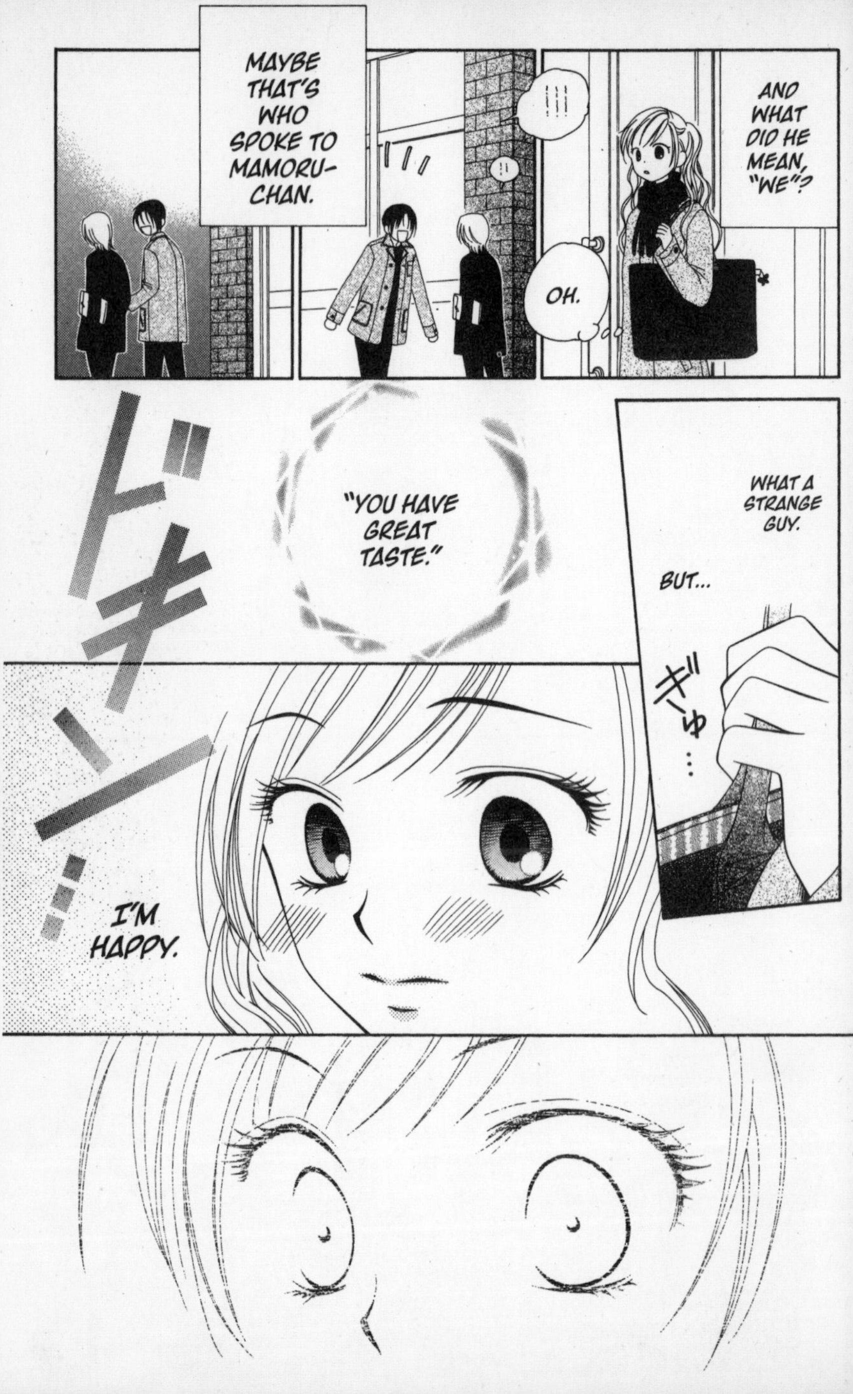
AND WHAT DID HE MEAN, "WE"?
OH.
!!!
!!
MAYBE THAT'S WHO SPOKE TO MAMORU-CHAN.
WHAT A STRANGE GUY.
BUT...
ギゅ…
"YOU HAVE GREAT TASTE."
ドキーン…
I'M HAPPY.

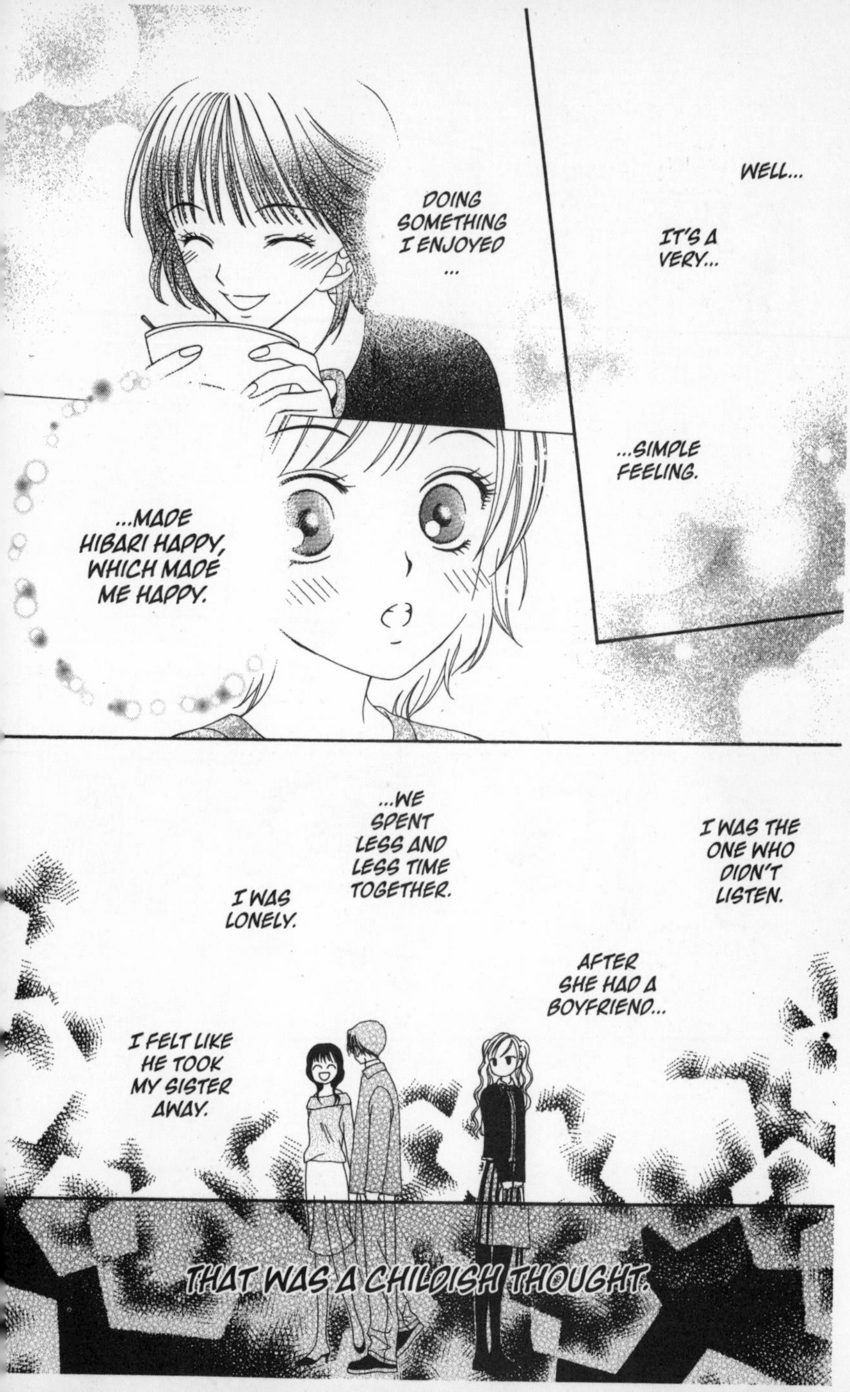
WELL...
IT'S A VERY...
...SIMPLE FEELING.
DOING SOMETHING I ENJOYED ...
...MADE HIBARI HAPPY, WHICH MADE ME HAPPY.
I WAS THE ONE WHO DIDN'T LISTEN.
...WE SPENT LESS AND LESS TIME TOGETHER.
I WAS LONELY.
AFTER SHE HAD A BOYFRIEND...
I FELT LIKE HE TOOK MY SISTER AWAY.
THAT WAS A CHILDISH THOUGHT.

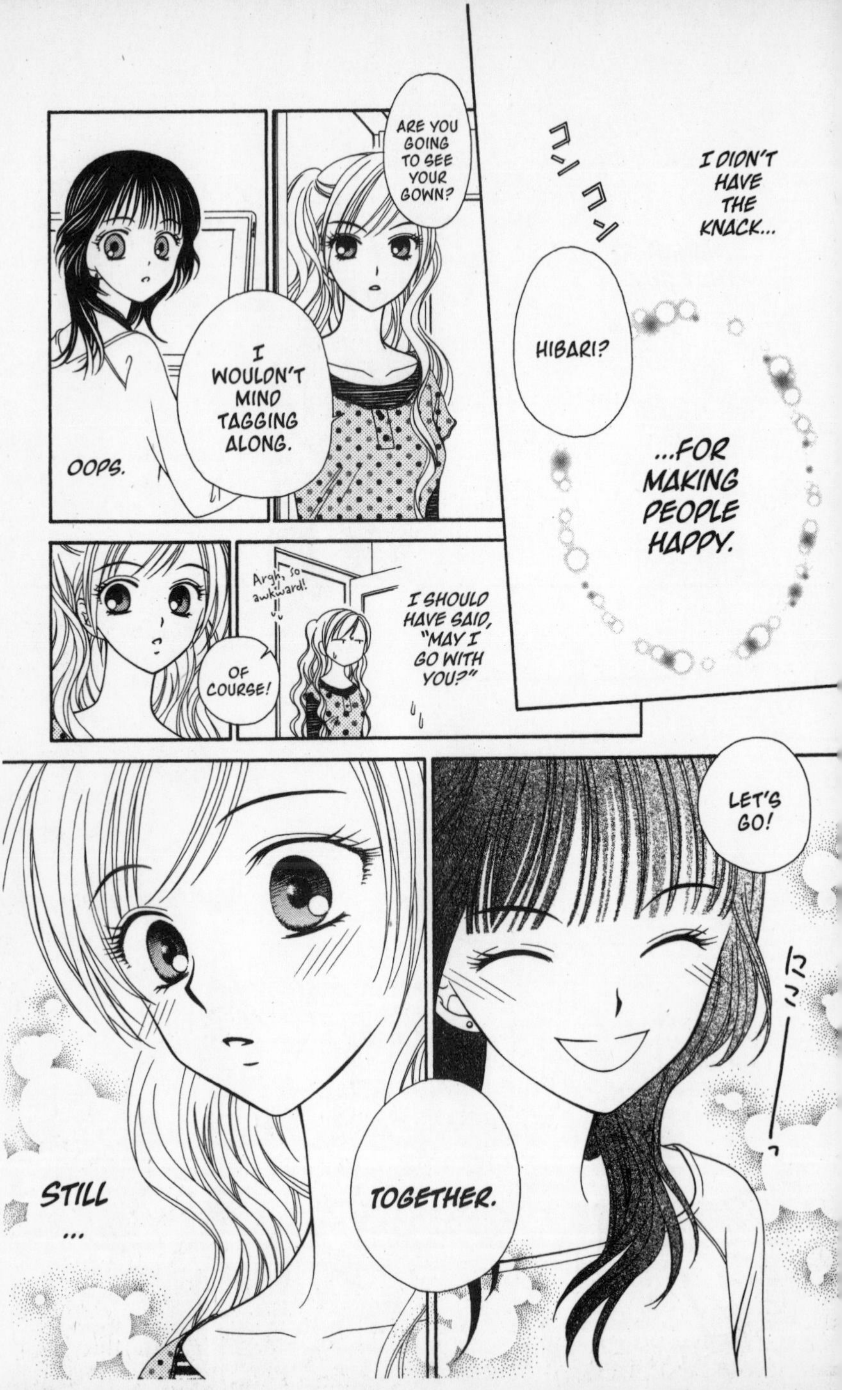
I DIDN'T HAVE THE KNACK...
コンコン
HIBARI?
...FOR MAKING PEOPLE HAPPY.
ARE YOU GOING TO SEE YOUR GOWN?
I WOULDN'T MIND TAGGING ALONG.
OOPS.
I SHOULD HAVE SAID, "MAY I GO WITH YOU?"
Argh, so awkward!
OF COURSE!
LET'S GO!
にこーっ
TOGETHER.
STILL ...

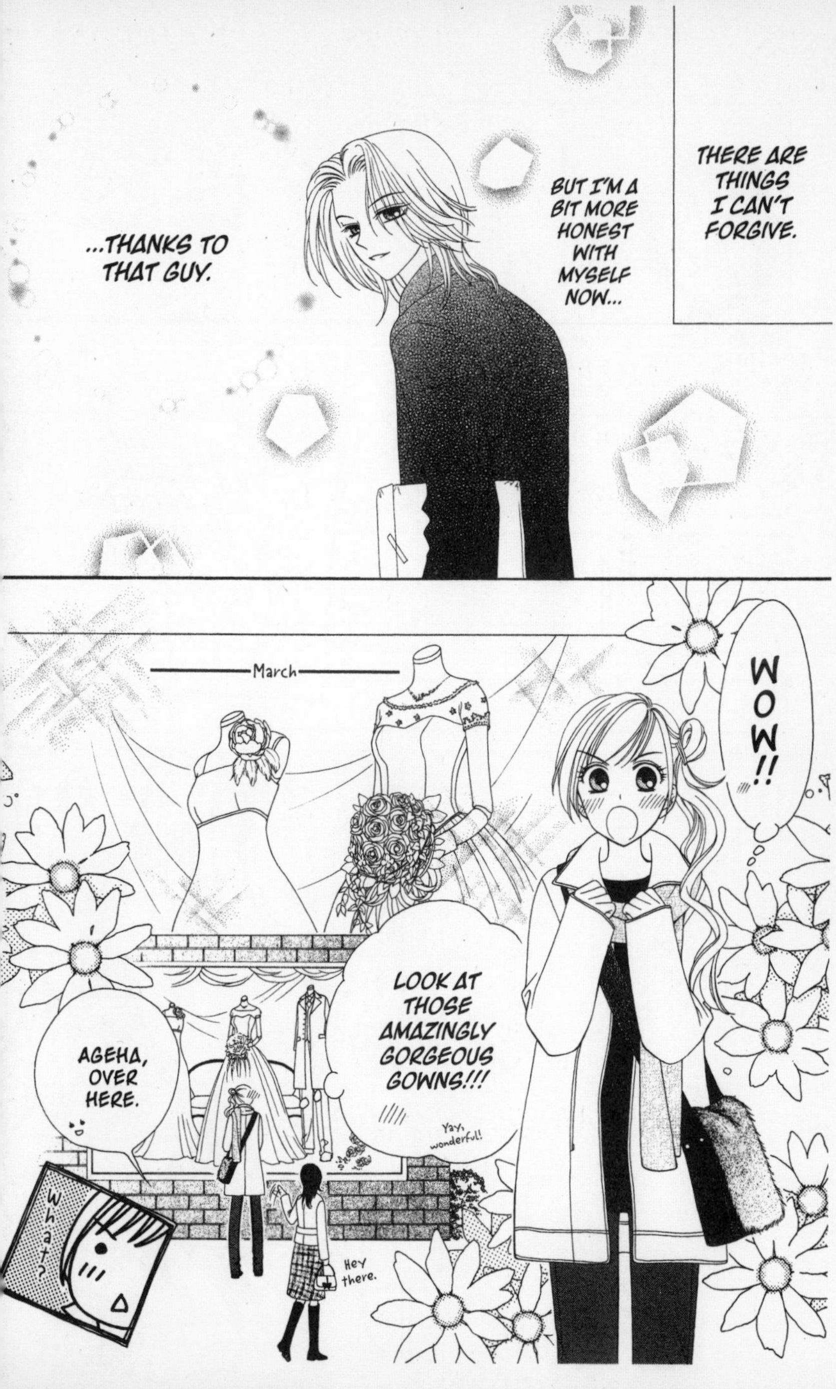
THERE ARE THINGS I CAN'T FORGIVE.
BUT I'M A BIT MORE HONEST WITH MYSELF NOW...
...THANKS TO THAT GUY.
WOW!!
March
LOOK AT THOSE AMAZINGLY GORGEOUS GOWNS!!!
Yay, wonderful!
AGEHA, OVER HERE.
Hey there.
What?

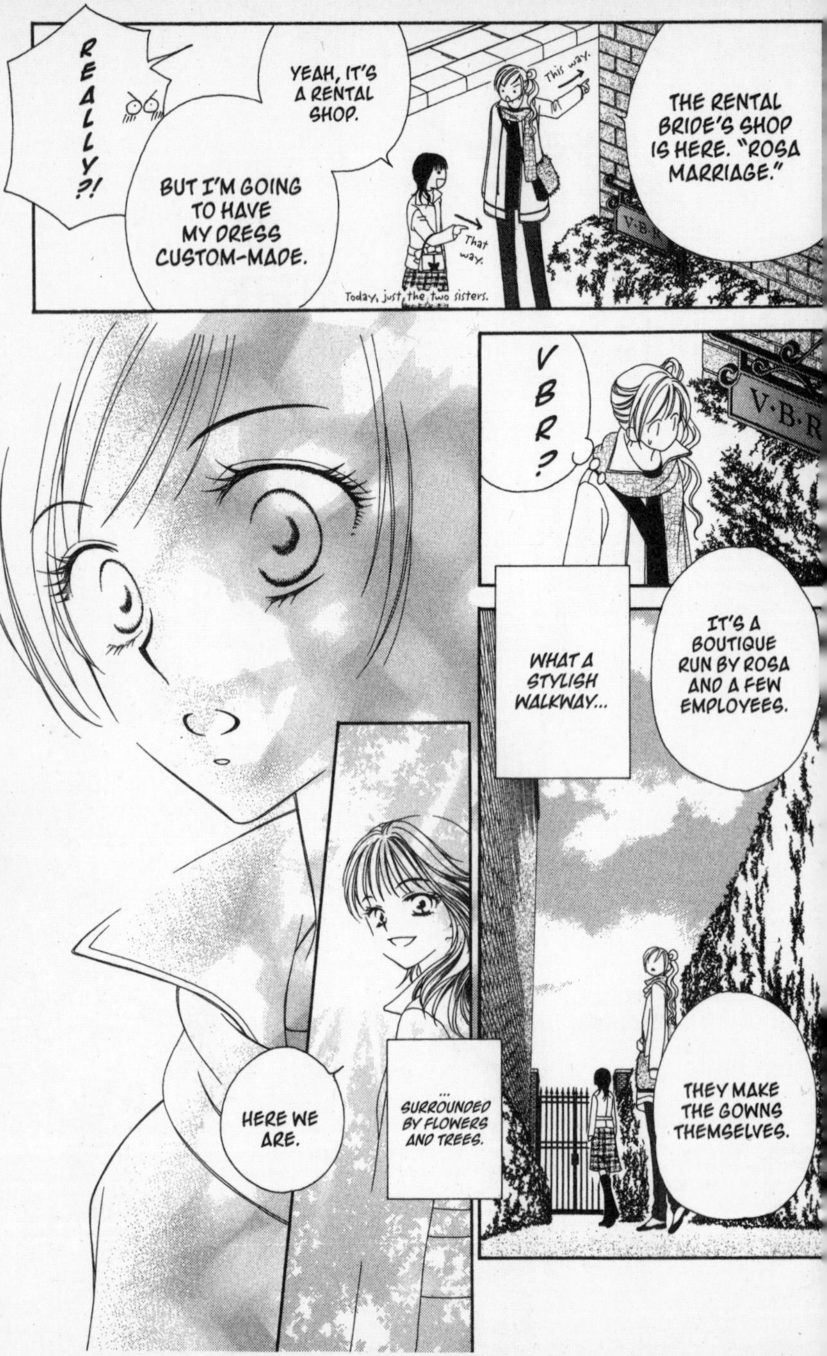
THE RENTAL BRIDE'S SHOP IS HERE. "ROSA MARRIAGE."
V·B·R
This way.
YEAH, IT'S A RENTAL SHOP.
That way.
BUT I'M GOING TO HAVE MY DRESS CUSTOM-MADE.
Today, just the two sisters.
REALLY?!
V·B·R
VBR?
IT'S A BOUTIQUE RUN BY ROSA AND A FEW EMPLOYEES.
WHAT A STYLISH WALKWAY...
THEY MAKE THE GOWNS THEMSELVES.
...SURROUNDED BY FLOWERS AND TREES.
HERE WE ARE.

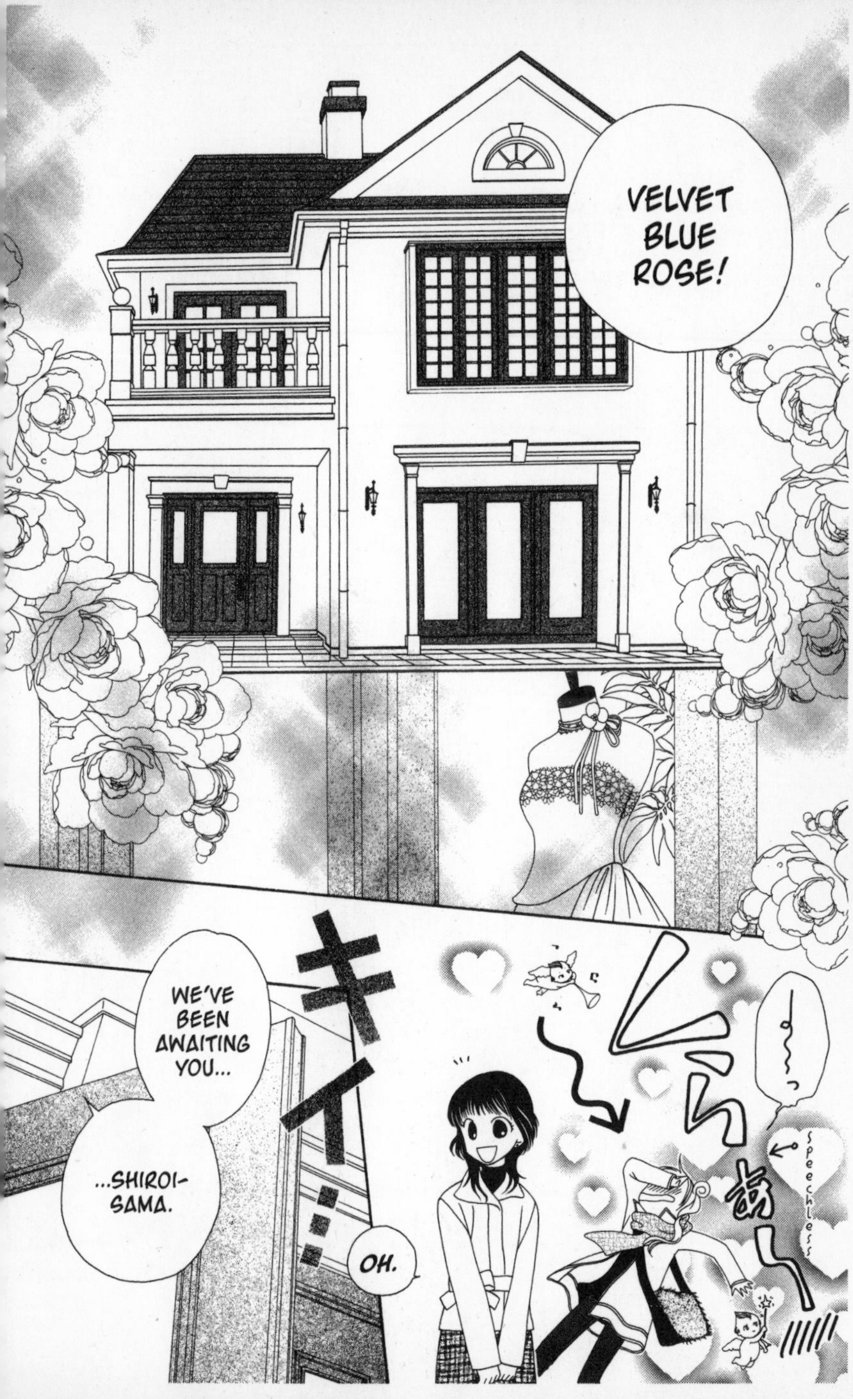
VELVET BLUE ROSE!
Speechless
WE'VE BEEN AWAITING YOU...
...SHIROI-SAMA.
OH.

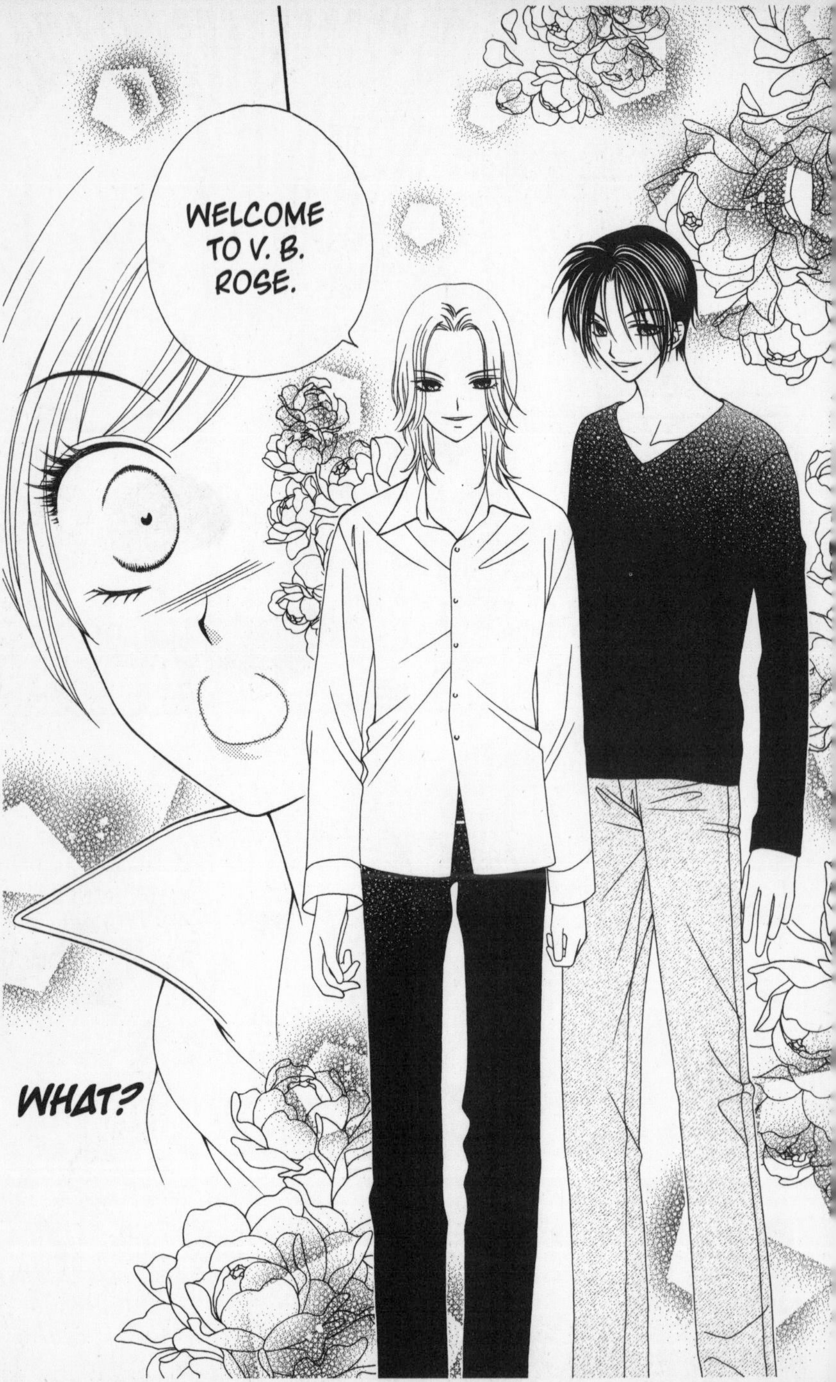
WELCOME TO V. B. ROSE.
WHAT?

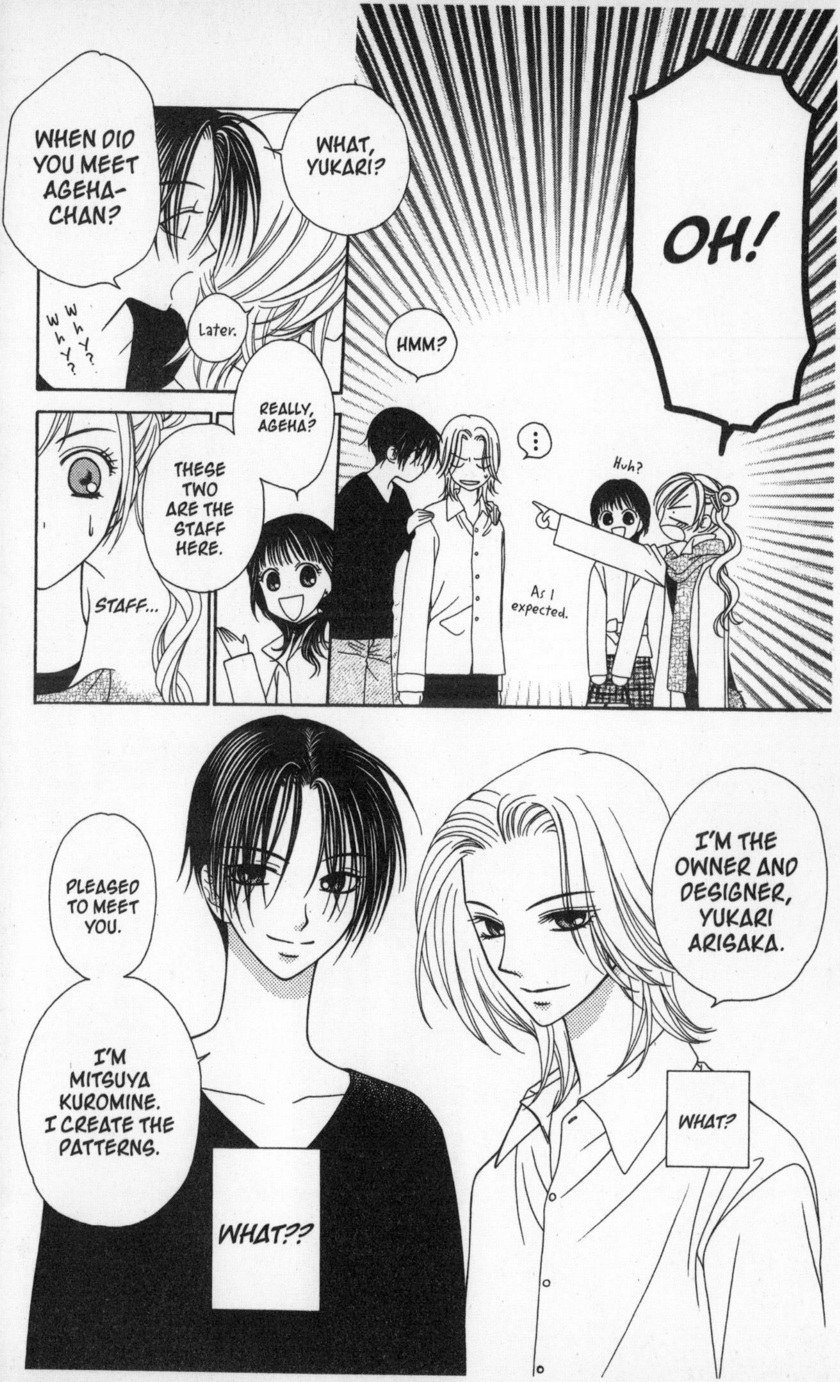
OH!
HMM?
...
Huh?
As I expected.
REALLY, AGEHA?
THESE TWO ARE THE STAFF HERE.
WHAT, YUKARI?
WHEN DID YOU MEET AGEHA-CHAN?
Later.
Why? Why?
STAFF...
I'M THE OWNER AND DESIGNER, YUKARI ARISAKA.
PLEASED TO MEET YOU.
I'M MITSUYA KUROMINE. I CREATE THE PATTERNS.
WHAT?
WHAT??

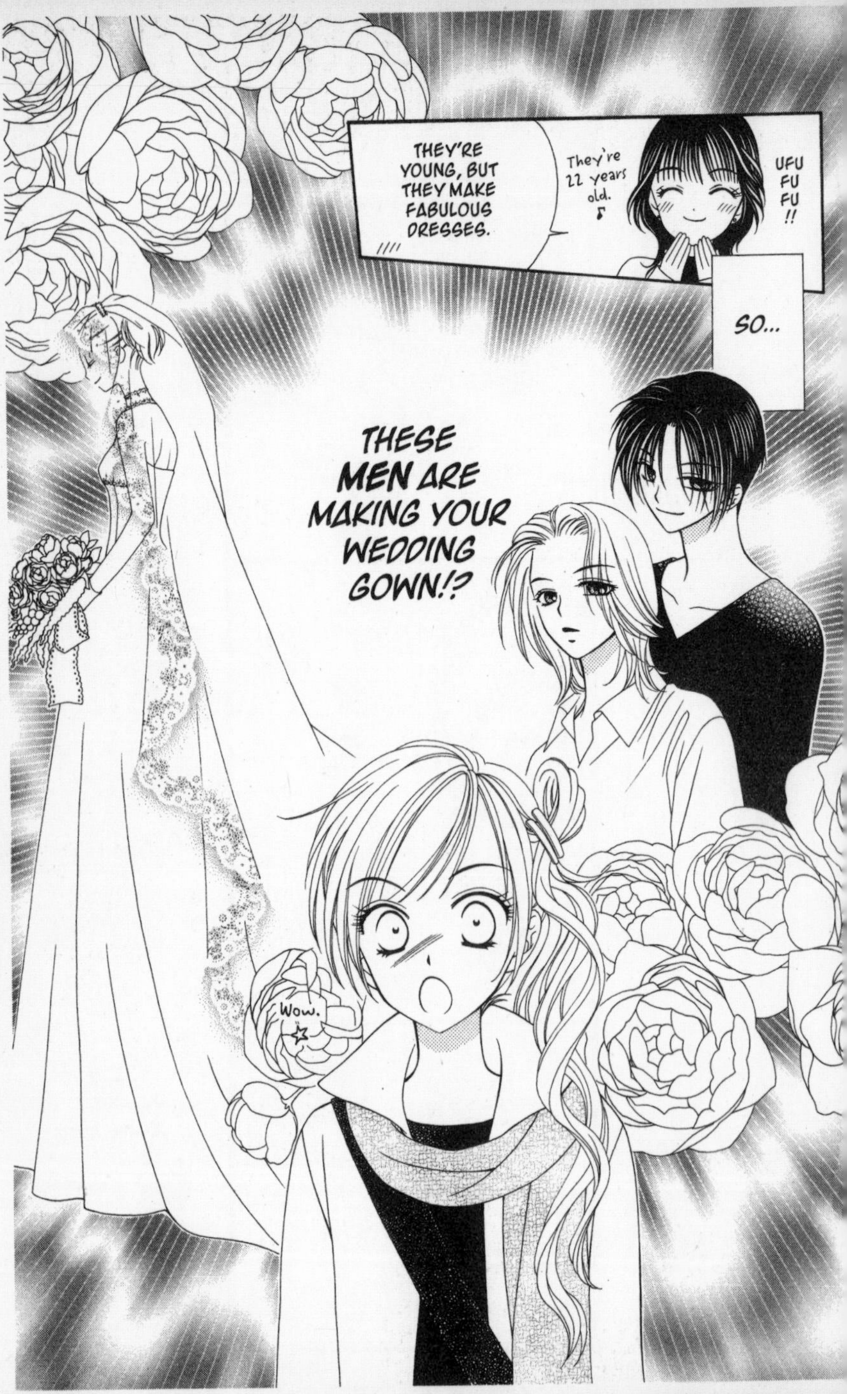
UFU FU FU !!
They're 22 years old. ♪
THEY'RE YOUNG, BUT THEY MAKE FABULOUS DRESSES.
SO...
THESE MEN ARE MAKING YOUR WEDDING GOWN!?
Wow. ☆

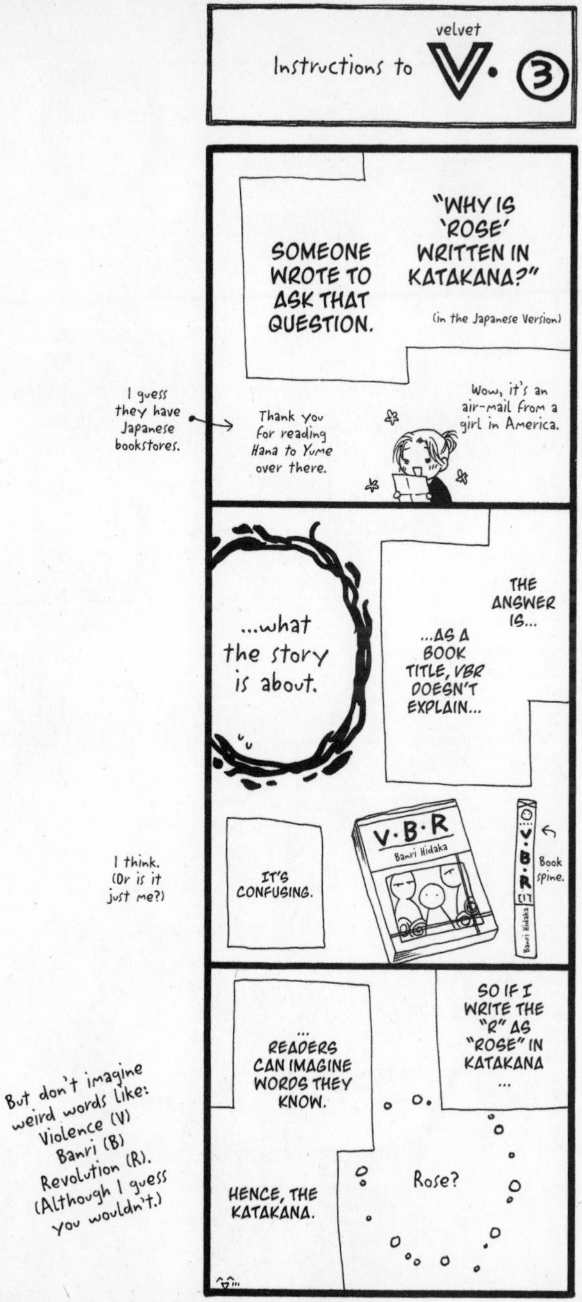
Instructions to velvet V. ③
"WHY IS 'ROSE' WRITTEN IN KATAKANA?"
(in the Japanese Version)
SOMEONE WROTE TO ASK THAT QUESTION.
Wow, it's an air-mail from a girl in America.
Thank you for reading Hana to Yume over there.
I guess they have Japanese bookstores.
THE ANSWER IS...
...AS A BOOK TITLE, VBR DOESN'T EXPLAIN...
...what the story is about.
V·B·R
Banri Hidaka
Book spine.
IT'S CONFUSING.
I think. (Or is it just me?)
SO IF I WRITE THE "R" AS "ROSE" IN KATAKANA ...
... READERS CAN IMAGINE WORDS THEY KNOW.
Rose?
HENCE, THE KATAKANA.
But don't imagine weird words like: Violence (V) Banri (B) Revolution (R). (Although I guess you wouldn't.)

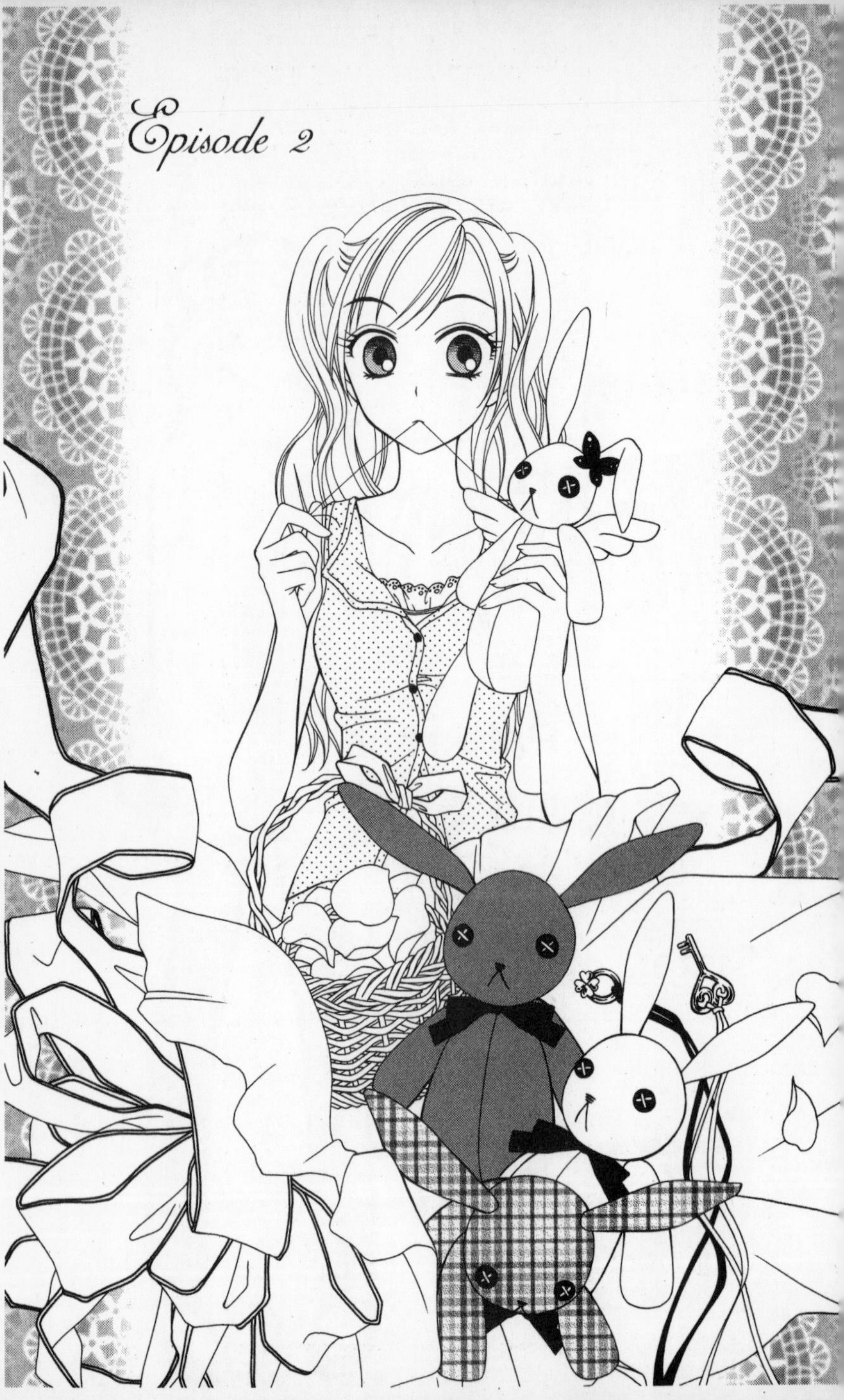
Episode 2

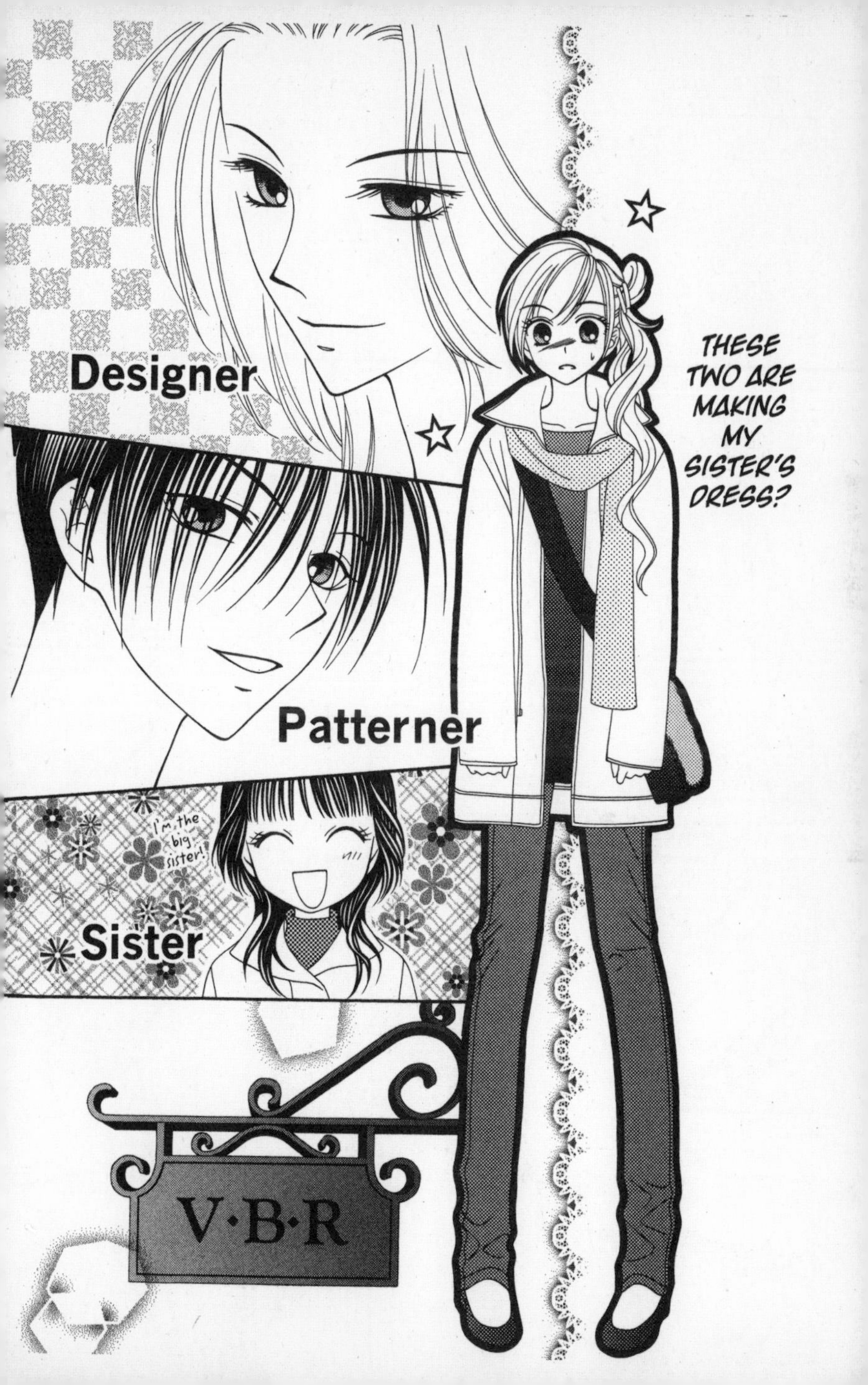
THESE TWO ARE MAKING MY SISTER'S DRESS?
Designer
Patterner
I'm the big sister!
Sister
V·B·R

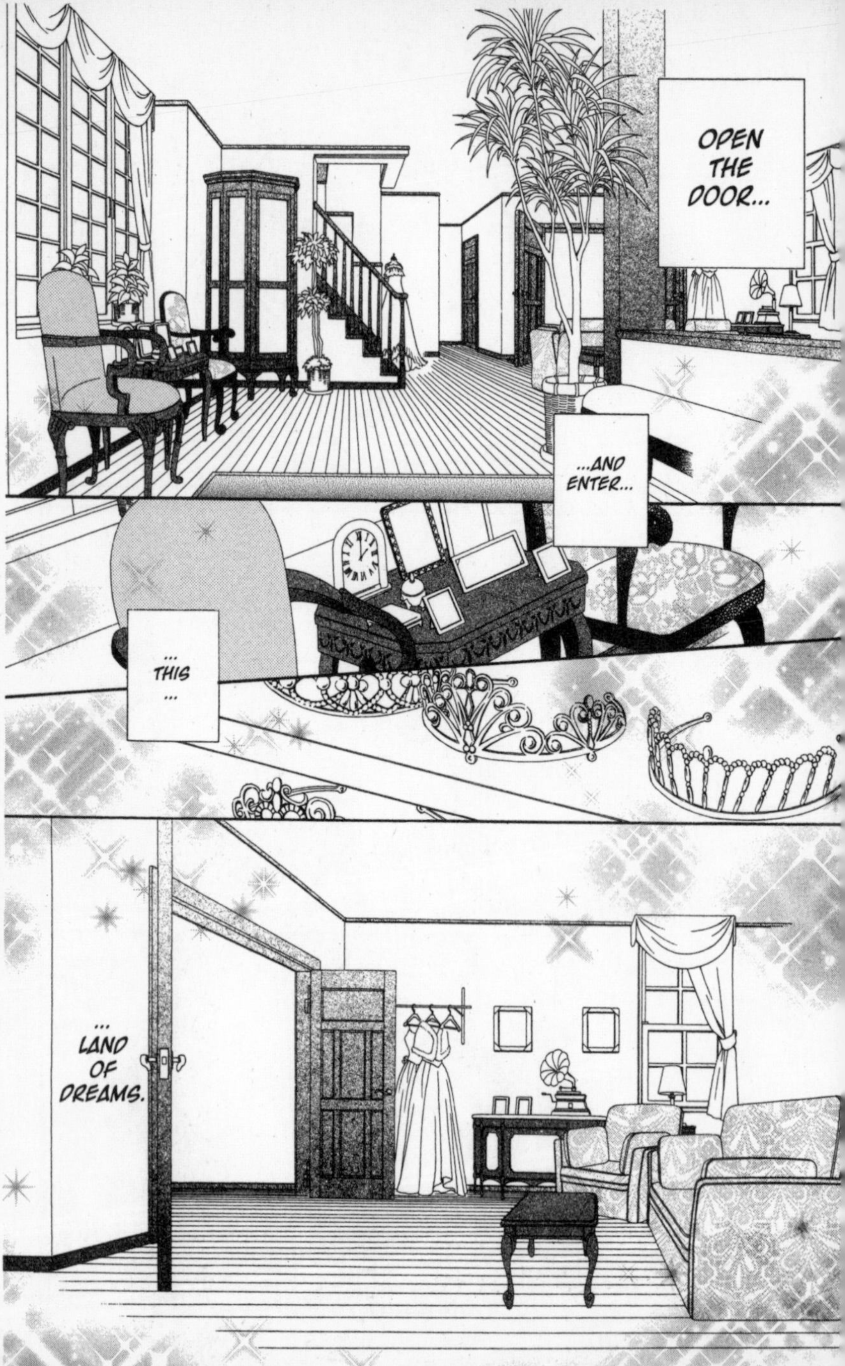
OPEN THE DOOR...
...AND ENTER...
... THIS ...
... LAND OF DREAMS.

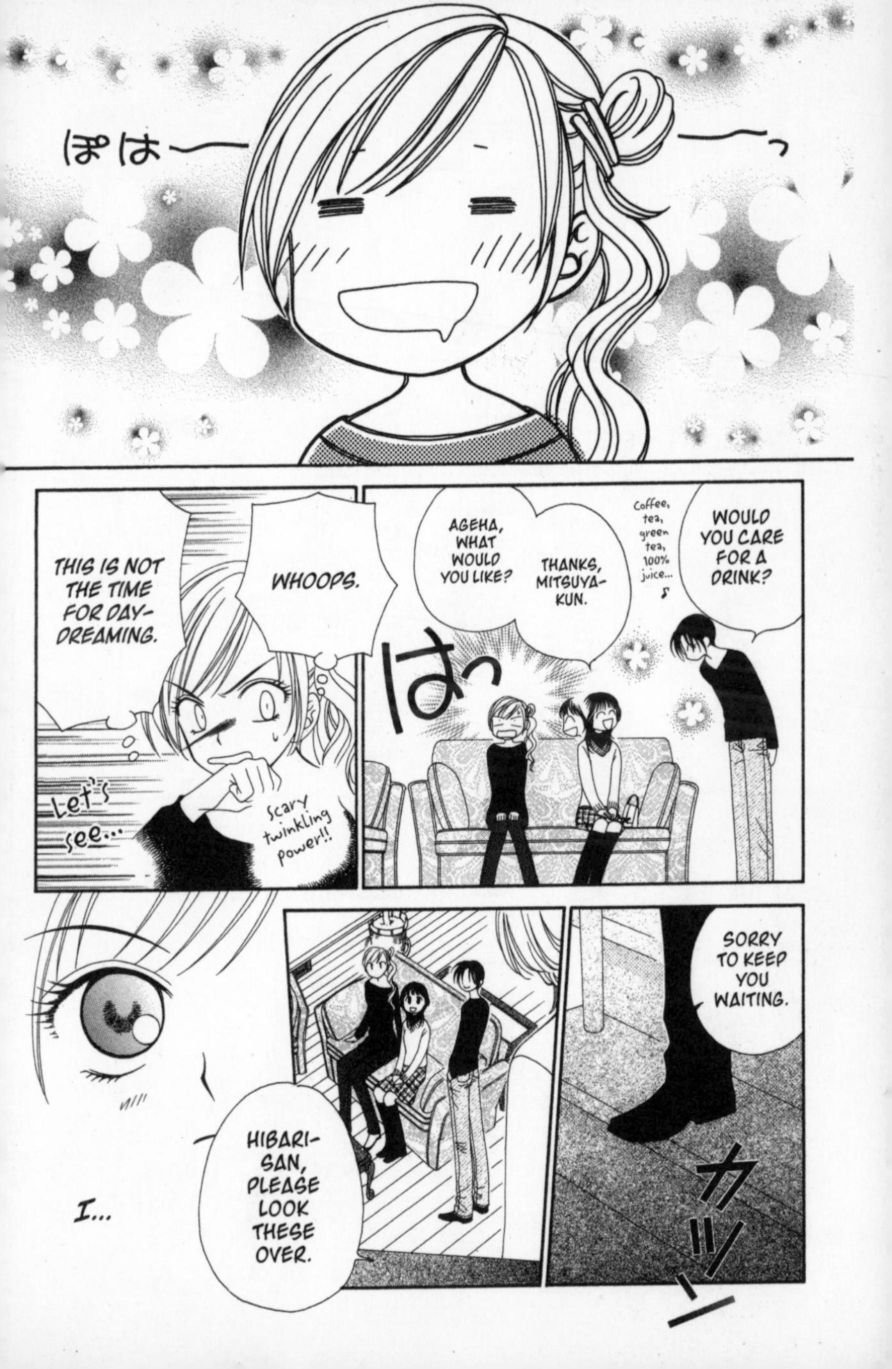
ぽは〜〜〜っ
WOULD YOU CARE FOR A DRINK?
Coffee, tea, green tea, 100% juice... ♪
AGEHA, WHAT WOULD YOU LIKE?
THANKS, MITSUYA-KUN.
はっ
WHOOPS.
THIS IS NOT THE TIME FOR DAY-DREAMING.
Let's see...
Scary twinkling power!!
SORRY TO KEEP YOU WAITING.
カツー
HIBARI-SAN, PLEASE LOOK THESE OVER.
I...

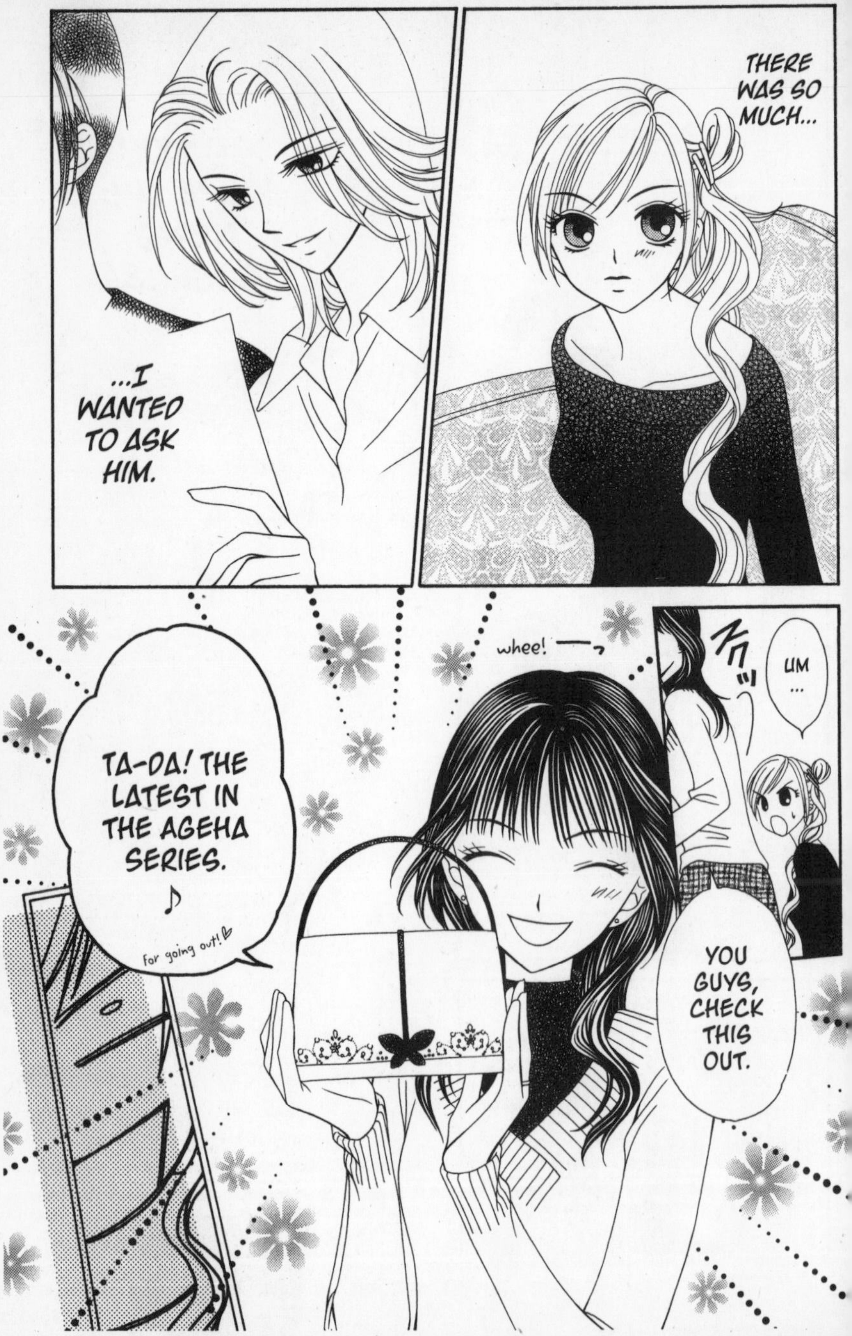
THERE WAS SO MUCH...
...I WANTED TO ASK HIM.
UM ...
whee!
YOU GUYS, CHECK THIS OUT.
TA-DA! THE LATEST IN THE AGEHA SERIES. ♪
for going out!♥

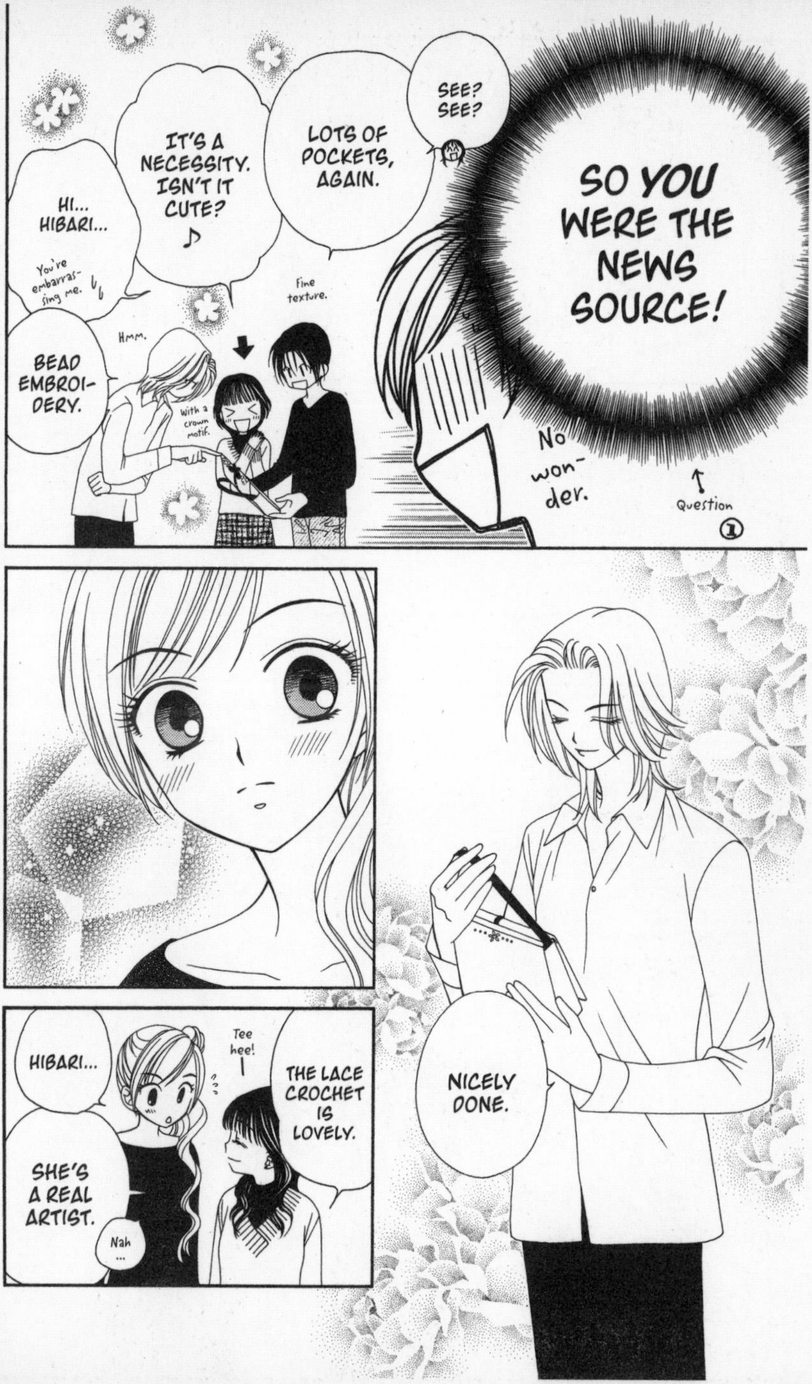
SEE? SEE?
SO YOU WERE THE NEWS SOURCE!
LOTS OF POCKETS, AGAIN.
IT'S A NECESSITY. ISN'T IT CUTE? ♪
HI... HIBARI...
You're embarras-sing me.
Fine texture.
Hmm.
BEAD EMBROI-DERY.
With a crown motif.
No won-der.
Question ①
NICELY DONE.
THE LACE CROCHET IS LOVELY.
Tee hee!
HIBARI...
SHE'S A REAL ARTIST.
Nah ...

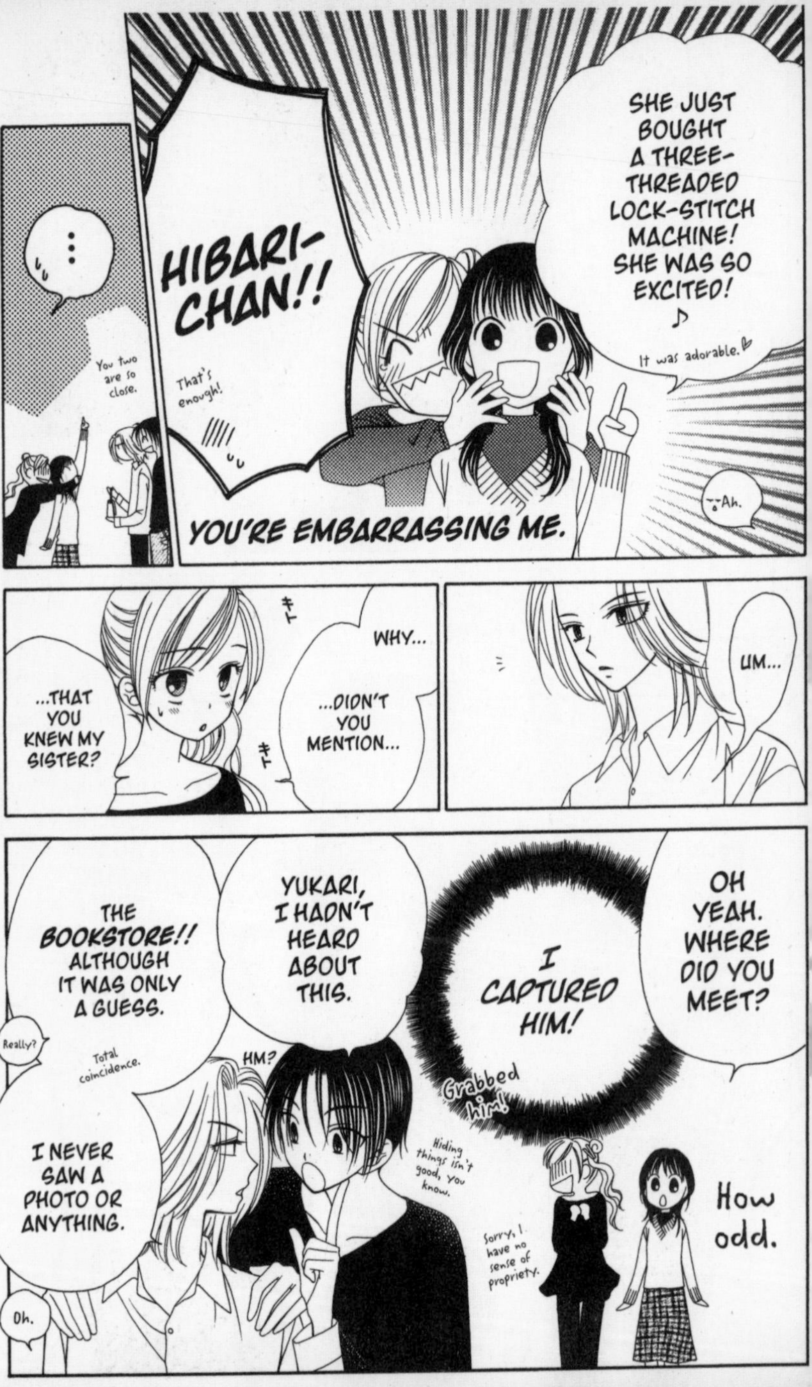
SHE JUST BOUGHT A THREE-THREADED LOCK-STITCH MACHINE! SHE WAS SO EXCITED! ♪
It was adorable.♥
Ah.
HIBARI-CHAN!!
That's enough!
YOU'RE EMBARRASSING ME.
...
You two are so close.
UM...
WHY...
...DIDN'T YOU MENTION...
...THAT YOU KNEW MY SISTER?
OH YEAH. WHERE DID YOU MEET?
I CAPTURED HIM!
Grabbed him!
How odd.
Hiding things isn't good, you know.
Sorry, I have no sense of propriety.
YUKARI, I HADN'T HEARD ABOUT THIS.
HM?
THE BOOKSTORE!! ALTHOUGH IT WAS ONLY A GUESS.
Really?
Total coincidence.
I NEVER SAW A PHOTO OR ANYTHING.
Oh.

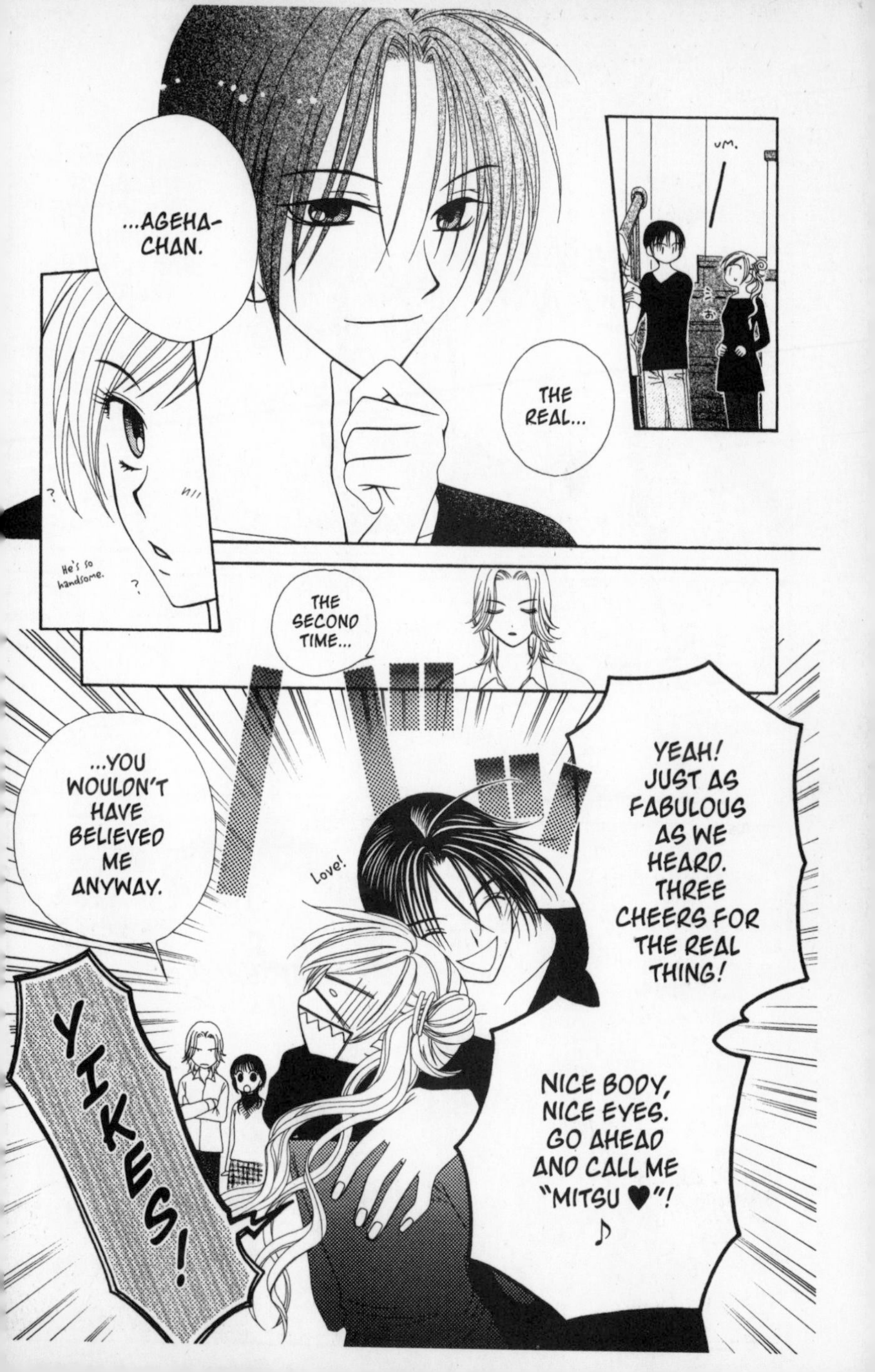
UM.
THE REAL...
...AGEHA-CHAN.
He's so handsome.
THE SECOND TIME...
YEAH! JUST AS FABULOUS AS WE HEARD. THREE CHEERS FOR THE REAL THING!
NICE BODY, NICE EYES. GO AHEAD AND CALL ME "MITSU ♥"! ♪
Love!
...YOU WOULDN'T HAVE BELIEVED ME ANYWAY.
YIKES!

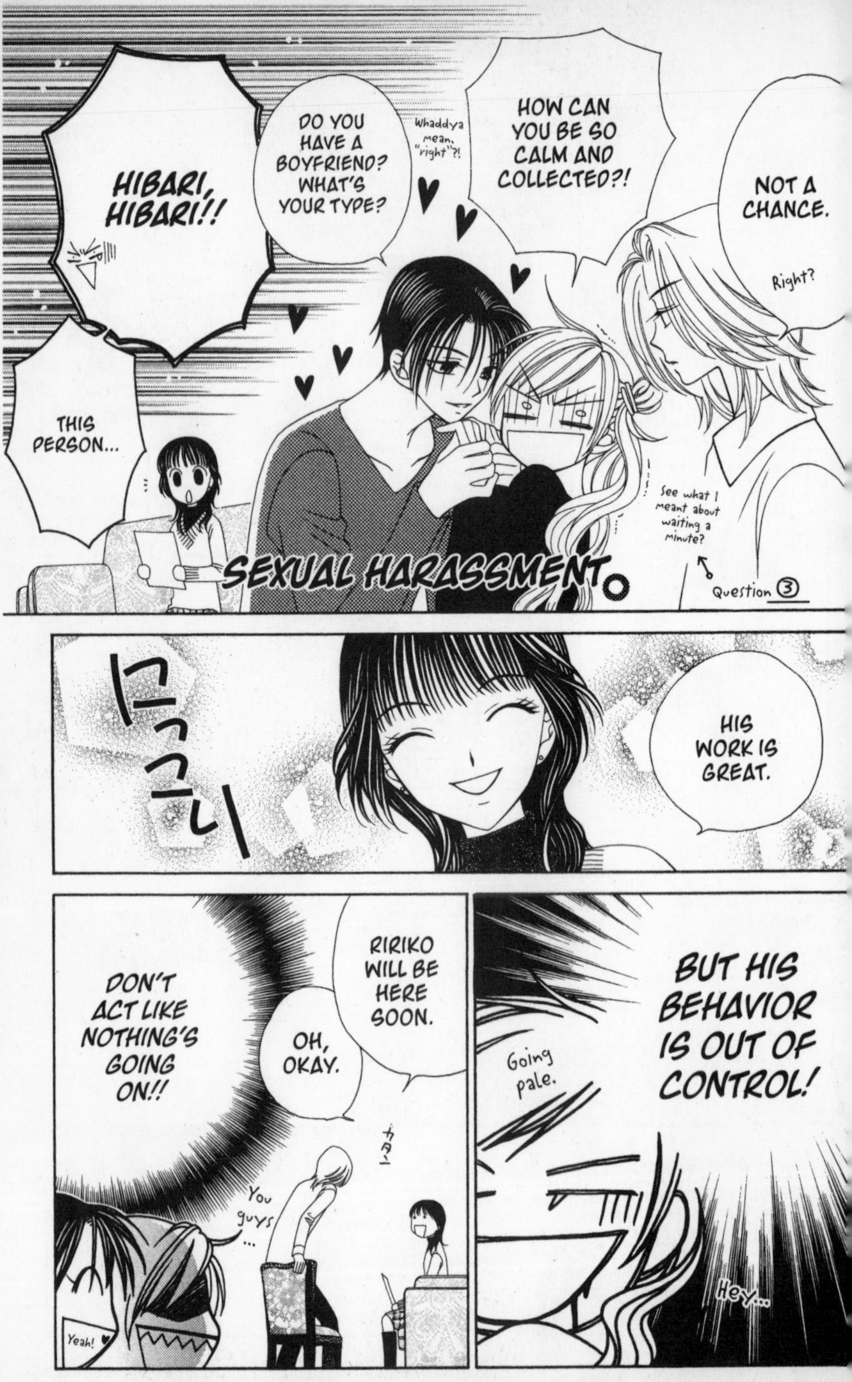
NOT A CHANCE.
Right?
HOW CAN YOU BE SO CALM AND COLLECTED?!
Whaddya mean, "right"?!
DO YOU HAVE A BOYFRIEND? WHAT'S YOUR TYPE?
HIBARI, HIBARI!!
See what I meant about waiting a minute?
Question 3
THIS PERSON...
SEXUAL HARASSMENT.
HIS WORK IS GREAT.
BUT HIS BEHAVIOR IS OUT OF CONTROL!
Going pale.
Hey...
RIRIKO WILL BE HERE SOON.
OH, OKAY.
DON'T ACT LIKE NOTHING'S GOING ON!!
You guys ...
Yeah! ♥

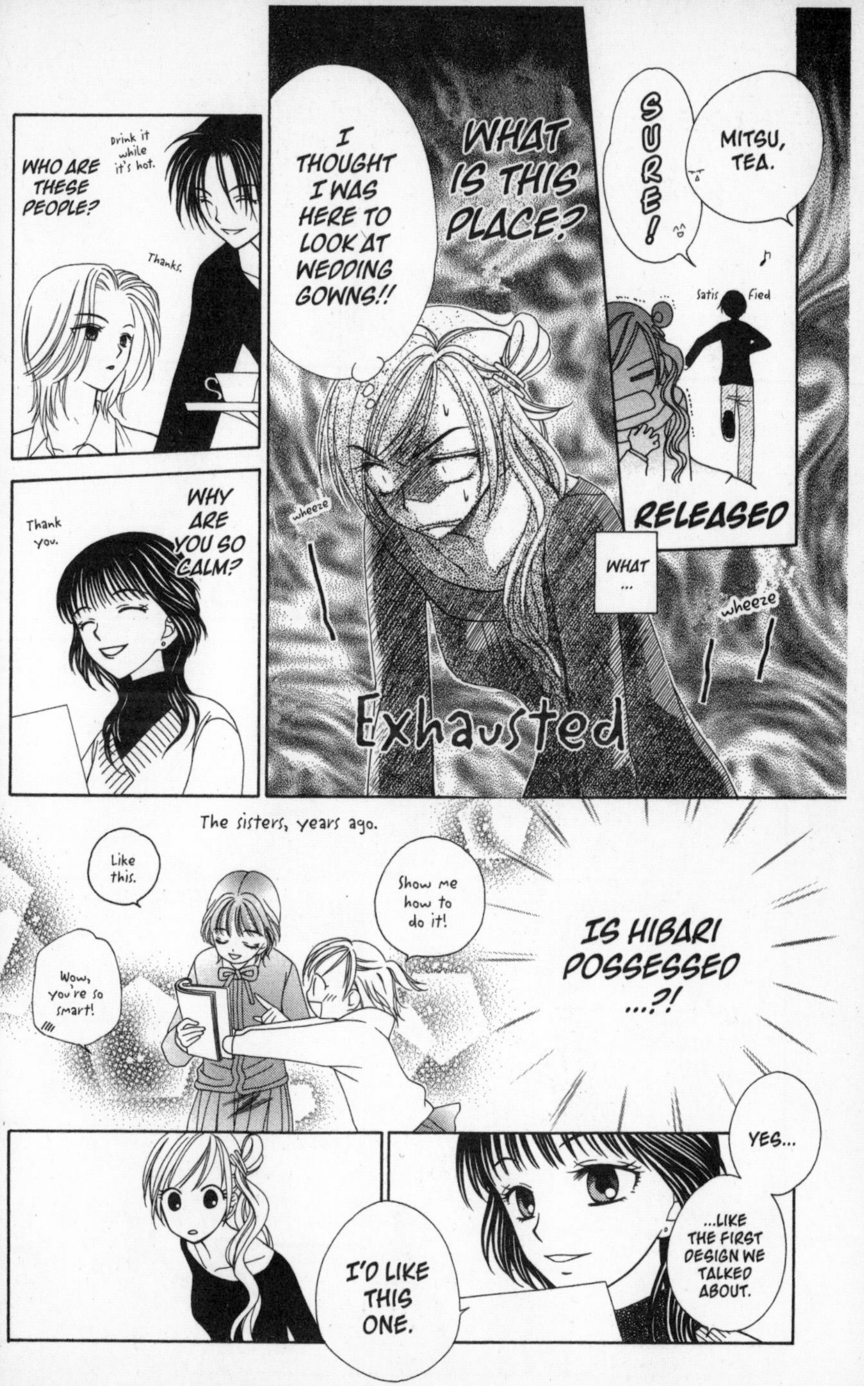
MITSU, TEA.
SURE!
Satisfied
RELEASED
WHAT IS THIS PLACE?
I THOUGHT I WAS HERE TO LOOK AT WEDDING GOWNS!!
WHAT ...
wheeze
wheeze
Exhausted
WHO ARE THESE PEOPLE?
Drink it while it's hot.
Thanks.
WHY ARE YOU SO CALM?
Thank you.
The sisters, years ago.
IS HIBARI POSSESSED ...?!
Show me how to do it!
Like this.
Wow, you're so smart!
YES...
...LIKE THE FIRST DESIGN WE TALKED ABOUT.
I'D LIKE THIS ONE.

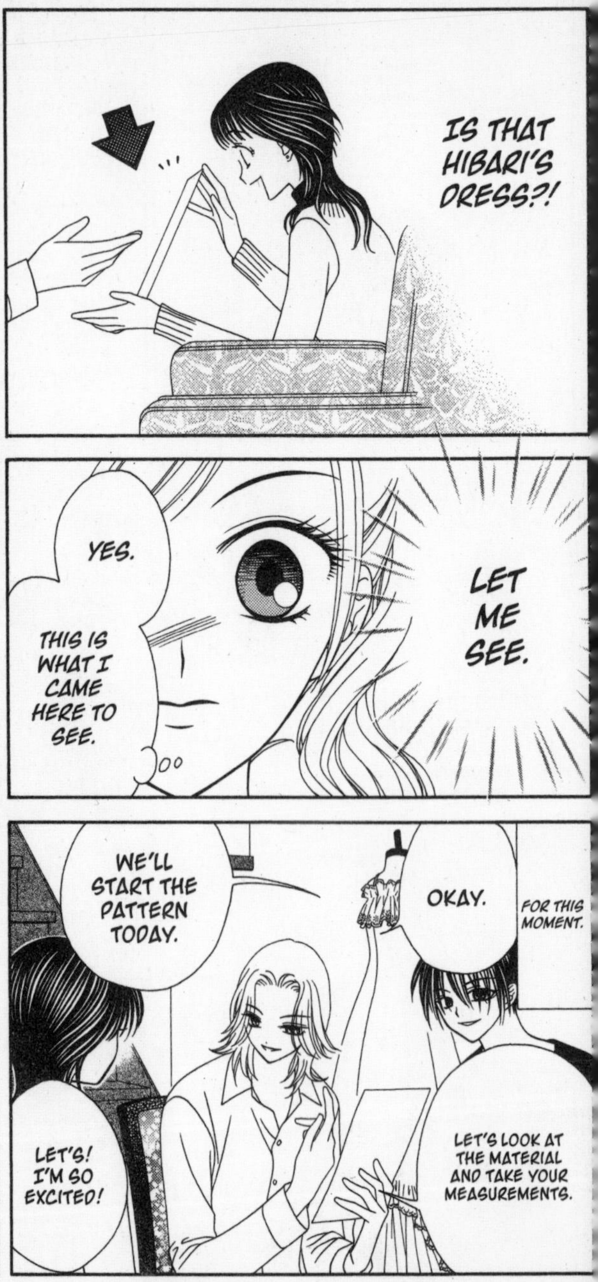
IS THAT HIBARI'S DRESS?!
LET ME SEE.
YES.
THIS IS WHAT I CAME HERE TO SEE.
FOR THIS MOMENT.
OKAY.
WE'LL START THE PATTERN TODAY.
LET'S LOOK AT THE MATERIAL AND TAKE YOUR MEASUREMENTS.
LET'S! I'M SO EXCITED!

I started *VB Rose* in February, but to tell you the truth, I didn't finish the pencils until November. I began writing it right after I finished *Tears of a Lamb*.

My first art book was released this March. (Thank you to everyone who bought it!) But as late as mid-October, I still didn't know how to structure it or how many pages it would have.

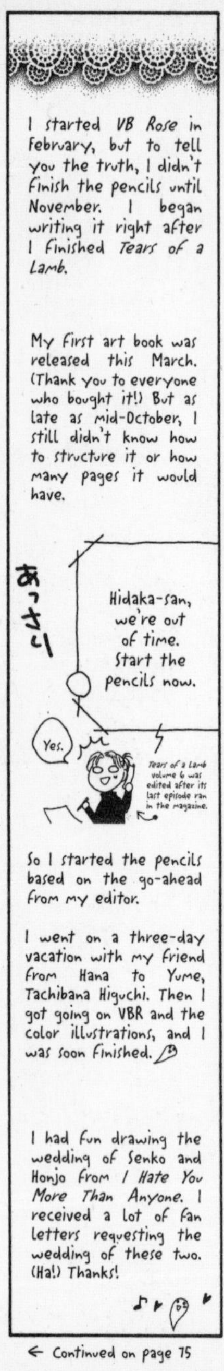
あっさり
Hidaka-san, we're out of time. Start the pencils now.
Yes.
Tears of a Lamb volume 6 was edited after its last episode ran in the magazine.

So I started the pencils based on the go-ahead from my editor.

I went on a three-day vacation with my friend from Hana to Yume, Tachibana Higuchi. Then I got going on VBR and the color illustrations, and I was soon finished.

I had fun drawing the wedding of Senko and Honjo from *I Hate You More Than Anyone*. I received a lot of fan letters requesting the wedding of these two. (Ha!) Thanks!

← Continued on page 75

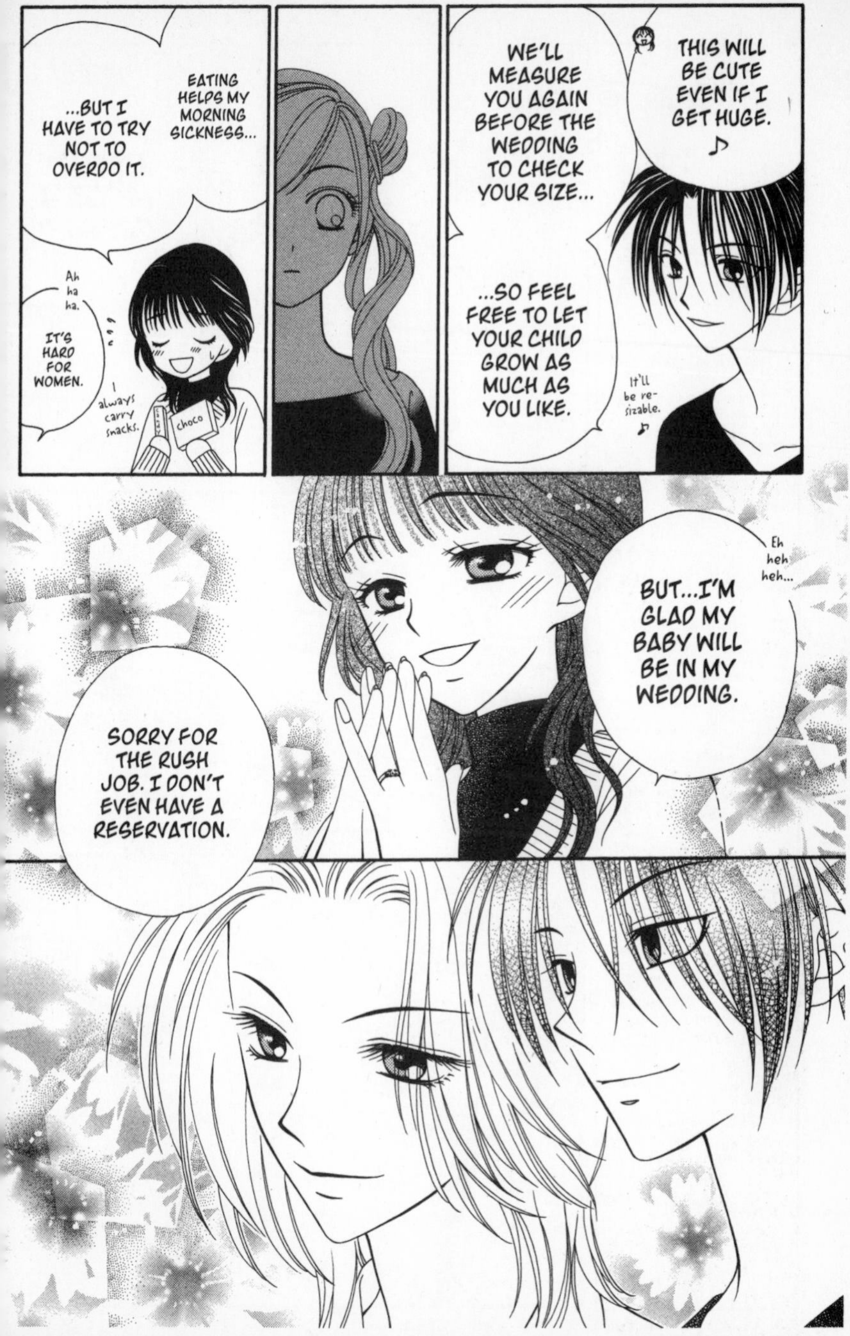
THIS WILL BE CUTE EVEN IF I GET HUGE. ♪
WE'LL MEASURE YOU AGAIN BEFORE THE WEDDING TO CHECK YOUR SIZE...
...SO FEEL FREE TO LET YOUR CHILD GROW AS MUCH AS YOU LIKE.
It'll be re-sizable. ♪
EATING HELPS MY MORNING SICKNESS...
...BUT I HAVE TO TRY NOT TO OVERDO IT.
I always carry snacks.
choco
Ah ha ha.
IT'S HARD FOR WOMEN.
Eh heh heh...
BUT...I'M GLAD MY BABY WILL BE IN MY WEDDING.
SORRY FOR THE RUSH JOB. I DON'T EVEN HAVE A RESERVATION.

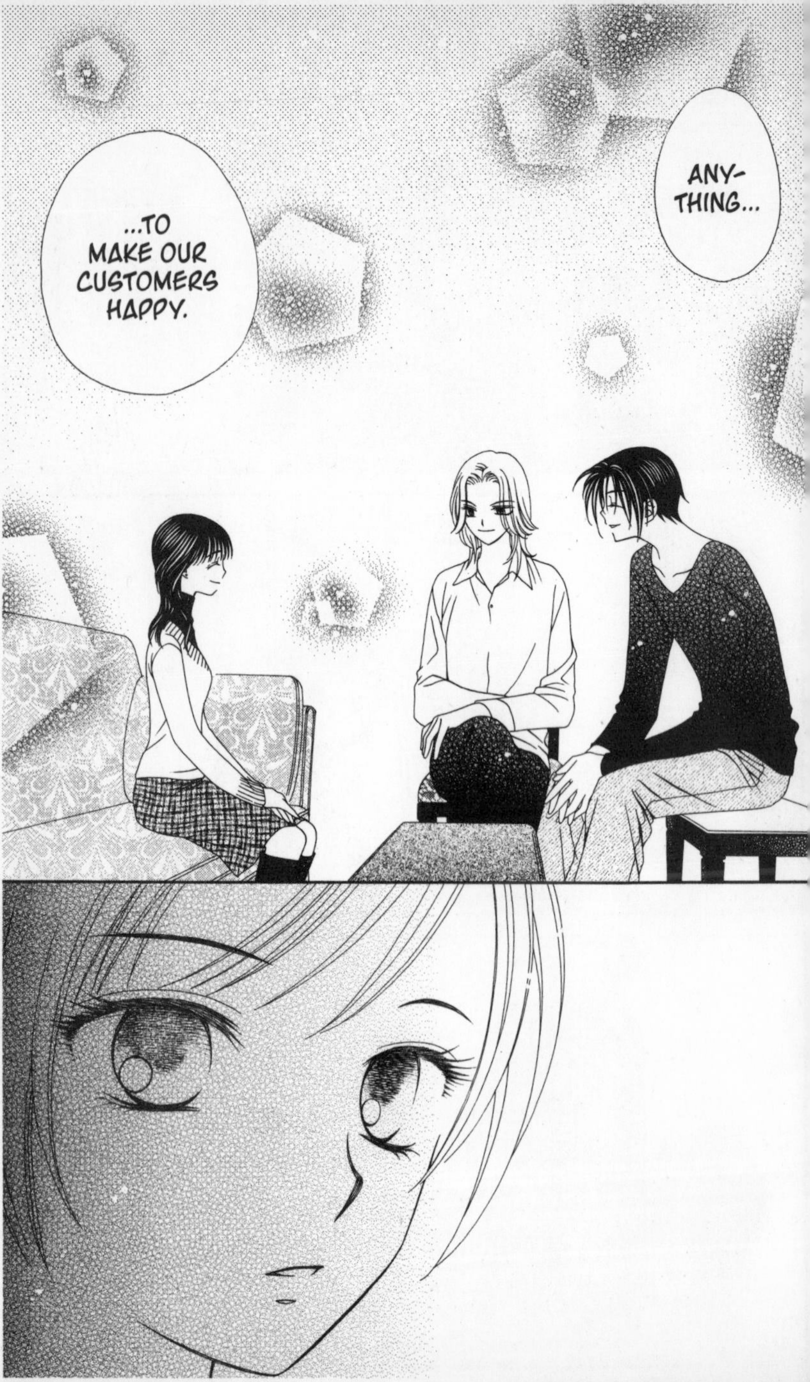
ANY-THING...
...TO MAKE OUR CUSTOMERS HAPPY.

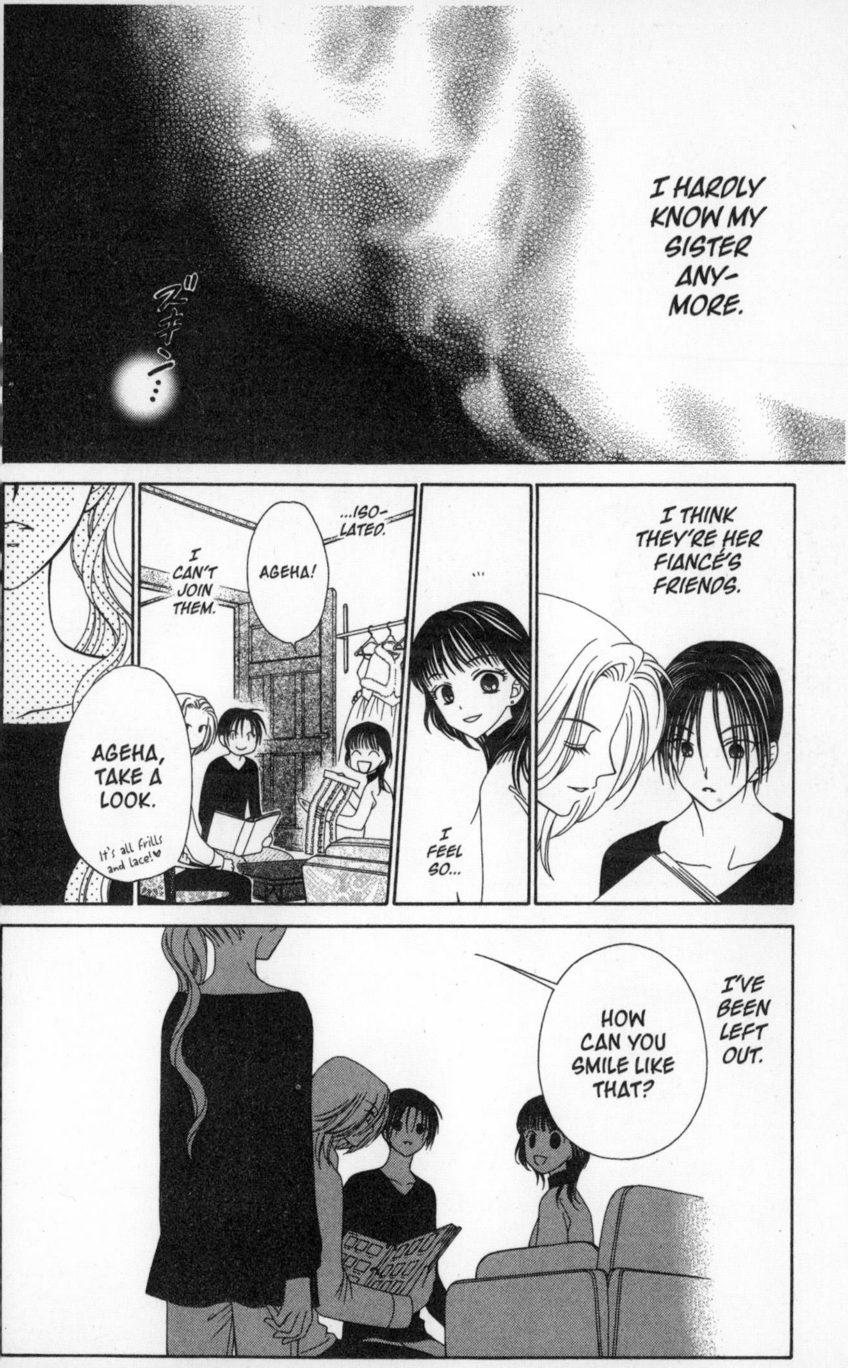
I HARDLY KNOW MY SISTER ANYMORE.
ズキッ…
I THINK THEY'RE HER FIANCÉ'S FRIENDS.
...
I FEEL SO...
...ISO-LATED.
AGEHA!
I CAN'T JOIN THEM.
AGEHA, TAKE A LOOK.
It's all frills and lace!♥
I'VE BEEN LEFT OUT.
HOW CAN YOU SMILE LIKE THAT?

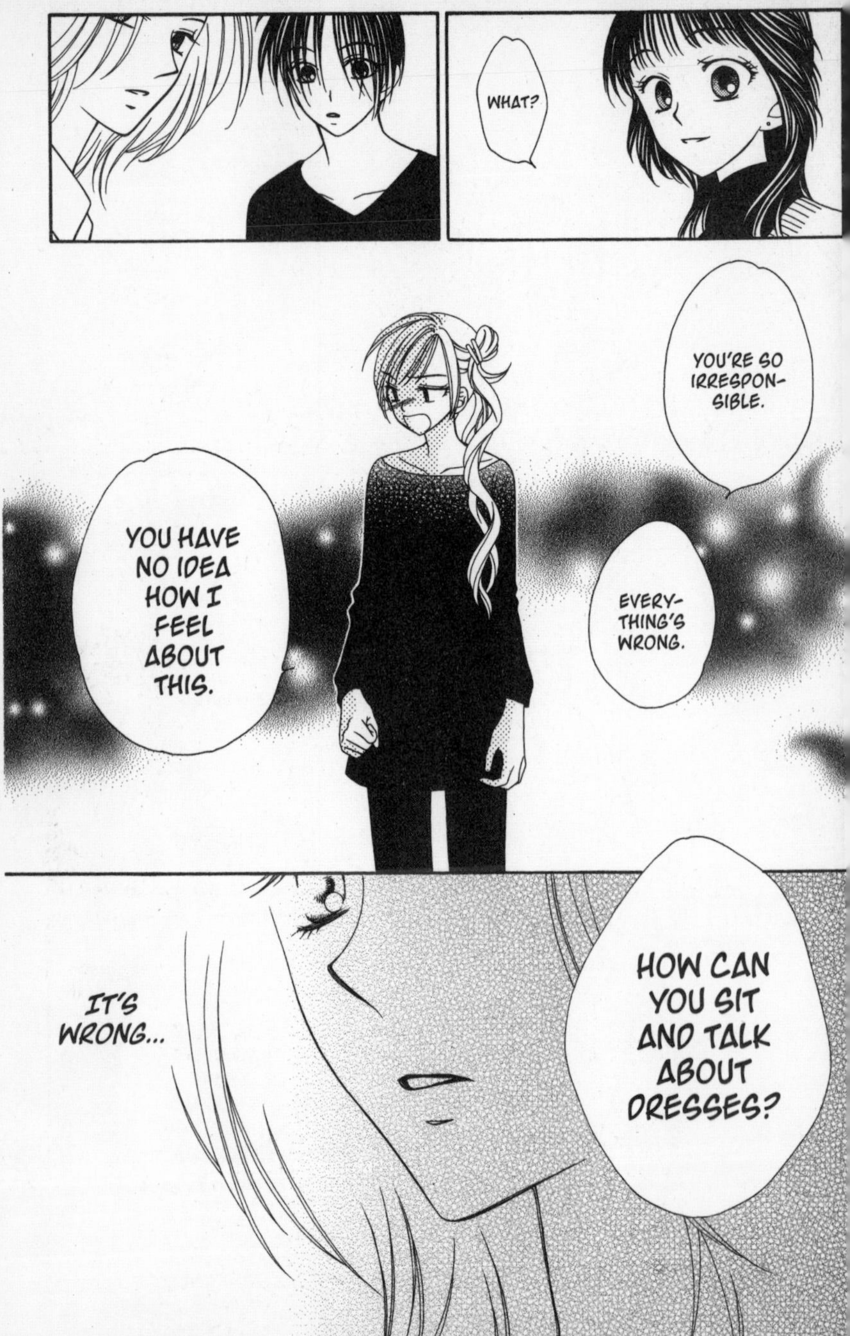
WHAT?
YOU'RE SO IRRESPONSIBLE.
EVERYTHING'S WRONG.
YOU HAVE NO IDEA HOW I FEEL ABOUT THIS.
HOW CAN YOU SIT AND TALK ABOUT DRESSES?
IT'S WRONG...

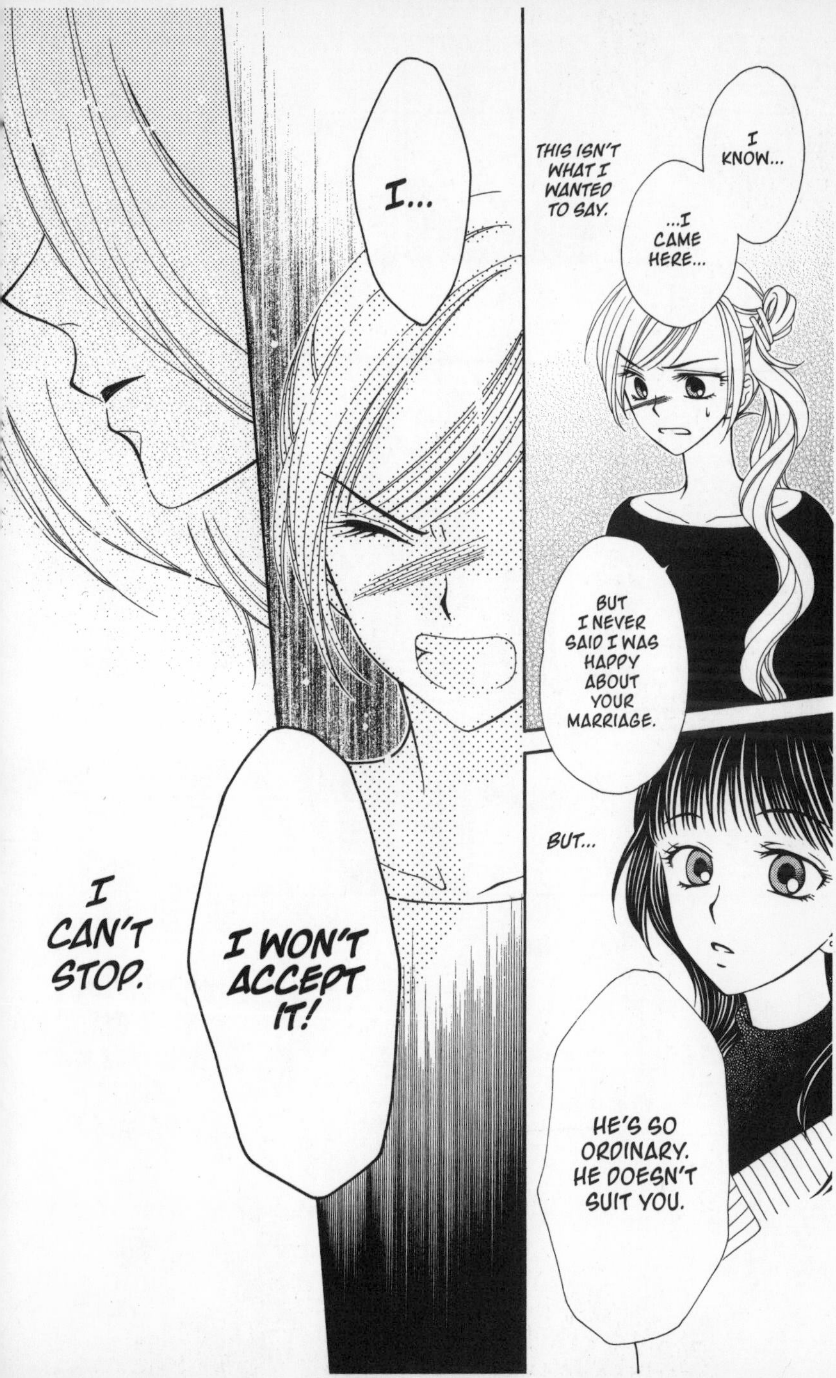
I KNOW...
...I CAME HERE...
THIS ISN'T WHAT I WANTED TO SAY.
BUT I NEVER SAID I WAS HAPPY ABOUT YOUR MARRIAGE.
BUT...
HE'S SO ORDINARY. HE DOESN'T SUIT YOU.
I...
I WON'T ACCEPT IT!
I CAN'T STOP.

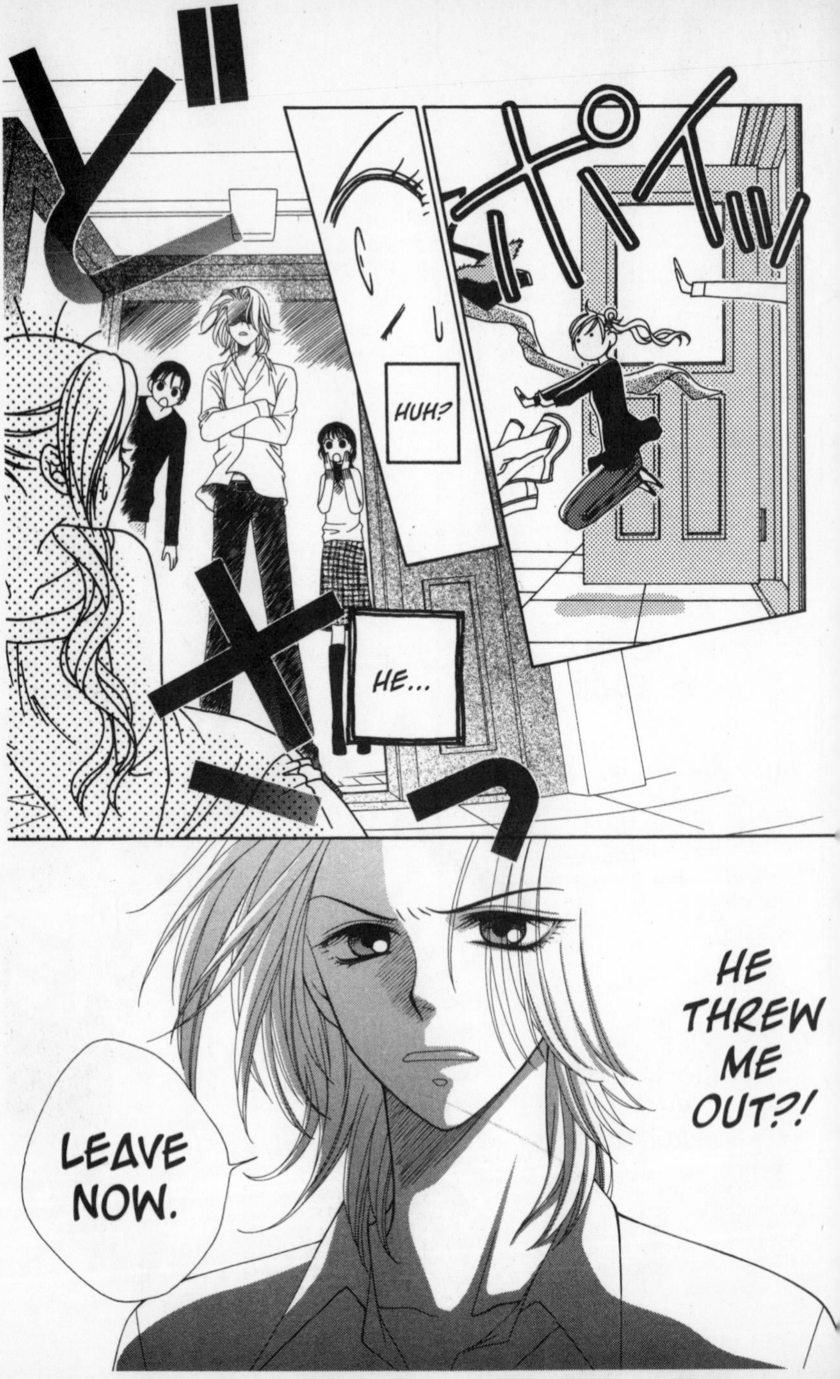
ポイッ
HUH?
HE...
HE THREW ME OUT?!
LEAVE NOW.

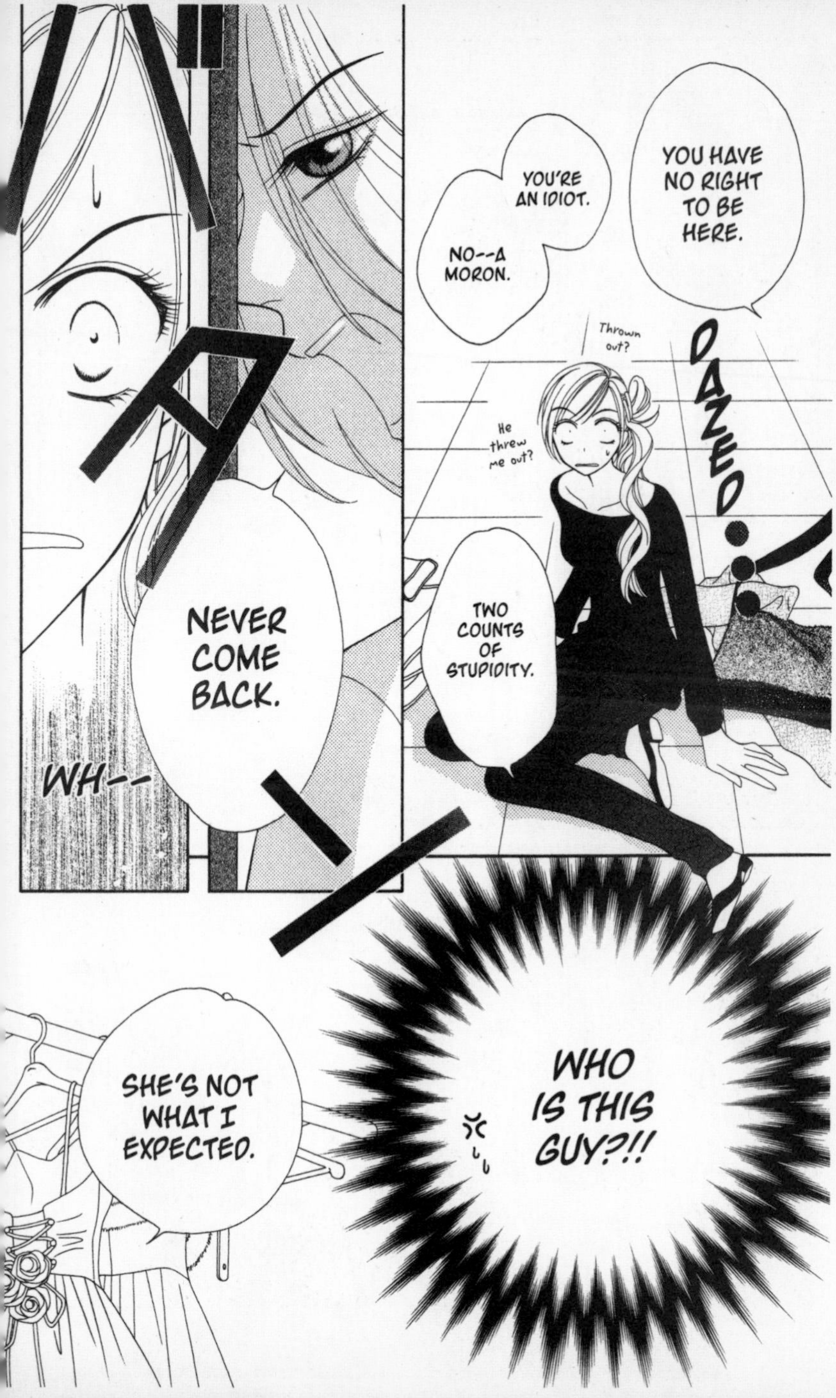
YOU HAVE NO RIGHT TO BE HERE.
YOU'RE AN IDIOT.
NO--A MORON.
Thrown out?
DAZED...
He threw me out?
TWO COUNTS OF STUPIDITY.
NEVER COME BACK.
WH--
WHO IS THIS GUY?!!
SHE'S NOT WHAT I EXPECTED.

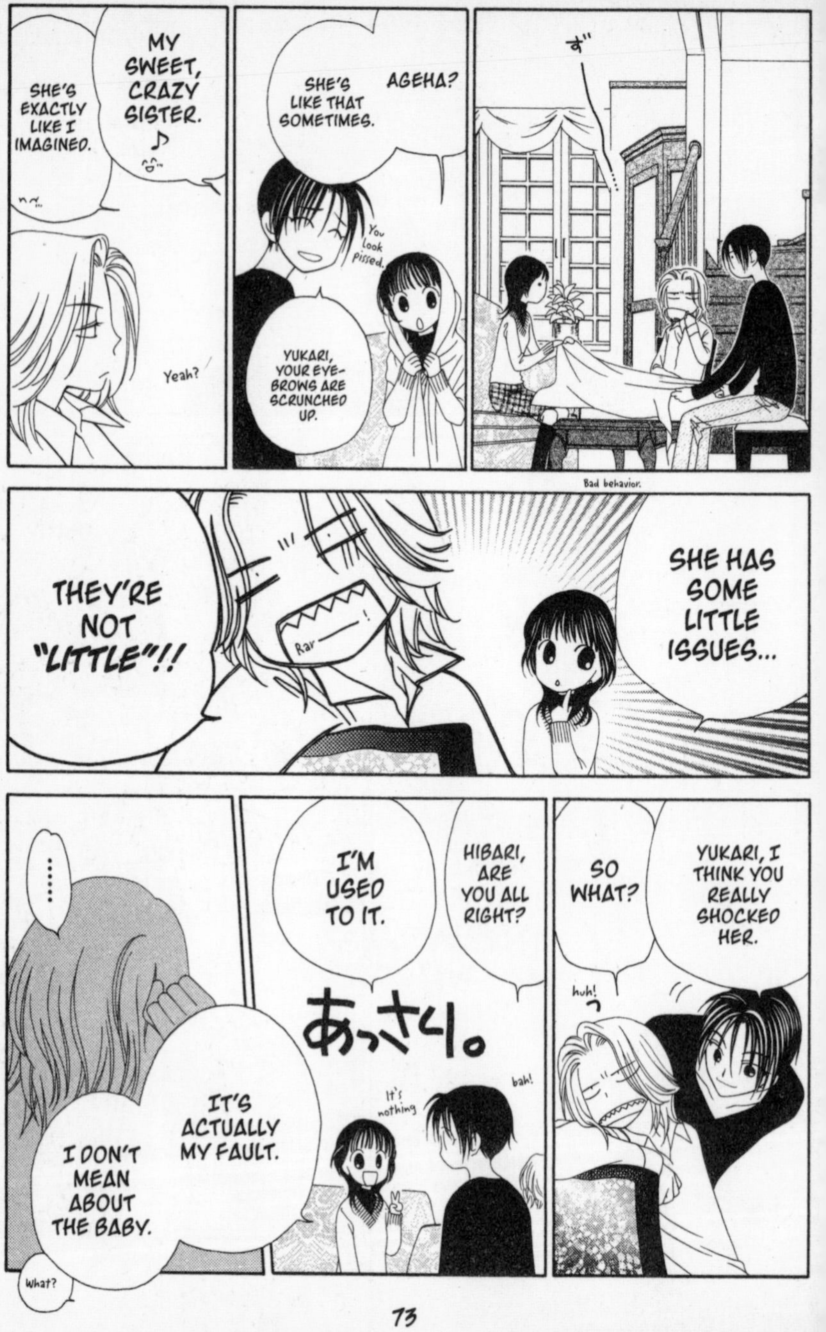
ず
Bad behavior.
AGEHA?
SHE'S LIKE THAT SOMETIMES.
You look pissed.
YUKARI, YOUR EYE-BROWS ARE SCRUNCHED UP.
MY SWEET, CRAZY SISTER. ♪
SHE'S EXACTLY LIKE I IMAGINED.
Yeah?
SHE HAS SOME LITTLE ISSUES...
Rar—!
THEY'RE NOT "LITTLE"!!
YUKARI, I THINK YOU REALLY SHOCKED HER.
SO WHAT?
huh!
HIBARI, ARE YOU ALL RIGHT?
I'M USED TO IT.
あっさり。
bah!
It's nothing
......
IT'S ACTUALLY MY FAULT.
I DON'T MEAN ABOUT THE BABY.
What?

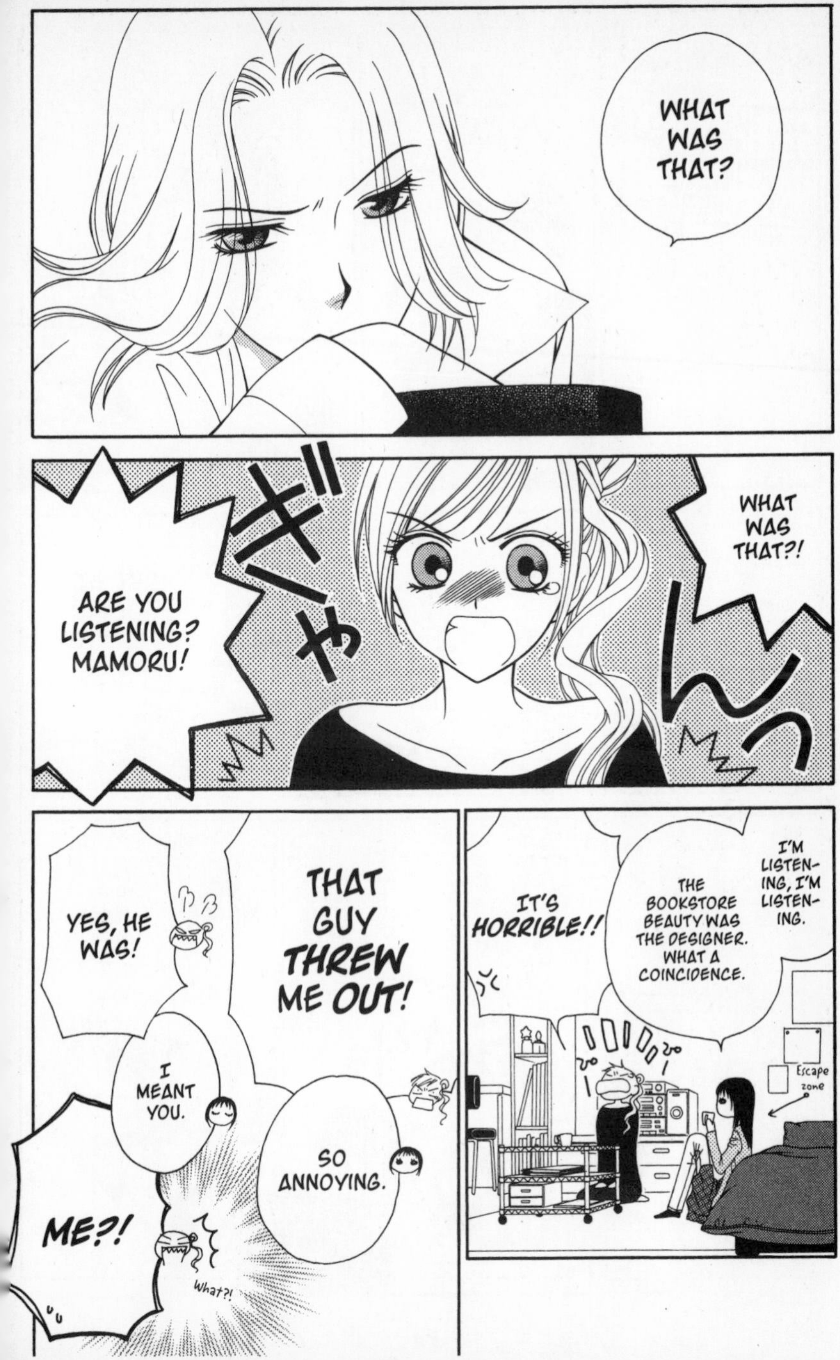
WHAT WAS THAT?
WHAT WAS THAT?!
ARE YOU LISTENING? MAMORU!
I'M LISTENING, I'M LISTENING.
THE BOOKSTORE BEAUTY WAS THE DESIGNER. WHAT A COINCIDENCE.
IT'S HORRIBLE!!
Escape zone
THAT GUY THREW ME OUT!
YES, HE WAS!
SO ANNOYING.
I MEANT YOU.
ME?!
What?!

YOU USUALLY WOULDN'T DO SOMETHING LIKE THAT.
NO WONDER HE WAS ANGRY.
I DIDN'T...
YOU'RE SAYING NONE OF IT WAS YOUR FAULT?
I CAN'T FACE MY SISTER NOW.
What did I say?
AWW~!
There, there.
YES, YOU SHOULD WAIT 'TIL YOU'VE COOLED OFF.
HIBARI PROBABLY DOESN'T MIND, THOUGH.
Heh.
Correct.

The pencils I started on November 4 were finished on the 12th. The first episode was supposed to be 40 pages, but it became 43. I assumed my editor, Yamaki, would make some cuts, but...

I read it. There's so much crammed in toward the end...

...you may as well make it longer.

Add more pages!

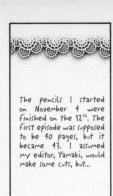

More pages ?!

I slept in and ran some errands the next day, and made the changes that night. I was so relaxed. It felt like vacation. And the page count increased to 45!

They were flexible about that because I turned it in early.

But including the color pages increased the count to 47!

← Continued on page 109.

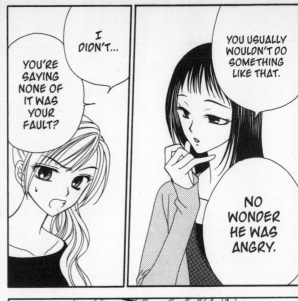

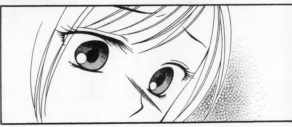

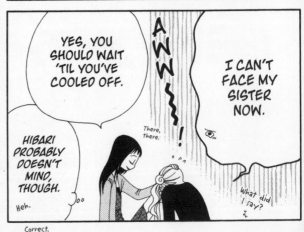

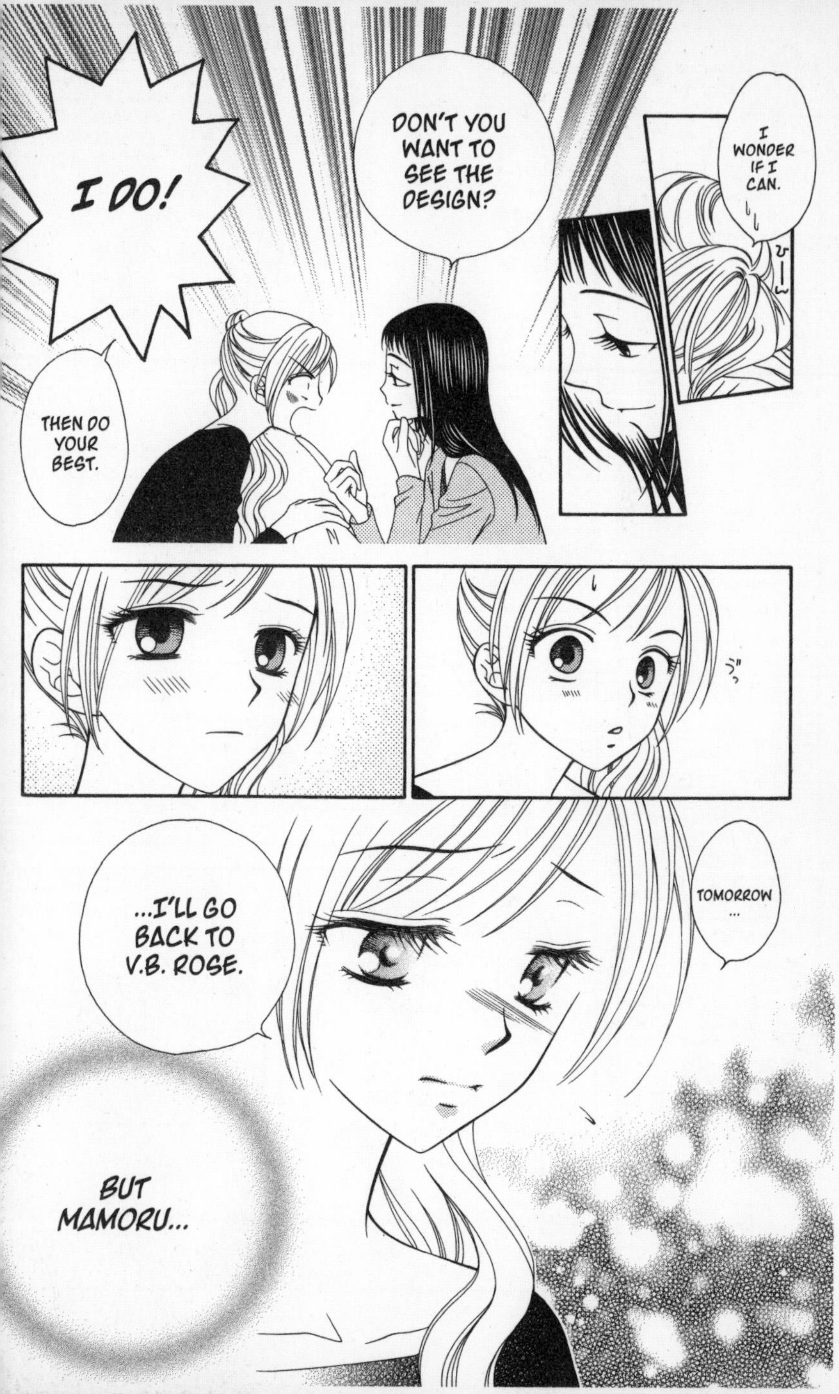
I WONDER IF I CAN.
DON'T YOU WANT TO SEE THE DESIGN?
I DO!
THEN DO YOUR BEST.
TOMORROW...
...I'LL GO BACK TO V.B. ROSE.
BUT MAMORU...

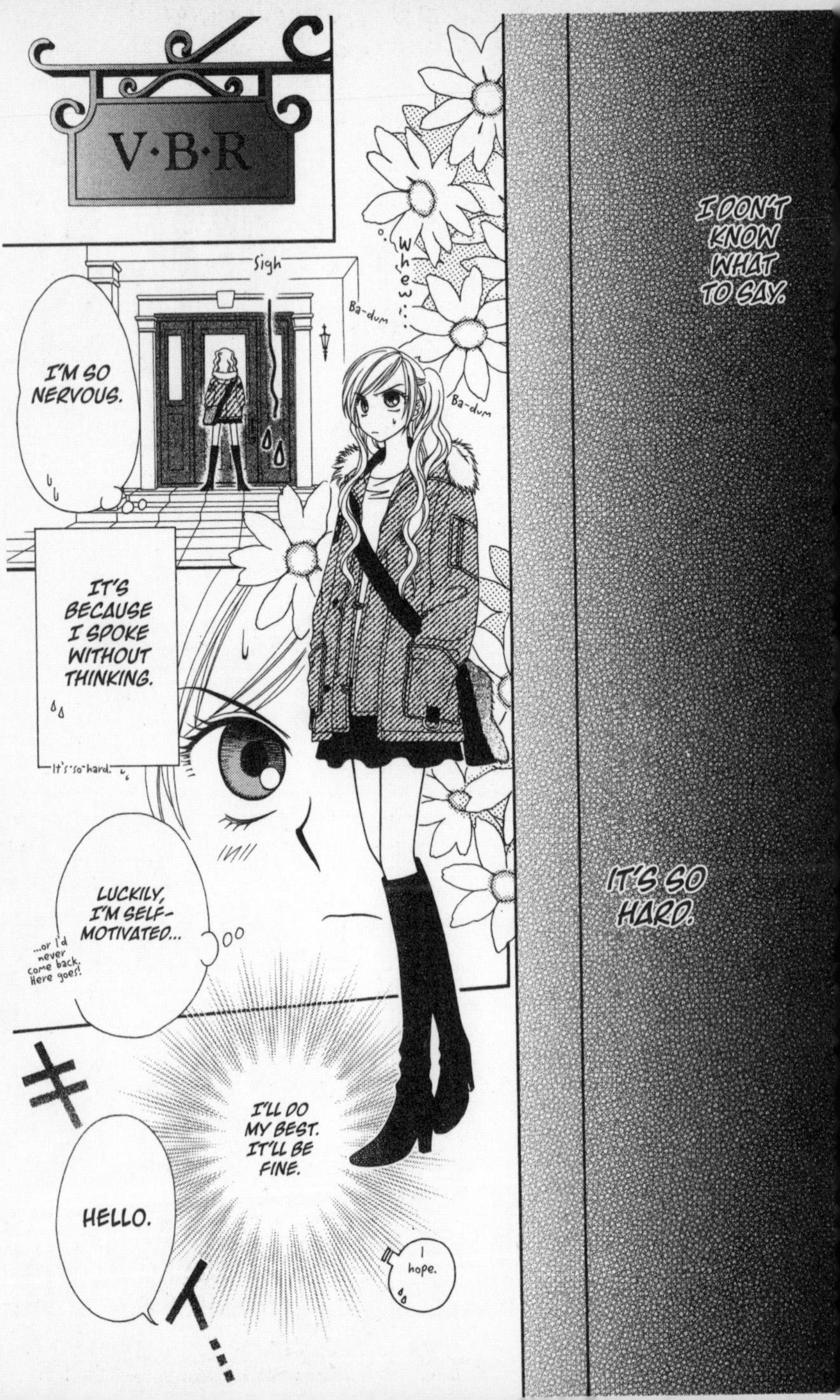
I DON'T KNOW WHAT TO SAY.
IT'S SO HARD.
V·B·R
Sigh
Whew...
Ba-dum
I'M SO NERVOUS.
Ba-dum
IT'S BECAUSE I SPOKE WITHOUT THINKING.
It's so hard.
LUCKILY, I'M SELF-MOTIVATED...
...or I'd never come back. Here goes!
I'LL DO MY BEST. IT'LL BE FINE.
I hope.
HELLO.

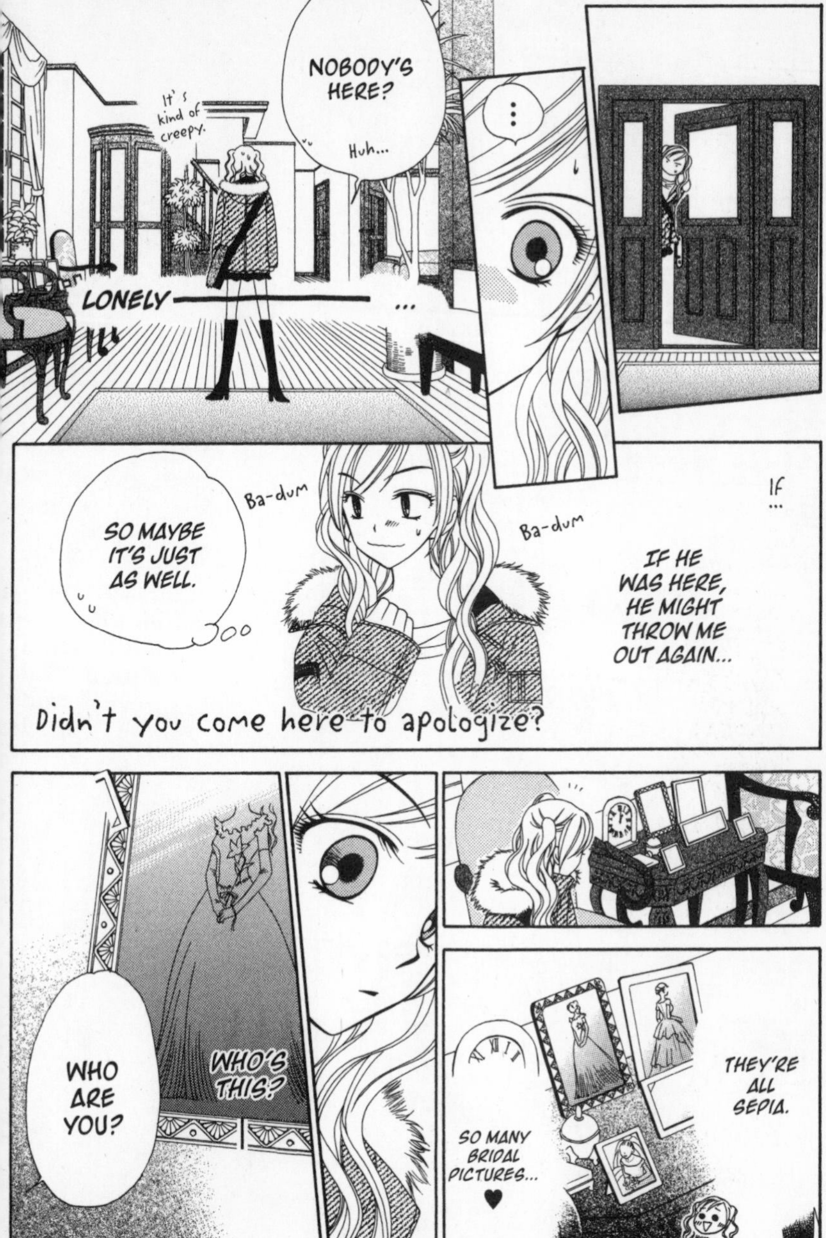
...
NOBODY'S HERE?
Huh...
It's kind of creepy.
LONELY
...
If...
IF HE WAS HERE, HE MIGHT THROW ME OUT AGAIN...
Ba-dum
Ba-dum
SO MAYBE IT'S JUST AS WELL.
Didn't you come here to apologize?
THEY'RE ALL SEPIA.
SO MANY BRIDAL PICTURES...
WHO'S THIS?
WHO ARE YOU?

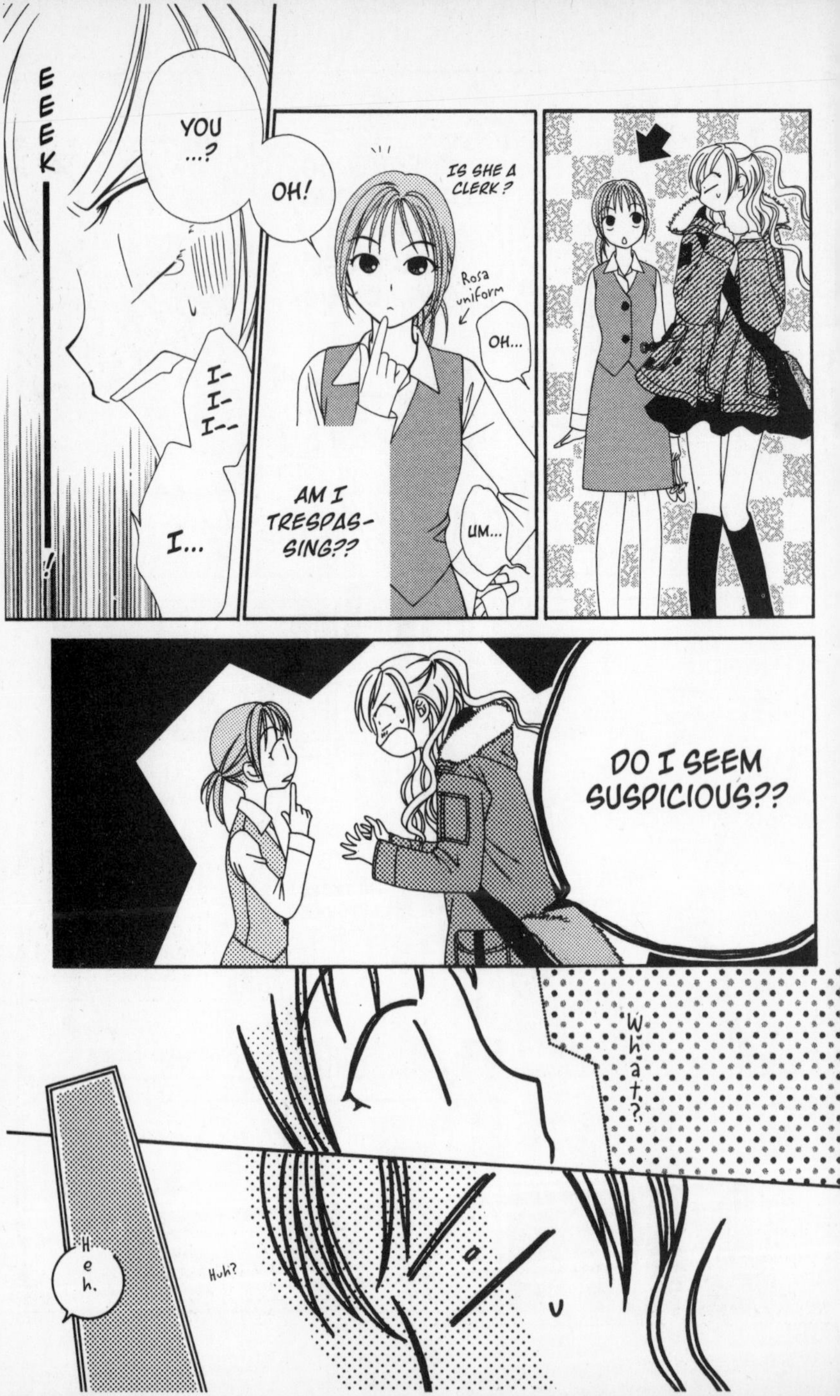
IS SHE A CLERK?
Rosa uniform
OH...
UM...
AM I TRESPAS-SING??
OH!
YOU ...?
EEEK!
I- I- I--
I...
DO I SEEM SUSPICIOUS??
What?
Huh?
Heh.

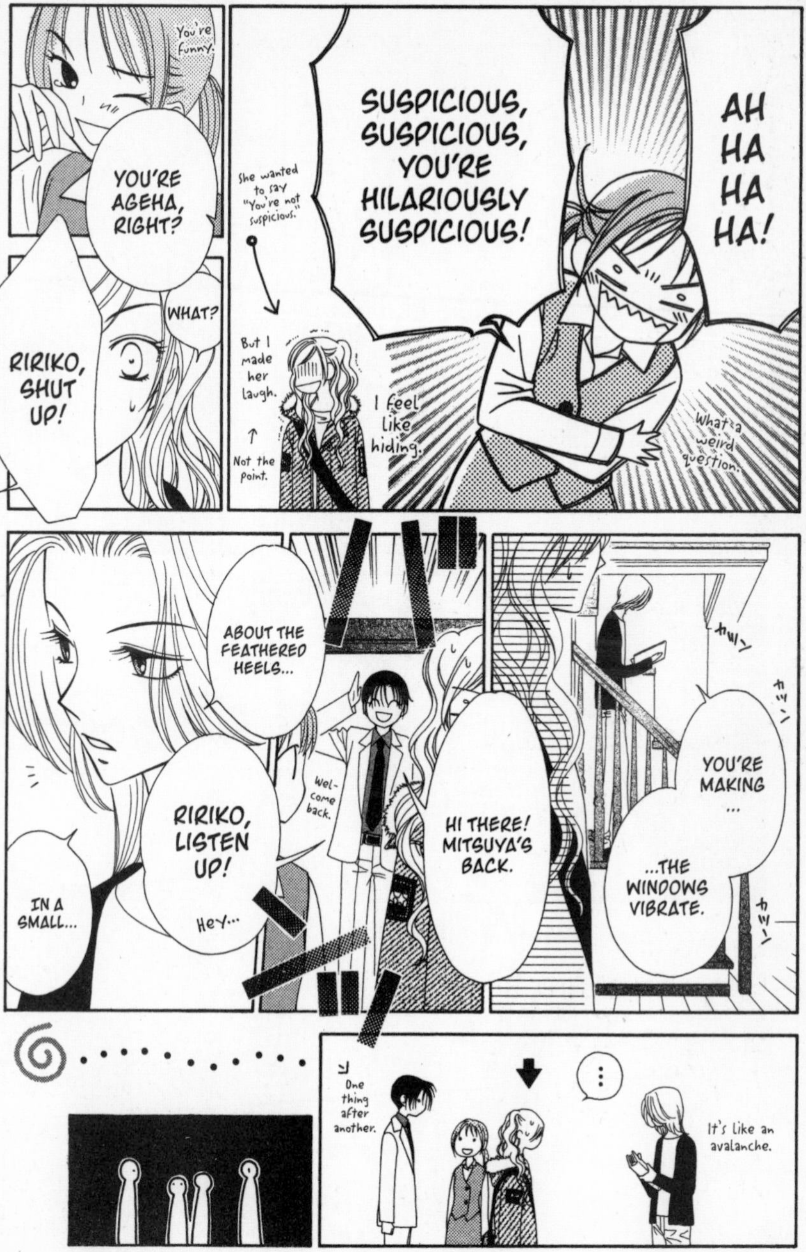
AH HA HA HA!
SUSPICIOUS, SUSPICIOUS, YOU'RE HILARIOUSLY SUSPICIOUS!
What a weird question.
I feel like hiding.
She wanted to say "You're not suspicious."
But I made her laugh.
Not the point.
You're funny.
YOU'RE AGEHA, RIGHT?
WHAT?
RIRIKO, SHUT UP!
YOU'RE MAKING...
...THE WINDOWS VIBRATE.
HI THERE! MITSUYA'S BACK.
Wel-come back.
ABOUT THE FEATHERED HEELS...
RIRIKO, LISTEN UP!
Hey...
IN A SMALL...
It's like an avalanche.
...
One thing after another.

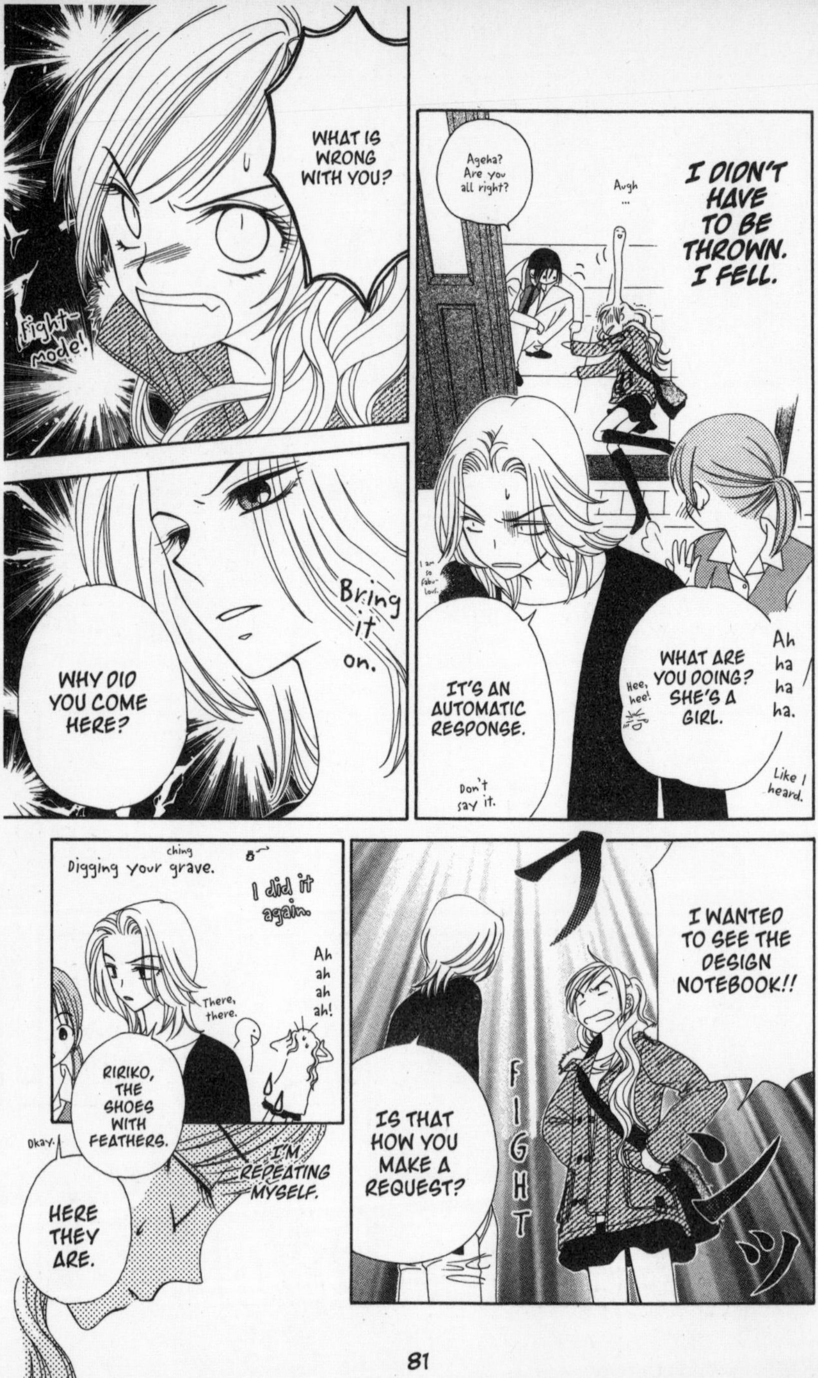
Ageha? Are you all right?
Augh ...
I DIDN'T HAVE TO BE THROWN. I FELL.
I am so fabulous.
Ah ha ha ha.
WHAT ARE YOU DOING? SHE'S A GIRL.
Hee, hee!
Like I heard.
IT'S AN AUTOMATIC RESPONSE.
Don't say it.
WHAT IS WRONG WITH YOU?
Fight-mode!
Bring it on.
WHY DID YOU COME HERE?
I WANTED TO SEE THE DESIGN NOTEBOOK!!
FIGHT
IS THAT HOW YOU MAKE A REQUEST?
ching
Digging your grave.
I did it again.
Ah ah ah ah!
There, there.
RIRIKO, THE SHOES WITH FEATHERS.
I'M REPEATING MYSELF.
Okay.
HERE THEY ARE.

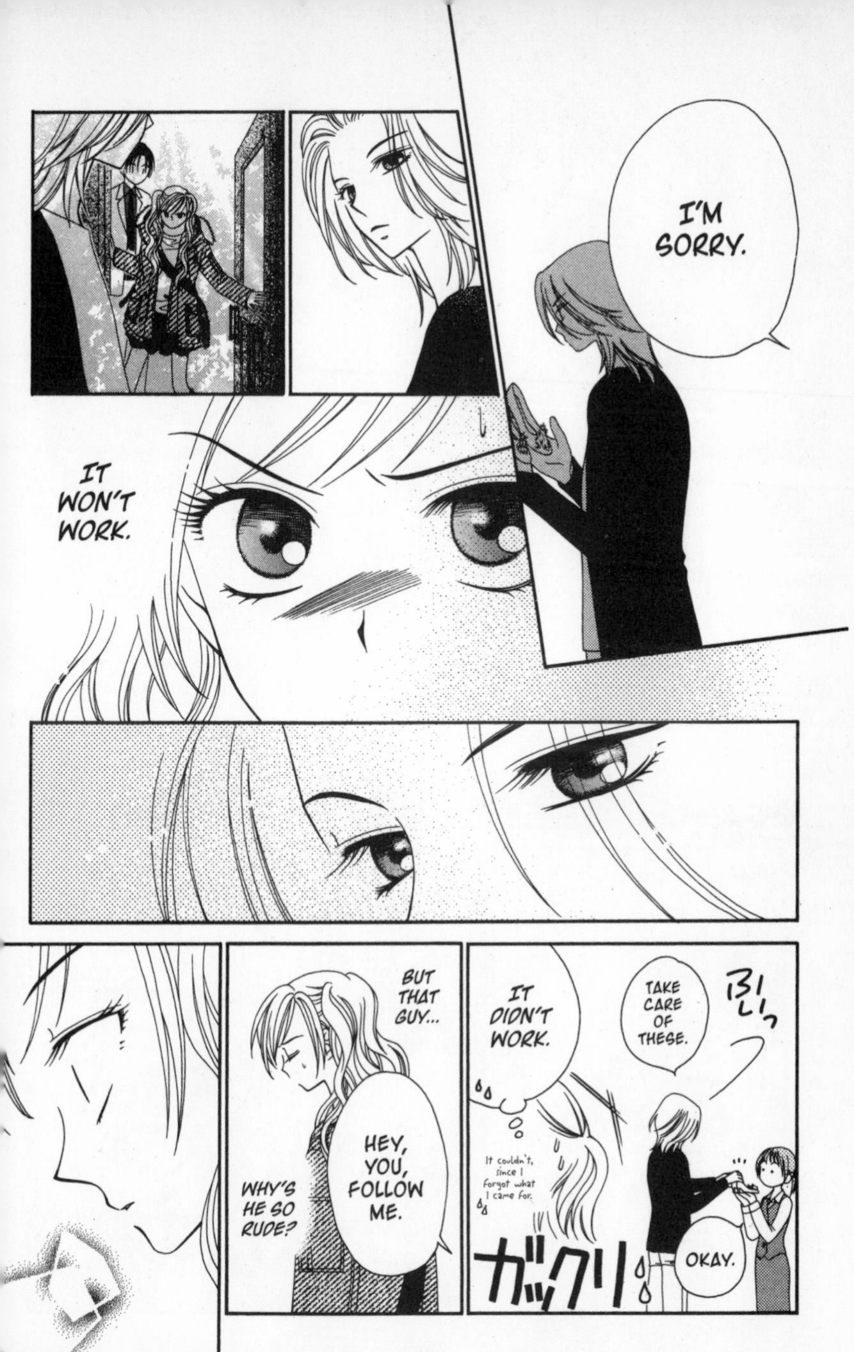
I'M SORRY.
IT WON'T WORK.
ふいっ
TAKE CARE OF THESE.
IT DIDN'T WORK.
It couldn't, since I forgot what I came for.
OKAY.
ガックリ
BUT THAT GUY...
HEY, YOU, FOLLOW ME.
WHY'S HE SO RUDE?

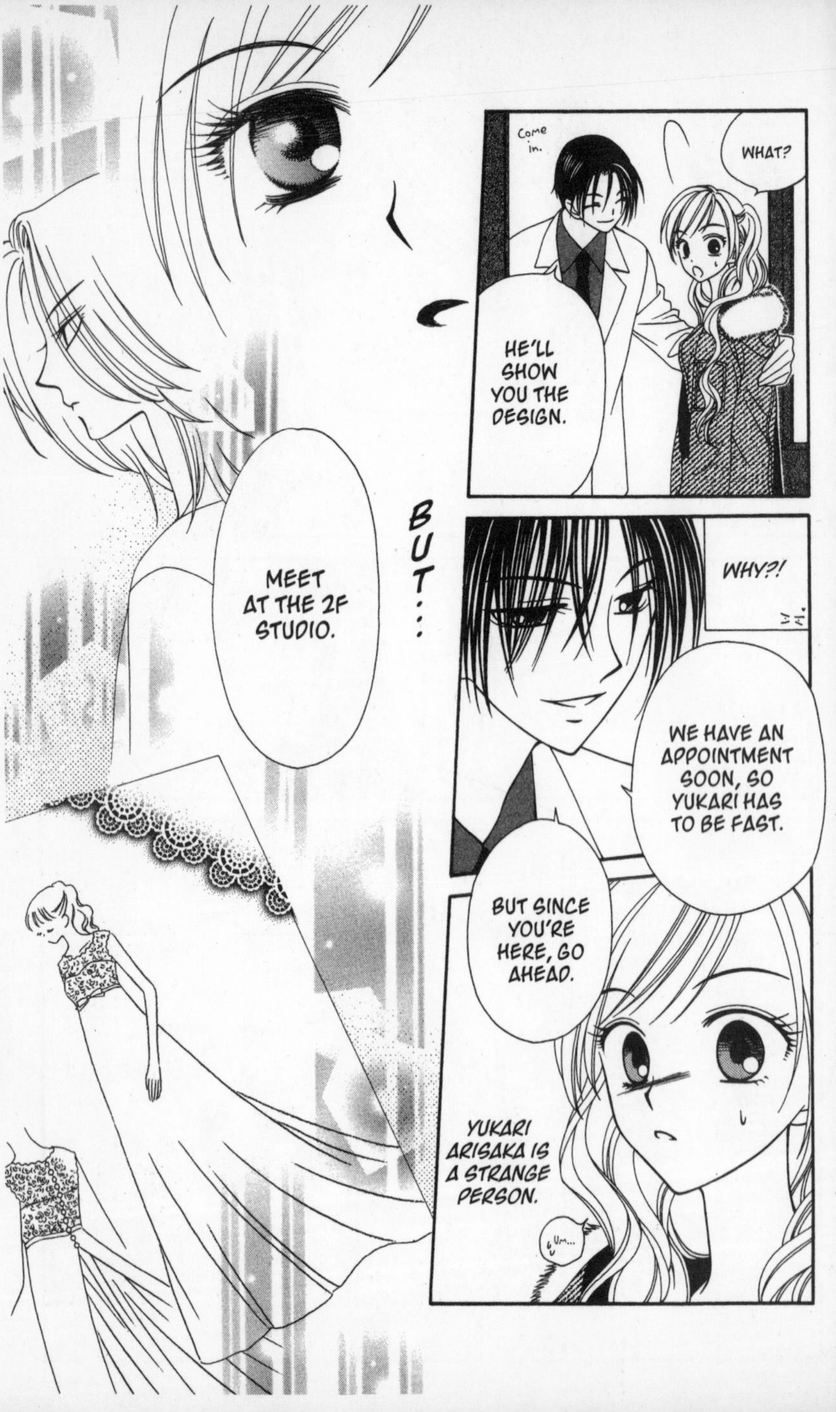
WHAT?
Come in.
HE'LL SHOW YOU THE DESIGN.
WHY?!
WE HAVE AN APPOINTMENT SOON, SO YUKARI HAS TO BE FAST.
BUT SINCE YOU'RE HERE, GO AHEAD.
YUKARI ARISAKA IS A STRANGE PERSON.
Um...
BUT...
MEET AT THE 2F STUDIO.

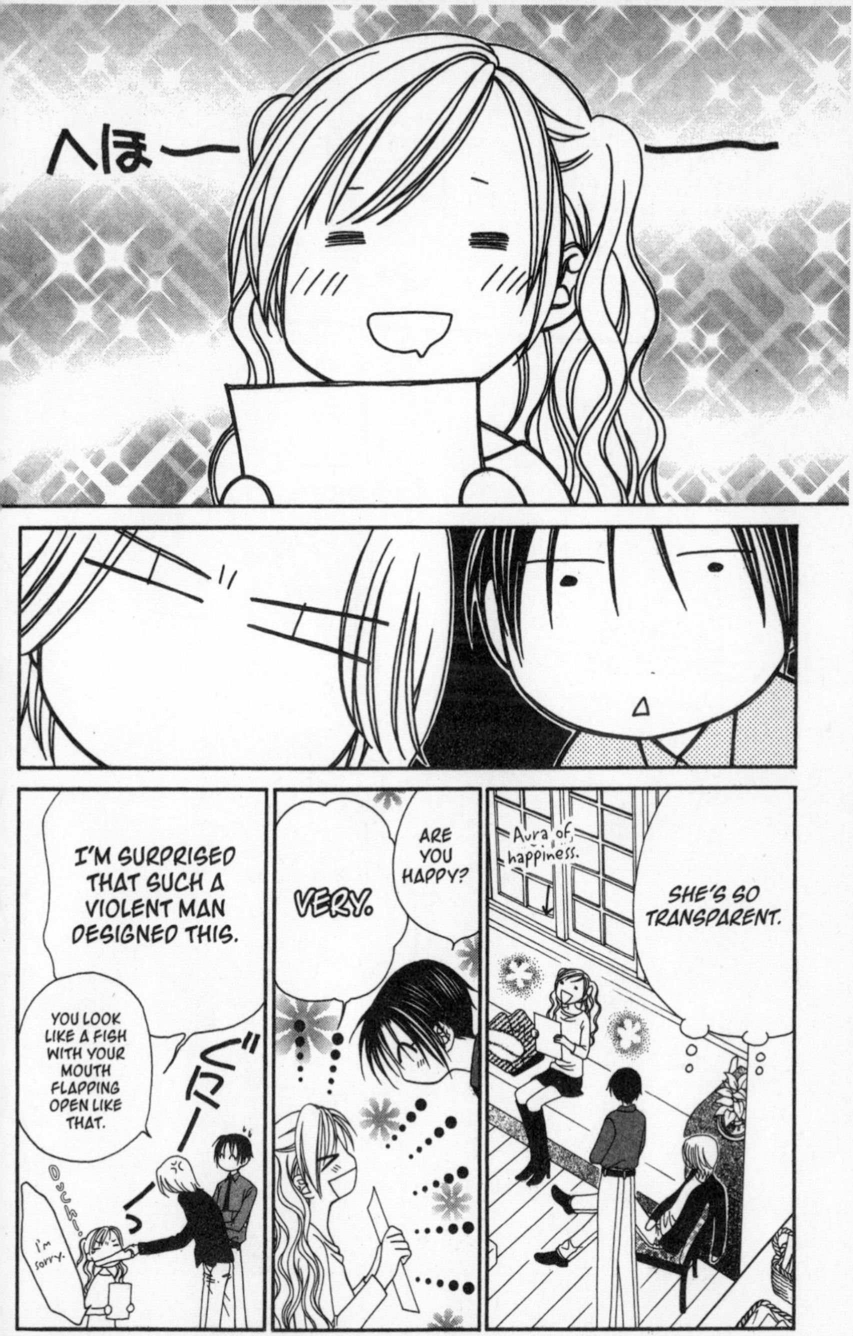
へほ〜〜
〜〜
Aura of happiness.
SHE'S SO TRANSPARENT.
ARE YOU HAPPY?
VERY.
I'M SURPRISED THAT SUCH A VIOLENT MAN DESIGNED THIS.
YOU LOOK LIKE A FISH WITH YOUR MOUTH FLAPPING OPEN LIKE THAT.
ぐにー
Ouch!
I'm sorry.

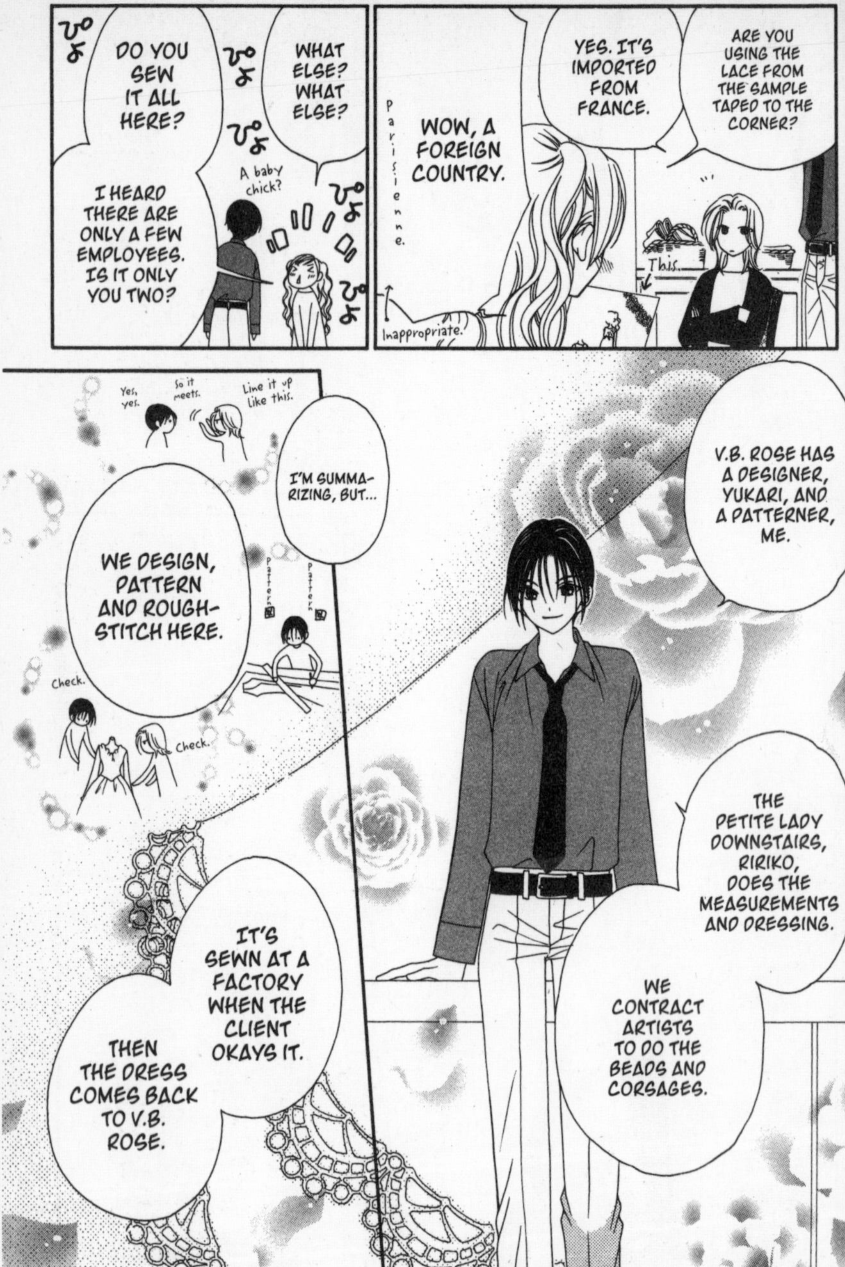
ARE YOU USING THE LACE FROM THE SAMPLE TAPED TO THE CORNER?
YES. IT'S IMPORTED FROM FRANCE.
...
This.
WOW, A FOREIGN COUNTRY.
Parisienne.
Inappropriate.
WHAT ELSE? WHAT ELSE?
ぴよ
ぴよ
ぴよ
DO YOU SEW IT ALL HERE?
ぴよ
ぴよ
ぴよ
I HEARD THERE ARE ONLY A FEW EMPLOYEES. IS IT ONLY YOU TWO?
A baby chick?
V.B. ROSE HAS A DESIGNER, YUKARI, AND A PATTERNER, ME.
THE PETITE LADY DOWNSTAIRS, RIRIKO, DOES THE MEASUREMENTS AND DRESSING.
WE CONTRACT ARTISTS TO DO THE BEADS AND CORSAGES.
I'M SUMMARIZING, BUT...
Line it up like this.
So it meets.
Yes, yes.
WE DESIGN, PATTERN AND ROUGH-STITCH HERE.
Pattern
Pattern
Check.
Check.
IT'S SEWN AT A FACTORY WHEN THE CLIENT OKAYS IT.
THEN THE DRESS COMES BACK TO V.B. ROSE.

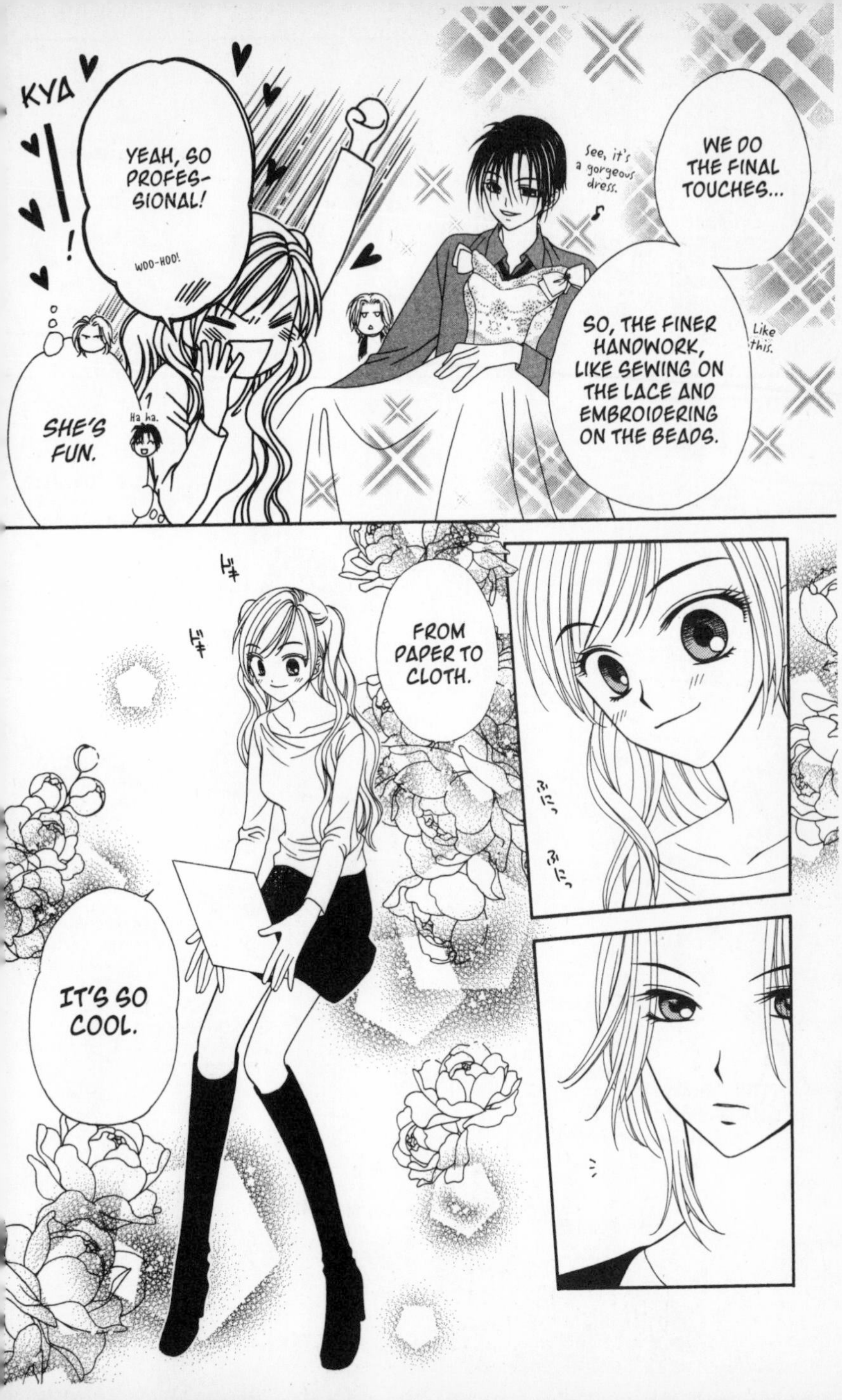
WE DO THE FINAL TOUCHES...
See, it's a gorgeous dress.
SO, THE FINER HANDWORK, LIKE SEWING ON THE LACE AND EMBROIDERING ON THE BEADS.
Like this.
YEAH, SO PROFES-SIONAL!
WOO-HOO!
KYA
SHE'S FUN.
Ha ha.
ふにっ
ふにっ
ドキ
ドキ
FROM PAPER TO CLOTH.
IT'S SO COOL.

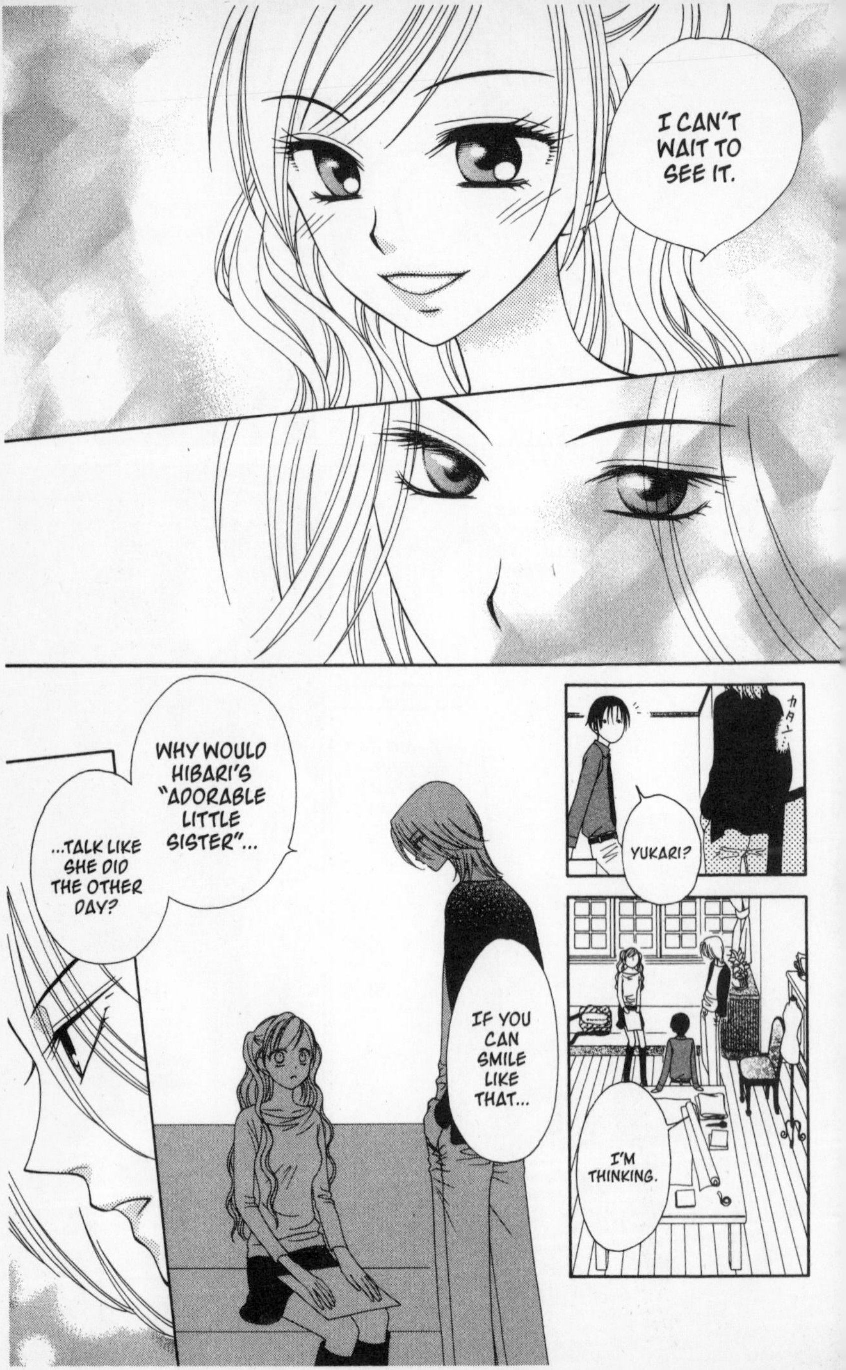

I CAN'T WAIT TO SEE IT.
YUKARI?
I'M THINKING.
IF YOU CAN SMILE LIKE THAT...
WHY WOULD HIBARI'S "ADORABLE LITTLE SISTER"...
...TALK LIKE SHE DID THE OTHER DAY?

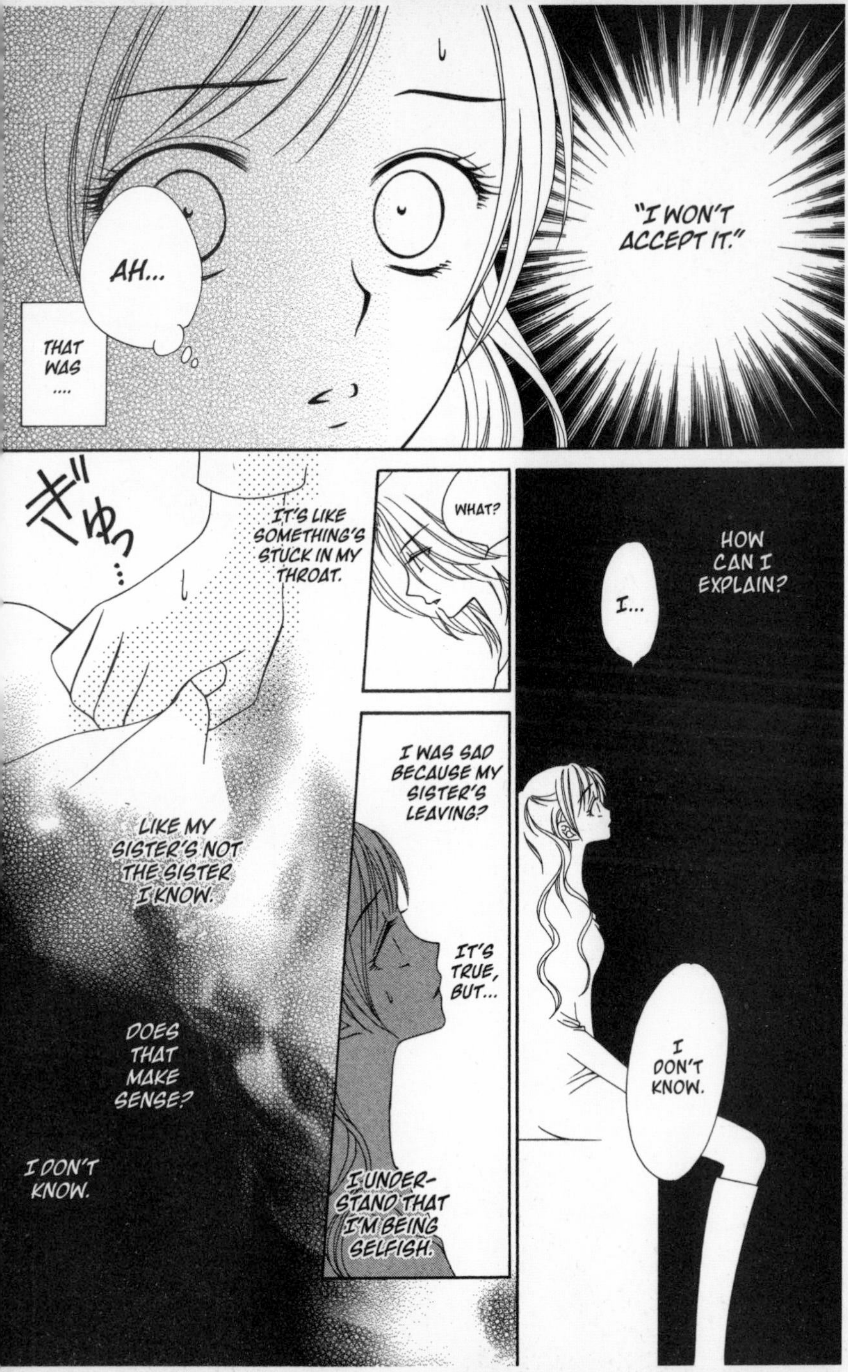
"I WON'T ACCEPT IT."
AH...
THAT WAS .....
HOW CAN I EXPLAIN?
I...
I DON'T KNOW.
WHAT?
I WAS SAD BECAUSE MY SISTER'S LEAVING?
IT'S TRUE, BUT...
I UNDER-STAND THAT I'M BEING SELFISH.
ぎゅっ...
IT'S LIKE SOMETHING'S STUCK IN MY THROAT.
LIKE MY SISTER'S NOT THE SISTER I KNOW.
DOES THAT MAKE SENSE?
I DON'T KNOW.

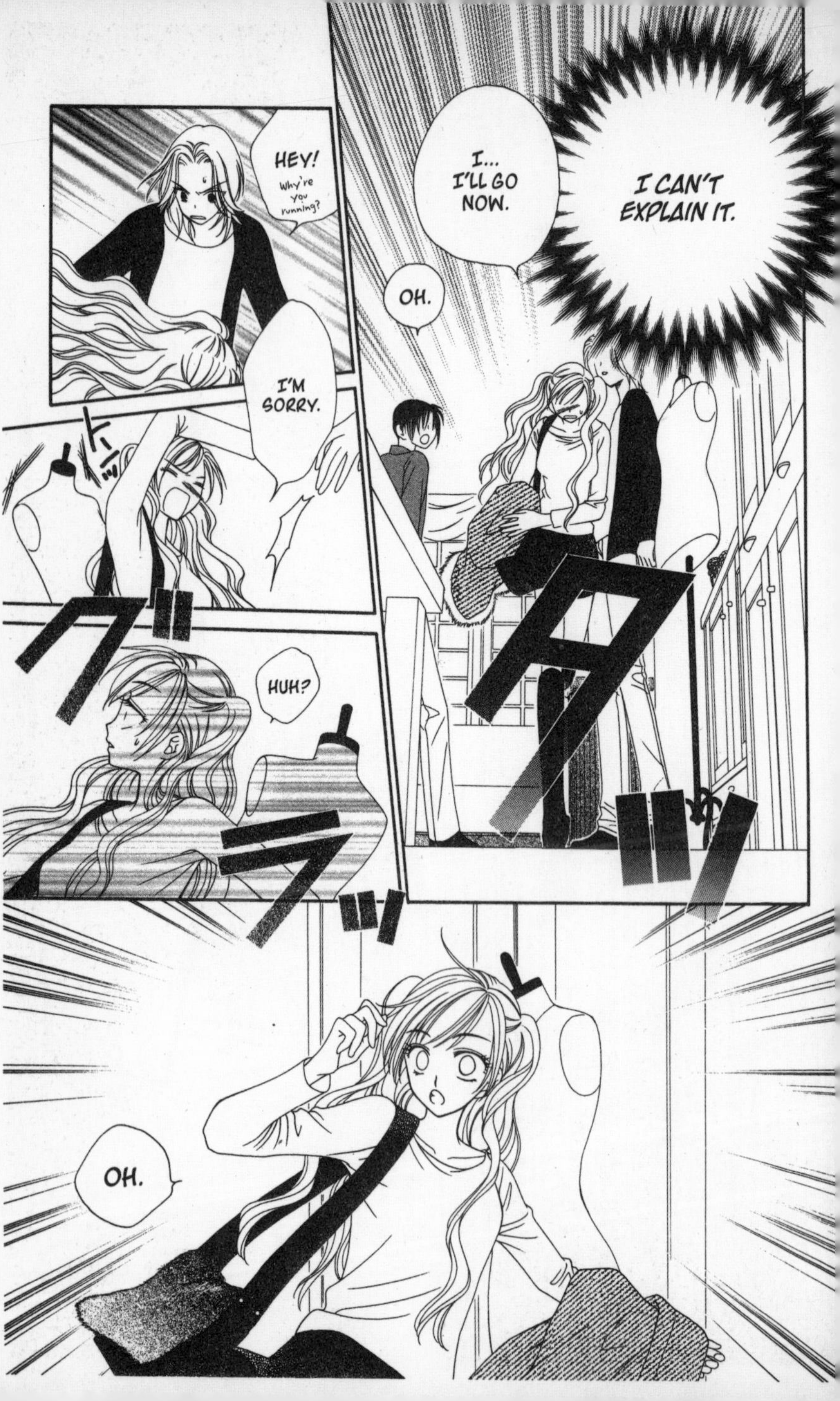

I CAN'T EXPLAIN IT.
I... I'LL GO NOW.
OH.
HEY!
Why're you running?
I'M SORRY.
HUH?
OH.

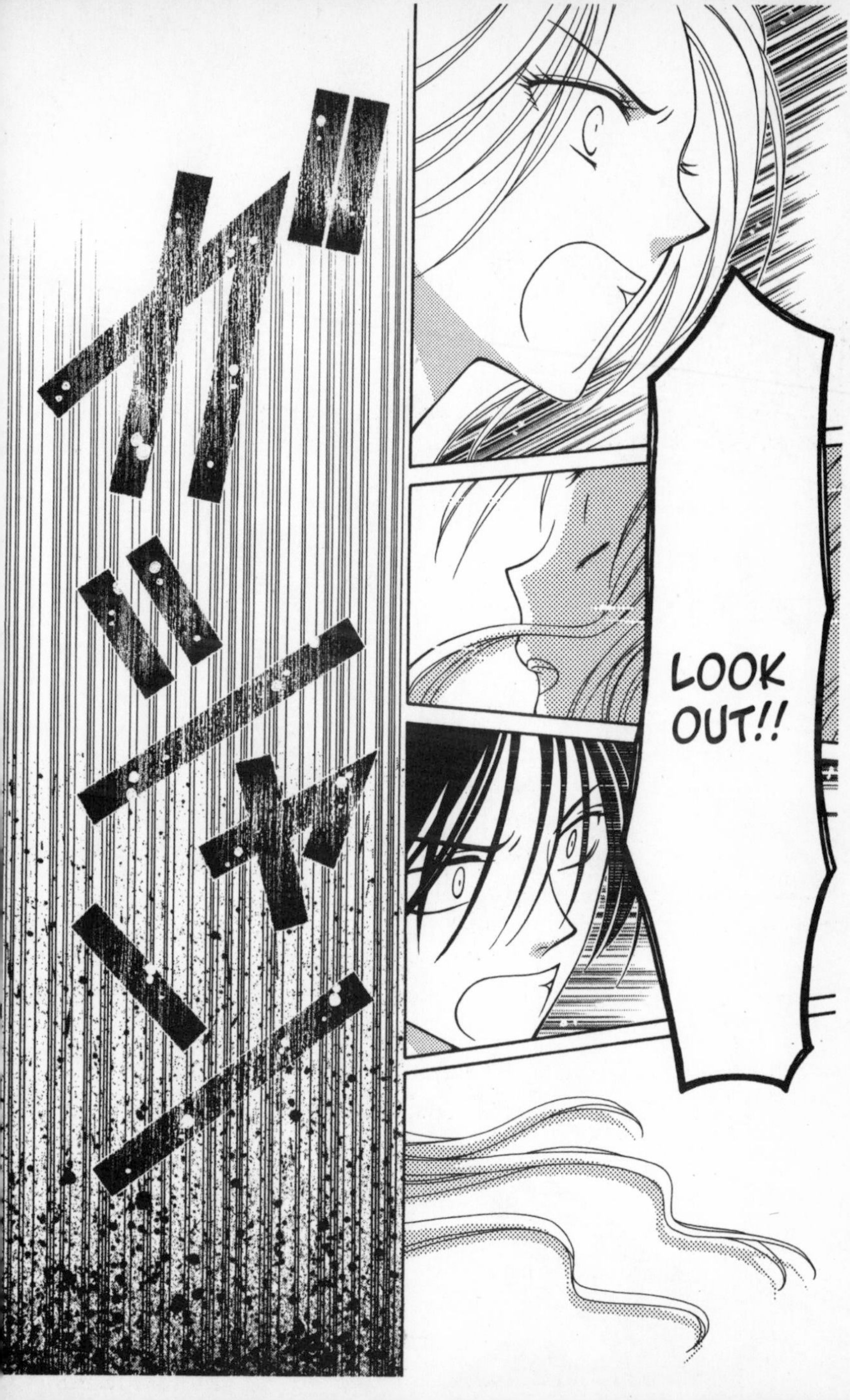
LOOK OUT!!

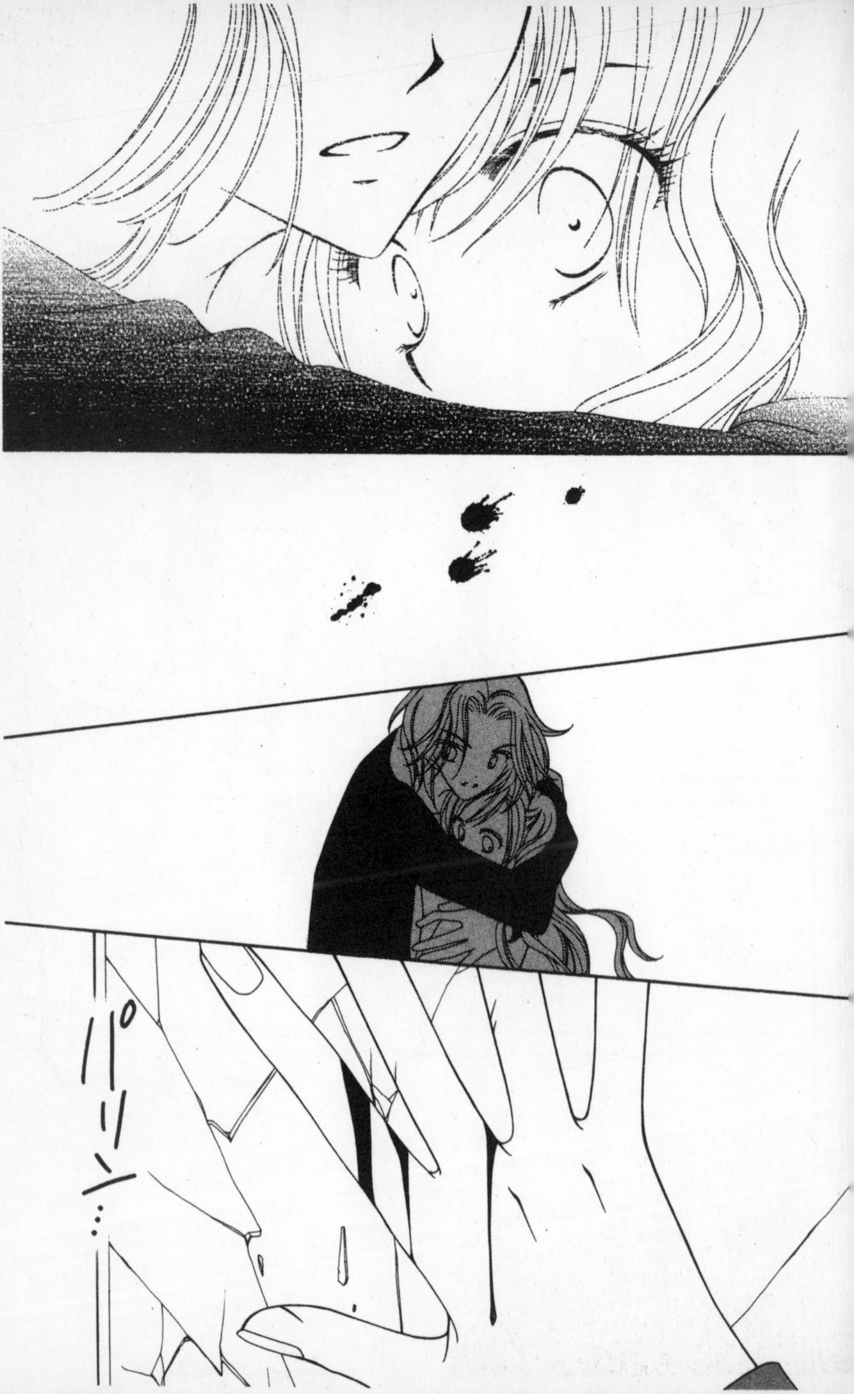
パリン…

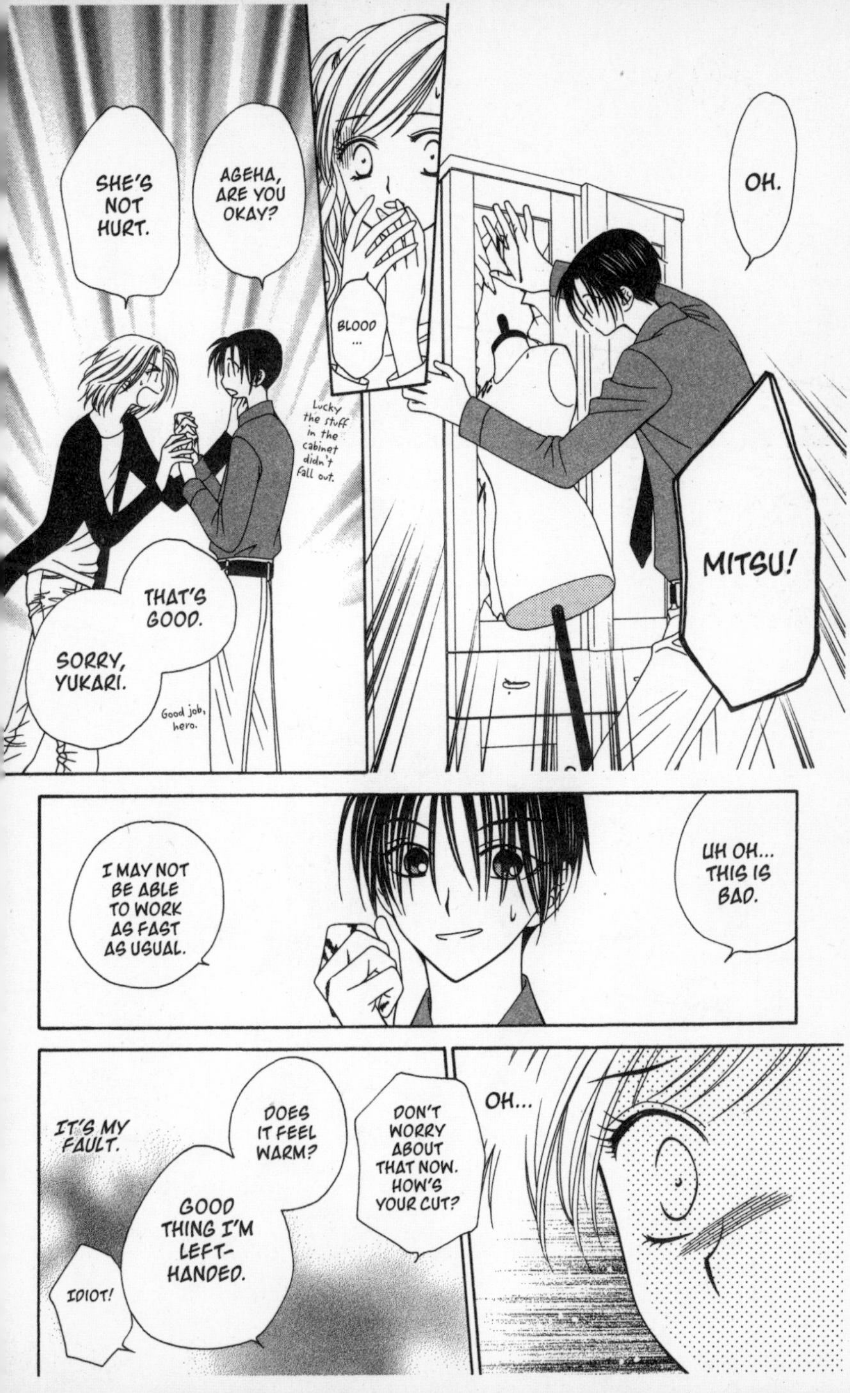
OH.
MITSU!
BLOOD ...
AGEHA, ARE YOU OKAY?
SHE'S NOT HURT.
Lucky the stuff in the cabinet didn't fall out.
THAT'S GOOD.
SORRY, YUKARI.
Good job, hero.
UH OH... THIS IS BAD.
I MAY NOT BE ABLE TO WORK AS FAST AS USUAL.
OH...
DON'T WORRY ABOUT THAT NOW. HOW'S YOUR CUT?
DOES IT FEEL WARM?
GOOD THING I'M LEFT-HANDED.
IT'S MY FAULT.
IDIOT!

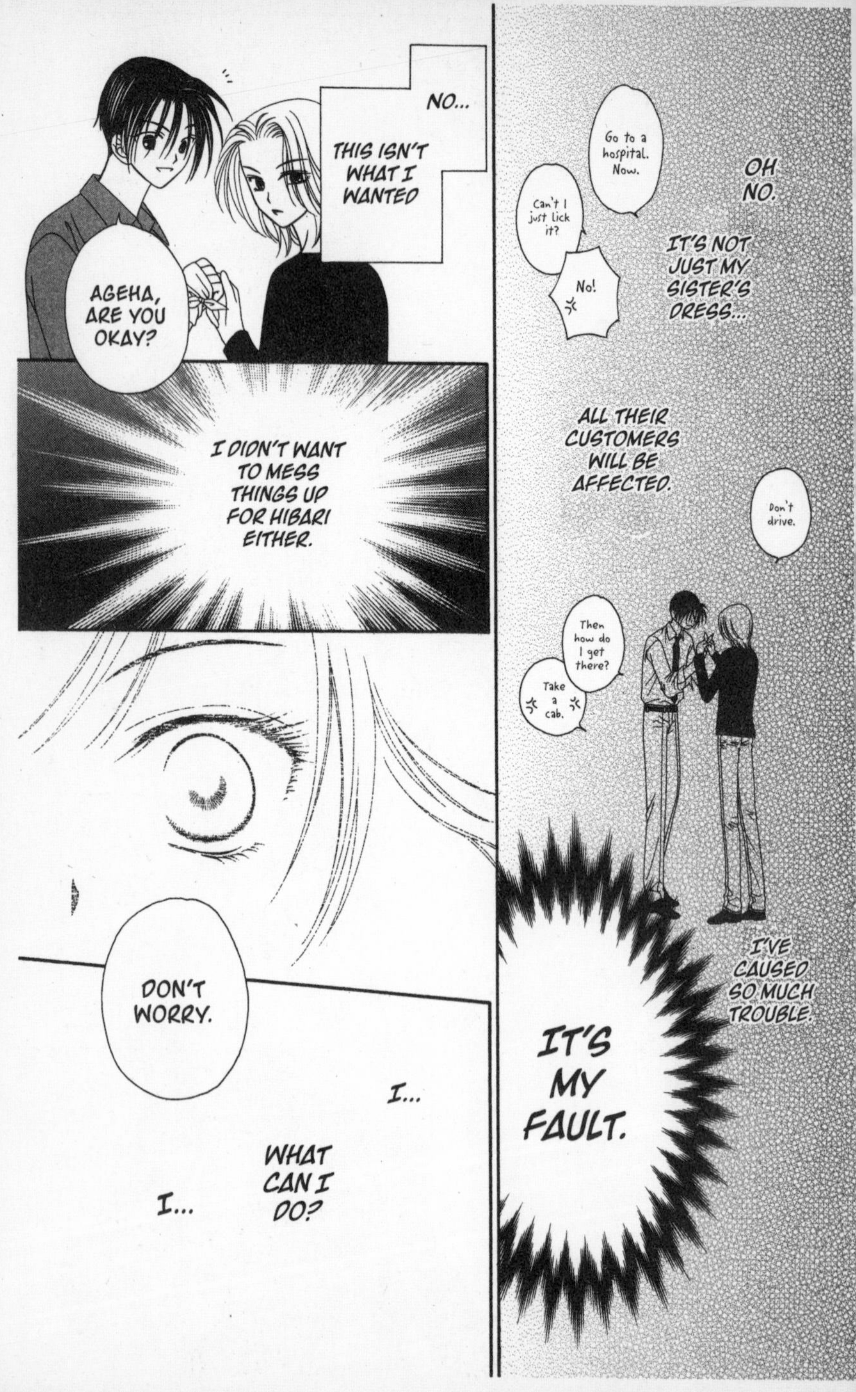
OH NO.
Go to a hospital. Now.
Can't I just lick it?
No!
IT'S NOT JUST MY SISTER'S DRESS...
ALL THEIR CUSTOMERS WILL BE AFFECTED.
Don't drive.
Then how do I get there?
Take a cab.
I'VE CAUSED SO MUCH TROUBLE.
IT'S MY FAULT.
NO...
THIS ISN'T WHAT I WANTED
AGEHA, ARE YOU OKAY?
I DIDN'T WANT TO MESS THINGS UP FOR HIBARI EITHER.
DON'T WORRY.
I...
WHAT CAN I DO?
I...

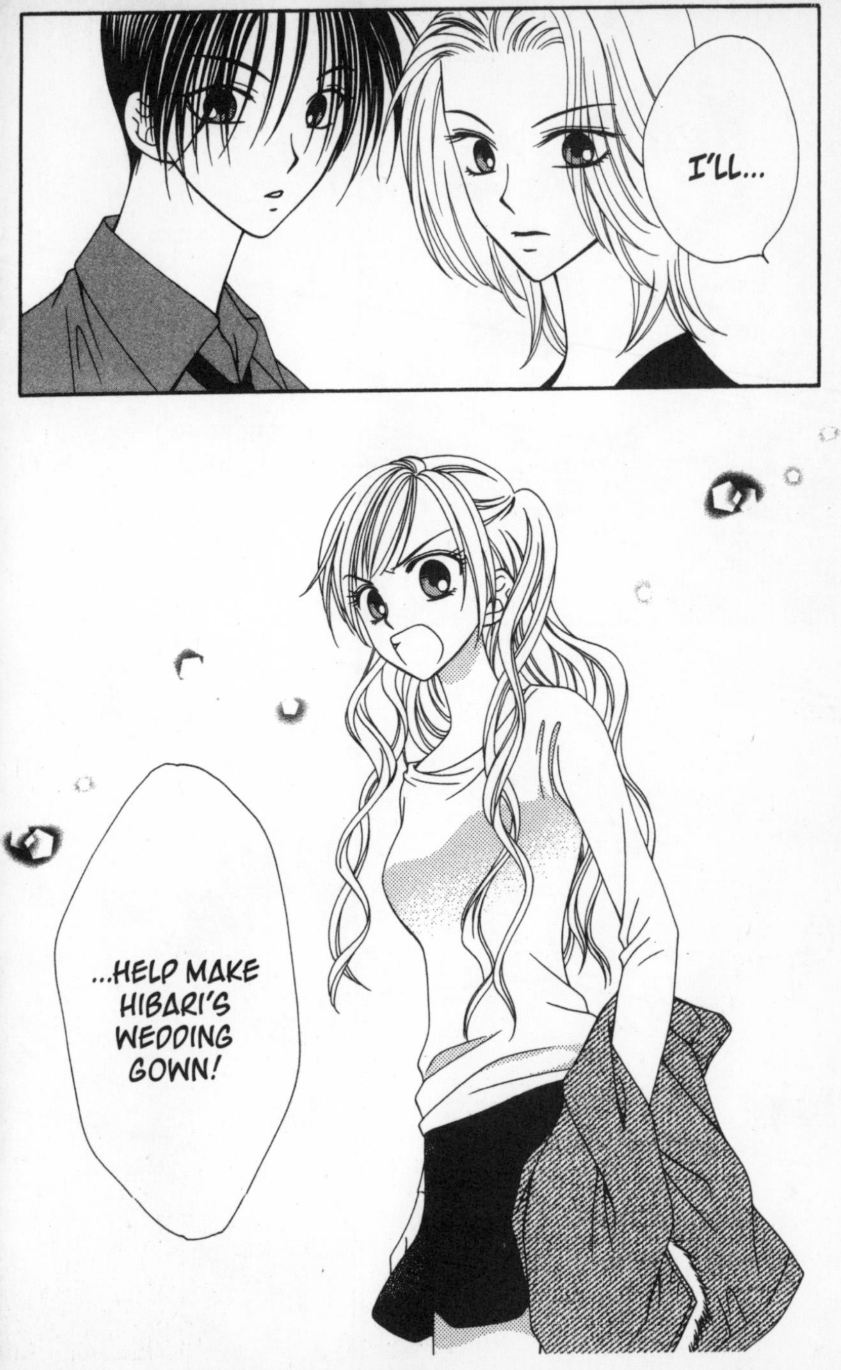
I'LL...
...HELP MAKE HIBARI'S WEDDING GOWN!

Episode 3

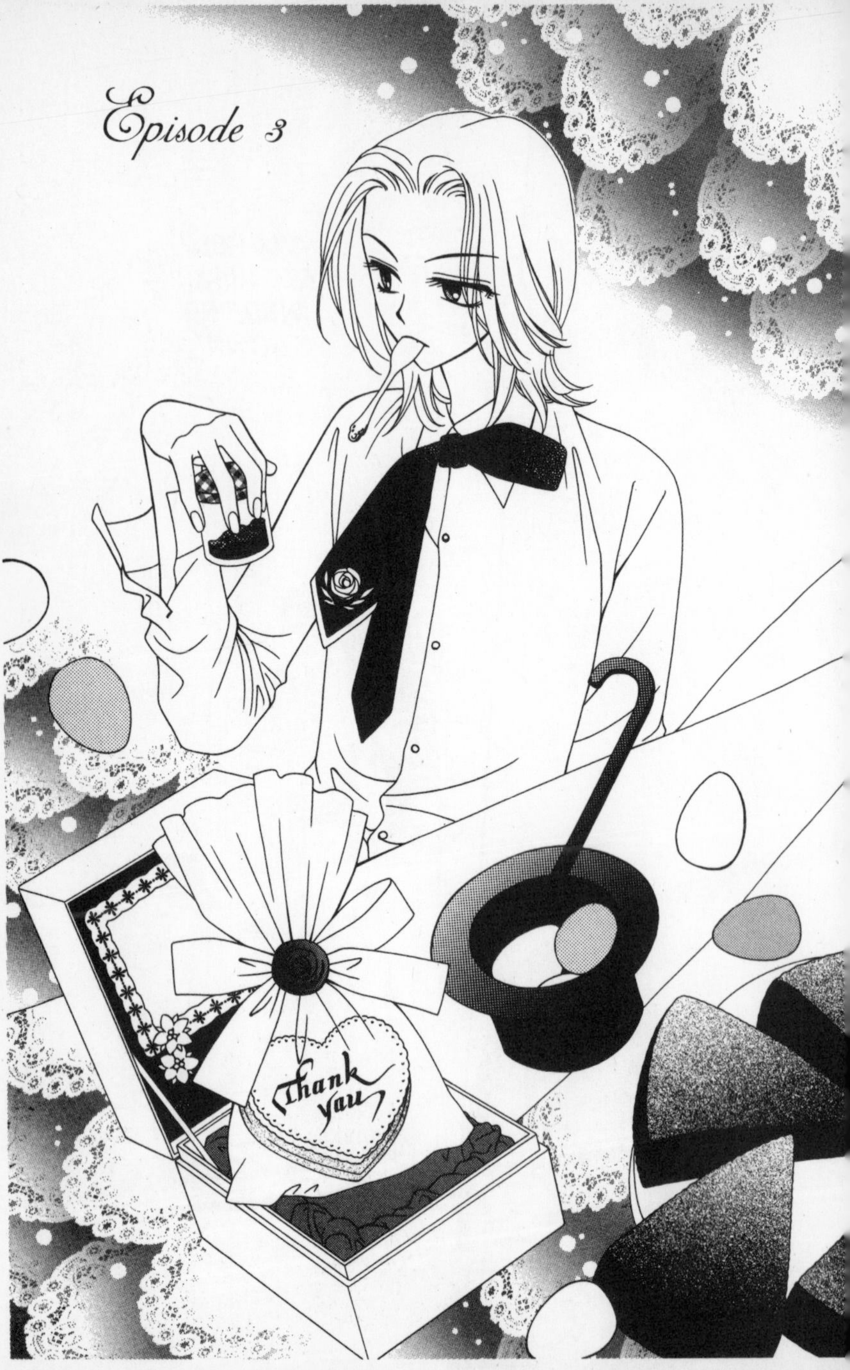
Thank yau

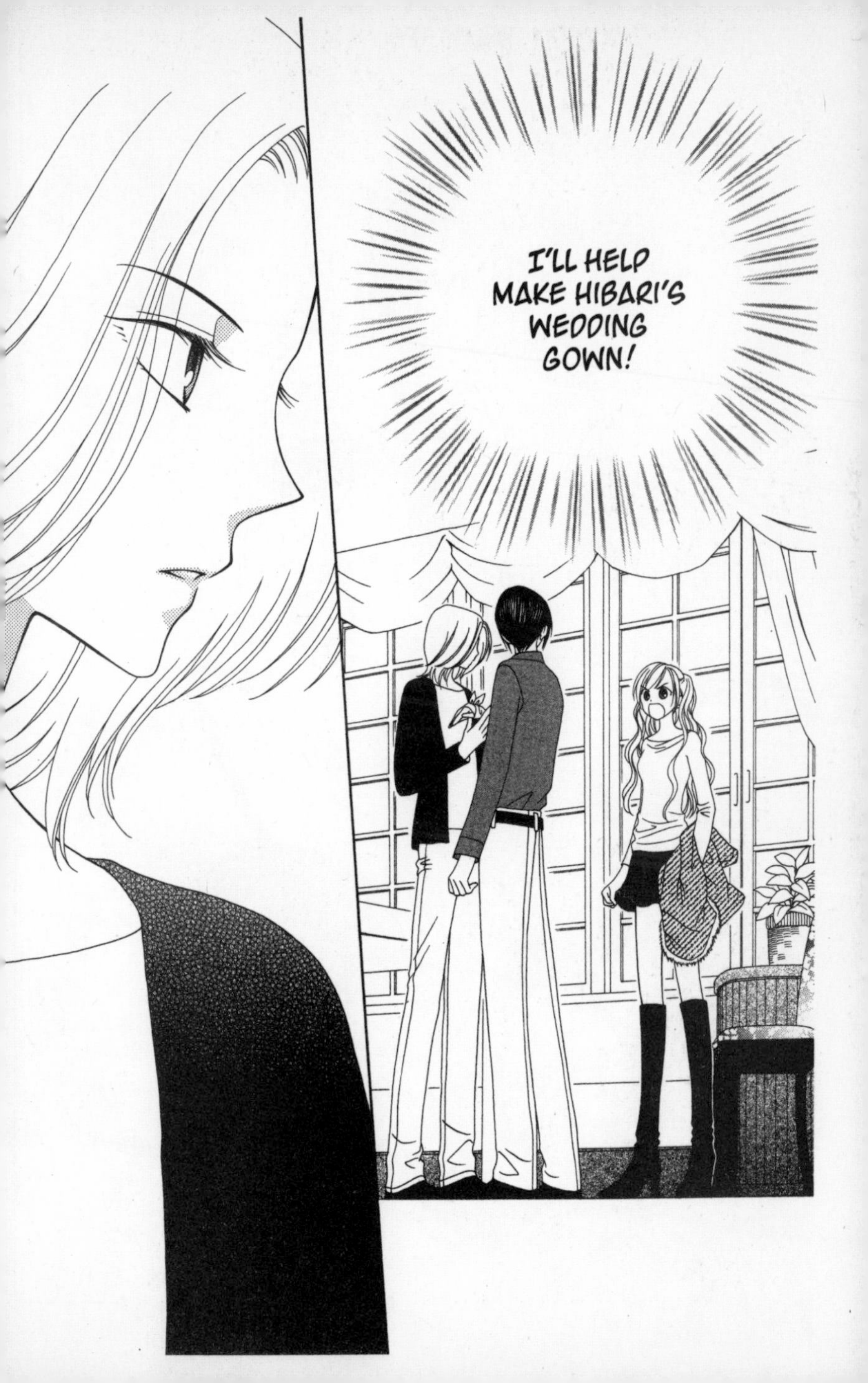
I'LL HELP MAKE HIBARI'S WEDDING GOWN!

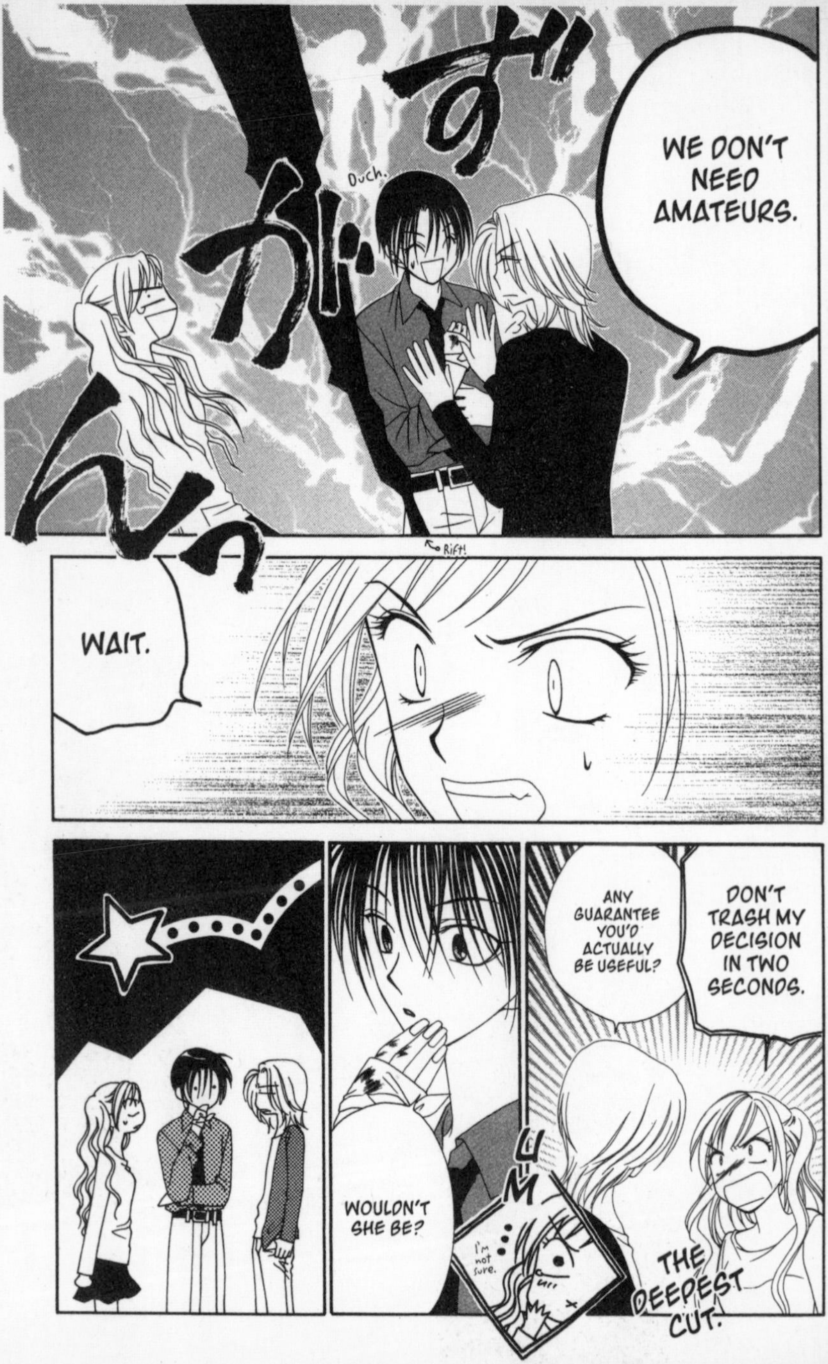
WE DON'T NEED AMATEURS.
Ouch.
Rift!
WAIT.
DON'T TRASH MY DECISION IN TWO SECONDS.
ANY GUARANTEE YOU'D ACTUALLY BE USEFUL?
THE DEEPEST CUT.
UM
I'm not sure.
WOULDN'T SHE BE?

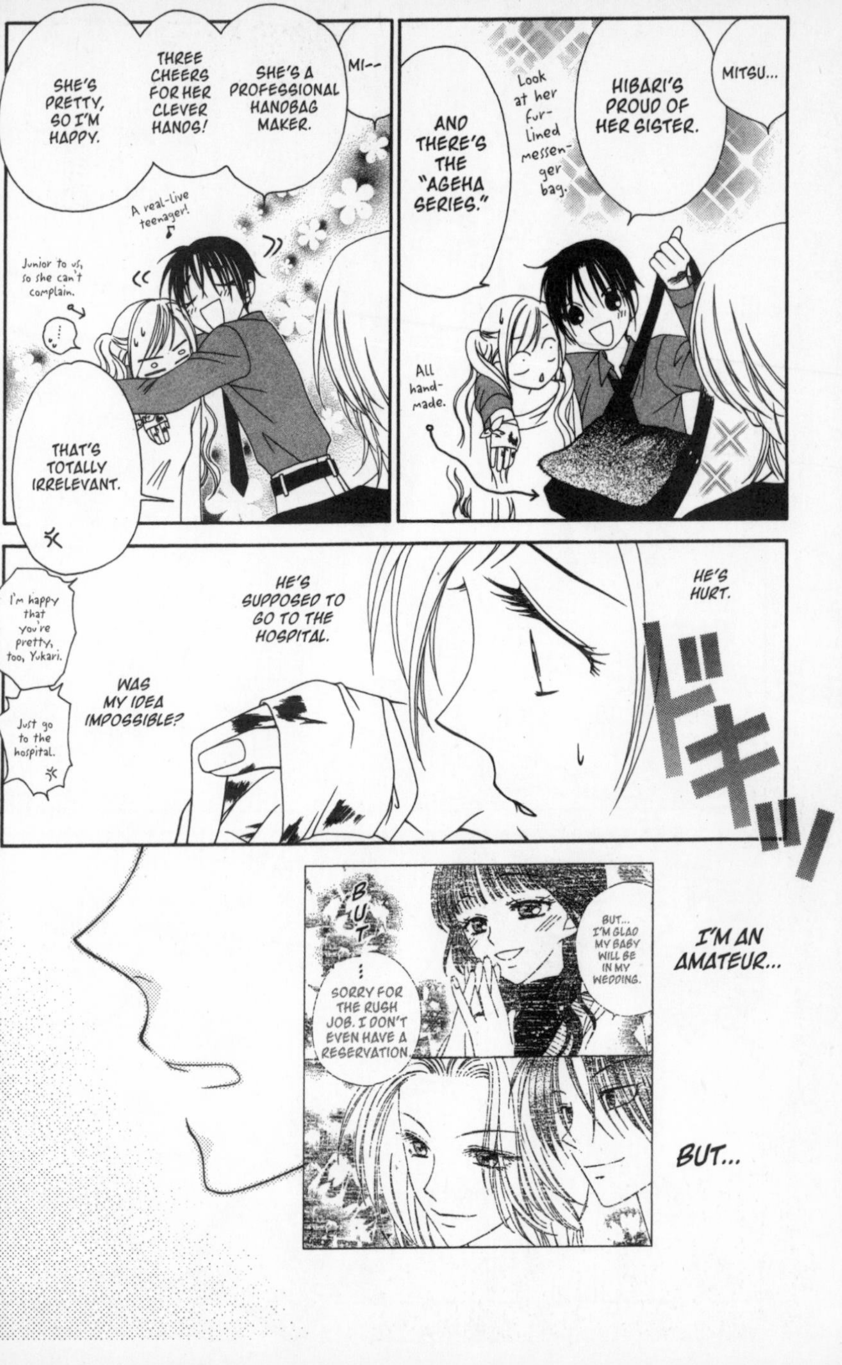
MITSU...
HIBARI'S PROUD OF HER SISTER.
Look at her fur-lined messenger bag.
AND THERE'S THE "AGEHA SERIES."
All handmade.
MI--
SHE'S A PROFESSIONAL HANDBAG MAKER.
THREE CHEERS FOR HER CLEVER HANDS!
SHE'S PRETTY, SO I'M HAPPY.
A real-live teenager!
Junior to us, so she can't complain.
...
THAT'S TOTALLY IRRELEVANT.
HE'S HURT.
ドキッ
HE'S SUPPOSED TO GO TO THE HOSPITAL.
WAS MY IDEA IMPOSSIBLE?
I'm happy that you're pretty, too, Yukari.
Just go to the hospital.
I'M AN AMATEUR...
BUT... I'M GLAD MY BABY WILL BE IN MY WEDDING.
BUT...
SORRY FOR THE RUSH JOB. I DON'T EVEN HAVE A RESERVATION.
BUT...

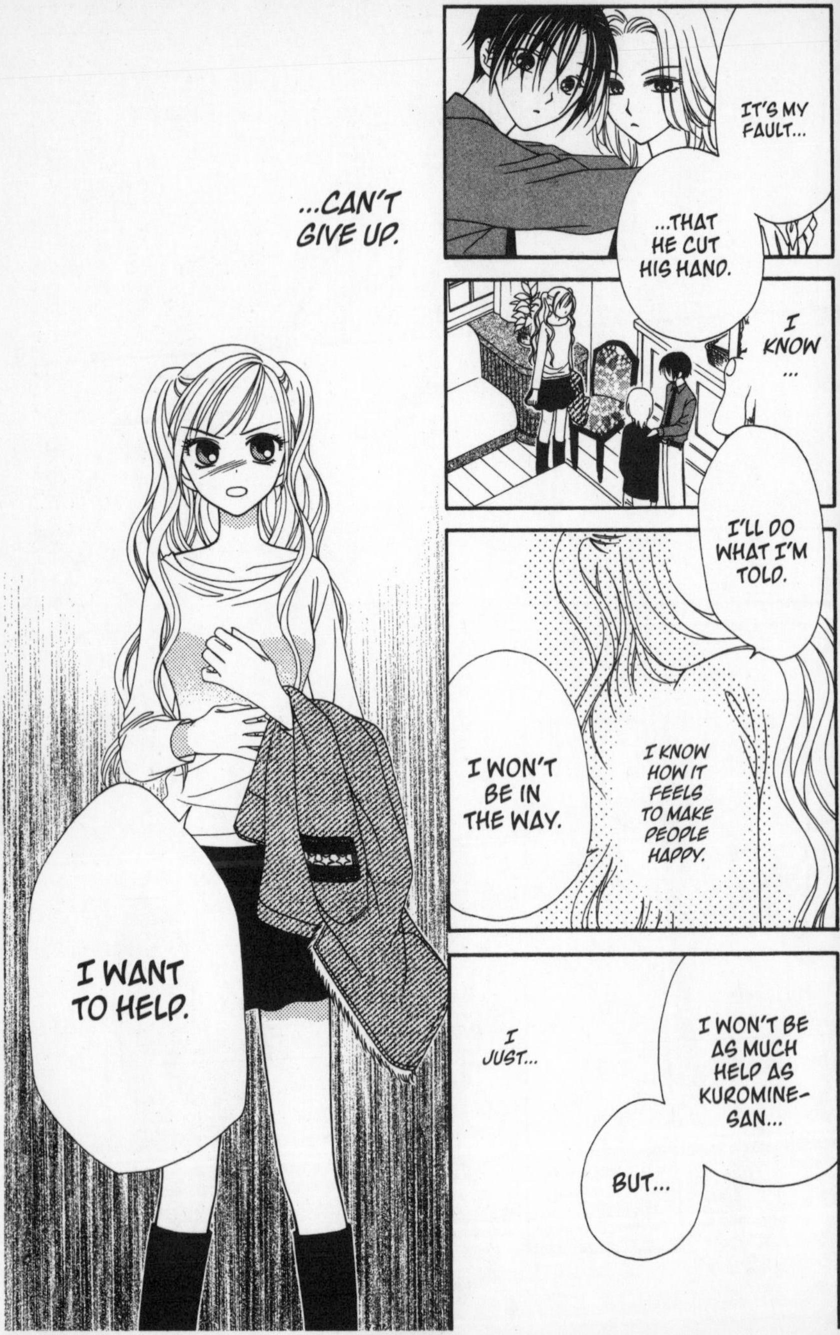
IT'S MY FAULT...
...THAT HE CUT HIS HAND.
I KNOW ...
I'LL DO WHAT I'M TOLD.
I KNOW HOW IT FEELS TO MAKE PEOPLE HAPPY.
I WON'T BE IN THE WAY.
I WON'T BE AS MUCH HELP AS KUROMINE-SAN...
BUT...
I JUST...
...CAN'T GIVE UP.
I WANT TO HELP.

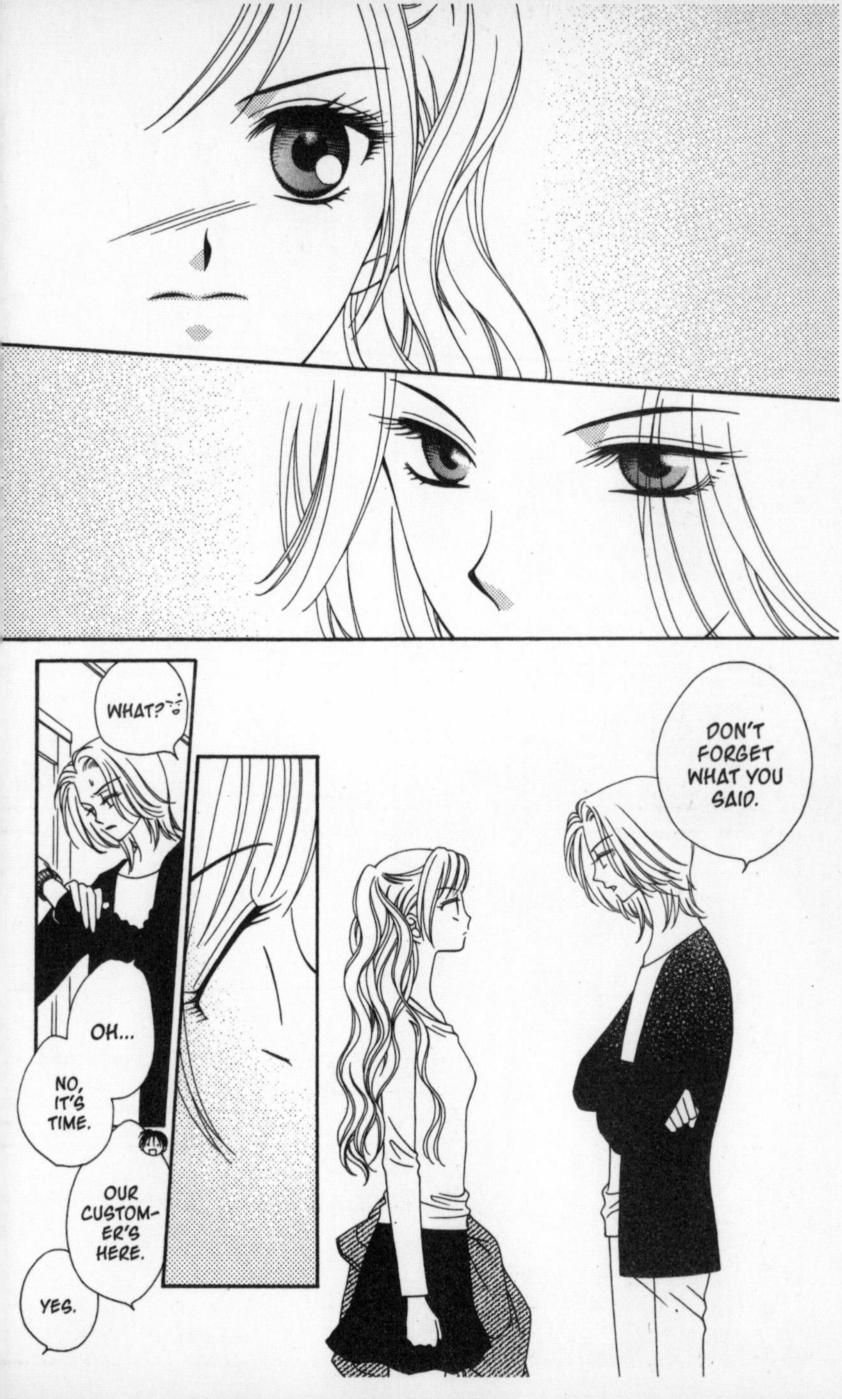
DON'T FORGET WHAT YOU SAID.
WHAT?
OH...
NO, IT'S TIME.
OUR CUSTOM-ER'S HERE.
YES.

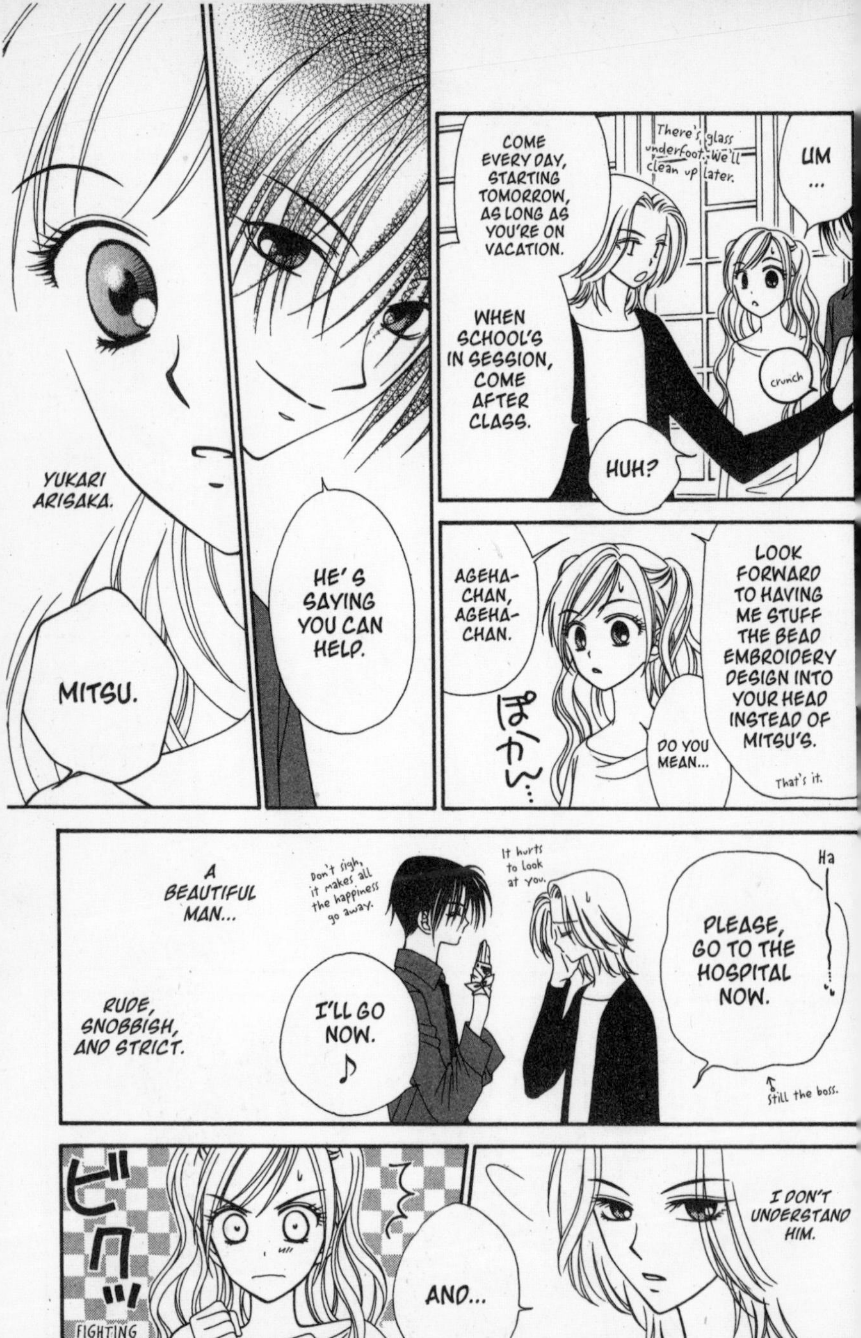
UM ...
COME EVERY DAY, STARTING TOMORROW, AS LONG AS YOU'RE ON VACATION.
There's glass underfoot. We'll clean up later.
crunch
WHEN SCHOOL'S IN SESSION, COME AFTER CLASS.
HUH?
LOOK FORWARD TO HAVING ME STUFF THE BEAD EMBROIDERY DESIGN INTO YOUR HEAD INSTEAD OF MITSU'S.
That's it.
AGEHA-CHAN, AGEHA-CHAN.
DO YOU MEAN...
ぽかん…
HE'S SAYING YOU CAN HELP.
YUKARI ARISAKA.
MITSU.
Ha......
PLEASE, GO TO THE HOSPITAL NOW.
still the boss.
It hurts to look at you.
Don't sigh, it makes all the happiness go away.
I'LL GO NOW. ♪
A BEAUTIFUL MAN...
RUDE, SNOBBISH, AND STRICT.
I DON'T UNDERSTAND HIM.
AND...
ビクッ
FIGHTING POSE

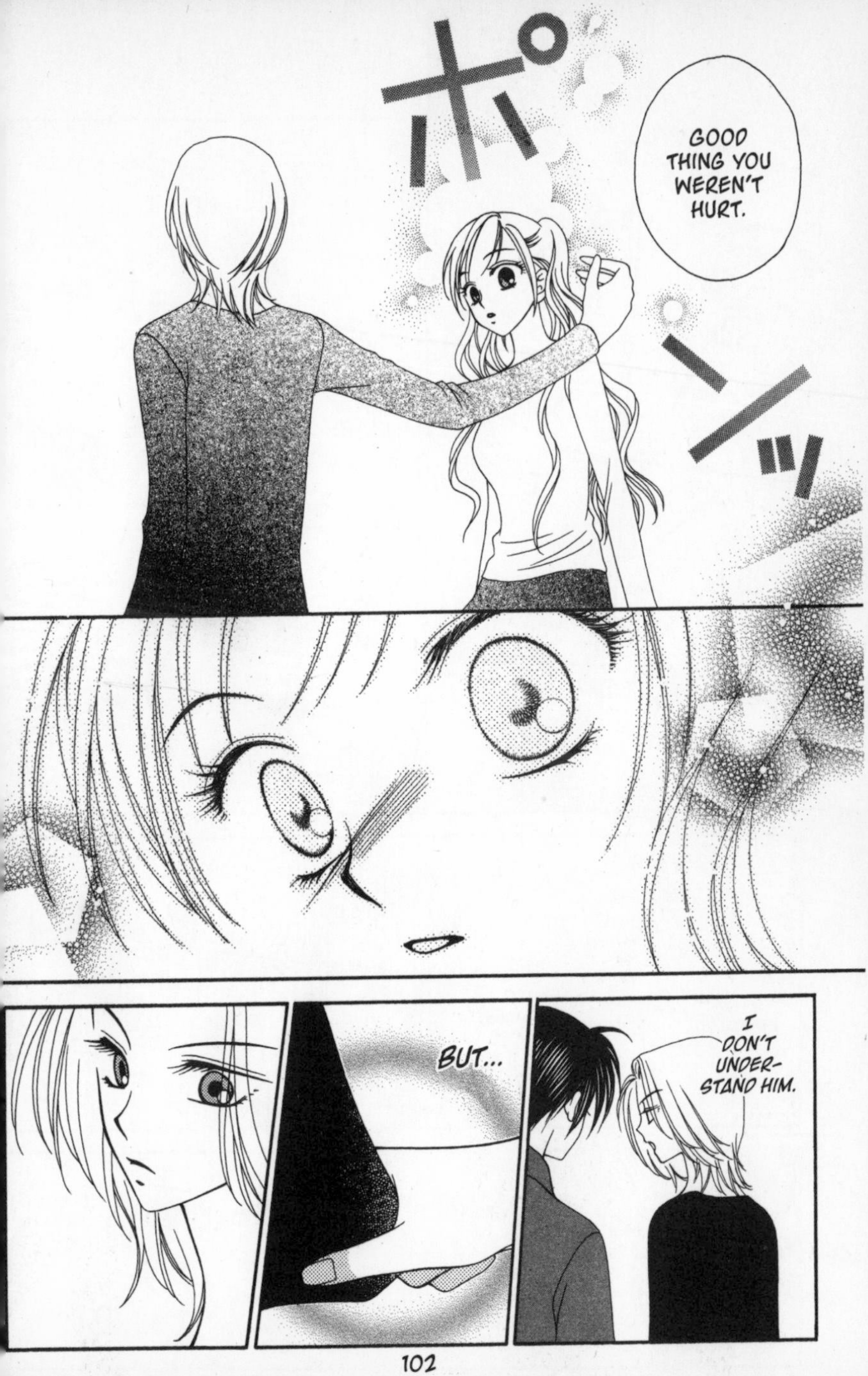
ポーンッ
GOOD THING YOU WEREN'T HURT.
I DON'T UNDER-STAND HIM.
BUT...

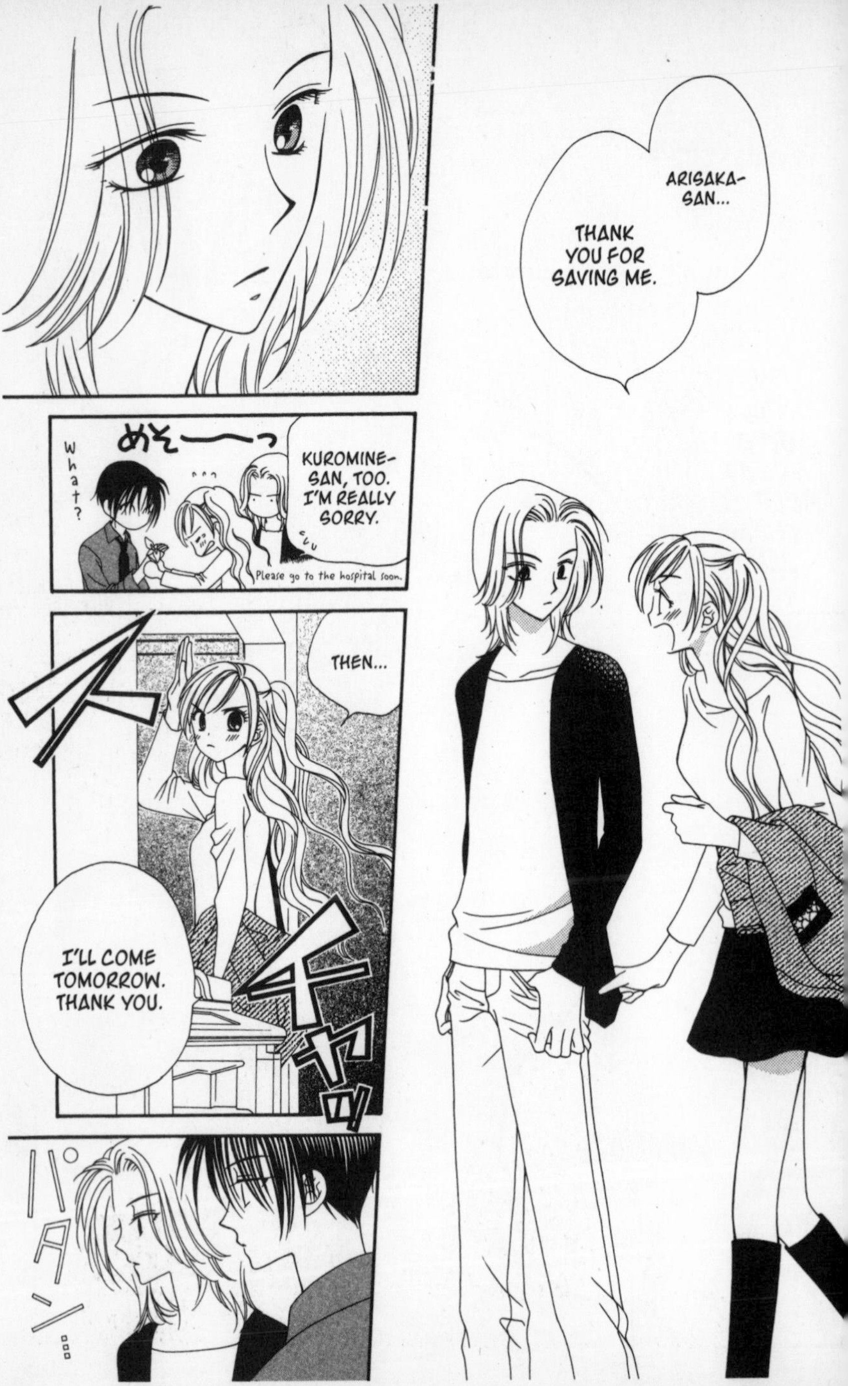
ARISAKA-SAN...
THANK YOU FOR SAVING ME.
めそーーっ
What?
KUROMINE-SAN, TOO. I'M REALLY SORRY.
Please go to the hospital soon.
THEN...
I'LL COME TOMORROW. THANK YOU.
パタン...

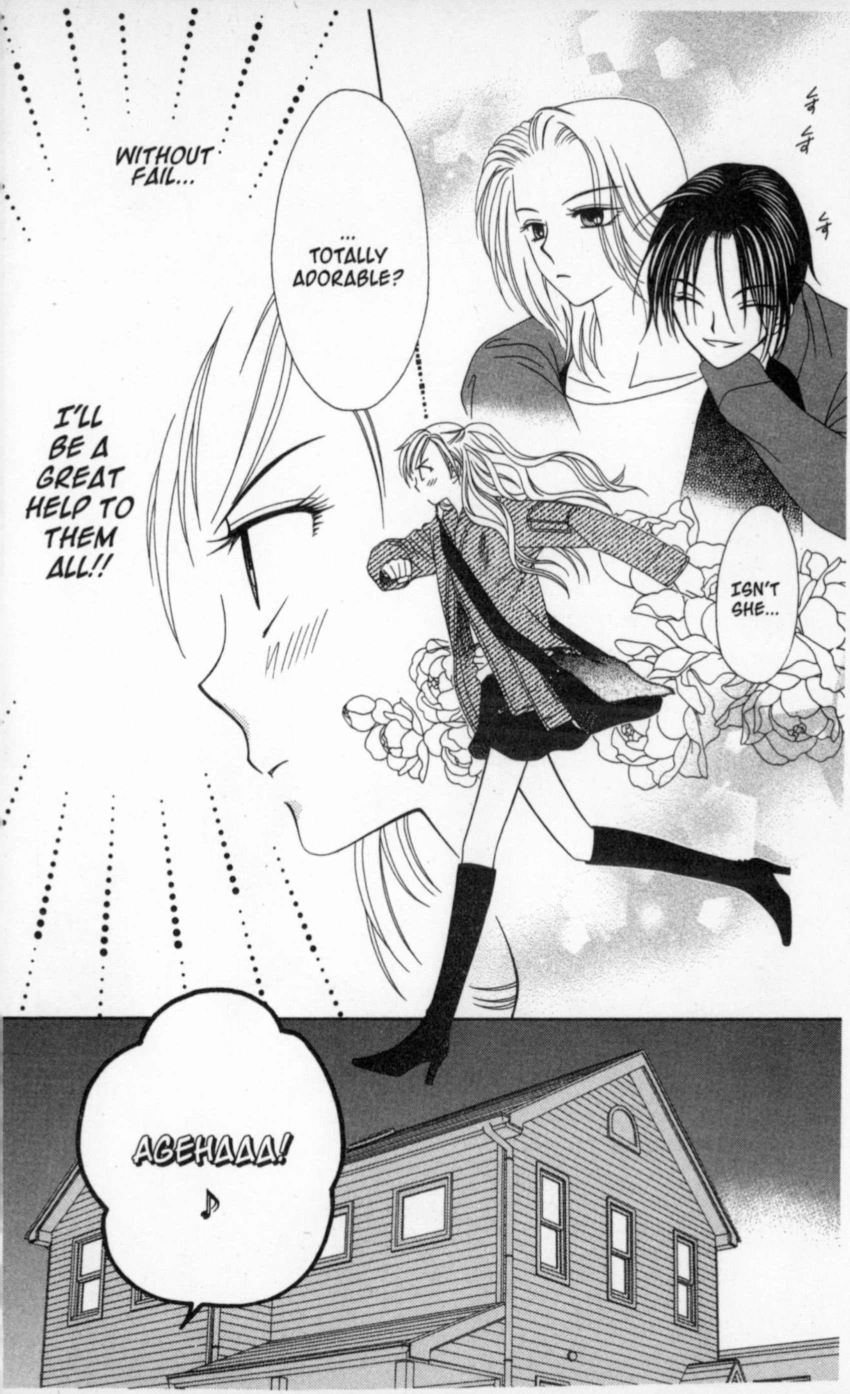

くすくす
ISN'T SHE...
... TOTALLY ADORABLE?
WITHOUT FAIL...
I'LL BE A GREAT HELP TO THEM ALL!!
AGEHAAA! ♪

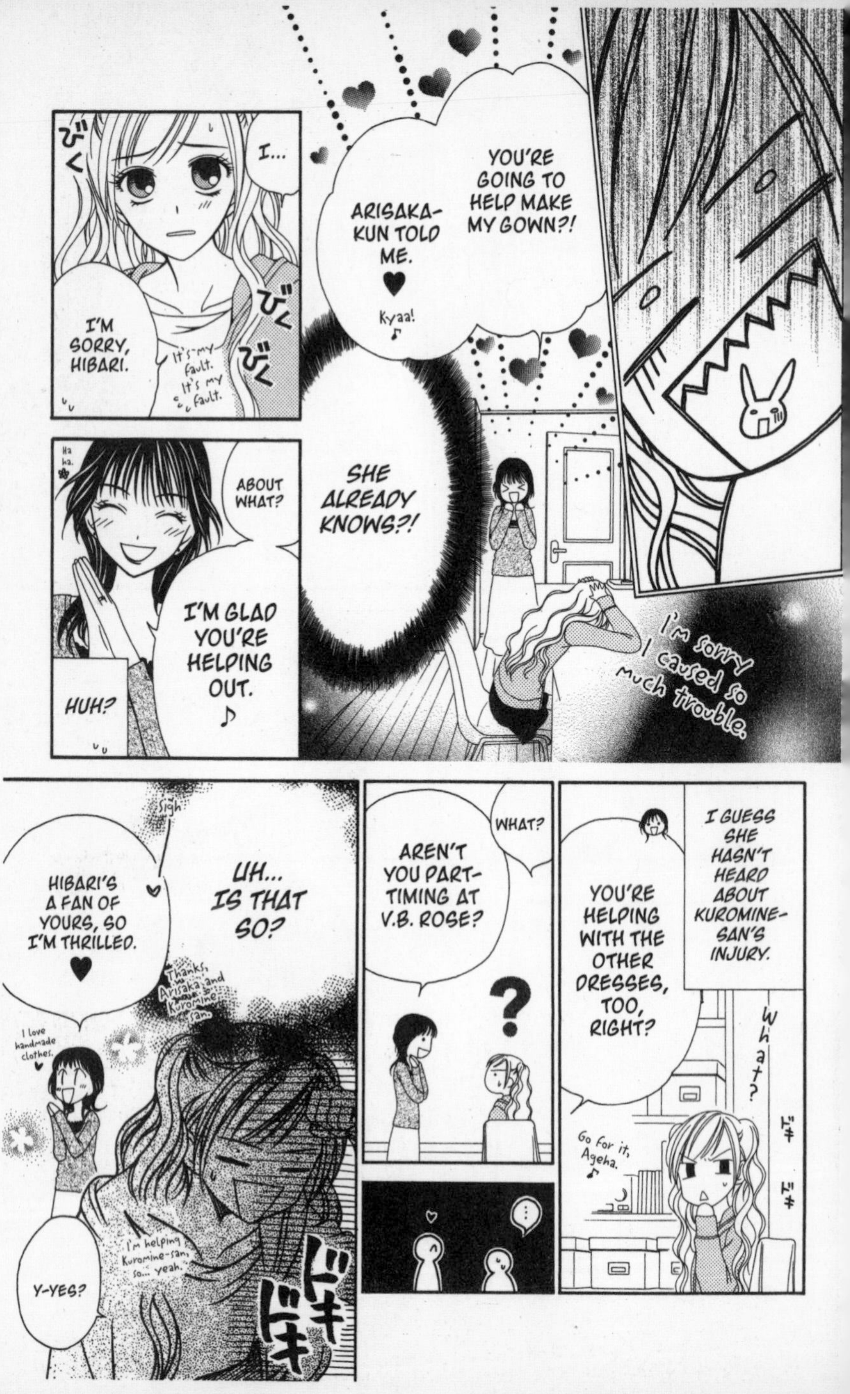
YOU'RE GOING TO HELP MAKE MY GOWN?!
ARISAKA-KUN TOLD ME. ♥
Kyaa! ♪
SHE ALREADY KNOWS?!
I'm sorry I caused so much trouble.
I...
I'M SORRY, HIBARI.
It's my fault. It's my fault.
ABOUT WHAT?
Ha ha.
I'M GLAD YOU'RE HELPING OUT. ♪
HUH?
I GUESS SHE HASN'T HEARD ABOUT KUROMINE-SAN'S INJURY.
YOU'RE HELPING WITH THE OTHER DRESSES, TOO, RIGHT?
What?
Go for it, Ageha. ♪
WHAT?
AREN'T YOU PART-TIMING AT V.B. ROSE?
?
UH... IS THAT SO?
Sigh
HIBARI'S A FAN OF YOURS, SO I'M THRILLED. ♥
Thanks, Arisaka and Kuromine-san.
I love handmade clothes.
I'm helping Kuromine-san, so... yeah.
Y-YES?

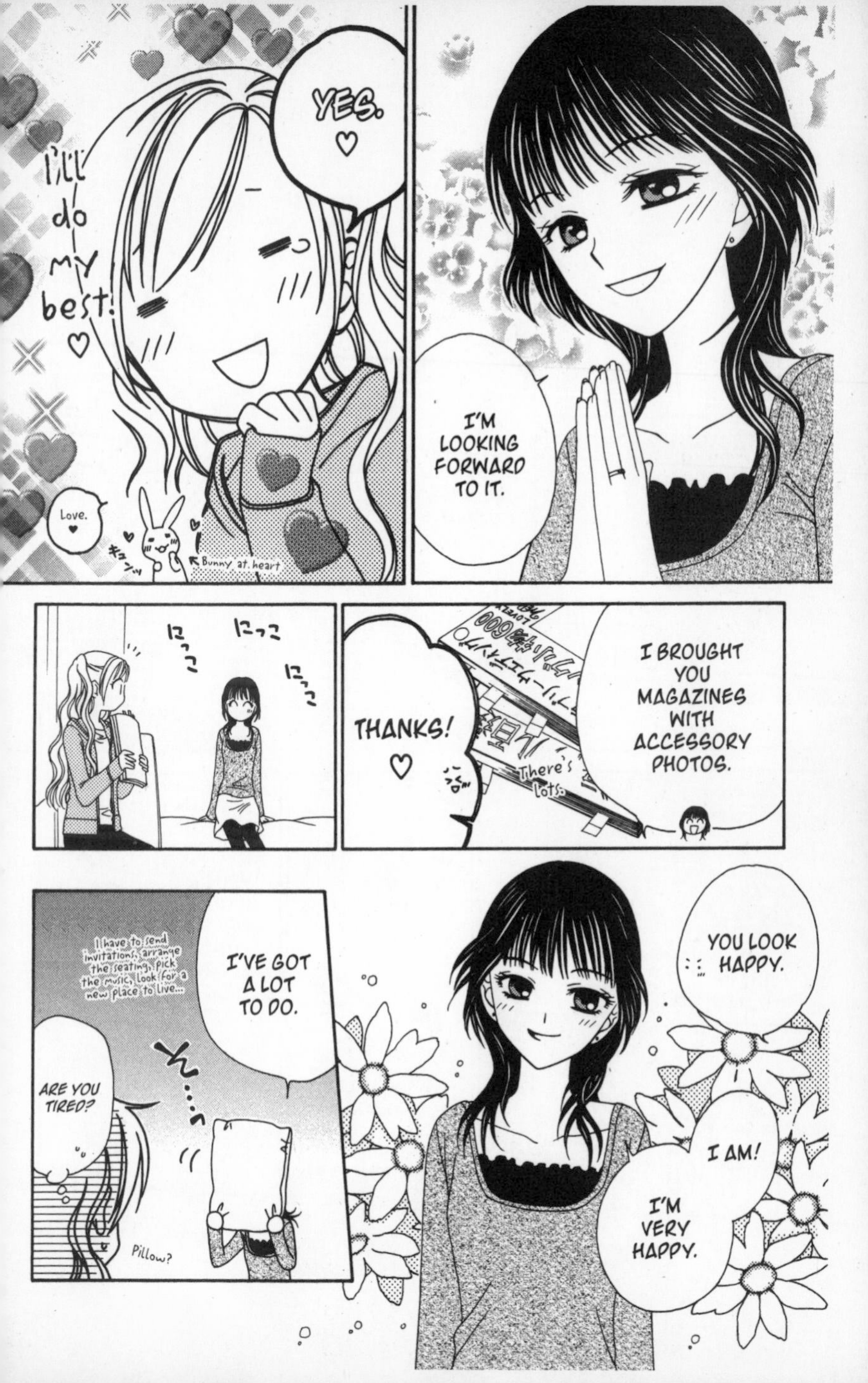
I'M LOOKING FORWARD TO IT.
YES. ♡
I'll do my best! ♡
Love. ♥
Bunny at heart
I BROUGHT YOU MAGAZINES WITH ACCESSORY PHOTOS.
There's lots.
THANKS! ♡
にっこ
にっこ
にっこ
YOU LOOK HAPPY.
I AM!
I'M VERY HAPPY.
I'VE GOT A LOT TO DO.
I have to send invitations, arrange the seating, pick the music, look for a new place to live...
ARE YOU TIRED?
Pillow?

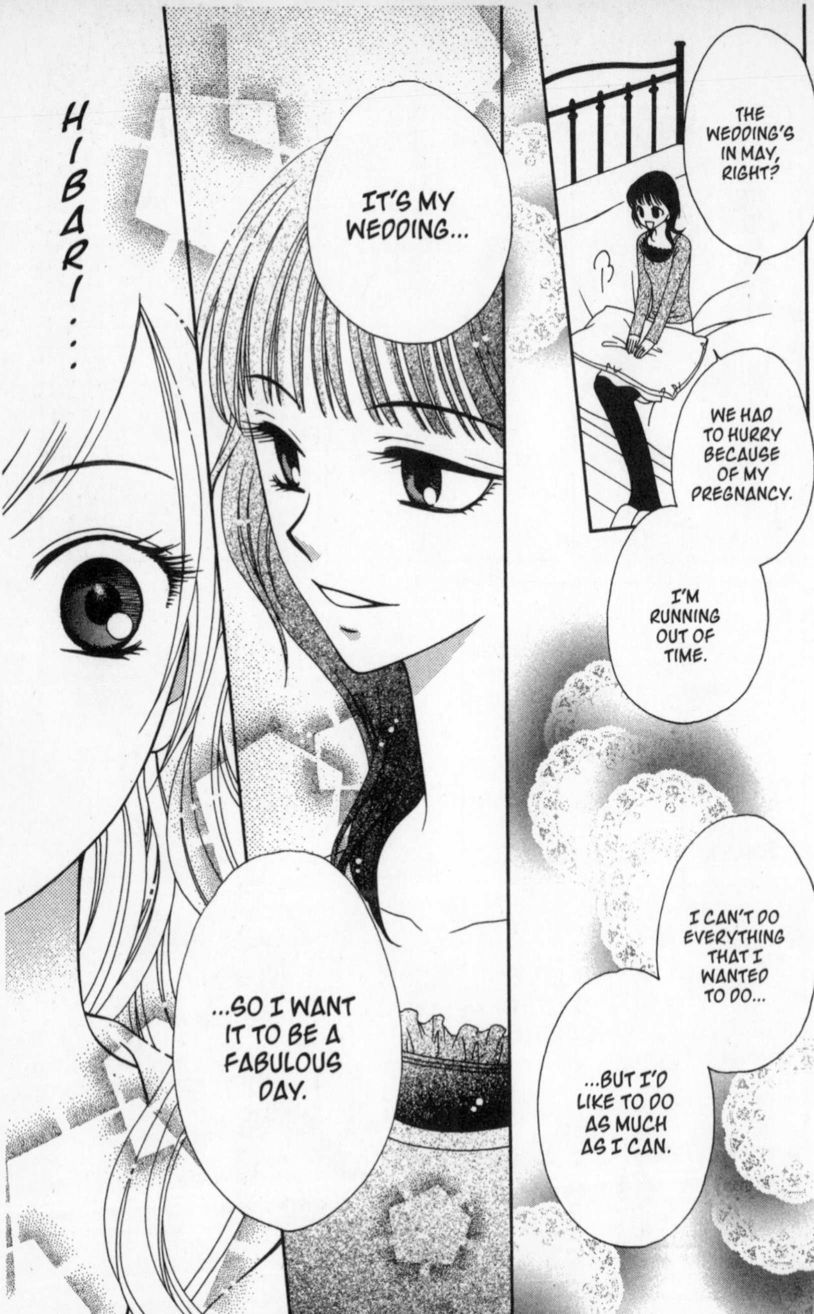
THE WEDDING'S IN MAY, RIGHT?
WE HAD TO HURRY BECAUSE OF MY PREGNANCY.
I'M RUNNING OUT OF TIME.
I CAN'T DO EVERYTHING THAT I WANTED TO DO...
...BUT I'D LIKE TO DO AS MUCH AS I CAN.
IT'S MY WEDDING...
...SO I WANT IT TO BE A FABULOUS DAY.
HIBARI...

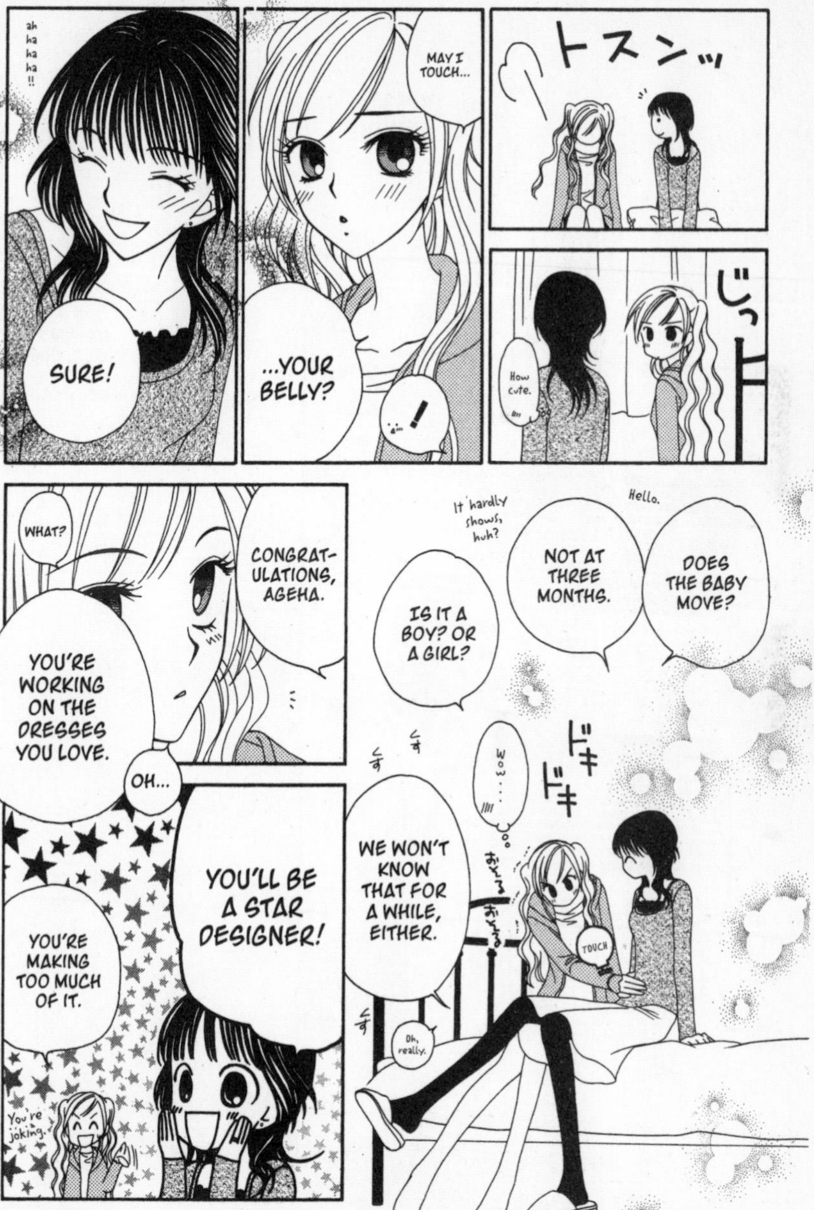

トスンッ
じっ
How cute.
MAY I TOUCH...
...YOUR BELLY?
!
SURE!
ah ha ha ha!!
Hello.
DOES THE BABY MOVE?
It hardly shows, huh?
NOT AT THREE MONTHS.
IS IT A BOY? OR A GIRL?
ドキドキ
Wow...
おそるおそる
TOUCH
WE WON'T KNOW THAT FOR A WHILE, EITHER.
くすくす
Oh, really.
CONGRAT-ULATIONS, AGEHA.
WHAT?
YOU'RE WORKING ON THE DRESSES YOU LOVE.
OH...
YOU'LL BE A STAR DESIGNER!
YOU'RE MAKING TOO MUCH OF IT.
You're joking.

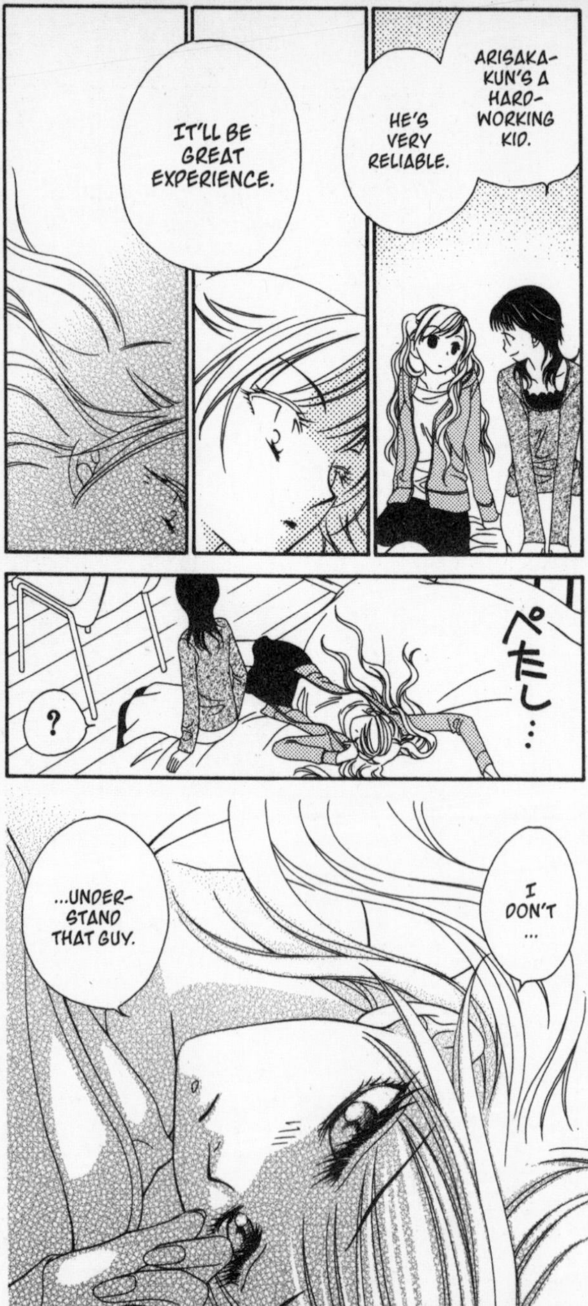
ARISAKA-KUN'S A HARD-WORKING KID.
HE'S VERY RELIABLE.
IT'LL BE GREAT EXPERIENCE.
ぺたし…
?
I DON'T...
...UNDER-STAND THAT GUY.

November 13, nighttime: re-faxed changes to editor.

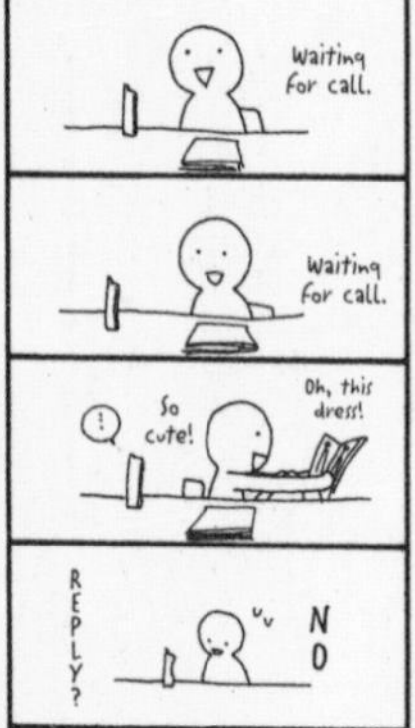
Waiting for call.
Waiting for call.
Oh, this dress!
So cute!
!
REPLY?
NO

I cleaned my desk and went to sleep.

November 14: Went to an eye doctor, who put drops in my eyes.

Did you know that our pupils adjust to let in the right amount of light?

I can explain better with cat's eyes.

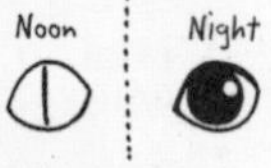
Noon
Night

I love cat's eyes at night. So cute!

My pupils were dilated all day. Too much light! My eyes really hurt on the drive home. I borrowed clip-on shades from the doctor, but the light was still too bright.

← Continued on page 145.

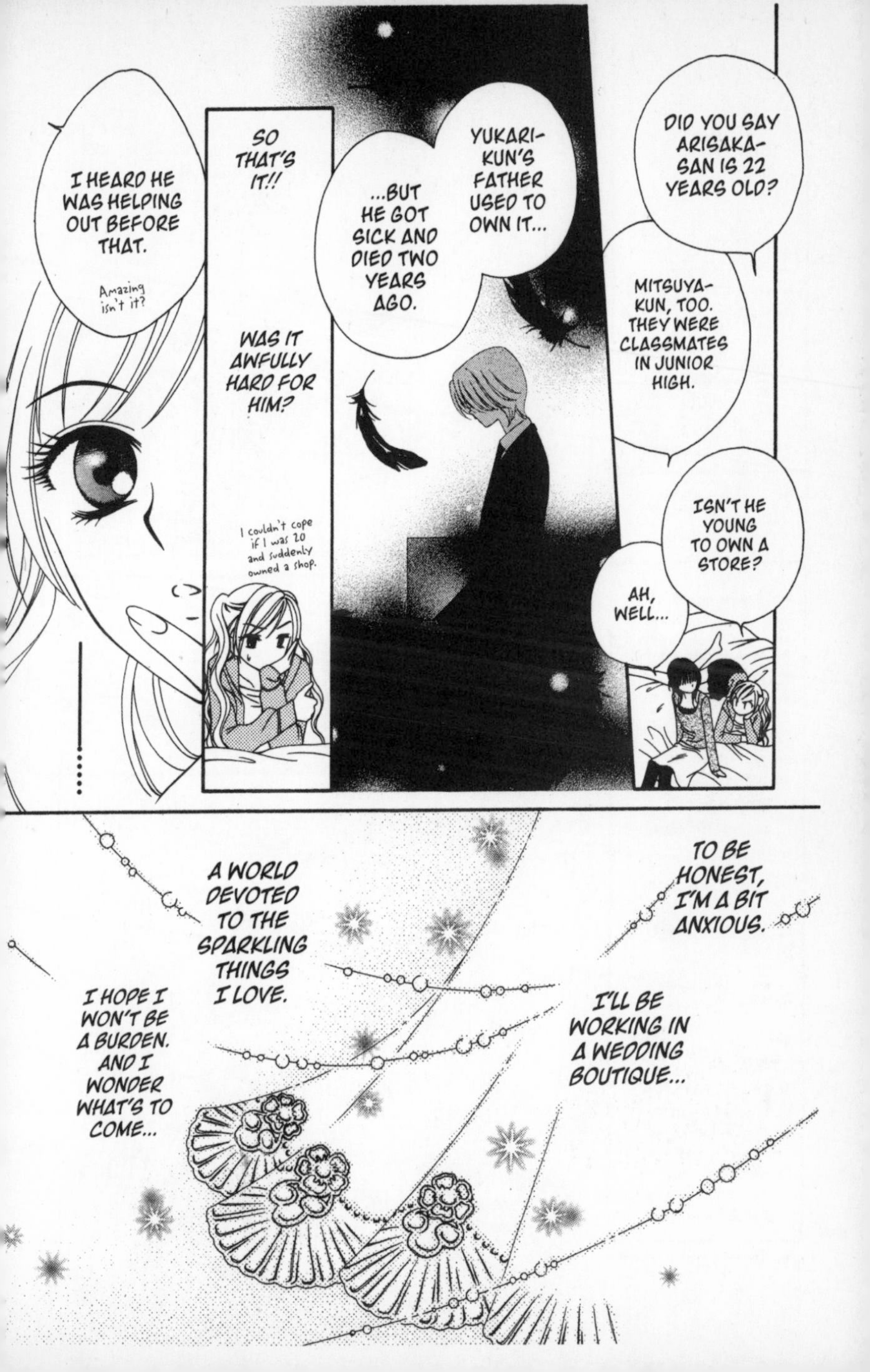
DID YOU SAY ARISAKA-SAN IS 22 YEARS OLD?
MITSUYA-KUN, TOO. THEY WERE CLASSMATES IN JUNIOR HIGH.
ISN'T HE YOUNG TO OWN A STORE?
AH, WELL...
YUKARI-KUN'S FATHER USED TO OWN IT...
...BUT HE GOT SICK AND DIED TWO YEARS AGO.
SO THAT'S IT!!
WAS IT AWFULLY HARD FOR HIM?
I couldn't cope if I was 20 and suddenly owned a shop.
I HEARD HE WAS HELPING OUT BEFORE THAT.
Amazing isn't it?
TO BE HONEST, I'M A BIT ANXIOUS.
I'LL BE WORKING IN A WEDDING BOUTIQUE...
A WORLD DEVOTED TO THE SPARKLING THINGS I LOVE.
I HOPE I WON'T BE A BURDEN. AND I WONDER WHAT'S TO COME...

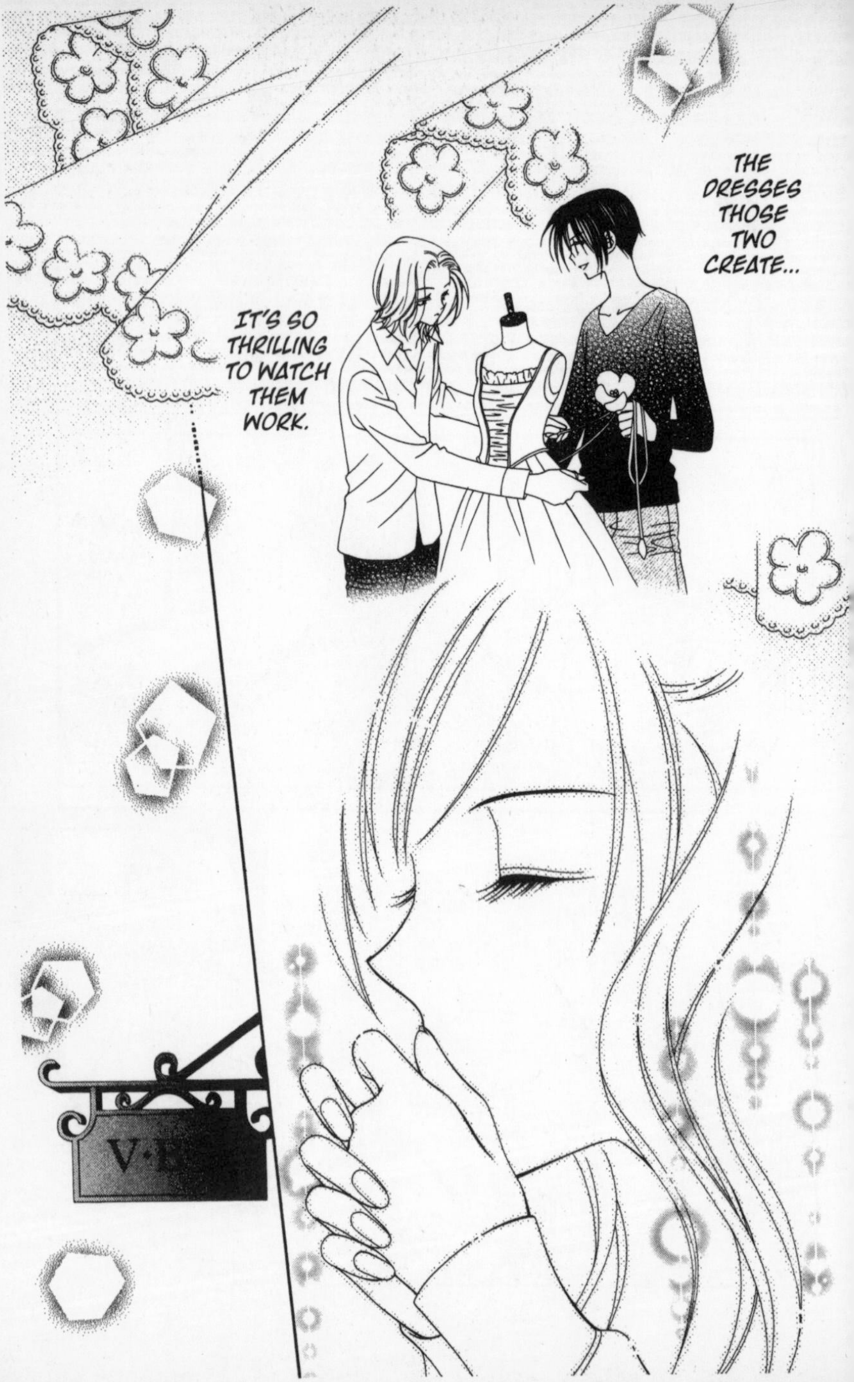
THE DRESSES THOSE TWO CREATE...
IT'S SO THRILLING TO WATCH THEM WORK.

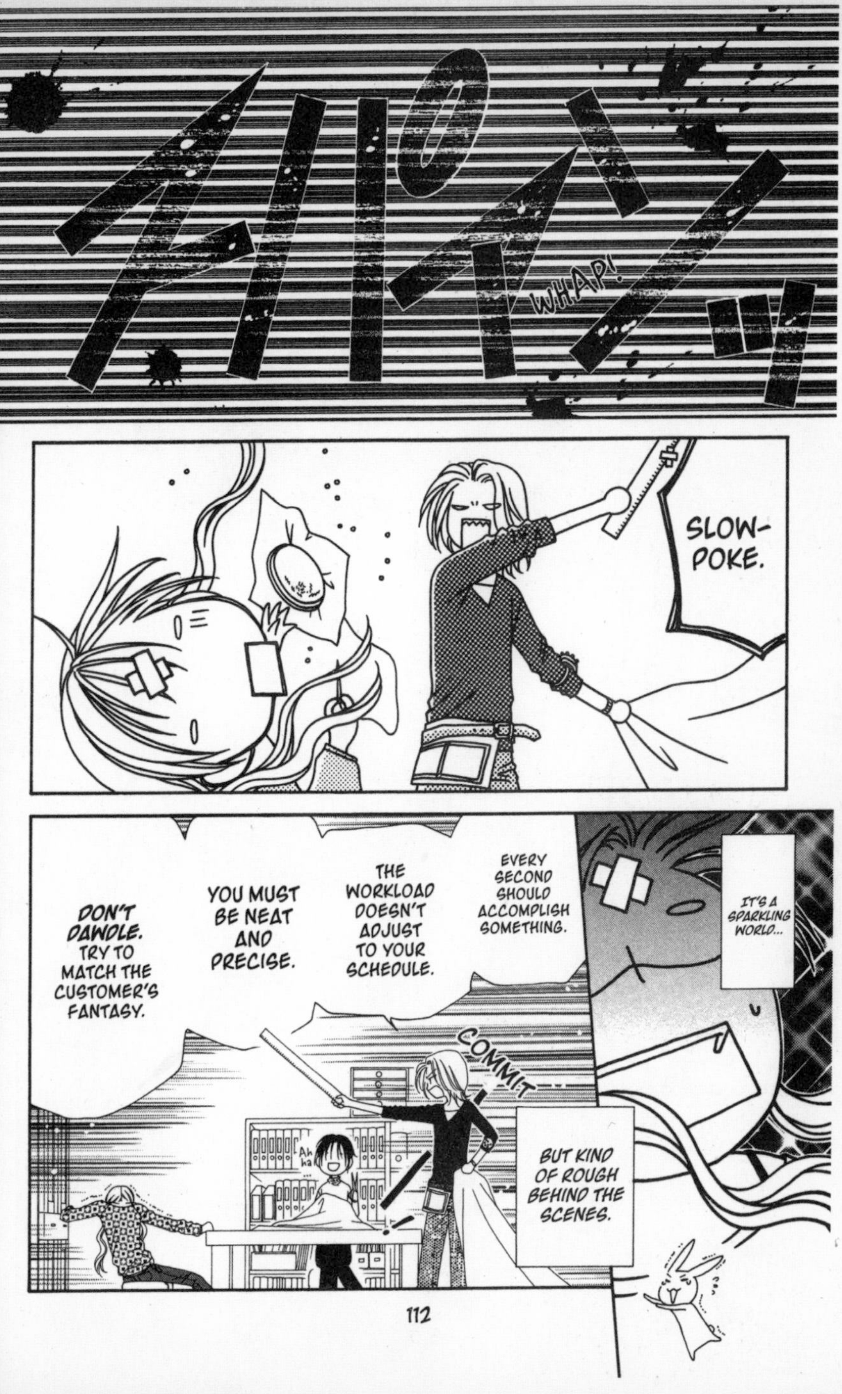
WHAP!
SLOW-POKE.
IT'S A SPARKLING WORLD...
EVERY SECOND SHOULD ACCOMPLISH SOMETHING.
THE WORKLOAD DOESN'T ADJUST TO YOUR SCHEDULE.
YOU MUST BE NEAT AND PRECISE.
DON'T DAWDLE. TRY TO MATCH THE CUSTOMER'S FANTASY.
COMMIT
BUT KIND OF ROUGH BEHIND THE SCENES.
Ah ha

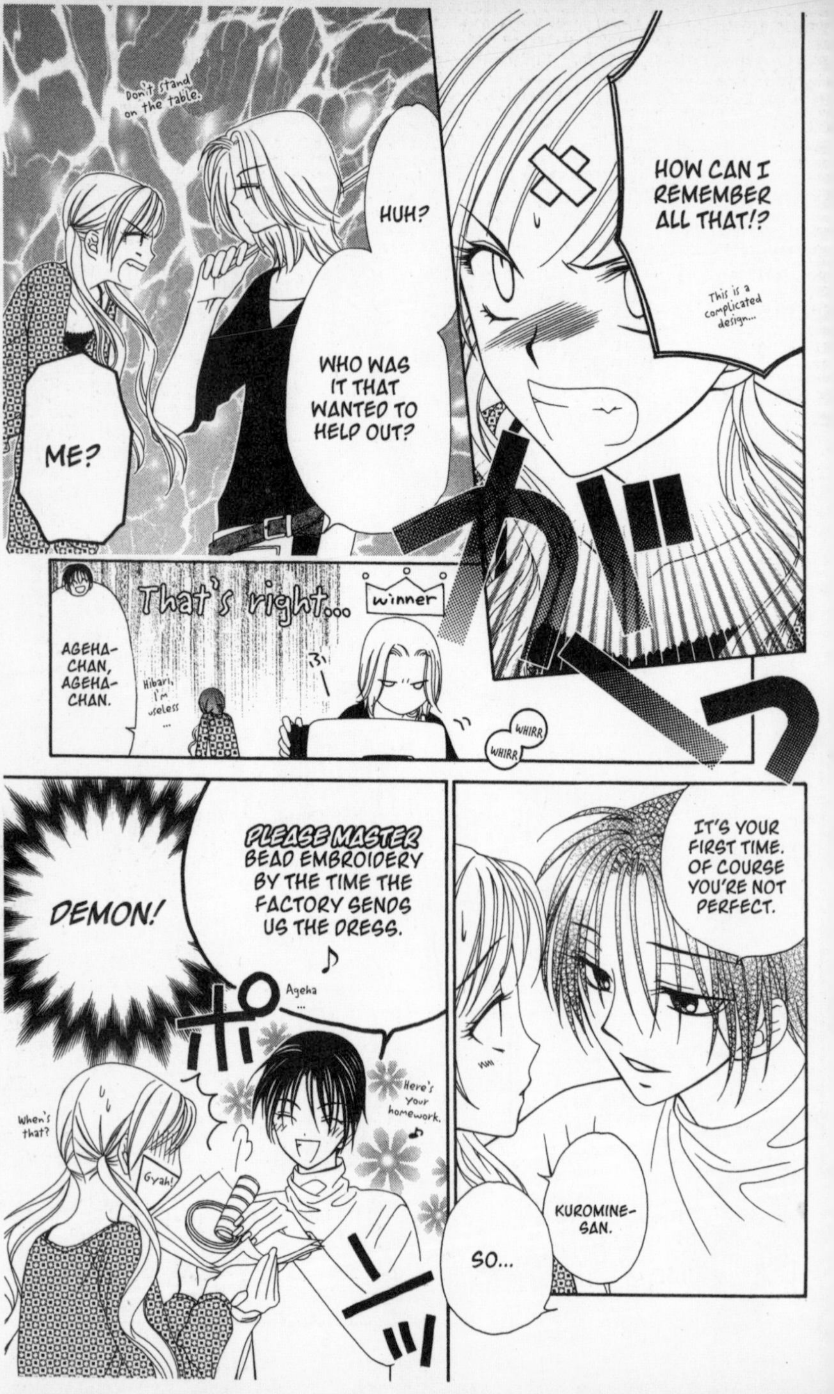
HOW CAN I REMEMBER ALL THAT!?
This is a complicated design...
Don't stand on the table.
HUH?
WHO WAS IT THAT WANTED TO HELP OUT?
ME?
That's right...
winner
AGEHA-CHAN, AGEHA-CHAN.
Hibari, I'm useless...
WHIRR
WHIRR
IT'S YOUR FIRST TIME. OF COURSE YOU'RE NOT PERFECT.
KUROMINE-SAN.
SO...
PLEASE MASTER BEAD EMBROIDERY BY THE TIME THE FACTORY SENDS US THE DRESS.
DEMON!
Ageha...
Here's your homework.
When's that?
Gyah!

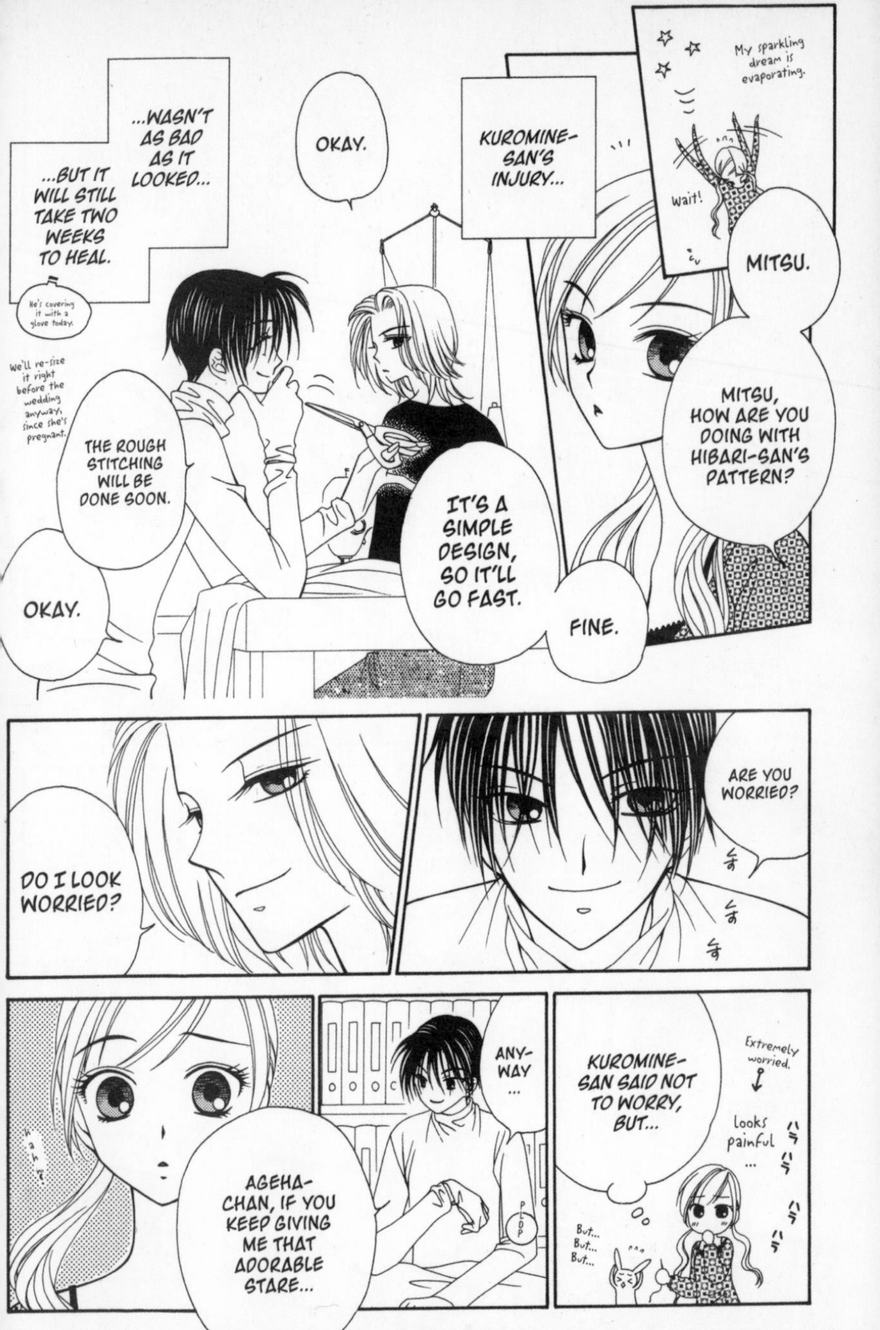

My sparkling dream is evaporating.
Wait!
MITSU.
MITSU, HOW ARE YOU DOING WITH HIBARI-SAN'S PATTERN?
FINE.
KUROMINE-SAN'S INJURY...
OKAY.
...WASN'T AS BAD AS IT LOOKED...
...BUT IT WILL STILL TAKE TWO WEEKS TO HEAL.
He's covering it with a glove today.
IT'S A SIMPLE DESIGN, SO IT'LL GO FAST.
We'll re-size it right before the wedding anyway, since she's pregnant.
THE ROUGH STITCHING WILL BE DONE SOON.
OKAY.
ARE YOU WORRIED?
くす くす くす
DO I LOOK WORRIED?
KUROMINE-SAN SAID NOT TO WORRY, BUT...
Extremely worried.
Looks painful...
ハラ ハラ ハラ ハラ
But... But... But...
ANY-WAY...
AGEHA-CHAN, IF YOU KEEP GIVING ME THAT ADORABLE STARE...

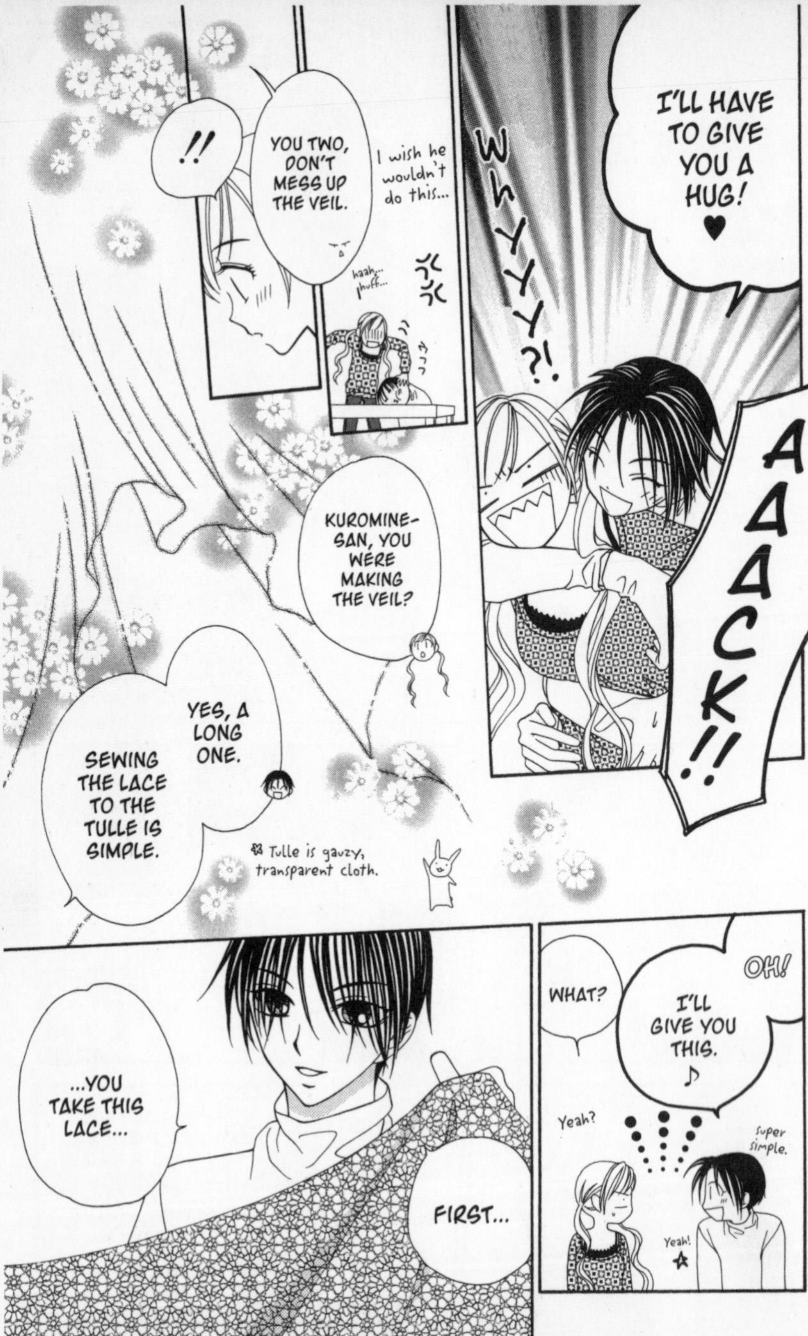
I'LL HAVE TO GIVE YOU A HUG! ♥
WHYYYY?!
AAACK!!
!!
YOU TWO, DON'T MESS UP THE VEIL.
I wish he wouldn't do this...
haah... huff...
KUROMINE-SAN, YOU WERE MAKING THE VEIL?
YES, A LONG ONE.
SEWING THE LACE TO THE TULLE IS SIMPLE.
✽ Tulle is gauzy, transparent cloth.
OH!
I'LL GIVE YOU THIS. ♪
WHAT?
super simple.
Yeah?
Yeah!
...YOU TAKE THIS LACE...
FIRST...

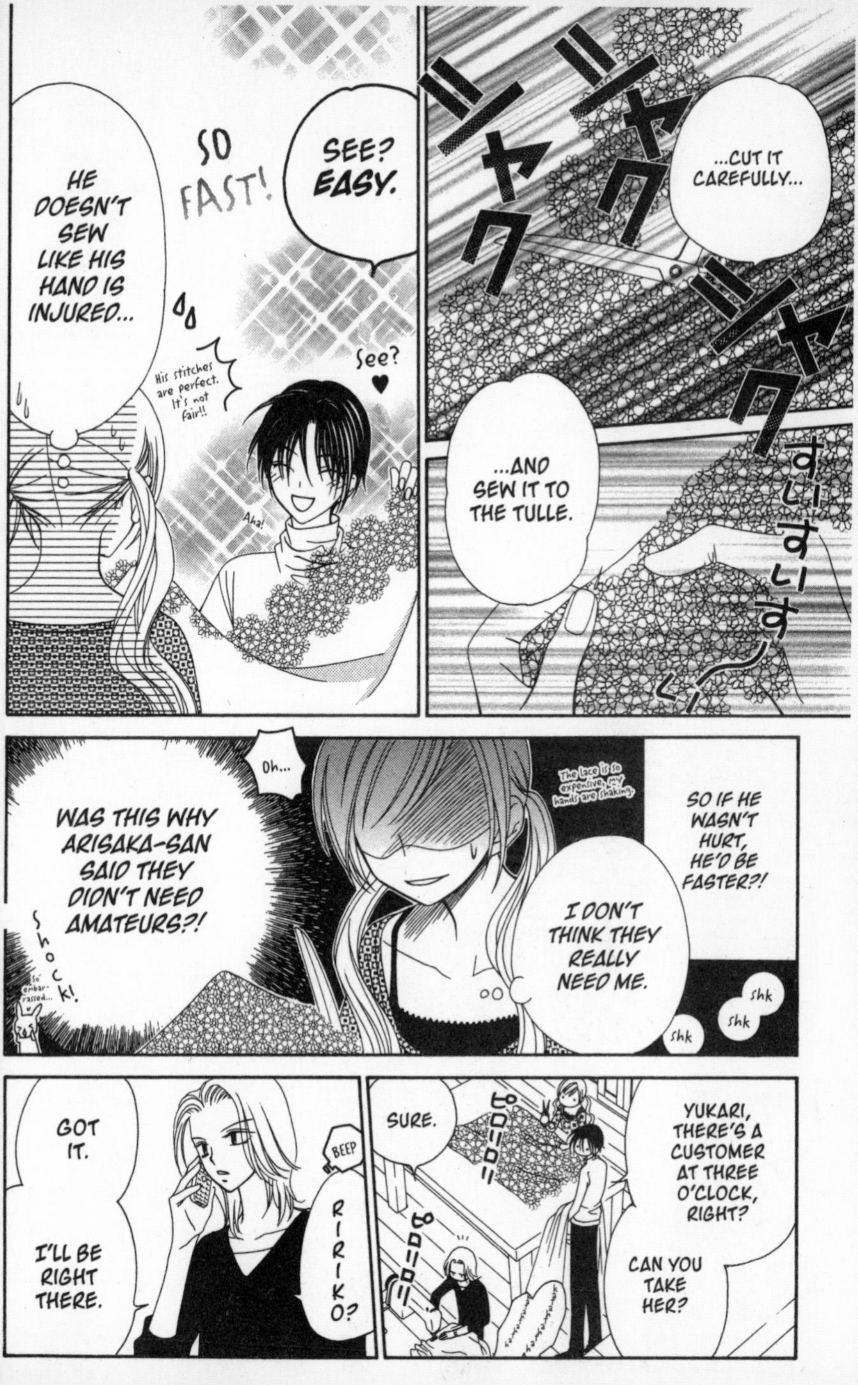
...CUT IT CAREFULLY...
...AND SEW IT TO THE TULLE.
SEE? EASY.
SO FAST!
HE DOESN'T SEW LIKE HIS HAND IS INJURED...
His stitches are perfect. It's not fair!!
See?
Aha!
SO IF HE WASN'T HURT, HE'D BE FASTER?!
The lace is so expensive, my hands are shaking.
I DON'T THINK THEY REALLY NEED ME.
shk
shk
shk
Oh...
WAS THIS WHY ARISAKA-SAN SAID THEY DIDN'T NEED AMATEURS?!
shock!
So embarrassed...
YUKARI, THERE'S A CUSTOMER AT THREE O'CLOCK, RIGHT?
CAN YOU TAKE HER?
SURE.
RIRIKO?
BEEP
GOT IT.
I'LL BE RIGHT THERE.

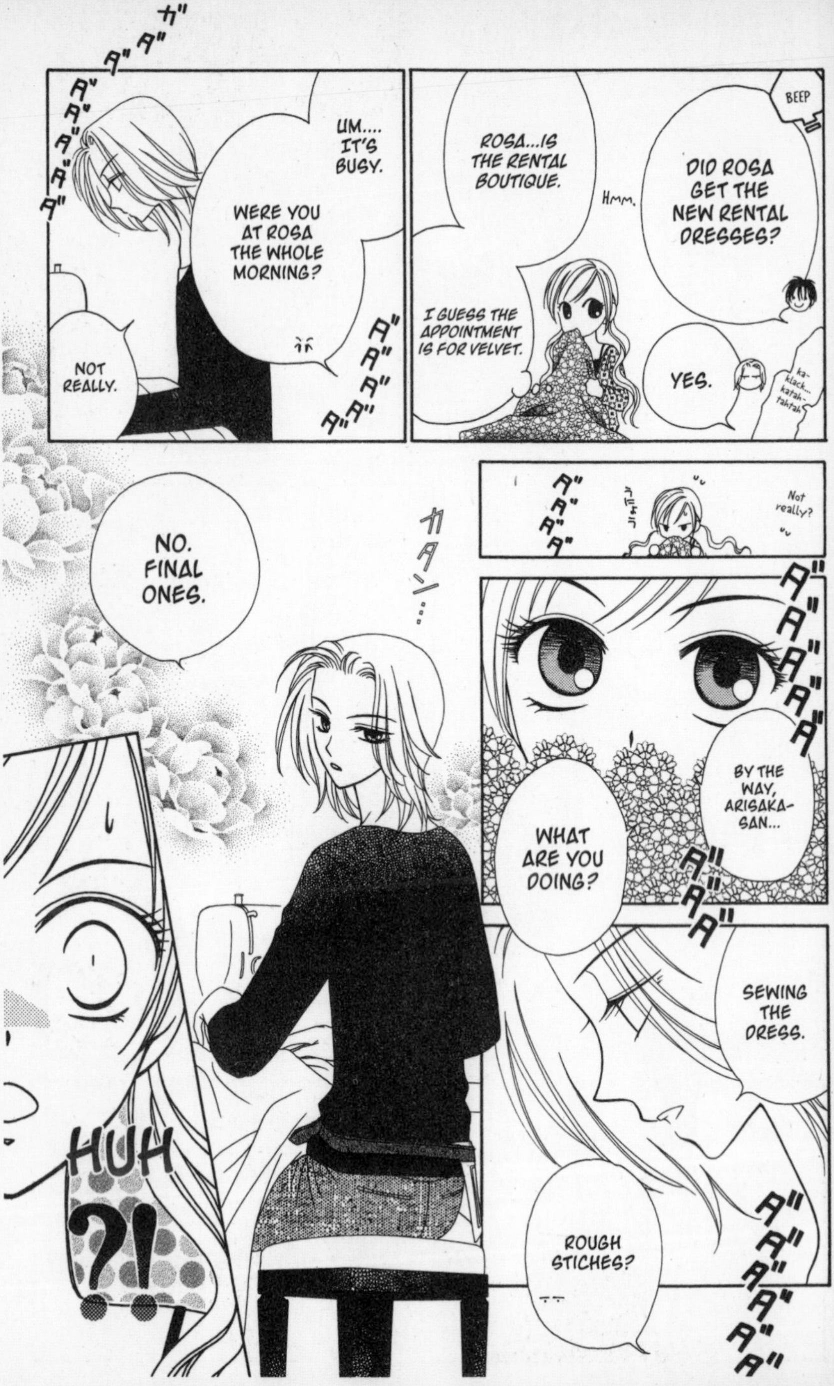
BEEP
DID ROSA GET THE NEW RENTAL DRESSES?
HMM.
ROSA...IS THE RENTAL BOUTIQUE.
YES.
ka-klack... katah-tahtah
I GUESS THE APPOINTMENT IS FOR VELVET.
ガダダダダダダダ
UM.... IT'S BUSY.
WERE YOU AT ROSA THE WHOLE MORNING?
ダダダダダ
NOT REALLY.
Not really?
ダダダダ
ダダダダダダ
BY THE WAY, ARISAKA-SAN...
ダダダ
WHAT ARE YOU DOING?
SEWING THE DRESS.
ダダダダダダ
ROUGH STICHES?
NO. FINAL ONES.
カタン...
HUH ?!

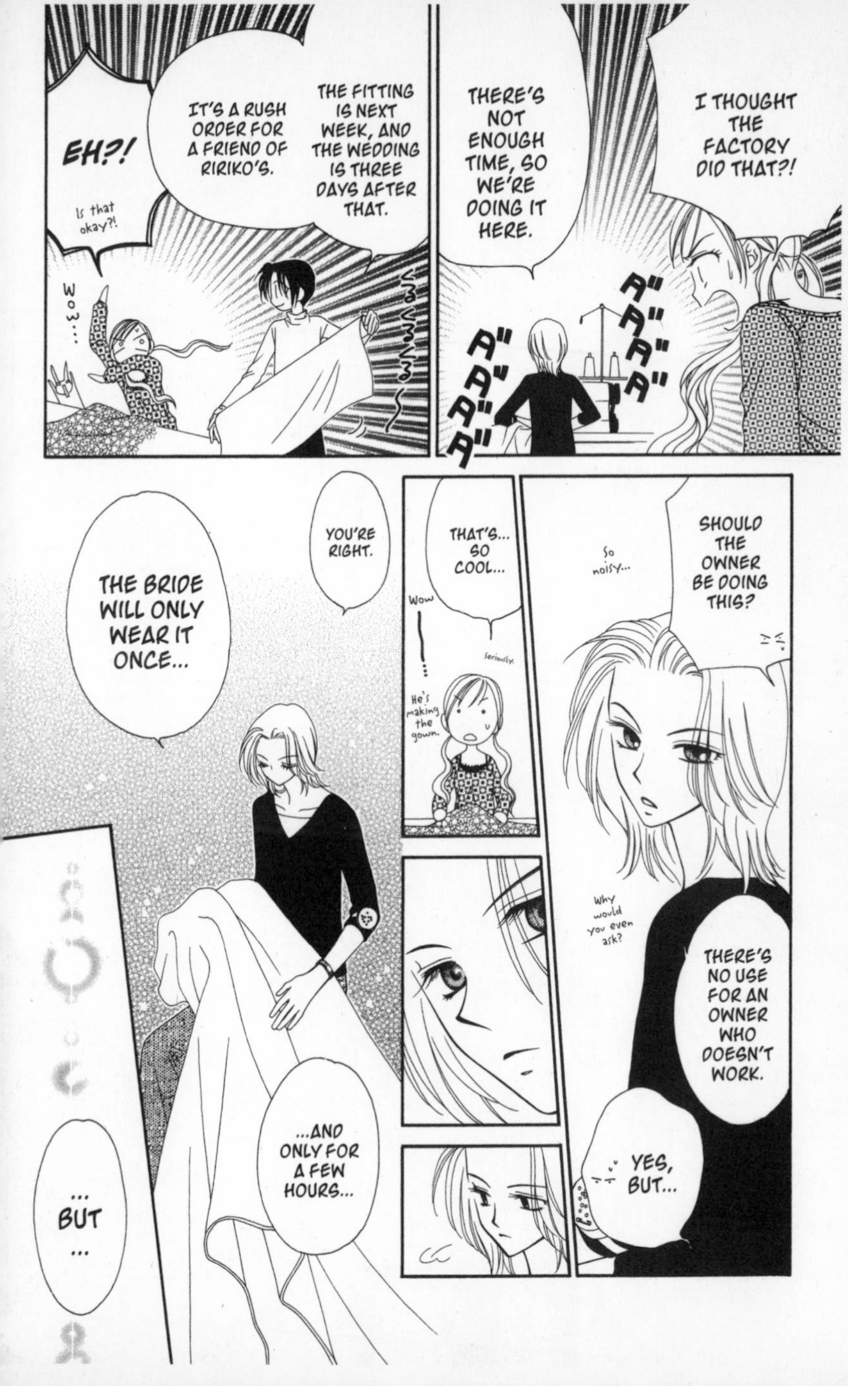
I THOUGHT THE FACTORY DID THAT?!
THERE'S NOT ENOUGH TIME, SO WE'RE DOING IT HERE.
THE FITTING IS NEXT WEEK, AND THE WEDDING IS THREE DAYS AFTER THAT.
IT'S A RUSH ORDER FOR A FRIEND OF RIRIKO'S.
EH?!
Is that okay?!
Wow...
SHOULD THE OWNER BE DOING THIS?
So noisy...
Why would you even ask?
THERE'S NO USE FOR AN OWNER WHO DOESN'T WORK.
YES, BUT...
THAT'S... SO COOL...
Wow—...
Seriously.
He's making the gown.
YOU'RE RIGHT.
THE BRIDE WILL ONLY WEAR IT ONCE...
...AND ONLY FOR A FEW HOURS...
... BUT ...

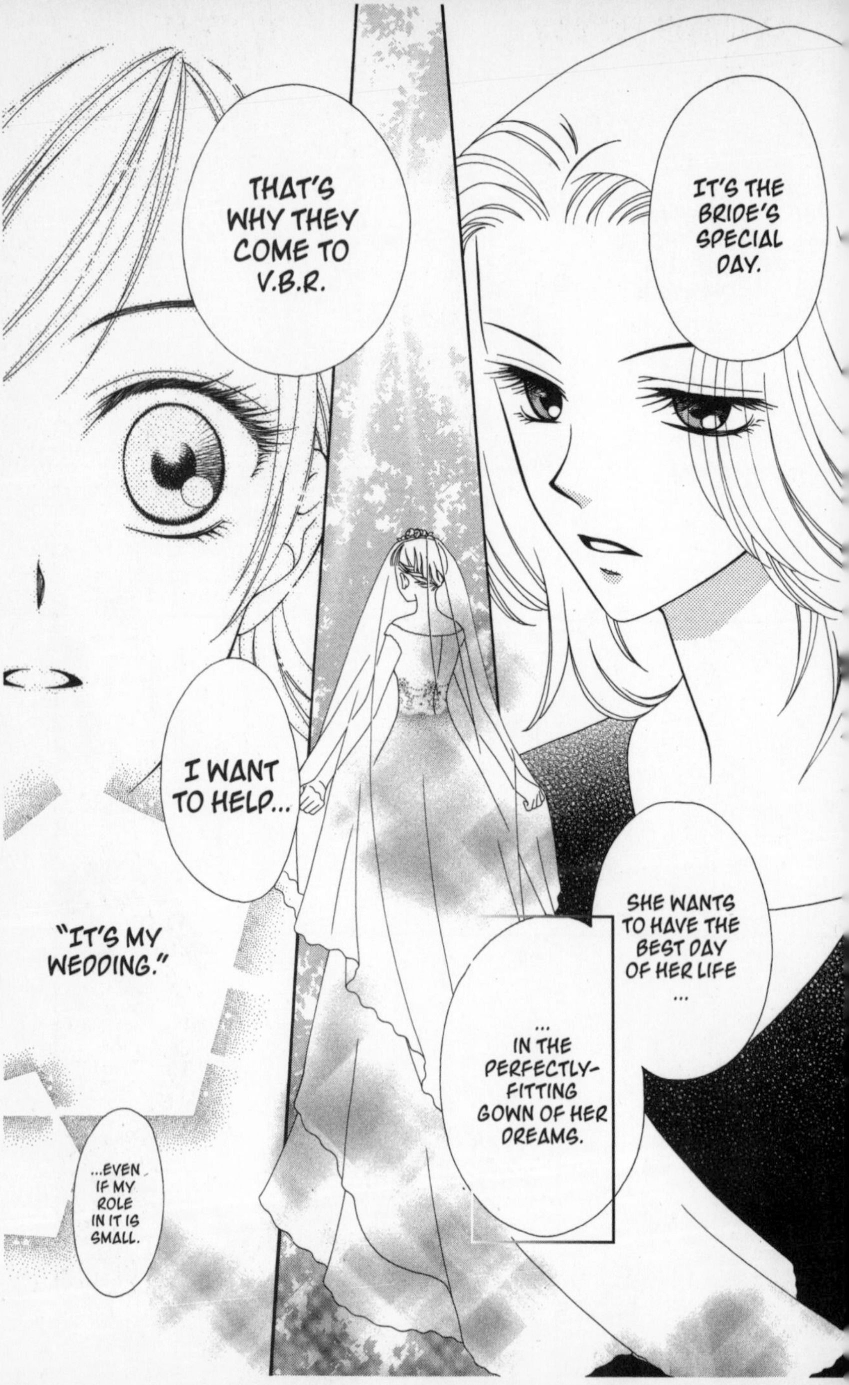
IT'S THE BRIDE'S SPECIAL DAY.
SHE WANTS TO HAVE THE BEST DAY OF HER LIFE ...
... IN THE PERFECTLY-FITTING GOWN OF HER DREAMS.
THAT'S WHY THEY COME TO V.B.R.
I WANT TO HELP...
"IT'S MY WEDDING."
...EVEN IF MY ROLE IN IT IS SMALL.

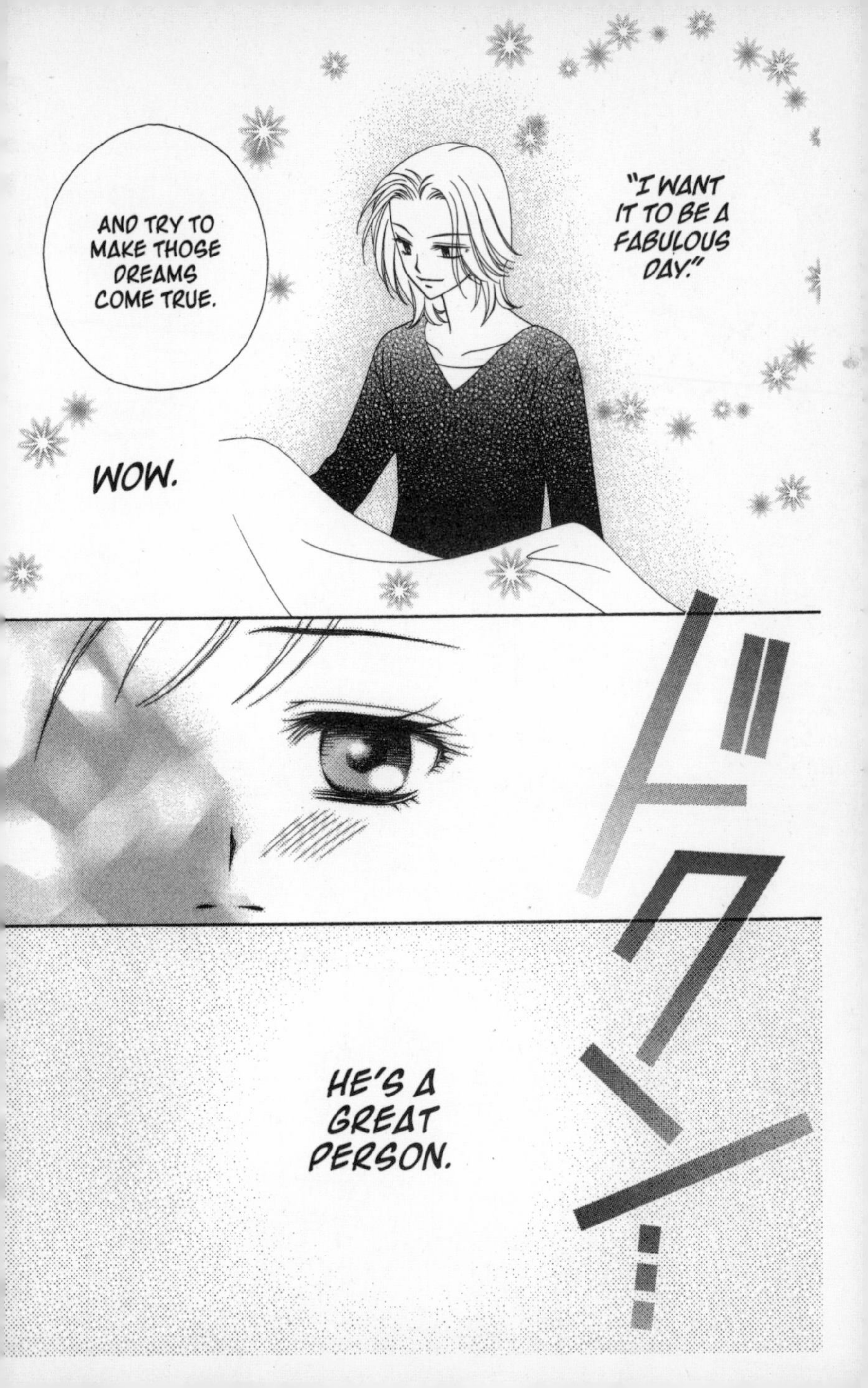
"I WANT IT TO BE A FABULOUS DAY."
AND TRY TO MAKE THOSE DREAMS COME TRUE.
WOW.
ドクン…
HE'S A GREAT PERSON.

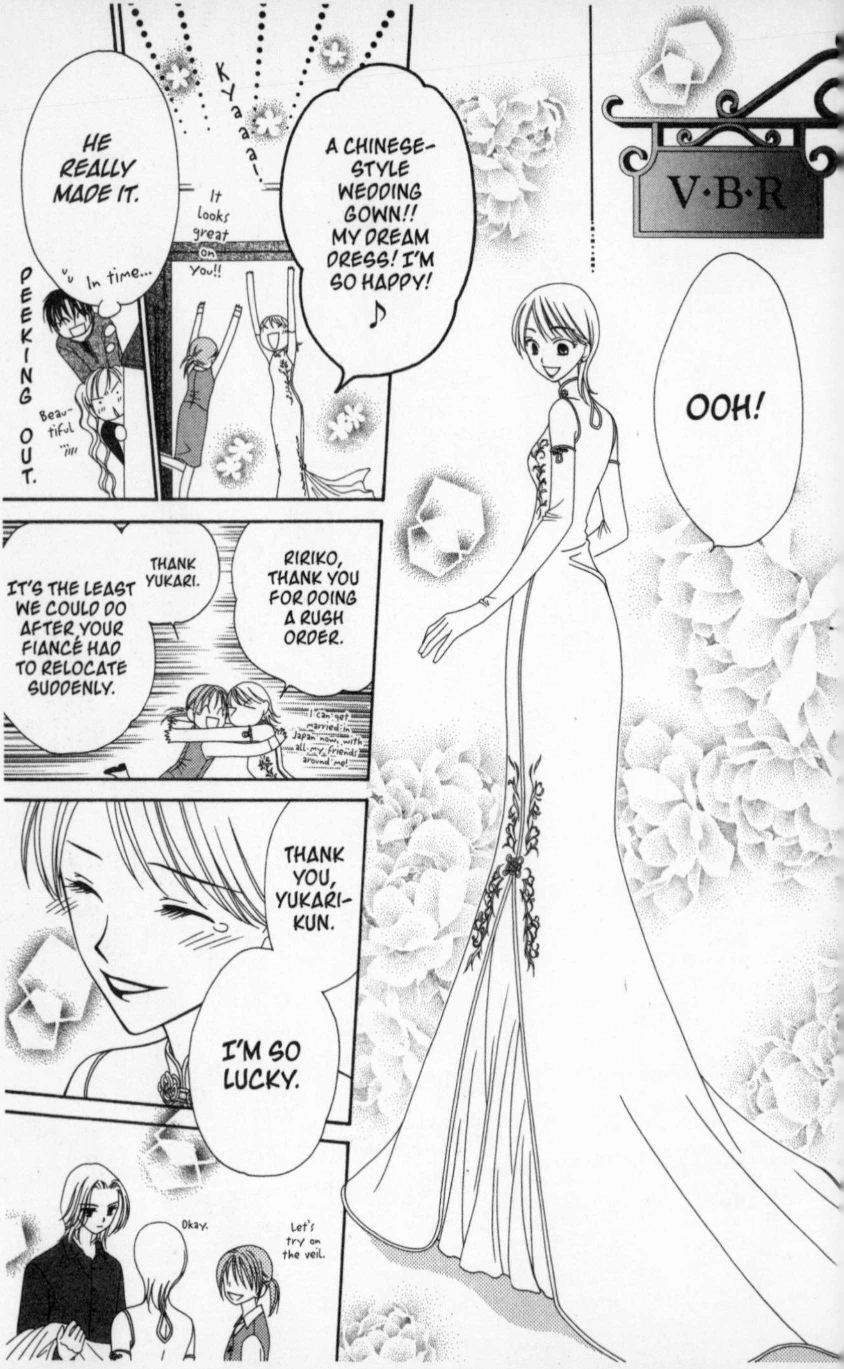
V·B·R
OOH!
Kyaaa!
A CHINESE-STYLE WEDDING GOWN!! MY DREAM DRESS! I'M SO HAPPY! ♪
It looks great on you!!
HE REALLY MADE IT.
In time...
PEEKING OUT.
Beautiful...
RIRIKO, THANK YOU FOR DOING A RUSH ORDER.
THANK YUKARI.
IT'S THE LEAST WE COULD DO AFTER YOUR FIANCÉ HAD TO RELOCATE SUDDENLY.
I can't get married in Japan now, with all my friends around me!
THANK YOU, YUKARI-KUN.
I'M SO LUCKY.
Let's try on the veil.
Okay.

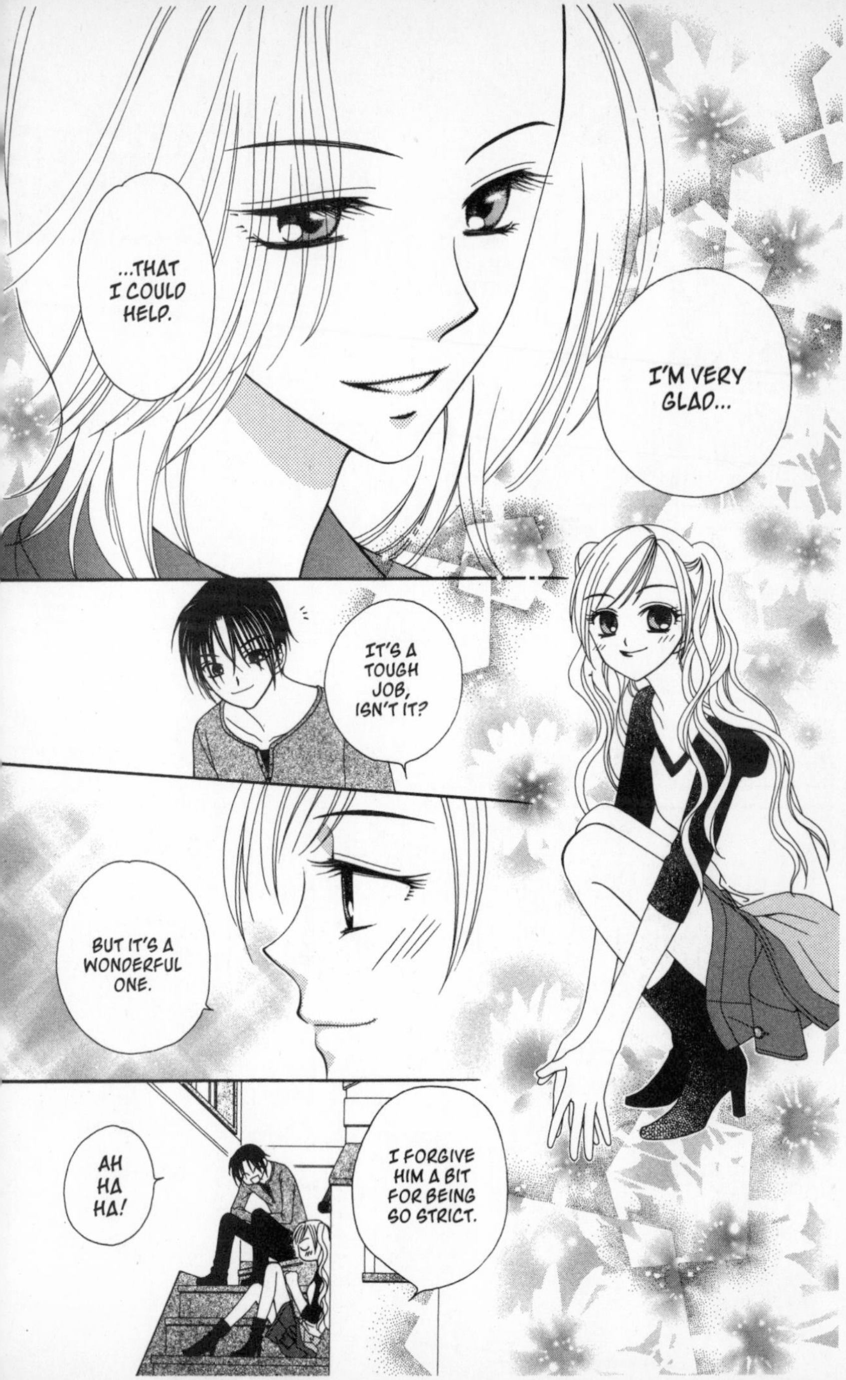
I'M VERY GLAD...
...THAT I COULD HELP.
IT'S A TOUGH JOB, ISN'T IT?
BUT IT'S A WONDERFUL ONE.
I FORGIVE HIM A BIT FOR BEING SO STRICT.
AH HA HA!

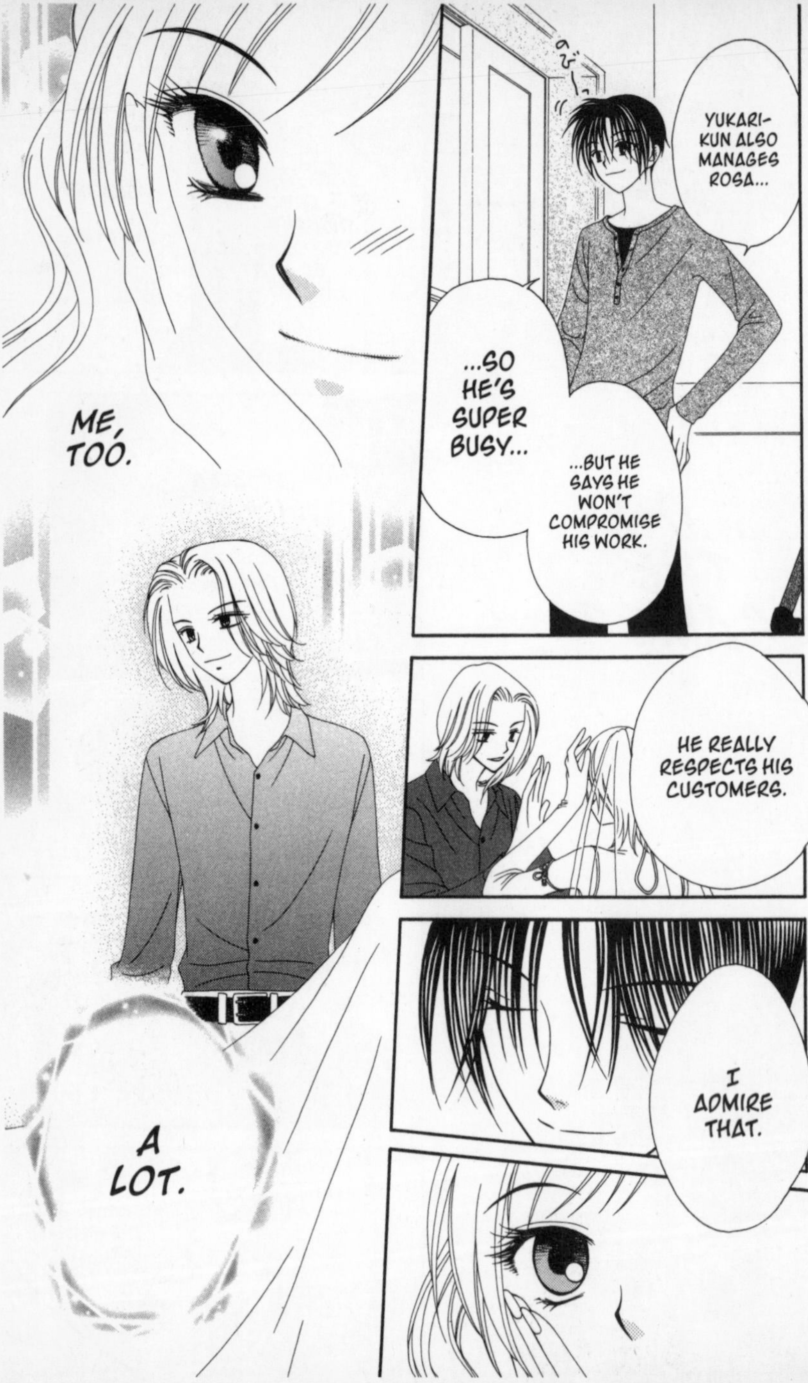
YUKARI-KUN ALSO MANAGES ROSA...
...SO HE'S SUPER BUSY...
...BUT HE SAYS HE WON'T COMPROMISE HIS WORK.
HE REALLY RESPECTS HIS CUSTOMERS.
I ADMIRE THAT.
ME, TOO.
A LOT.

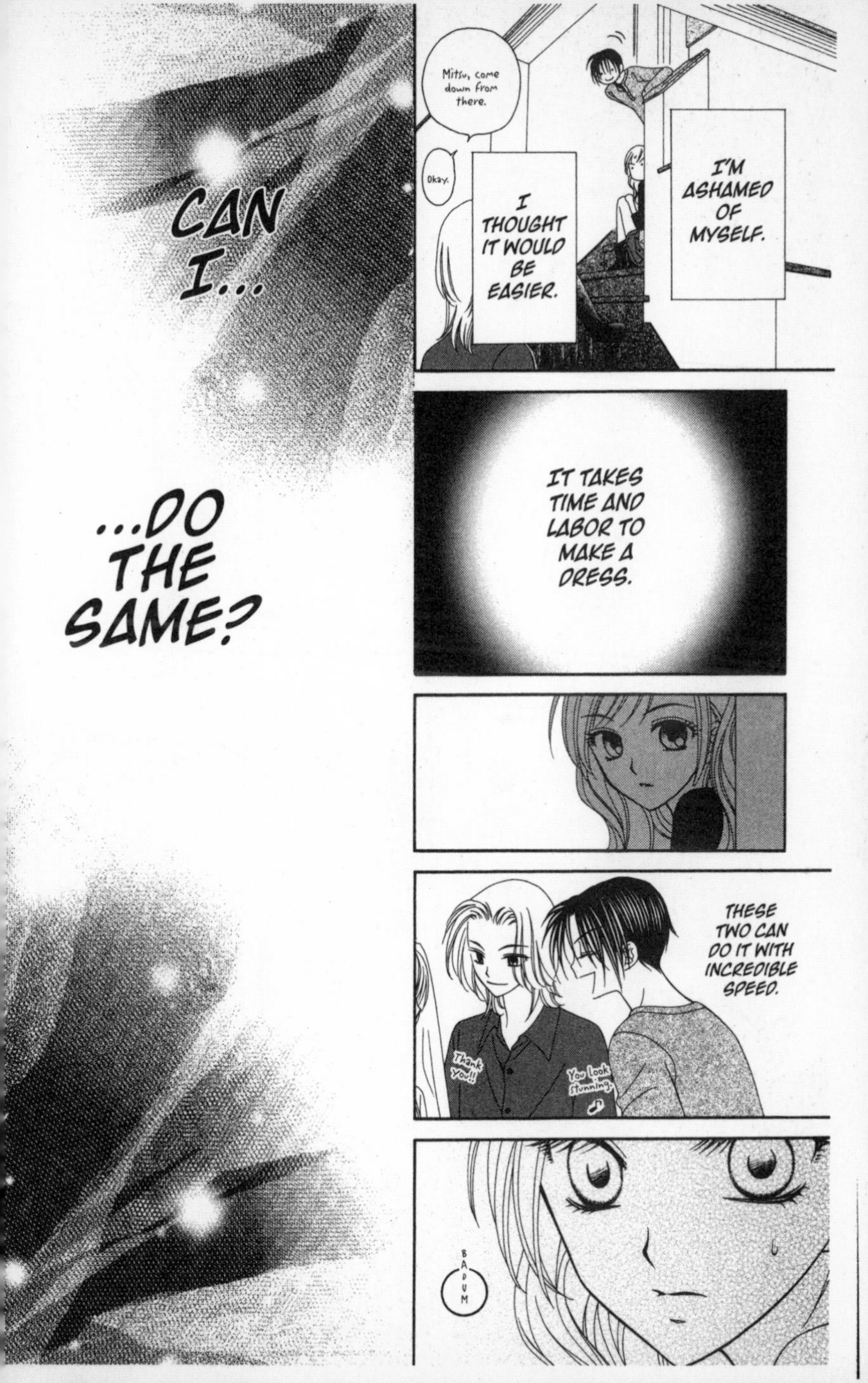
I'M ASHAMED OF MYSELF.
Mitsu, come down from there.
Okay.
I THOUGHT IT WOULD BE EASIER.
IT TAKES TIME AND LABOR TO MAKE A DRESS.
THESE TWO CAN DO IT WITH INCREDIBLE SPEED.
You look stunning.
Thank you!!
BADUM
CAN I...
...DO THE SAME?

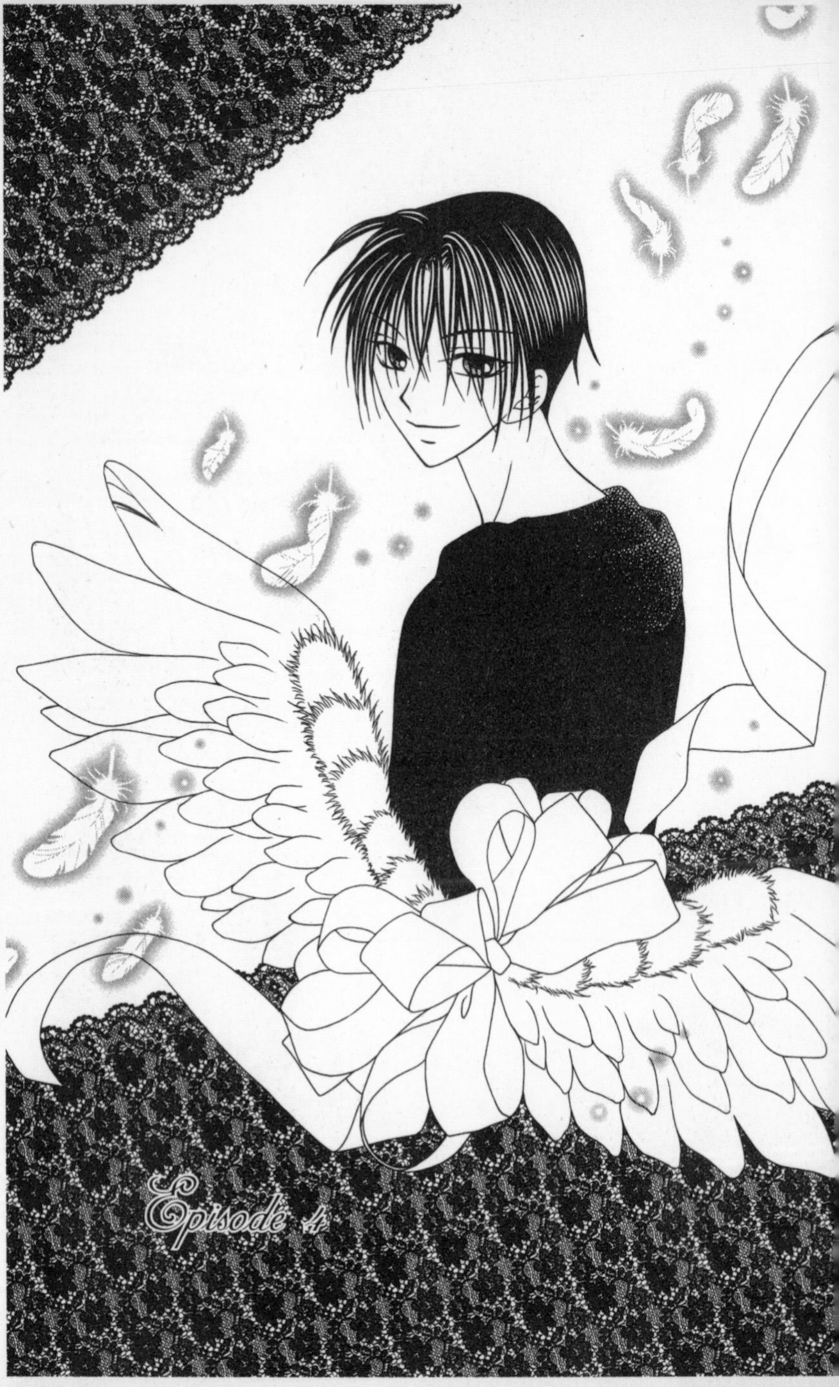
Episode 4

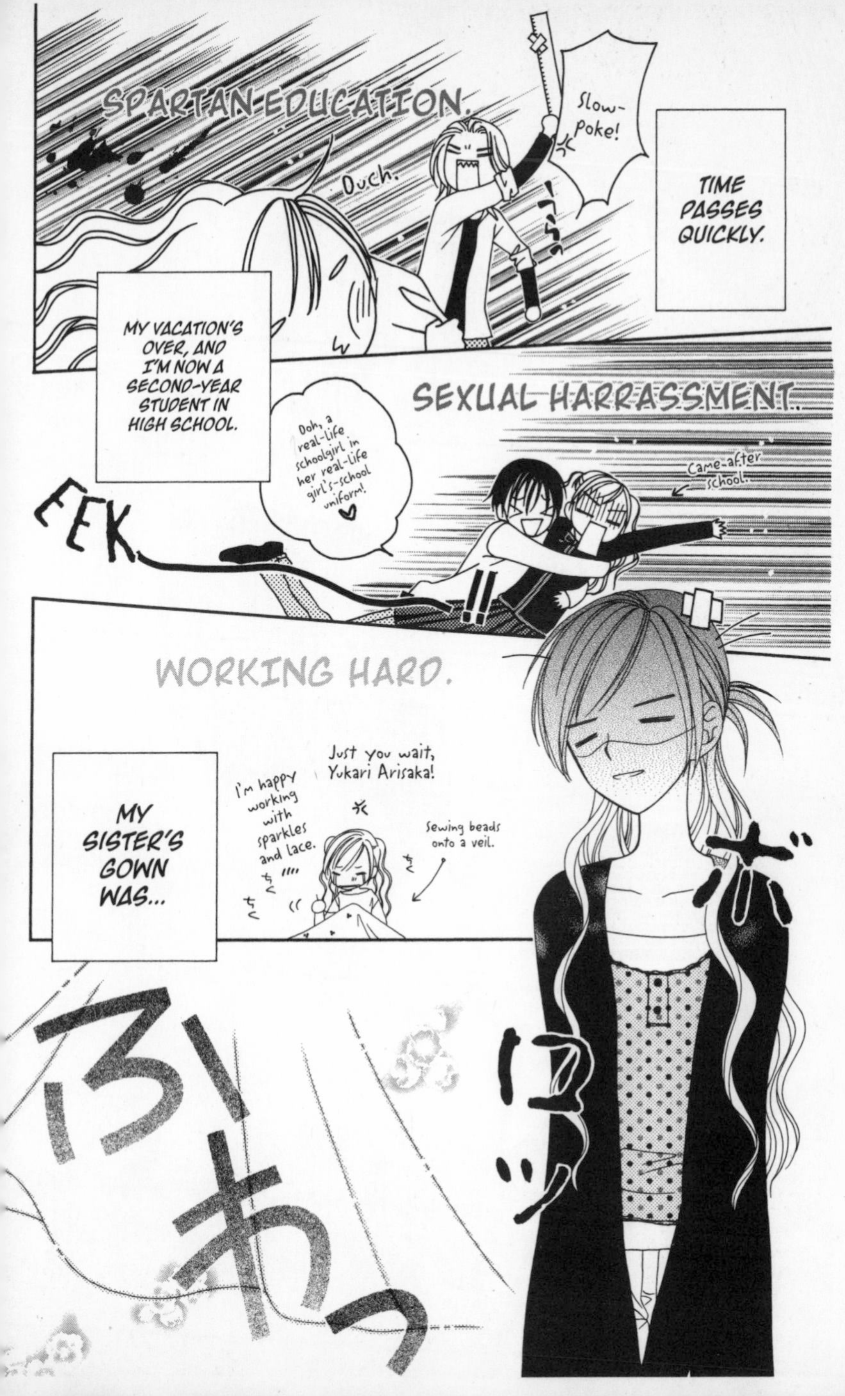

TIME PASSES QUICKLY.
Slow-poke!
SPARTAN EDUCATION.
Ouch.
MY VACATION'S OVER, AND I'M NOW A SECOND-YEAR STUDENT IN HIGH SCHOOL.
SEXUAL HARRASSMENT.
Came after school.
Ooh, a real-life schoolgirl in her real-life girl's-school uniform!
EEK
WORKING HARD.
Just you wait, Yukari Arisaka!
Sewing beads onto a veil.
I'm happy working with sparkles and lace.
MY SISTER'S GOWN WAS...
ふわっ

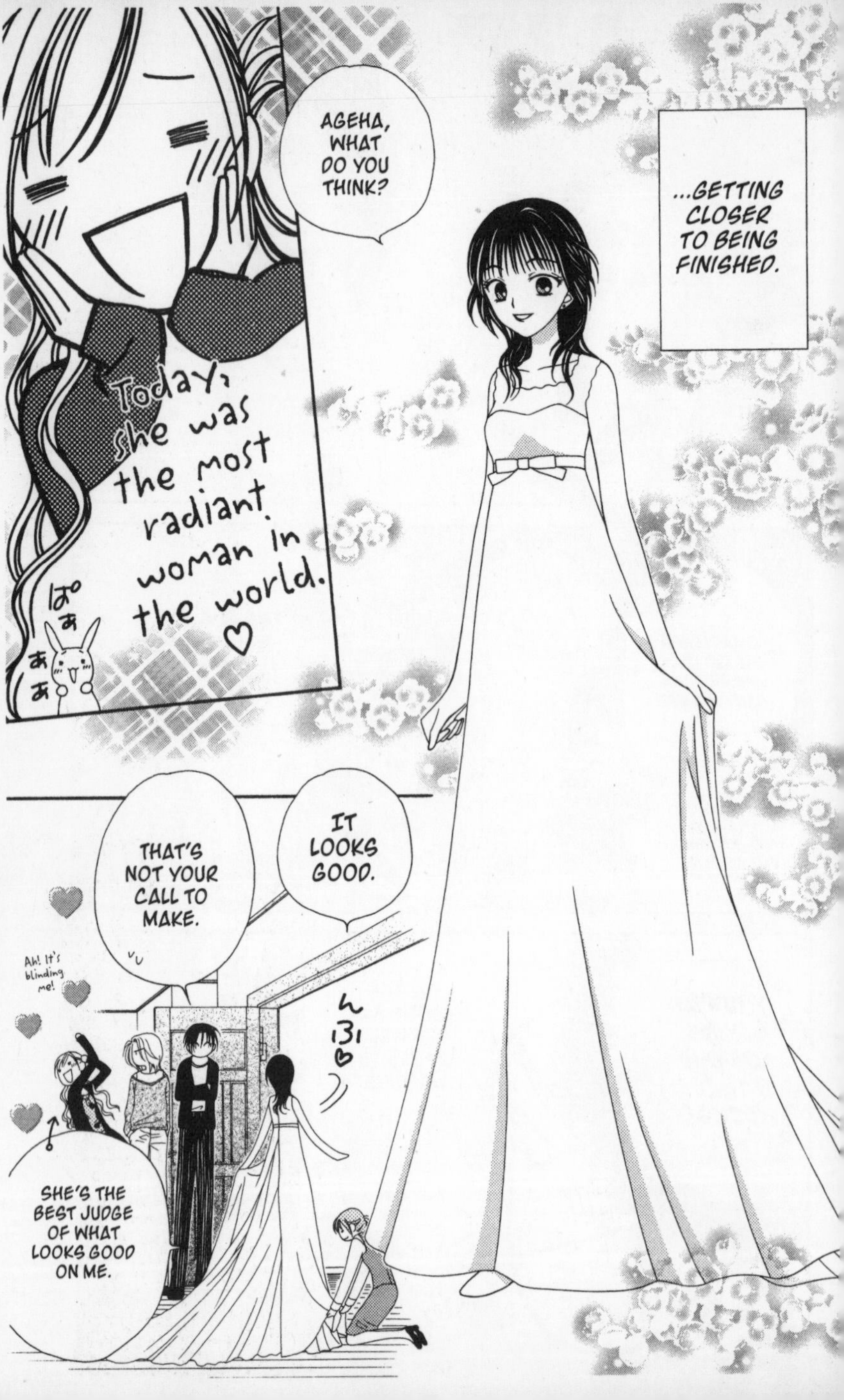
...GETTING CLOSER TO BEING FINISHED.
AGEHA, WHAT DO YOU THINK?
Today, she was the most radiant woman in the world. ♡
ぱあああ
IT LOOKS GOOD.
THAT'S NOT YOUR CALL TO MAKE.
んふ♡
Ah! It's blinding me!
SHE'S THE BEST JUDGE OF WHAT LOOKS GOOD ON ME.

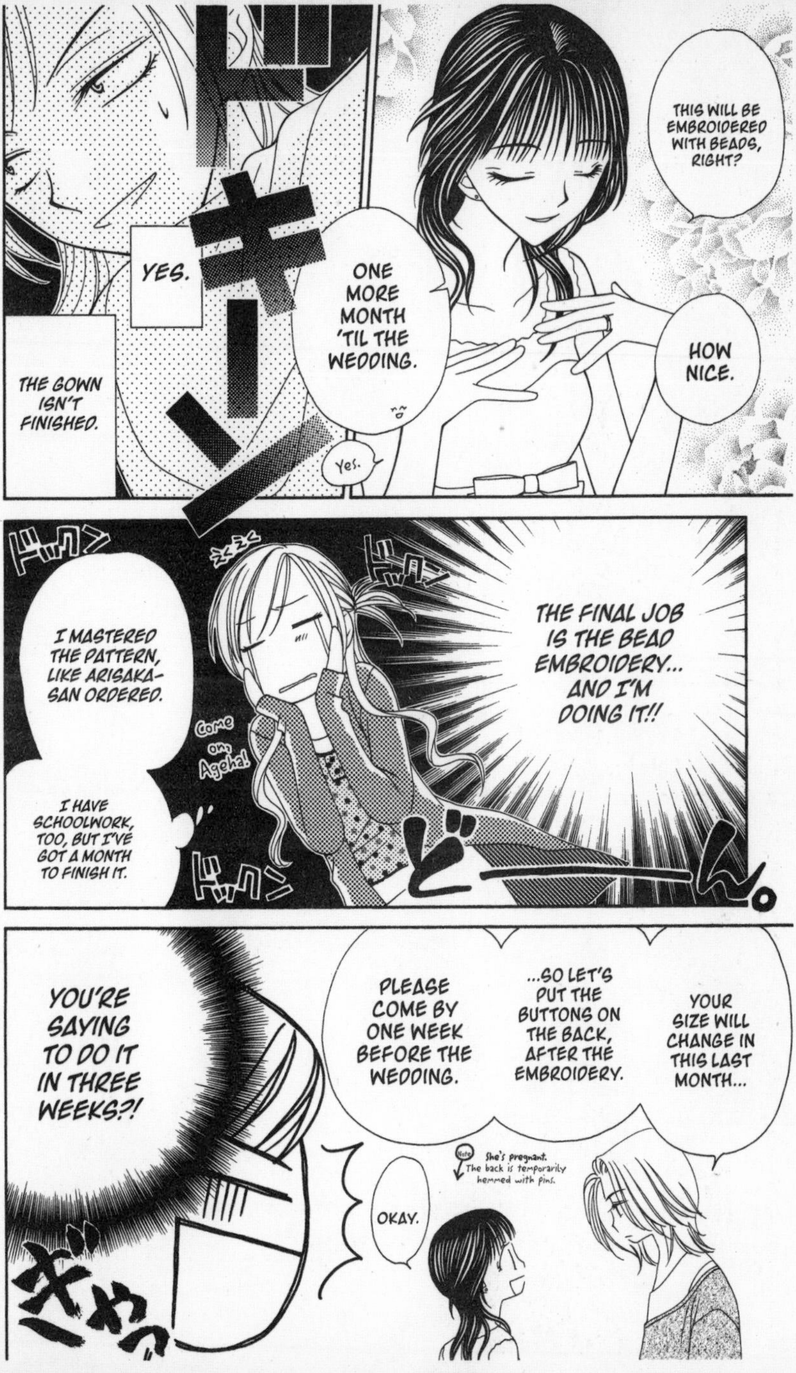
THIS WILL BE EMBROIDERED WITH BEADS, RIGHT?
HOW NICE.
ONE MORE MONTH 'TIL THE WEDDING.
Yes.
YES.
THE GOWN ISN'T FINISHED.
THE FINAL JOB IS THE BEAD EMBROIDERY... AND I'M DOING IT!!
I MASTERED THE PATTERN, LIKE ARISAKA-SAN ORDERED.
Come on, Ageha!
I HAVE SCHOOLWORK, TOO, BUT I'VE GOT A MONTH TO FINISH IT.
YOUR SIZE WILL CHANGE IN THIS LAST MONTH...
...SO LET'S PUT THE BUTTONS ON THE BACK, AFTER THE EMBROIDERY.
PLEASE COME BY ONE WEEK BEFORE THE WEDDING.
Note She's pregnant. The back is temporarily hemmed with pins.
OKAY.
YOU'RE SAYING TO DO IT IN THREE WEEKS?!

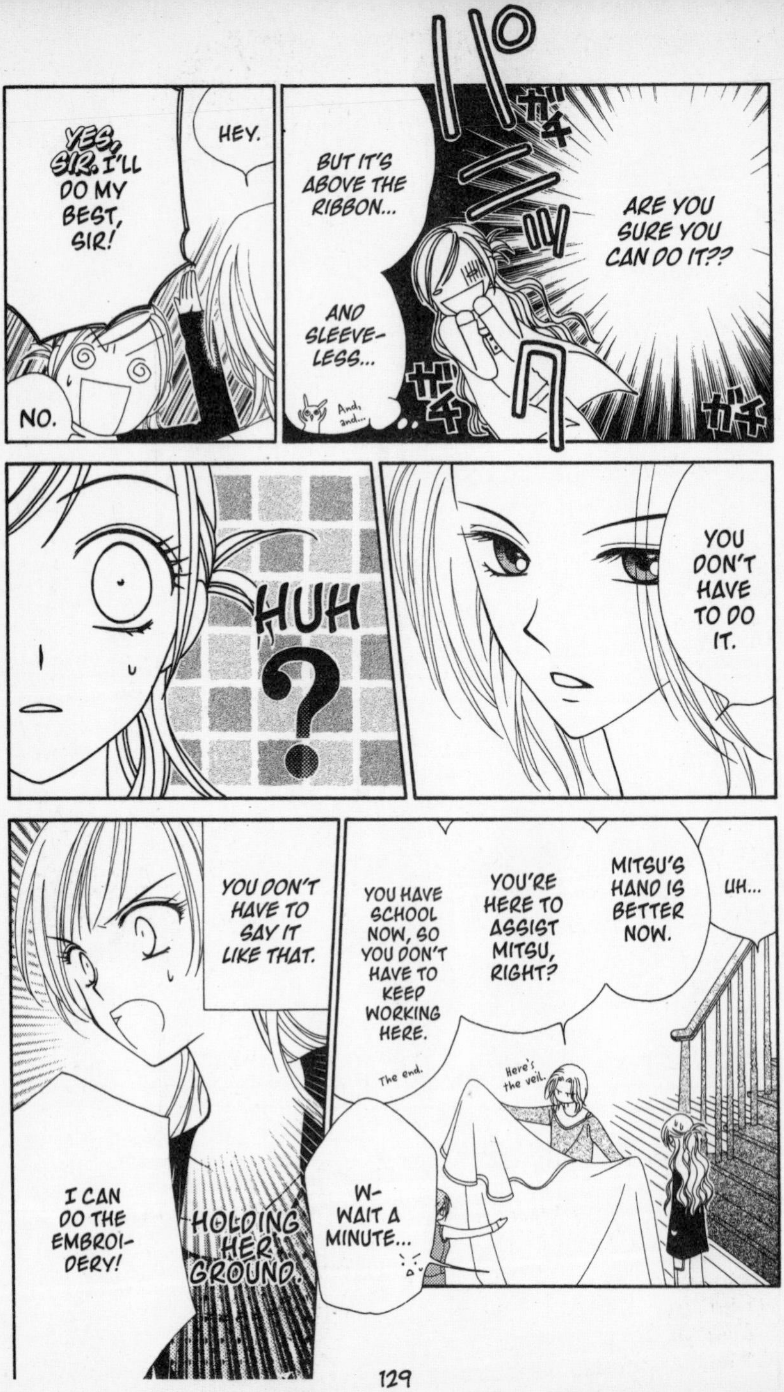
ARE YOU SURE YOU CAN DO IT??
ガチ
ガチ
BUT IT'S ABOVE THE RIBBON...
AND SLEEVE-LESS...
And, and...
ガチ
HEY.
YES, SIR. I'LL DO MY BEST, SIR!
NO.
YOU DON'T HAVE TO DO IT.
HUH ?
UH...
MITSU'S HAND IS BETTER NOW.
YOU'RE HERE TO ASSIST MITSU, RIGHT?
YOU HAVE SCHOOL NOW, SO YOU DON'T HAVE TO KEEP WORKING HERE.
Here's the veil.
The end.
W-WAIT A MINUTE...
YOU DON'T HAVE TO SAY IT LIKE THAT.
HOLDING HER GROUND.
I CAN DO THE EMBROIDERY!

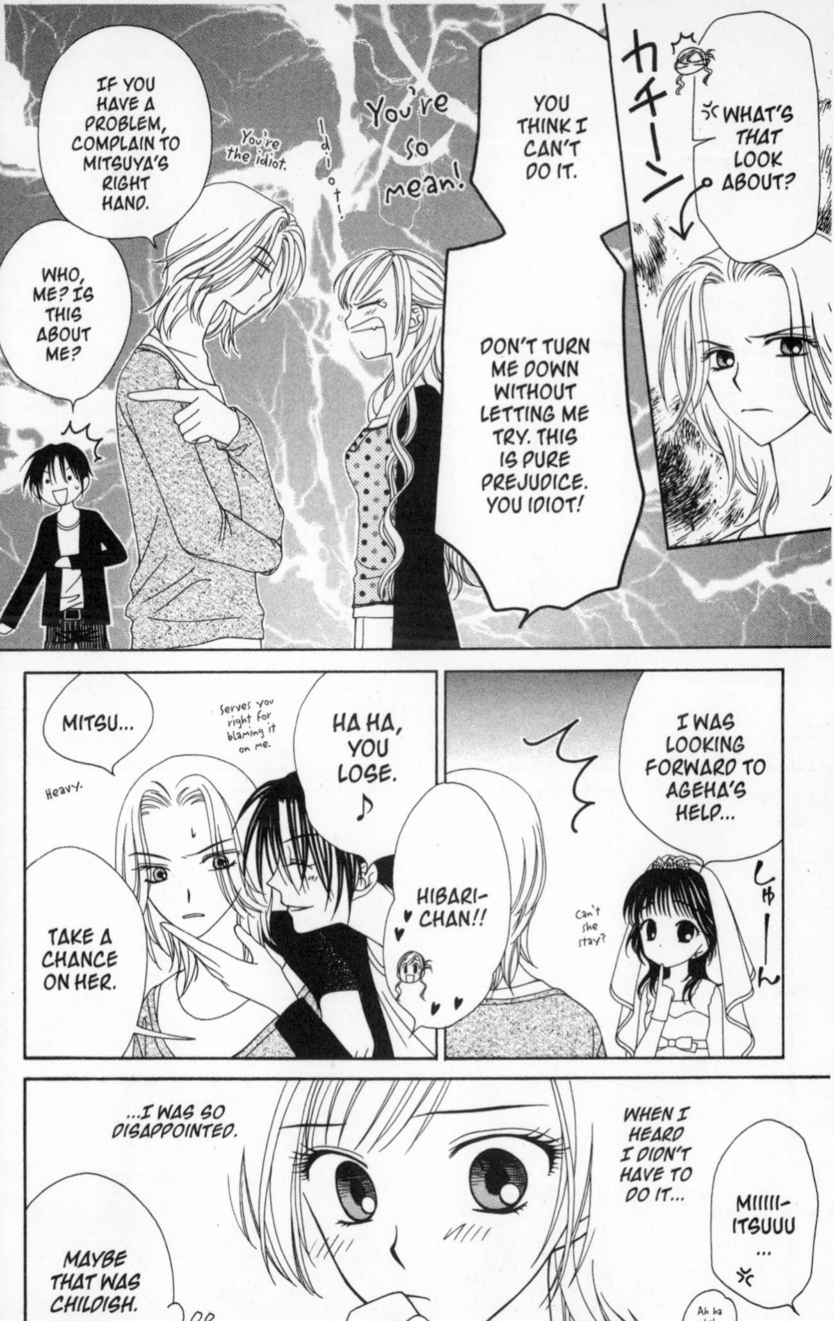

カチーン
WHAT'S THAT LOOK ABOUT?
YOU THINK I CAN'T DO IT.
DON'T TURN ME DOWN WITHOUT LETTING ME TRY. THIS IS PURE PREJUDICE. YOU IDIOT!
You're so mean!
idiot!
You're the idiot.
IF YOU HAVE A PROBLEM, COMPLAIN TO MITSUYA'S RIGHT HAND.
WHO, ME? IS THIS ABOUT ME?
I WAS LOOKING FORWARD TO AGEHA'S HELP...
しゅーん
Can't she stay?
HA HA, YOU LOSE. ♪
Serves you right for blaming it on me.
HIBARI-CHAN!!
MITSU...
Heavy.
TAKE A CHANCE ON HER.
WHEN I HEARD I DIDN'T HAVE TO DO IT...
...I WAS SO DISAPPOINTED.
MAYBE THAT WAS CHILDISH.
MIIIII-ITSUUU...
Ah ha ha!

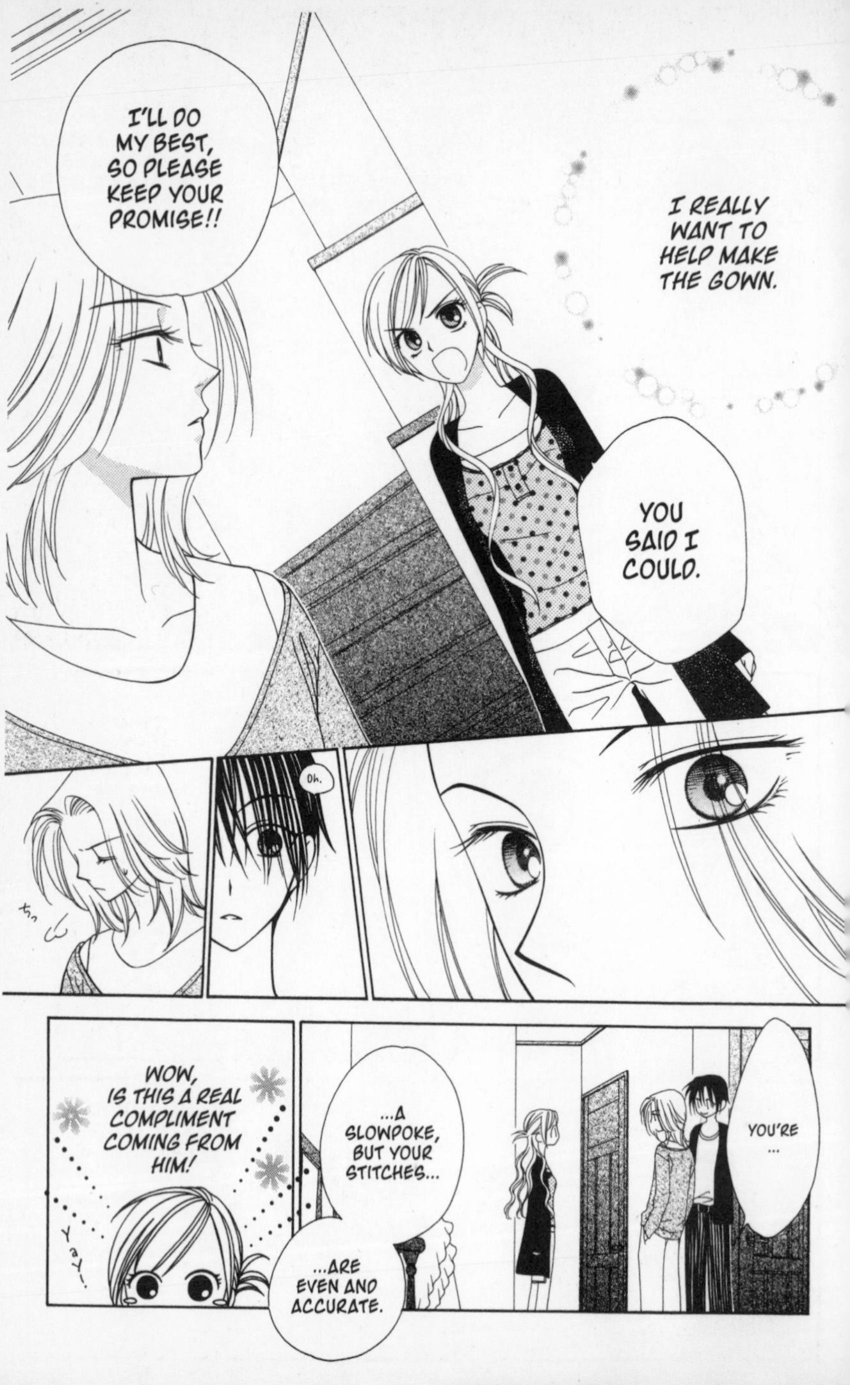
I REALLY WANT TO HELP MAKE THE GOWN.
YOU SAID I COULD.
I'LL DO MY BEST, SO PLEASE KEEP YOUR PROMISE!!
Oh.
YOU'RE ...
...A SLOWPOKE, BUT YOUR STITCHES...
...ARE EVEN AND ACCURATE.
WOW, IS THIS A REAL COMPLIMENT COMING FROM HIM!
Yay!

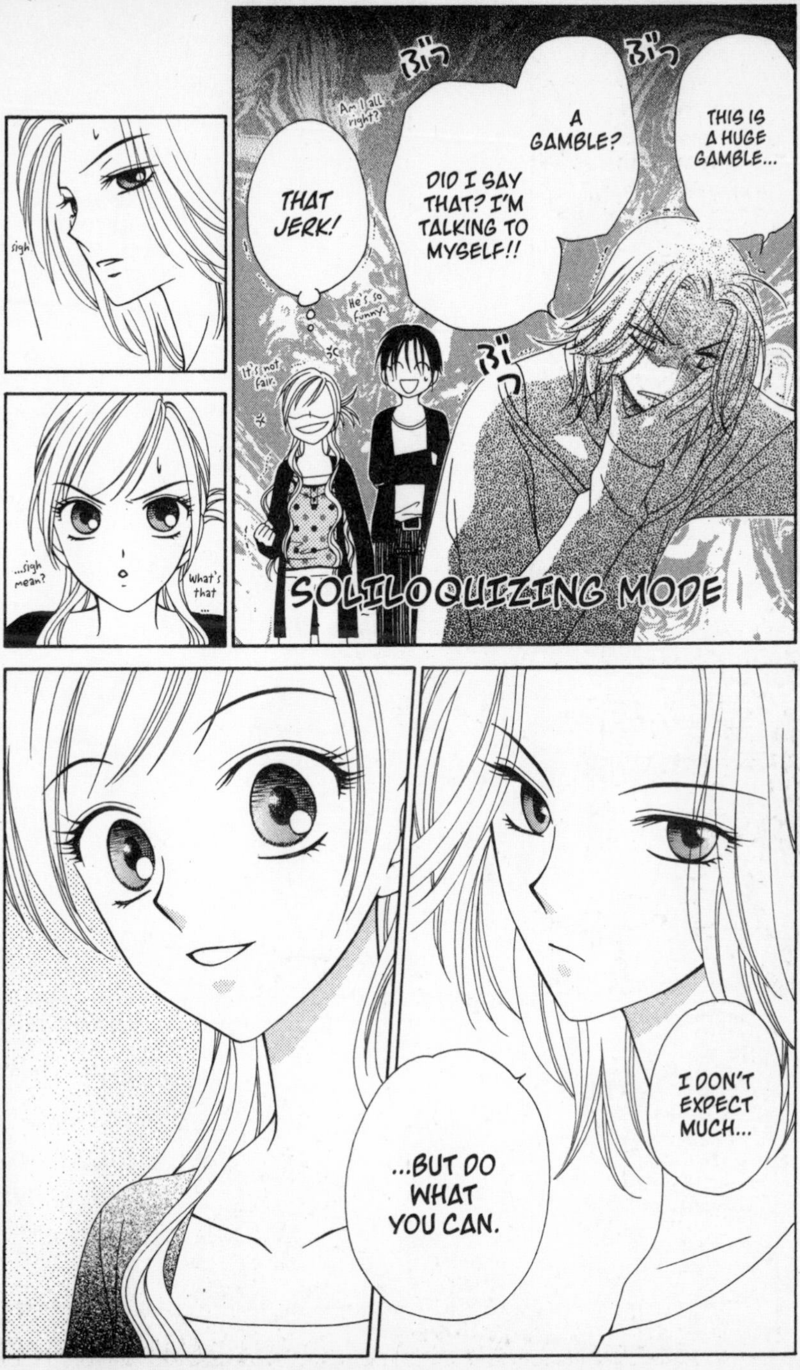
THIS IS A HUGE GAMBLE...
ぶっ
A GAMBLE?
ぶっ
Am I all right?
DID I SAY THAT? I'M TALKING TO MYSELF!!
THAT JERK!
He's so funny.
ぶっ
It's not fair.
SOLILOQUIZING MODE
sigh
What's that ...
...sigh mean?
I DON'T EXPECT MUCH...
...BUT DO WHAT YOU CAN.

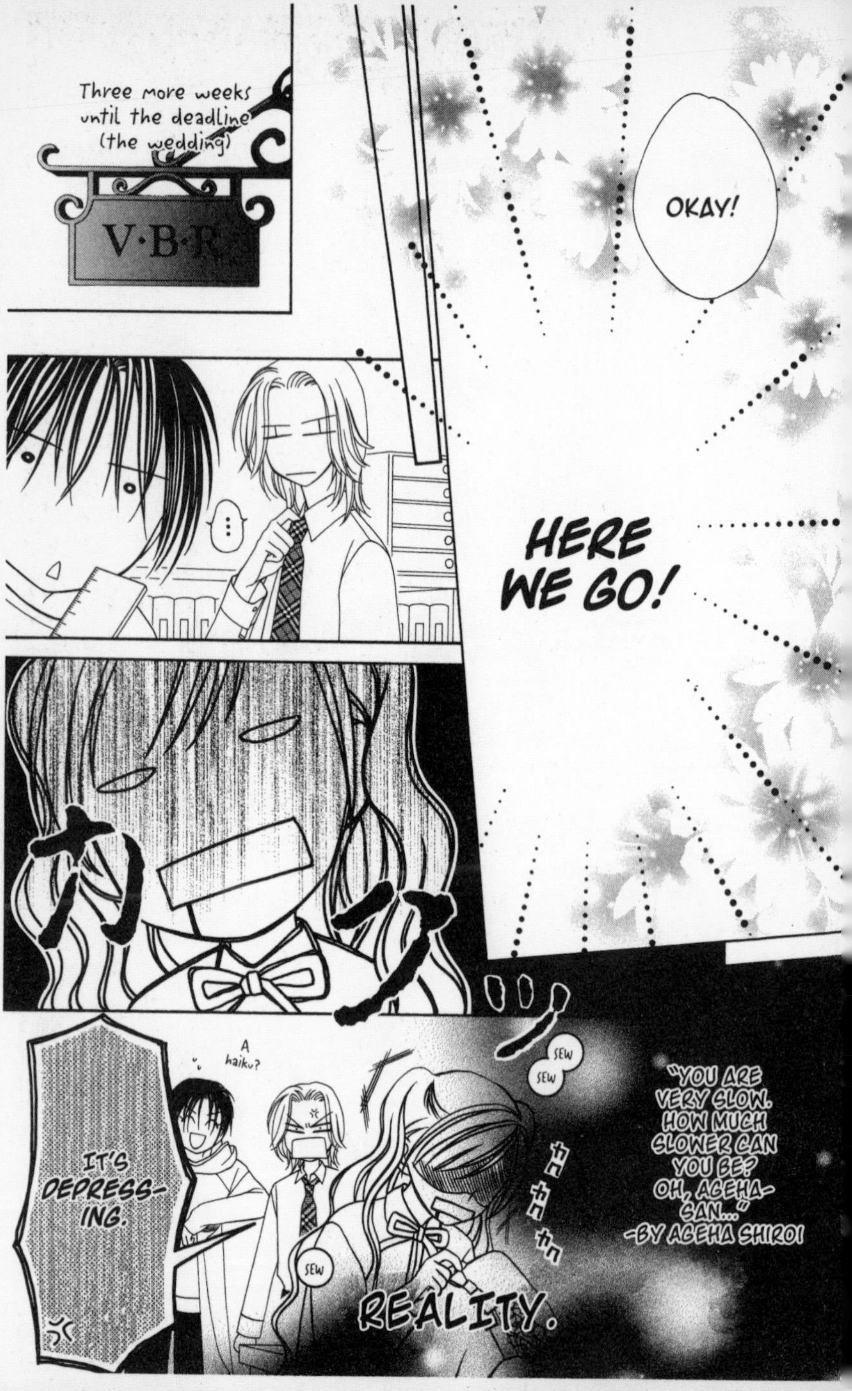
OKAY!
HERE WE GO!
Three more weeks until the deadline (the wedding)
V·B·R
...
"YOU ARE VERY SLOW. HOW MUCH SLOWER CAN YOU BE? OH, AGEHA-SAN..." -BY AGEHA SHIROI
SEW
SEW
A haiku?
IT'S DEPRESS-ING.
SEW
REALITY.

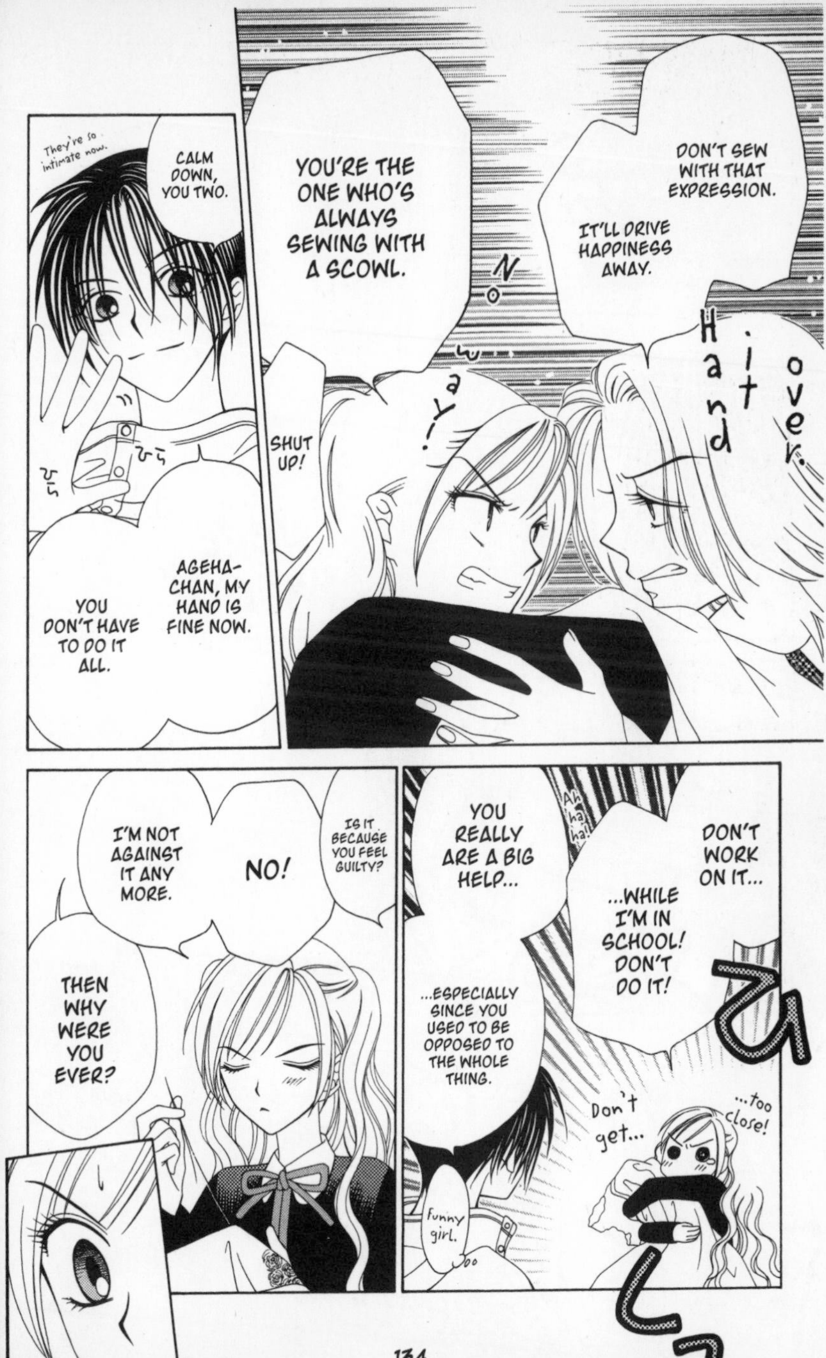
DON'T SEW WITH THAT EXPRESSION.
IT'LL DRIVE HAPPINESS AWAY.
Hand it over.
No way!
YOU'RE THE ONE WHO'S ALWAYS SEWING WITH A SCOWL.
SHUT UP!
CALM DOWN, YOU TWO.
They're so intimate now.
AGEHA-CHAN, MY HAND IS FINE NOW.
YOU DON'T HAVE TO DO IT ALL.
Ah ha ha!
DON'T WORK ON IT...
...WHILE I'M IN SCHOOL! DON'T DO IT!
YOU REALLY ARE A BIG HELP...
...ESPECIALLY SINCE YOU USED TO BE OPPOSED TO THE WHOLE THING.
...too close!
Don't get...
Funny girl.
IS IT BECAUSE YOU FEEL GUILTY?
NO!
I'M NOT AGAINST IT ANY MORE.
THEN WHY WERE YOU EVER?

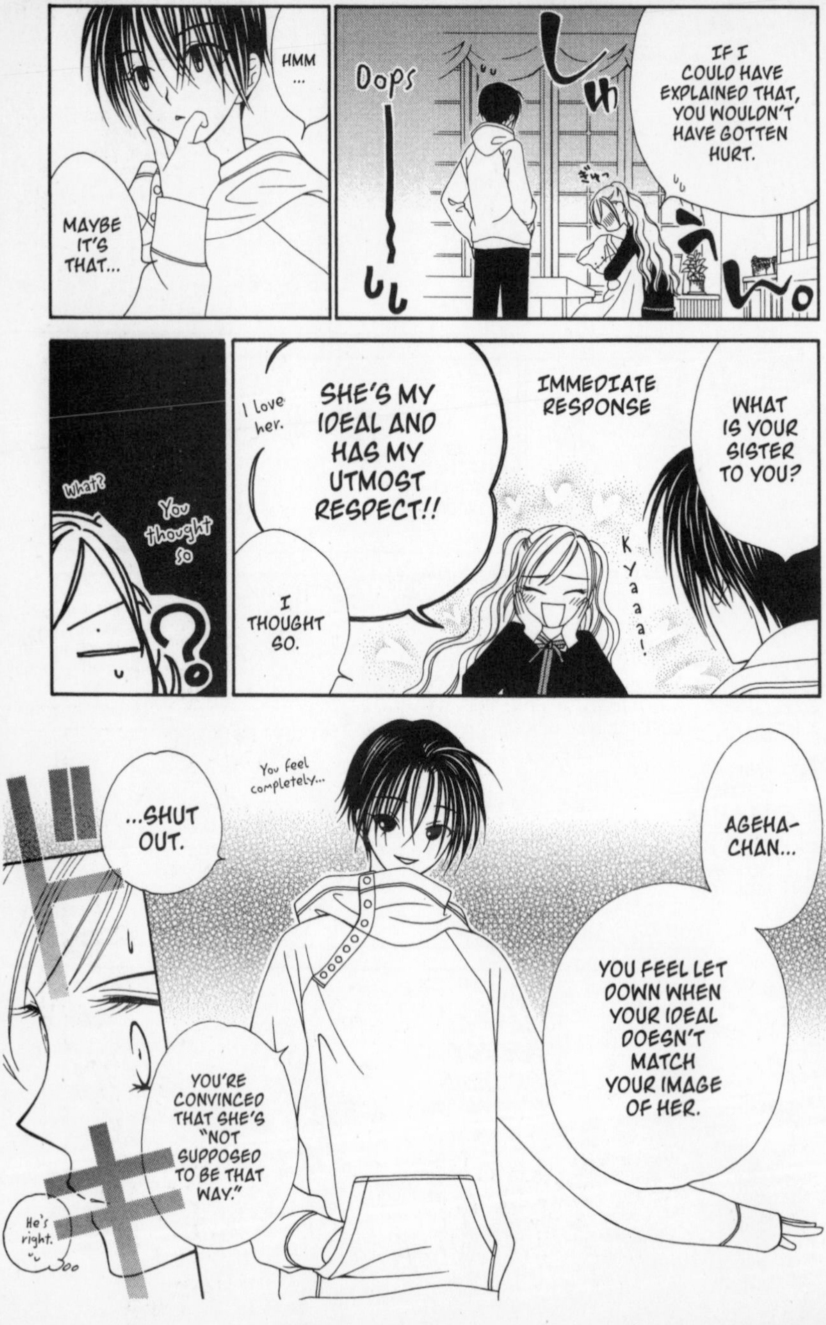
IF I COULD HAVE EXPLAINED THAT, YOU WOULDN'T HAVE GOTTEN HURT.
Oops
HMM ...
MAYBE IT'S THAT...
WHAT IS YOUR SISTER TO YOU?
IMMEDIATE RESPONSE
SHE'S MY IDEAL AND HAS MY UTMOST RESPECT!!
I love her.
Kyaaa!
I THOUGHT SO.
What?
You thought so
AGEHA-CHAN...
YOU FEEL LET DOWN WHEN YOUR IDEAL DOESN'T MATCH YOUR IMAGE OF HER.
YOU'RE CONVINCED THAT SHE'S "NOT SUPPOSED TO BE THAT WAY."
You feel completely...
...SHUT OUT.
He's right.

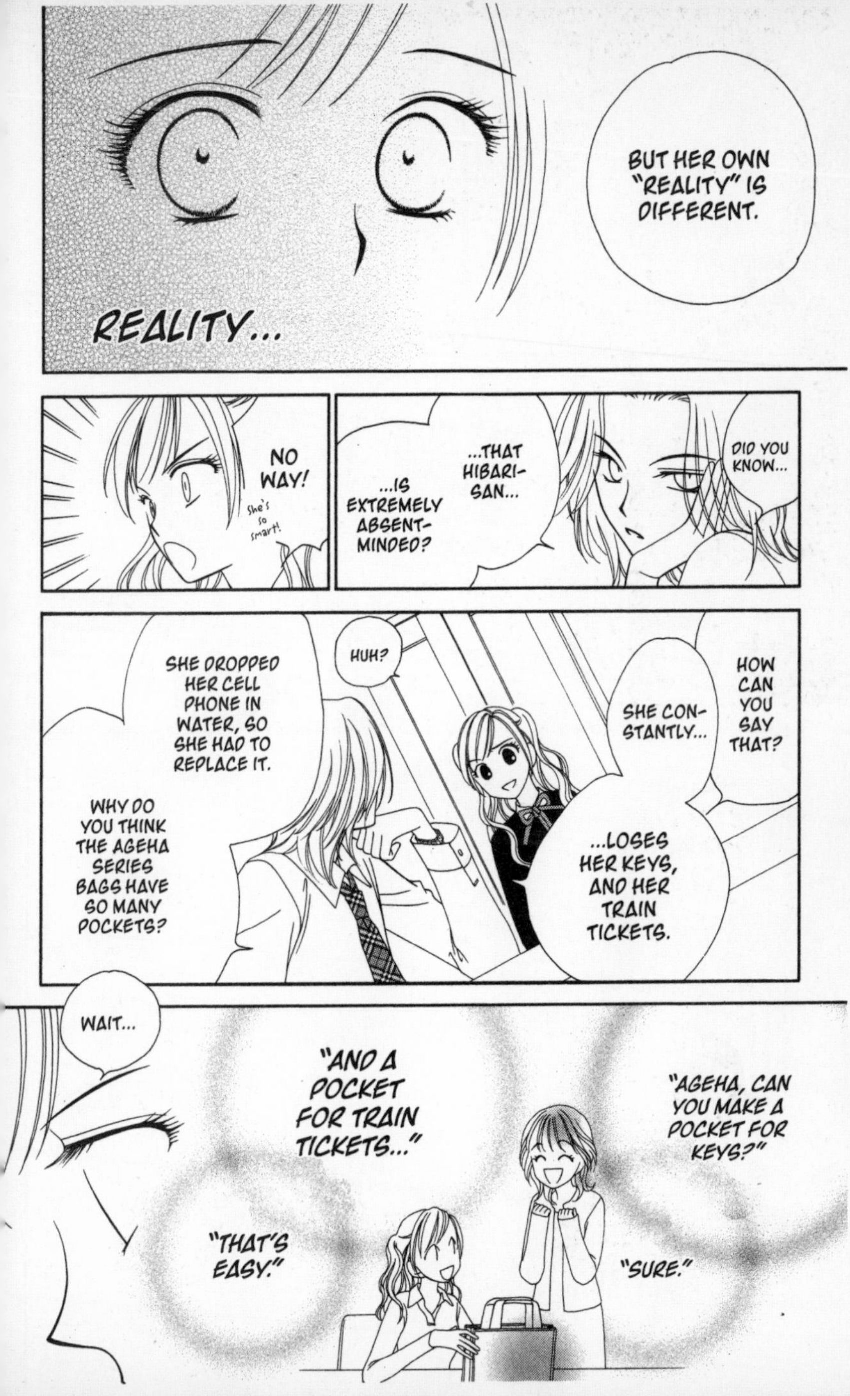
BUT HER OWN "REALITY" IS DIFFERENT.
REALITY...
DID YOU KNOW...
...THAT HIBARI-SAN...
...IS EXTREMELY ABSENT-MINDED?
NO WAY!
She's so smart!
HOW CAN YOU SAY THAT?
SHE CONSTANTLY...
...LOSES HER KEYS, AND HER TRAIN TICKETS.
HUH?
SHE DROPPED HER CELL PHONE IN WATER, SO SHE HAD TO REPLACE IT.
WHY DO YOU THINK THE AGEHA SERIES BAGS HAVE SO MANY POCKETS?
"AGEHA, CAN YOU MAKE A POCKET FOR KEYS?"
"SURE."
"AND A POCKET FOR TRAIN TICKETS..."
"THAT'S EASY."
WAIT...

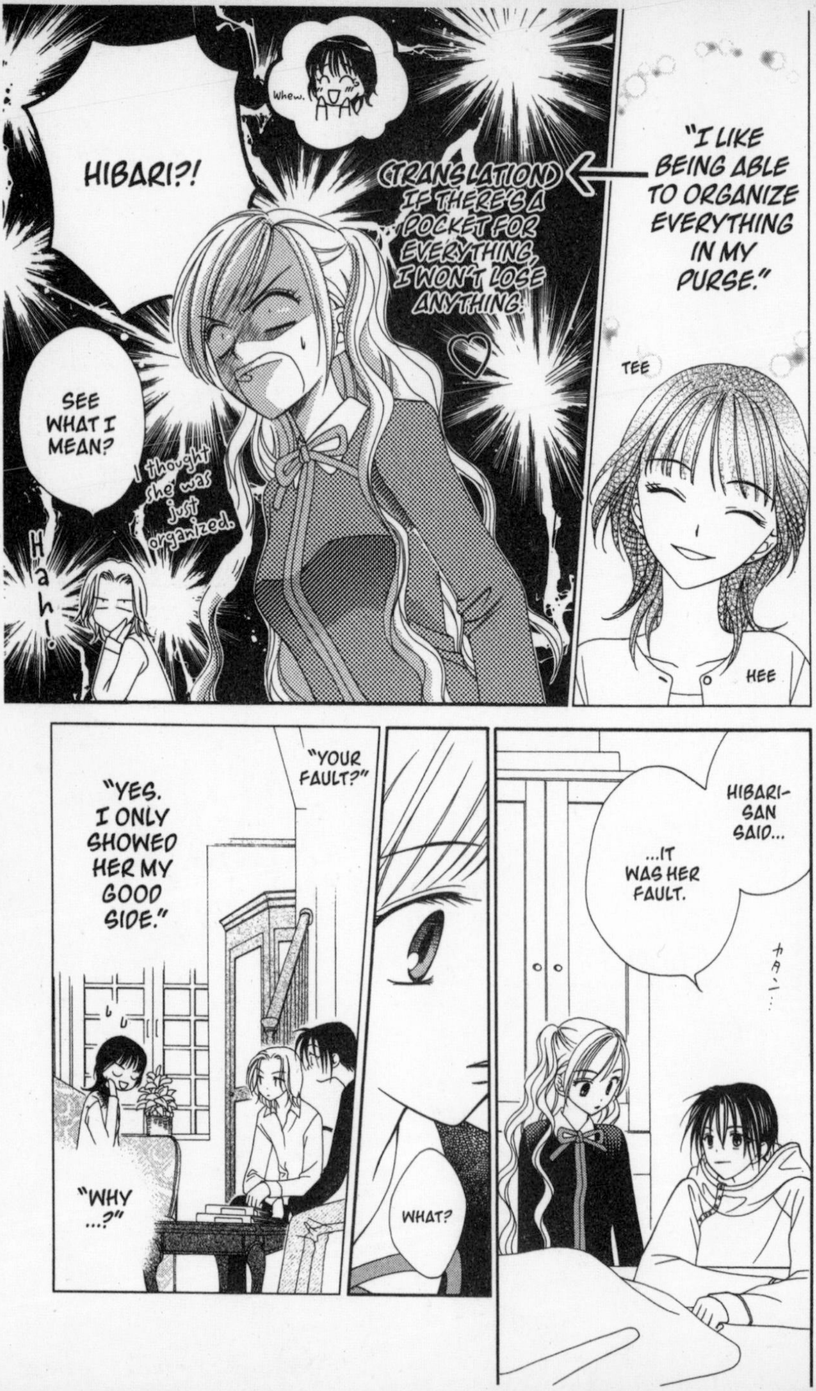
"I LIKE BEING ABLE TO ORGANIZE EVERYTHING IN MY PURSE."
TEE
HEE
(TRANSLATION) IF THERE'S A POCKET FOR EVERYTHING, I WON'T LOSE ANYTHING.
Whew.
HIBARI?!
SEE WHAT I MEAN?
I thought she was just organized.
Hah!
HIBARI-SAN SAID...
...IT WAS HER FAULT.
WHAT?
"YOUR FAULT?"
"YES. I ONLY SHOWED HER MY GOOD SIDE."
"WHY ...?"

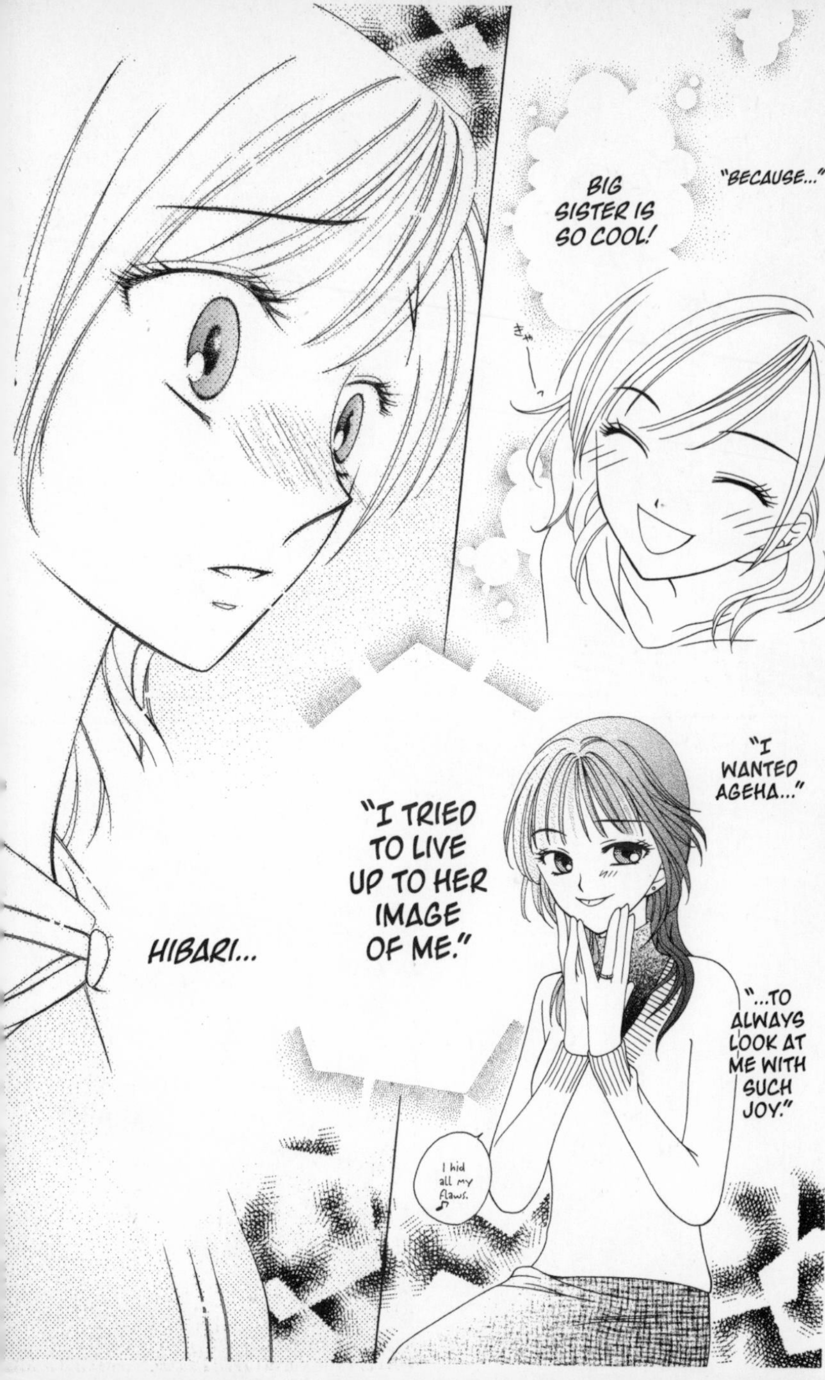
"BECAUSE..."
BIG SISTER IS SO COOL!
きゃー
"I WANTED AGEHA..."
"...TO ALWAYS LOOK AT ME WITH SUCH JOY."
"I TRIED TO LIVE UP TO HER IMAGE OF ME."
I hid all my flaws.
HIBARI...

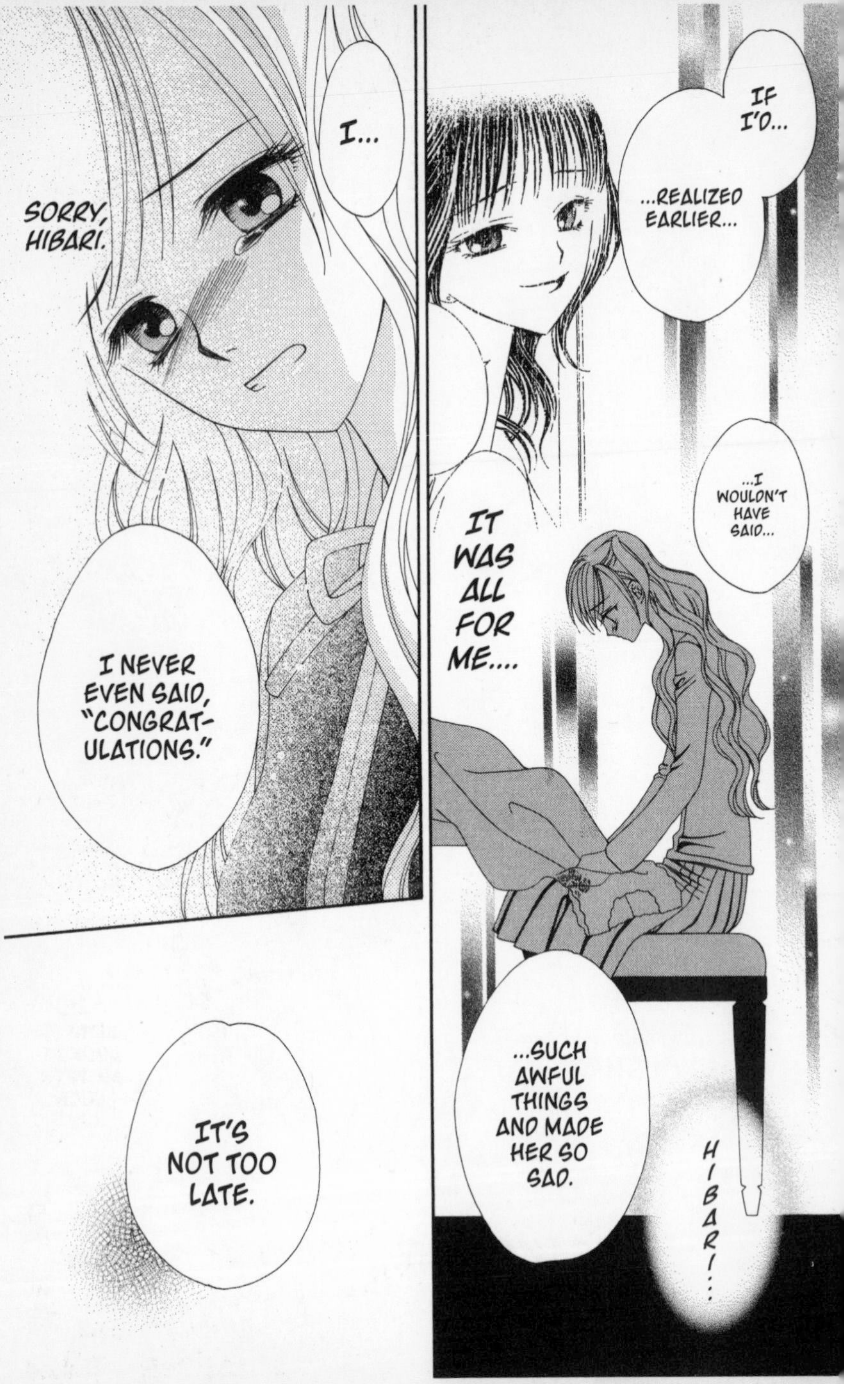
IF I'D...
...REALIZED EARLIER...
...I WOULDN'T HAVE SAID...
...SUCH AWFUL THINGS AND MADE HER SO SAD.
HIBARI...
IT WAS ALL FOR ME....
I...
SORRY, HIBARI.
I NEVER EVEN SAID, "CONGRAT-ULATIONS."
IT'S NOT TOO LATE.

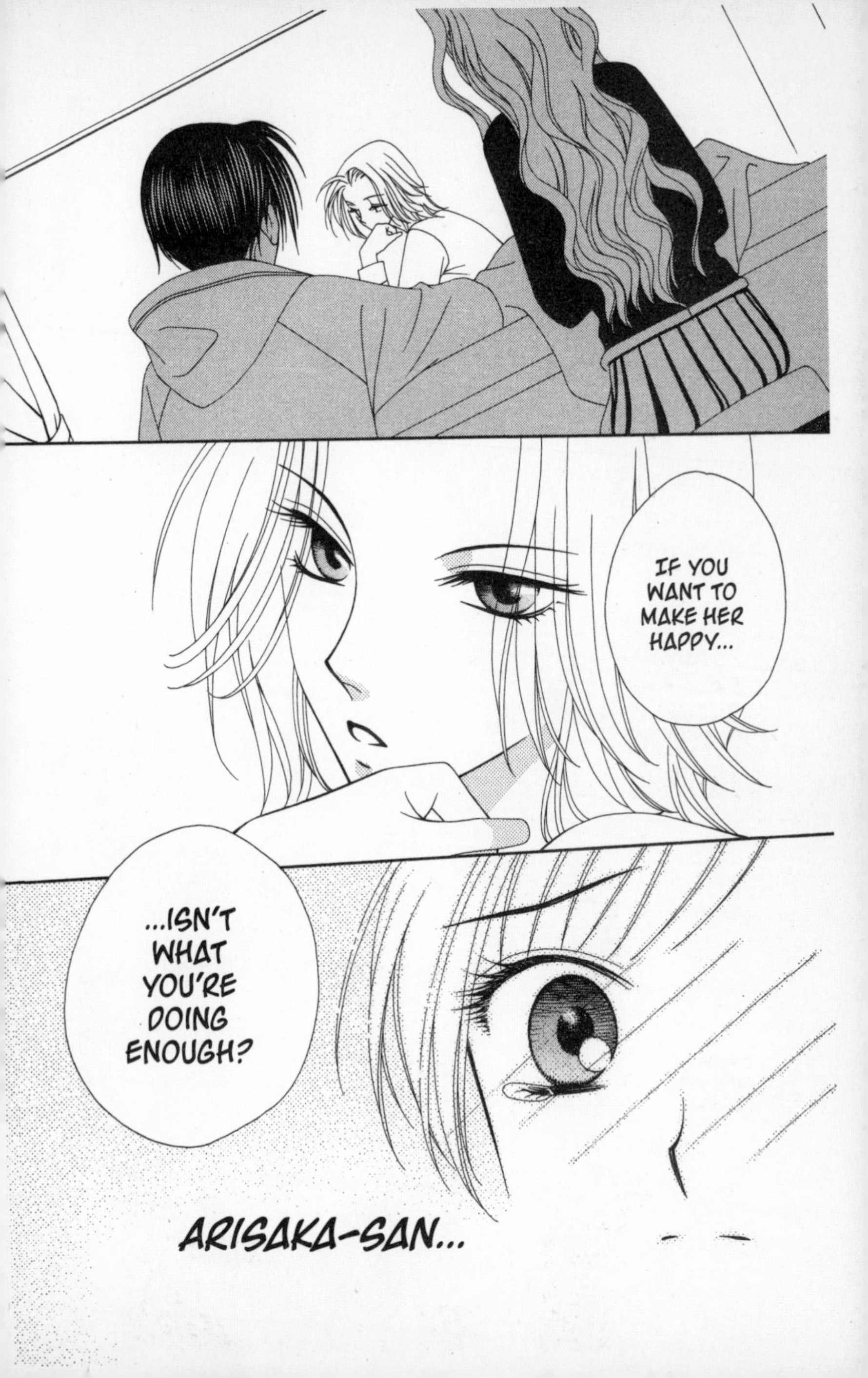
IF YOU WANT TO MAKE HER HAPPY...
...ISN'T WHAT YOU'RE DOING ENOUGH?
ARISAKA-SAN...

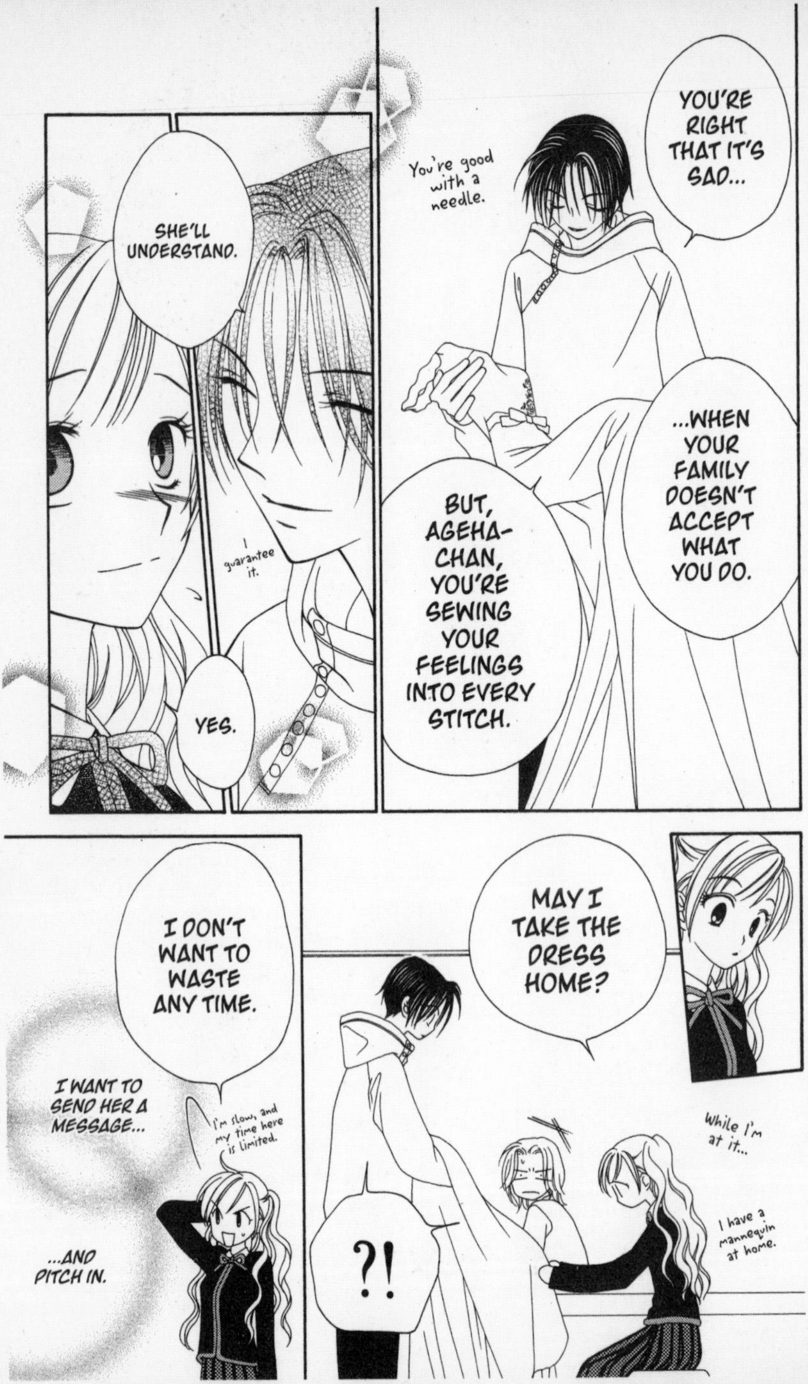
YOU'RE RIGHT THAT IT'S SAD...
You're good with a needle.
...WHEN YOUR FAMILY DOESN'T ACCEPT WHAT YOU DO.
BUT, AGEHA-CHAN, YOU'RE SEWING YOUR FEELINGS INTO EVERY STITCH.
SHE'LL UNDERSTAND.
I guarantee it.
YES.
MAY I TAKE THE DRESS HOME?
While I'm at it...
I have a mannequin at home.
?!
I DON'T WANT TO WASTE ANY TIME.
I'm slow, and my time here is limited.
I WANT TO SEND HER A MESSAGE...
...AND PITCH IN.

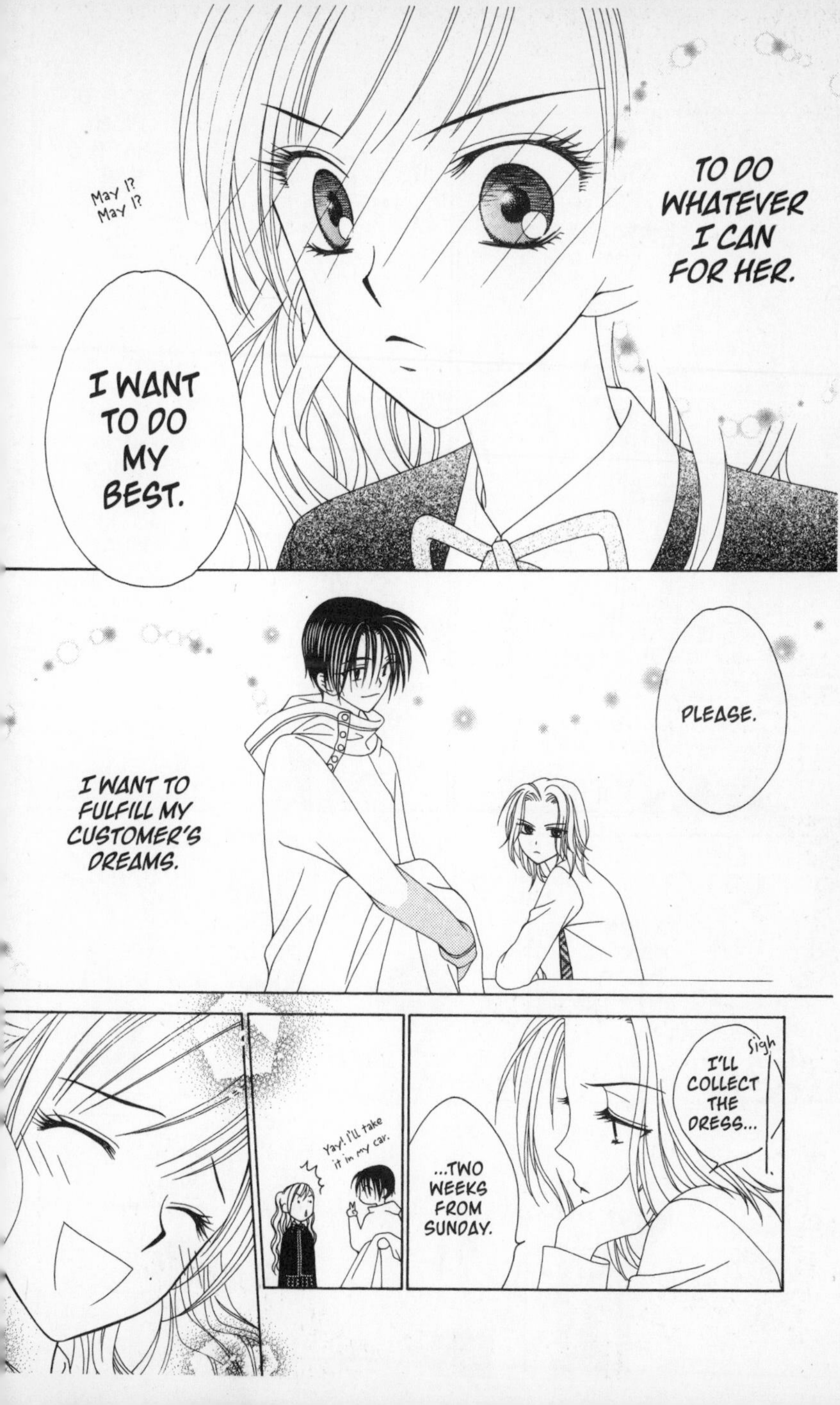
TO DO WHATEVER I CAN FOR HER.
May I? May I?
I WANT TO DO MY BEST.
PLEASE.
I WANT TO FULFILL MY CUSTOMER'S DREAMS.
Sigh
I'LL COLLECT THE DRESS...
...TWO WEEKS FROM SUNDAY.
Yay! I'll take it in my car.

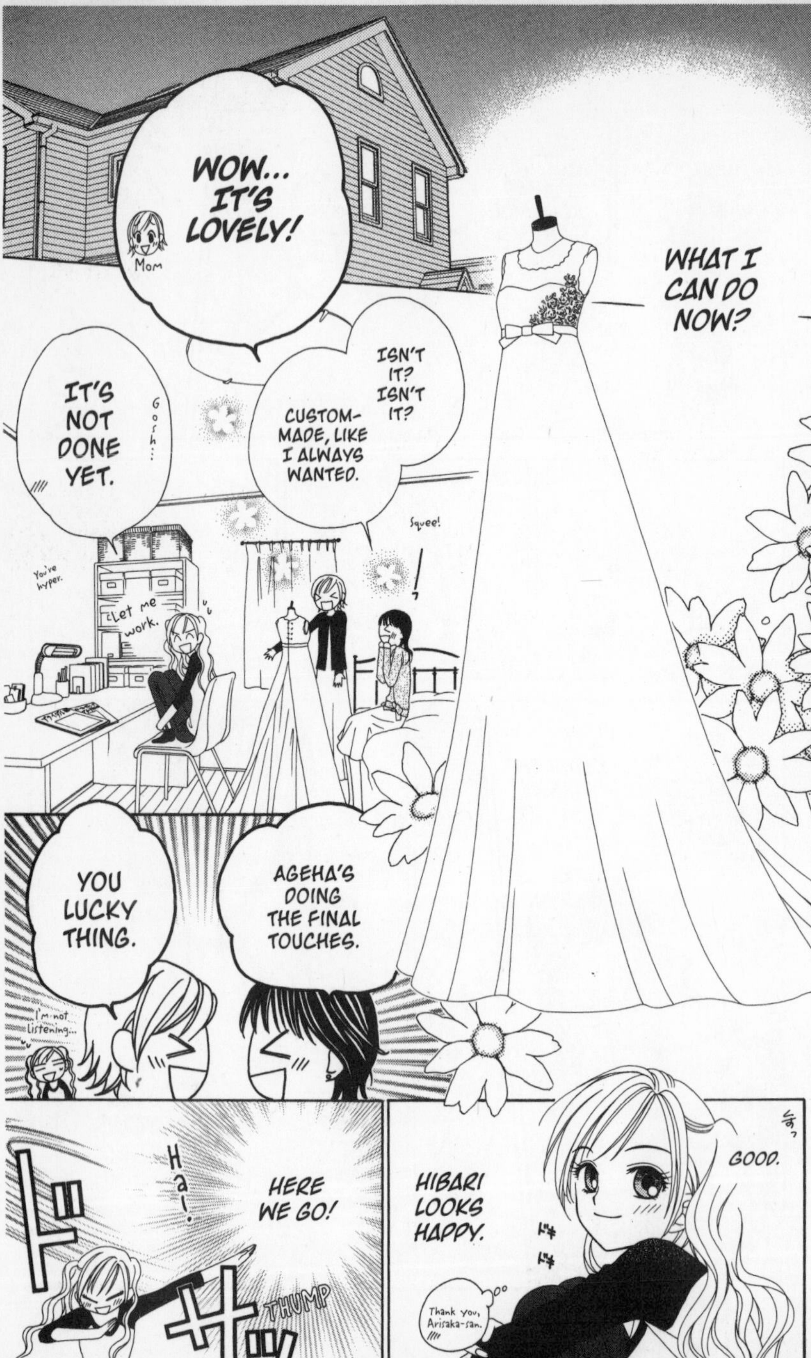

WHAT I CAN DO NOW?
WOW... IT'S LOVELY!
Mom
ISN'T IT? ISN'T IT?
CUSTOM-MADE, LIKE I ALWAYS WANTED.
Gosh...
IT'S NOT DONE YET.
Squee!
Let me work.
You're hyper.
AGEHA'S DOING THE FINAL TOUCHES.
YOU LUCKY THING.
I'm not listening...
GOOD.
HIBARI LOOKS HAPPY.
Thank you, Arisaka-san.
HERE WE GO!
Ha!
THUMP

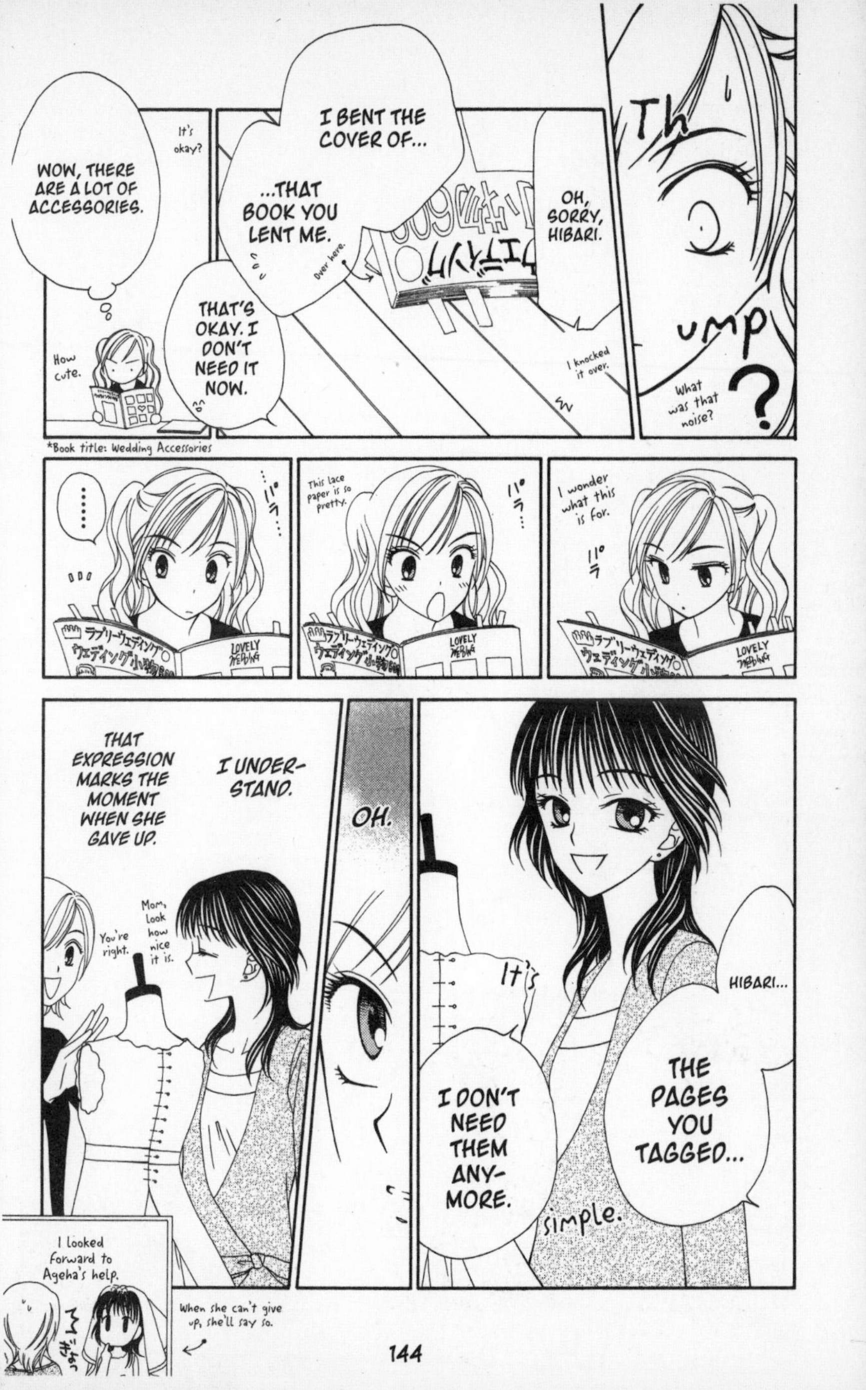
Th
ump
?
What was that noise?
Oh, sorry, Hibari.
I knocked it over.
I bent the cover of...
...that book you lent me.
Over here.
That's okay. I don't need it now.
It's okay?
Wow, there are a lot of accessories.
How cute.
*Book title: Wedding Accessories
I wonder what this is for.
パラ
This lace paper is so pretty.
パラ…
……
パラ…
Hibari...
The pages you tagged...
I don't need them anymore.
It's
simple.
Oh.
I under-stand.
That expression marks the moment when she gave up.
Mom, look how nice it is.
You're right.
I looked forward to Ageha's help.
When she can't give up, she'll say so.

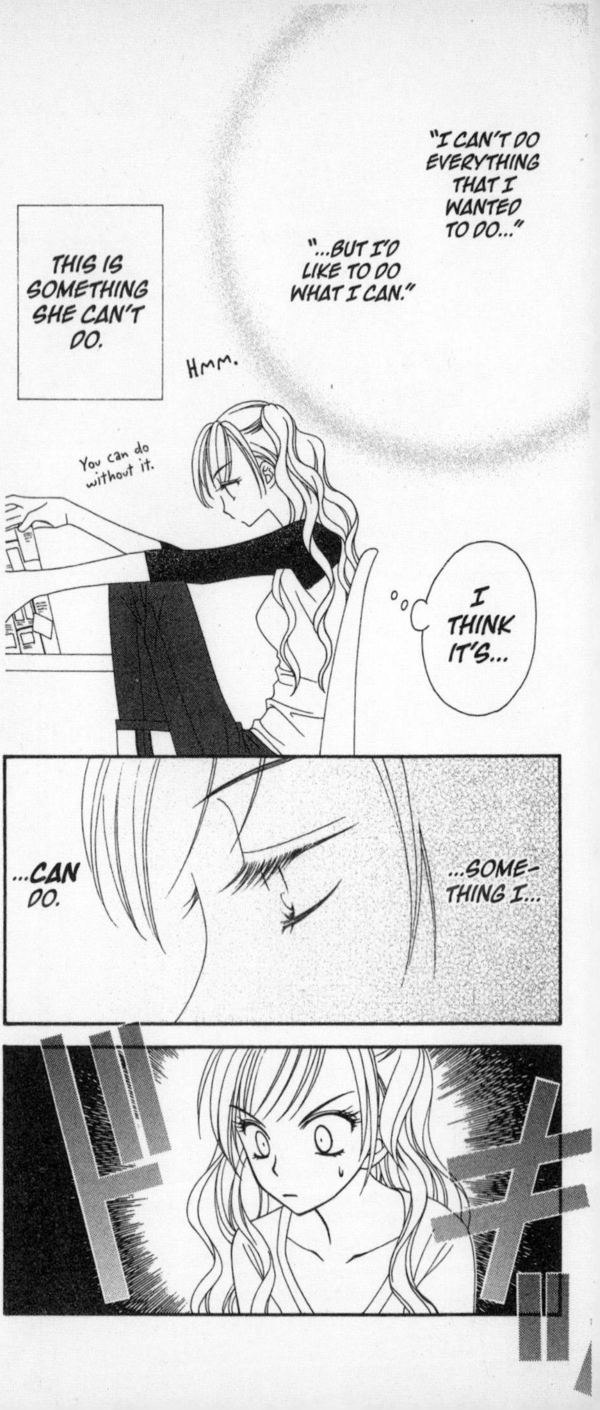

"I CAN'T DO EVERYTHING THAT I WANTED TO DO..."
"...BUT I'D LIKE TO DO WHAT I CAN."
THIS IS SOMETHING SHE CAN'T DO.
HMM.
You can do without it.
I THINK IT'S...
...SOME-THING I...
...CAN DO.

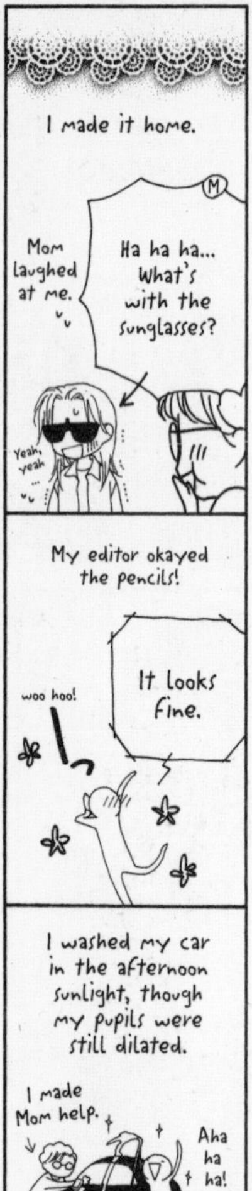

I made it home.
Ha ha ha... What's with the sunglasses?
Mom laughed at me.
Yeah, yeah...
My editor okayed the pencils!
It looks fine.
woo hoo!
I washed my car in the afternoon sunlight, though my pupils were still dilated.
I made Mom help.
Aha ha ha!
In the evening
Why I am so tired?
My eyes hurt.
Mom
You're silly.
Hidaka's silly story.

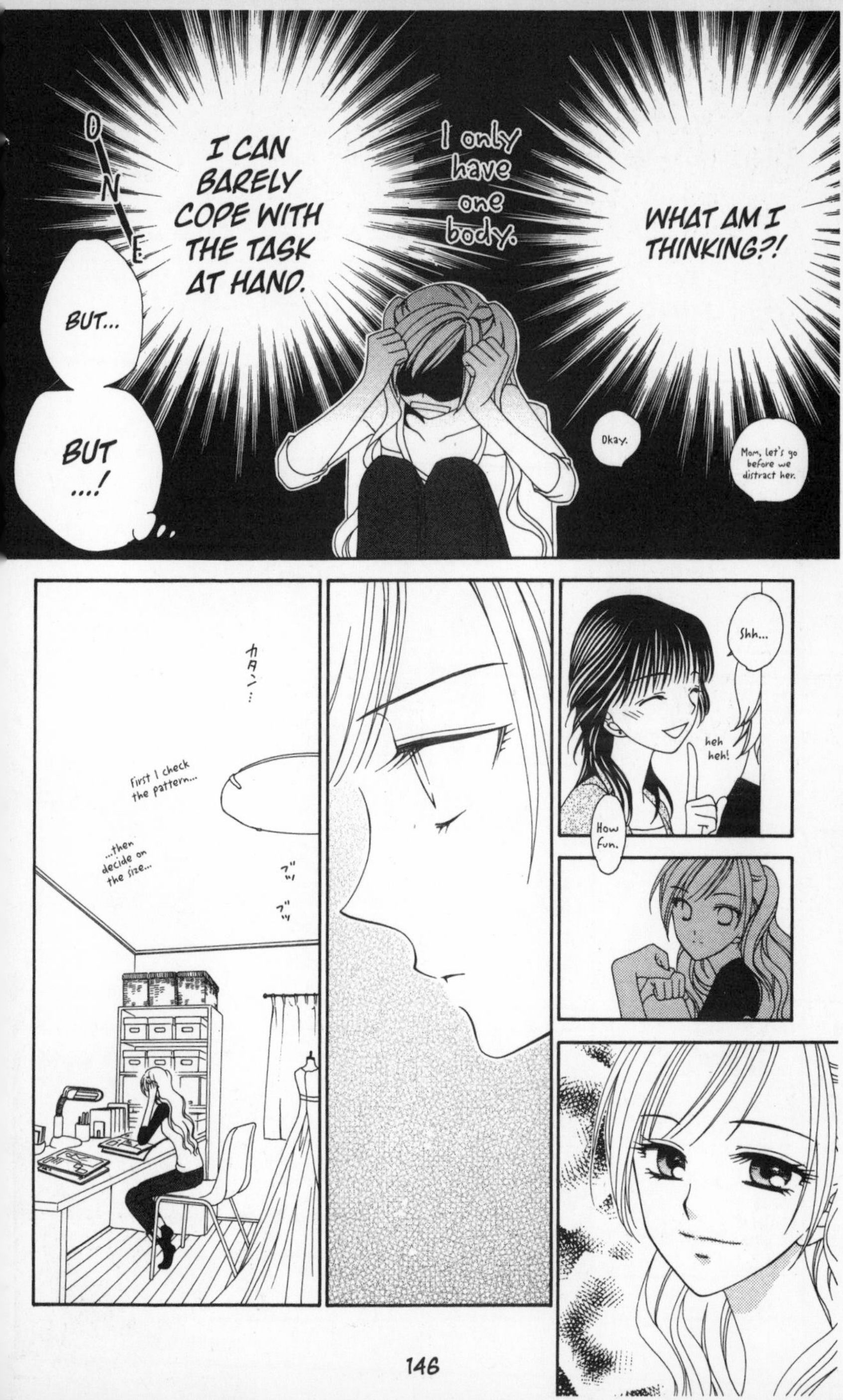
WHAT AM I THINKING?!
I only have one body.
I CAN BARELY COPE WITH THE TASK AT HAND.
ONE
BUT...
Mom, let's go before we distract her.
Okay.
BUT ...!
Shh...
heh heh!
How fun.
カタン…
First I check the pattern...
...then decide on the size...
ブツ
ブツ

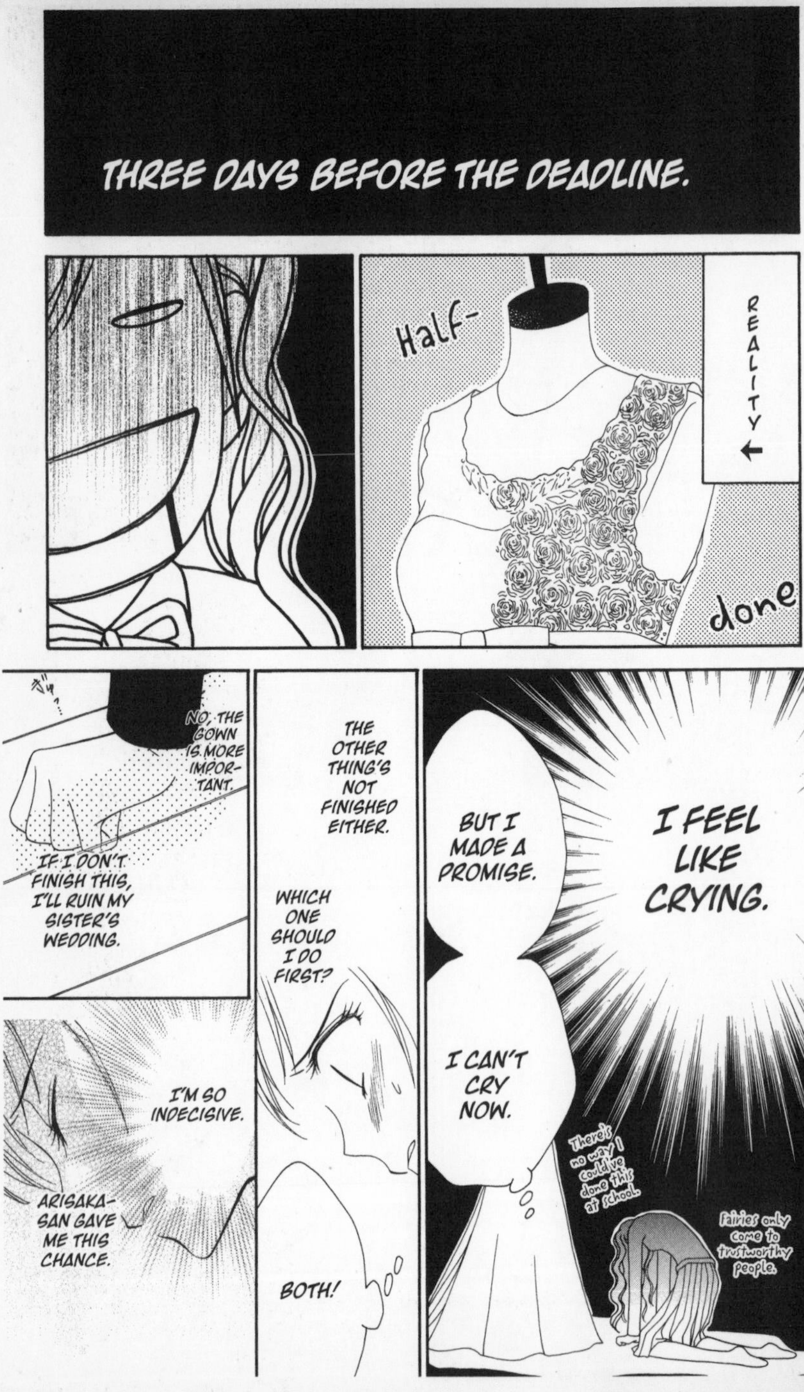
THREE DAYS BEFORE THE DEADLINE.
REALITY ←
Half-
done
I FEEL LIKE CRYING.
BUT I MADE A PROMISE.
I CAN'T CRY NOW.
There's no way I could've done this at school.
Fairies only come to trustworthy people.
THE OTHER THING'S NOT FINISHED EITHER.
WHICH ONE SHOULD I DO FIRST?
BOTH!
NO, THE GOWN IS MORE IMPORTANT.
IF I DON'T FINISH THIS, I'LL RUIN MY SISTER'S WEDDING.
I'M SO INDECISIVE.
ARISAKA-SAN GAVE ME THIS CHANCE.

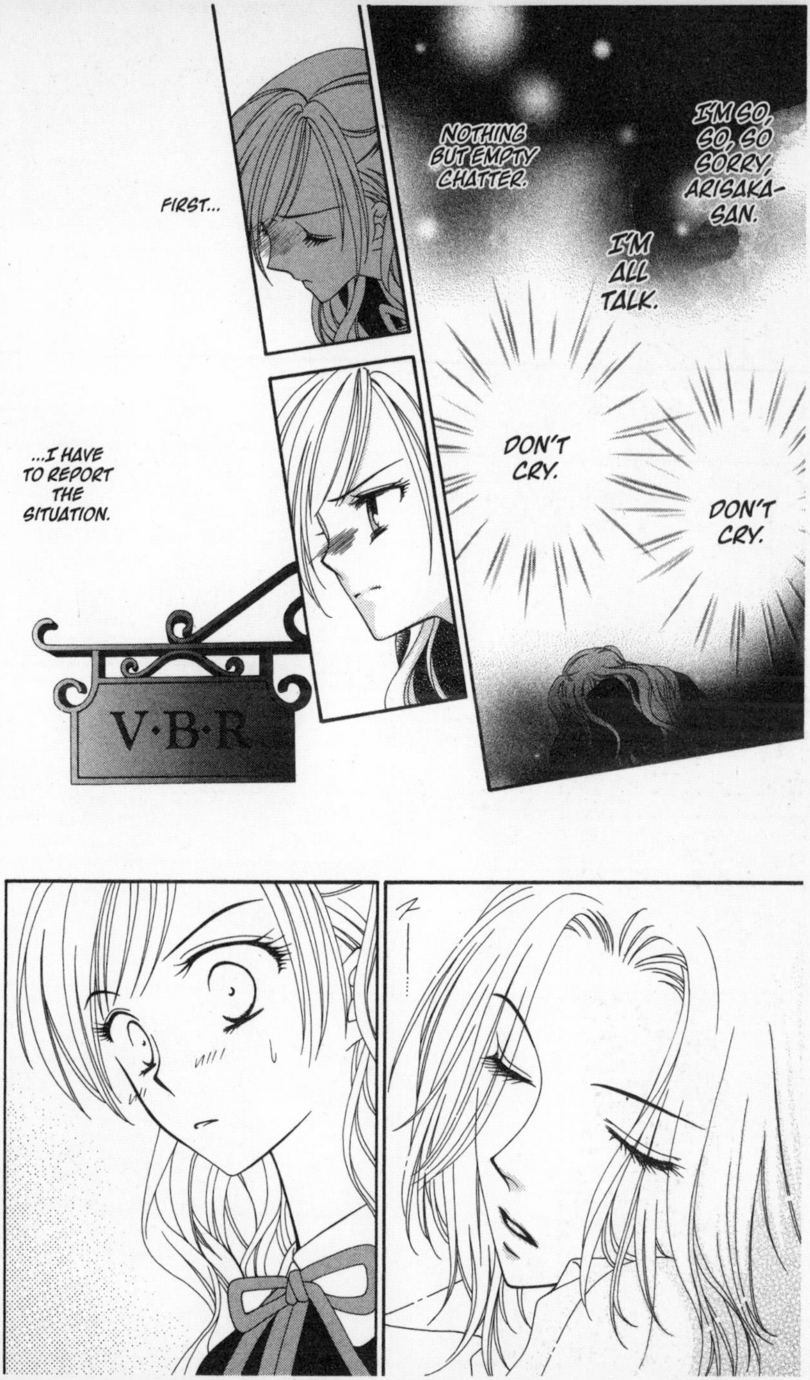
I'M SO, SO, SO SORRY, ARISAKA-SAN.
NOTHING BUT EMPTY CHATTER.
I'M ALL TALK.
DON'T CRY.
DON'T CRY.
FIRST...
...I HAVE TO REPORT THE SITUATION.
V·B·R

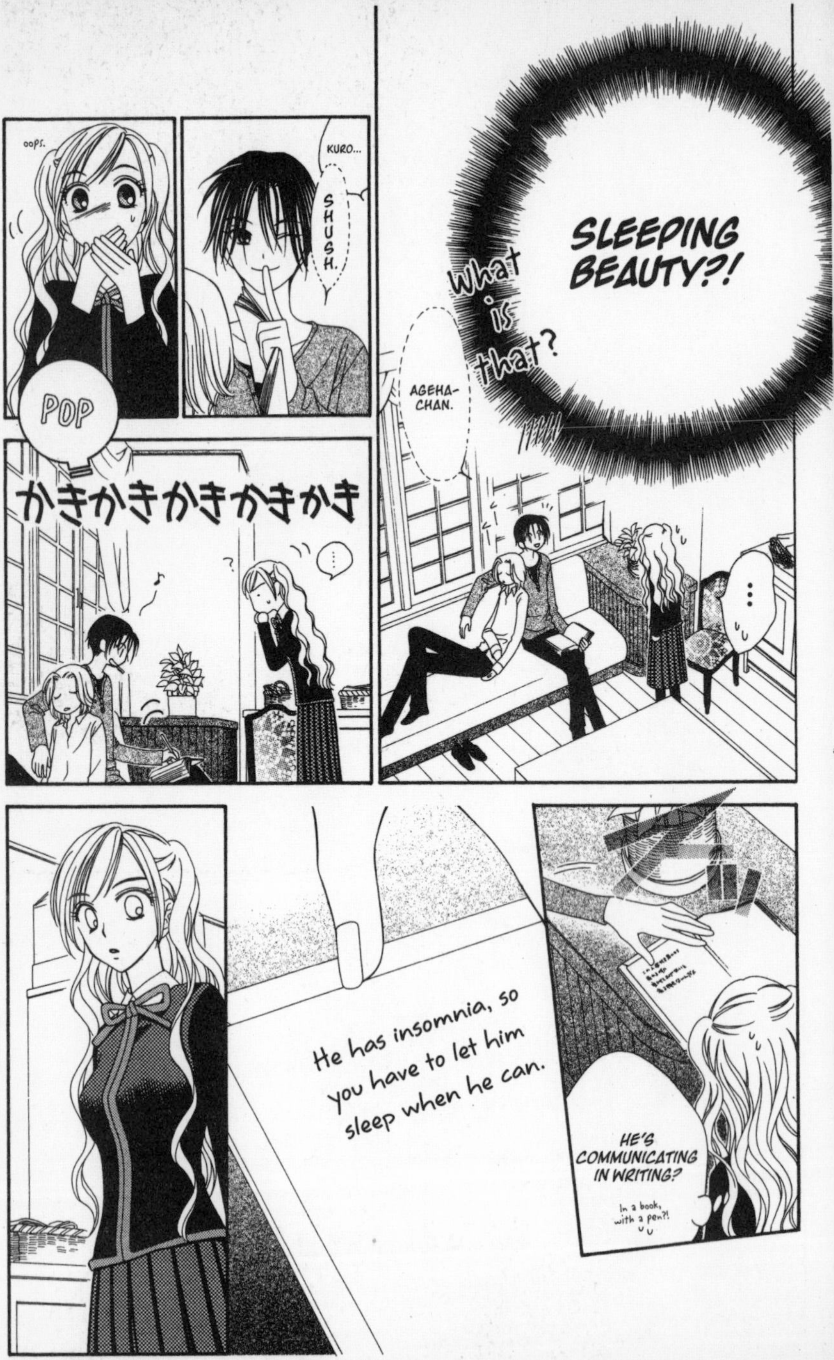

SLEEPING BEAUTY?!
What is that?
AGEHA-CHAN.
...
KURO...
SHUSH.
oops.
POP
かきかきかきかきかき
...
He has insomnia, so you have to let him sleep when he can.
HE'S COMMUNICATING IN WRITING?
In a book, with a pen?!

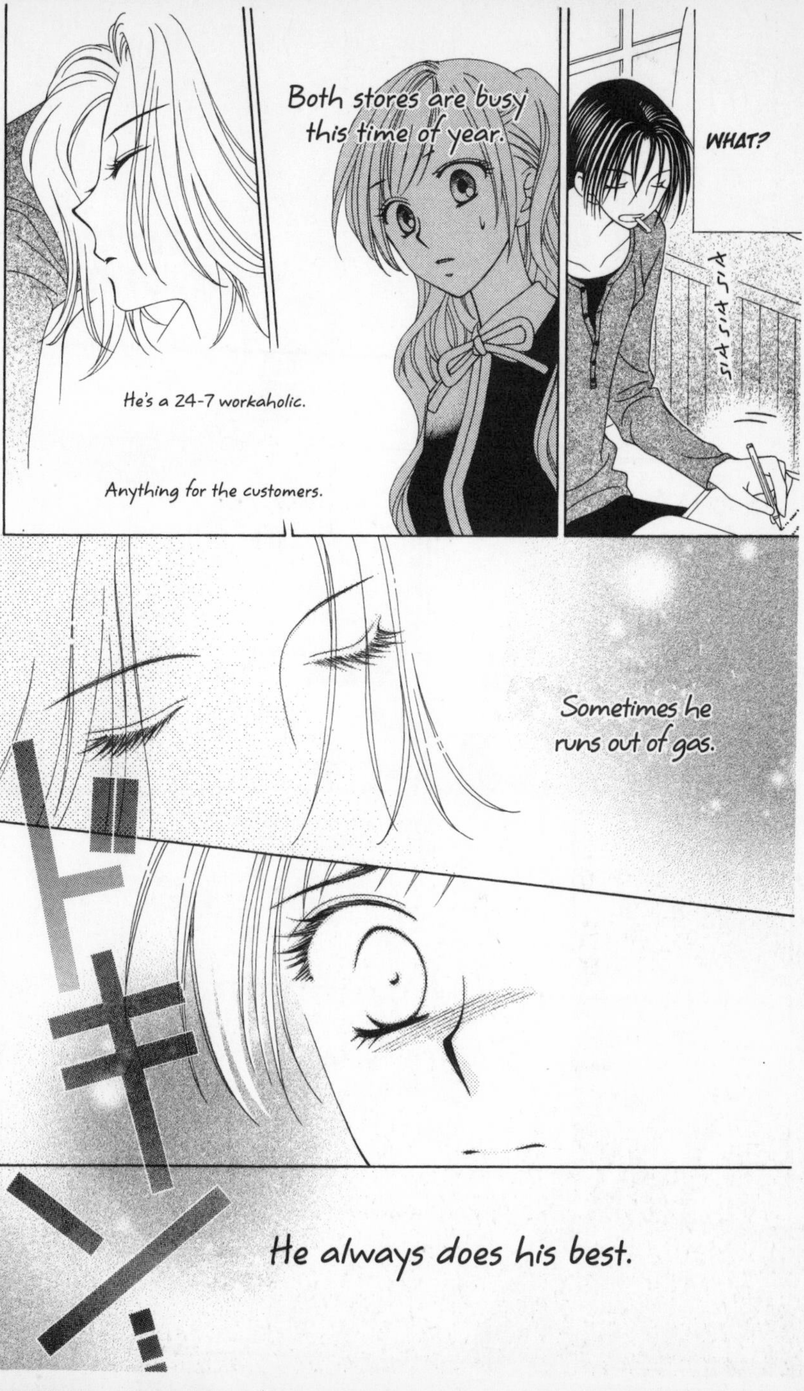
WHAT?
Both stores are busy this time of year.
He's a 24-7 workaholic.
Anything for the customers.
Sometimes he runs out of gas.
ドキン
He always does his best.

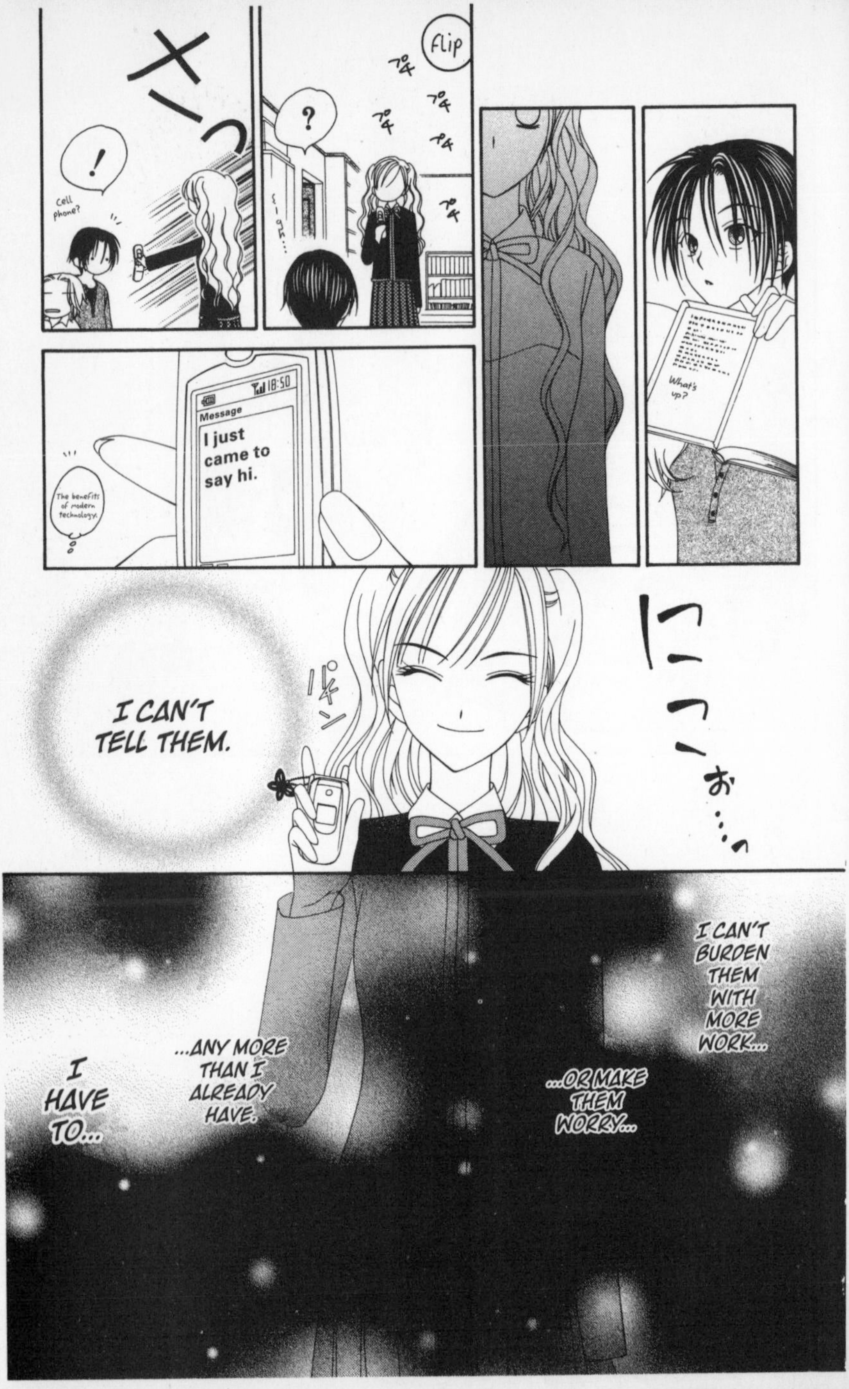
What's up?
Flip
?
sigh...
さっ
!
Cell phone?
18:50
Message
I just came to say hi.
The benefits of modern technology.
にっこぉ…
I CAN'T TELL THEM.
I CAN'T BURDEN THEM WITH MORE WORK...
...OR MAKE THEM WORRY...
...ANY MORE THAN I ALREADY HAVE.
I HAVE TO...

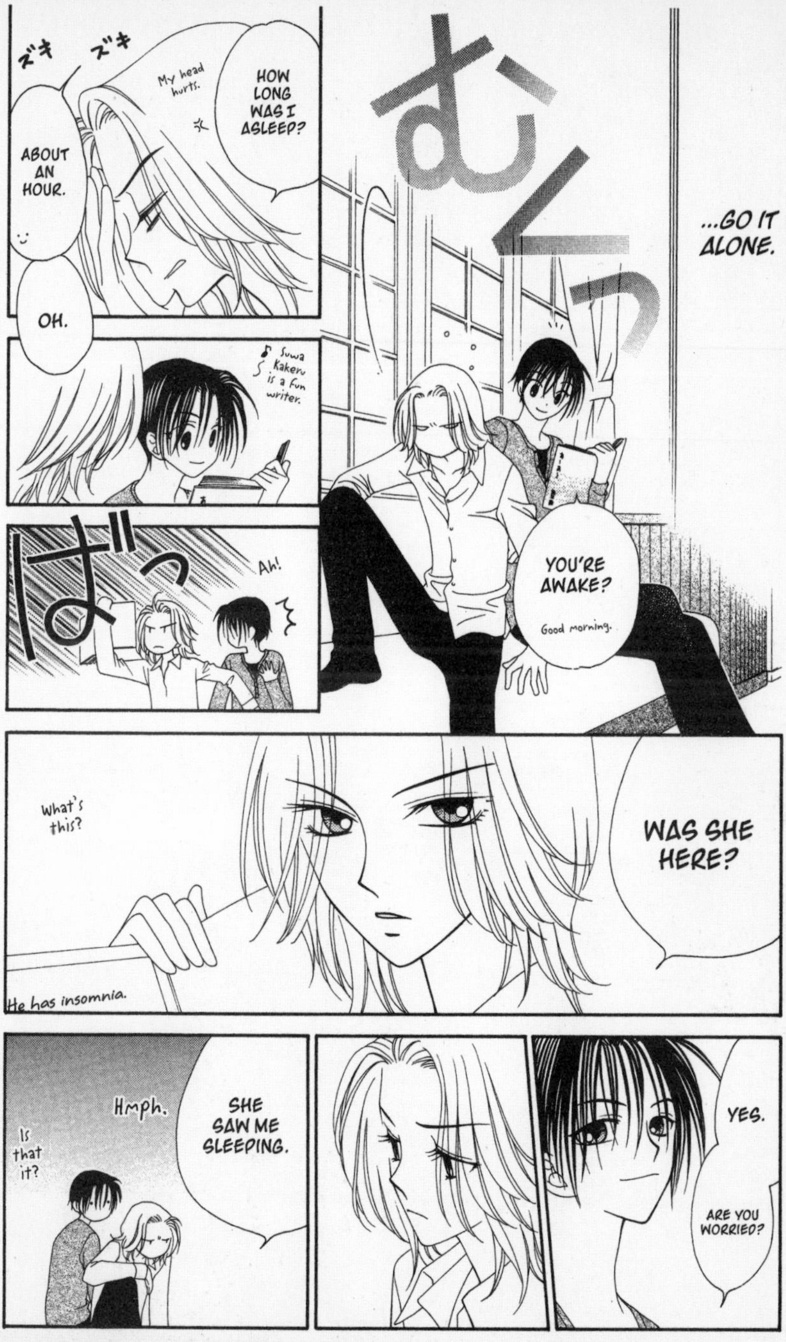
...GO IT ALONE.
むくっ
YOU'RE AWAKE?
Good morning.
ズキ ズキ
HOW LONG WAS I ASLEEP?
My head hurts.
ABOUT AN HOUR.
OH.
Suwa Kakeru is a fun writer.
ばっ
Ah!
WAS SHE HERE?
What's this?
He has insomnia.
YES.
ARE YOU WORRIED?
SHE SAW ME SLEEPING.
Hmph.
Is that it?

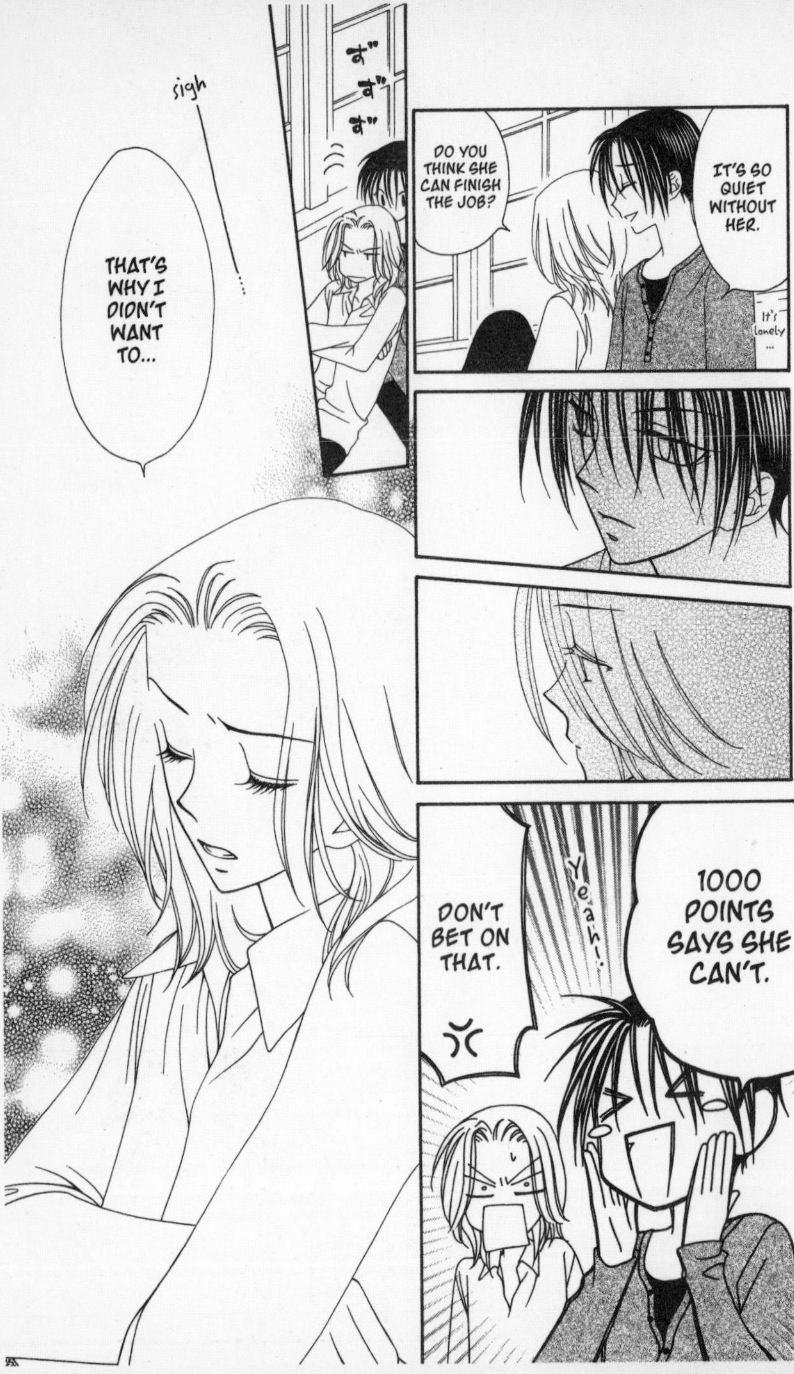
IT'S SO QUIET WITHOUT HER.
It's lonely...
DO YOU THINK SHE CAN FINISH THE JOB?
1000 POINTS SAYS SHE CAN'T.
Yeah!
DON'T BET ON THAT.
ずずず
sigh
THAT'S WHY I DIDN'T WANT TO...

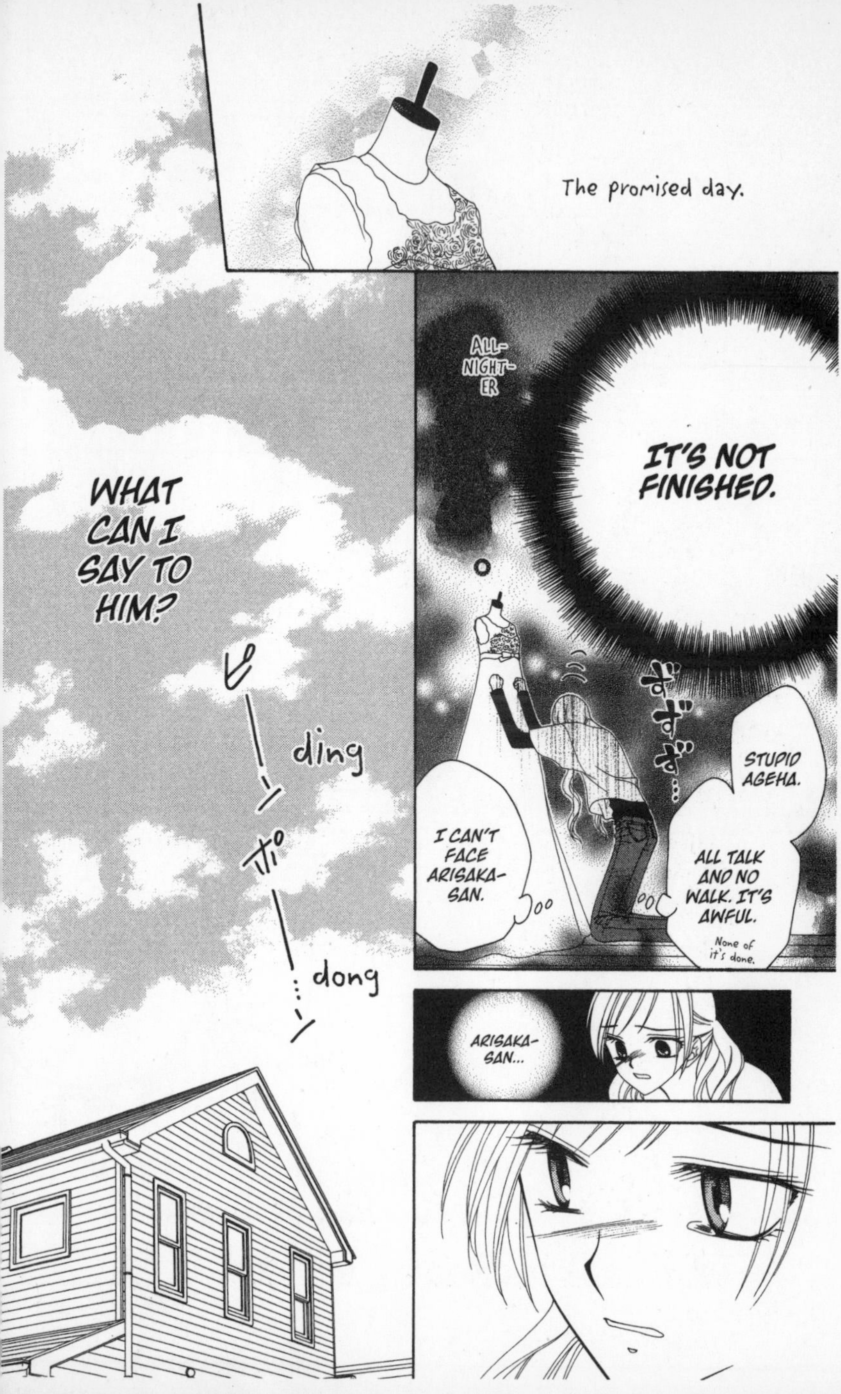

The promised day.
ALL-NIGHTER
IT'S NOT FINISHED.
ずずず…
STUPID AGEHA.
ALL TALK AND NO WALK. IT'S AWFUL.
None of it's done.
I CAN'T FACE ARISAKA-SAN.
ARISAKA-SAN...
WHAT CAN I SAY TO HIM?
ピーンポーン…
ding
dong

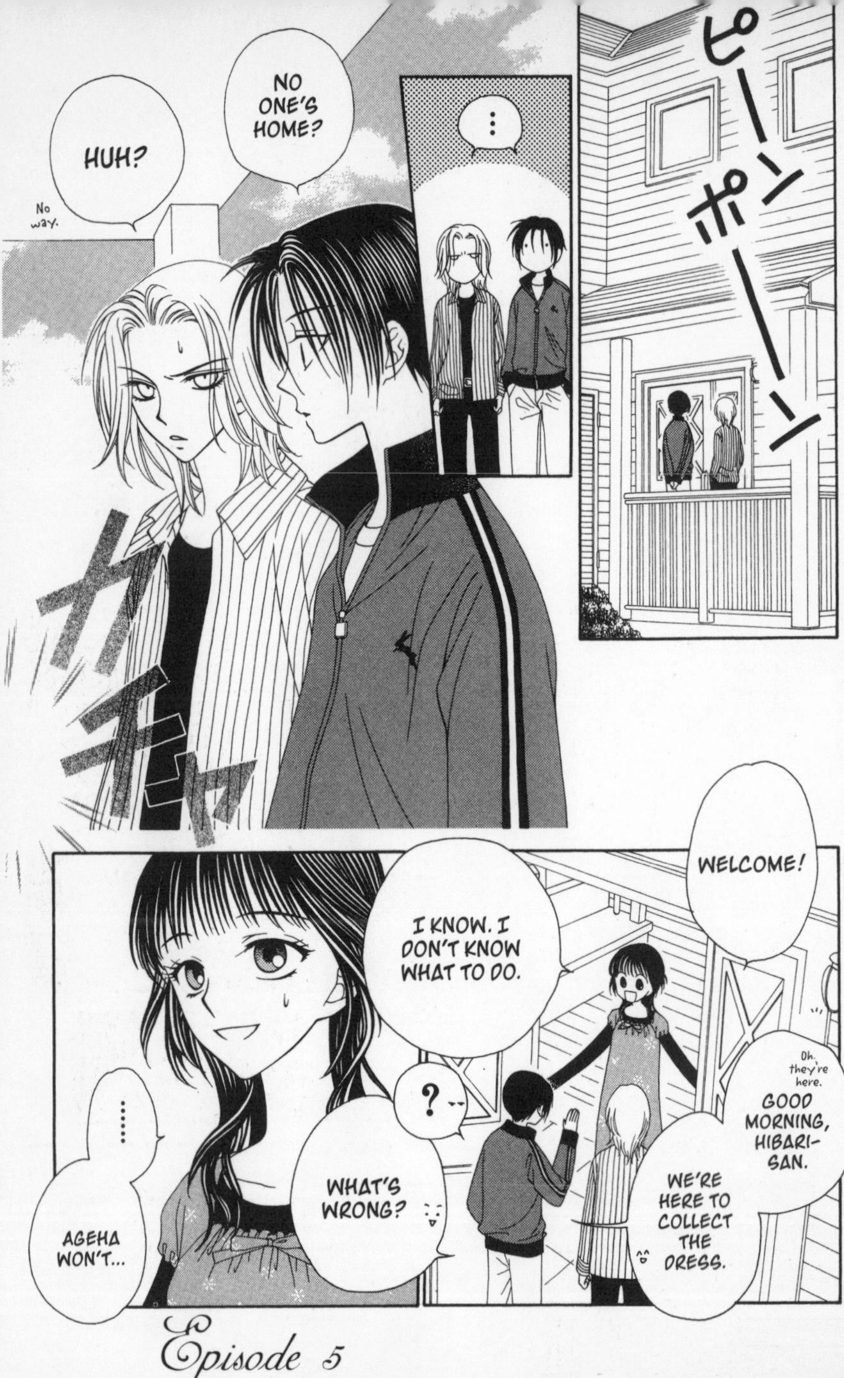
ピーンポーン
...
NO ONE'S HOME?
HUH?
No way.
ガチャ
WELCOME!
Oh. they're here.
GOOD MORNING, HIBARI-SAN.
WE'RE HERE TO COLLECT THE DRESS.
I KNOW. I DON'T KNOW WHAT TO DO.
?
WHAT'S WRONG?
......
AGEHA WON'T...

Episode 5

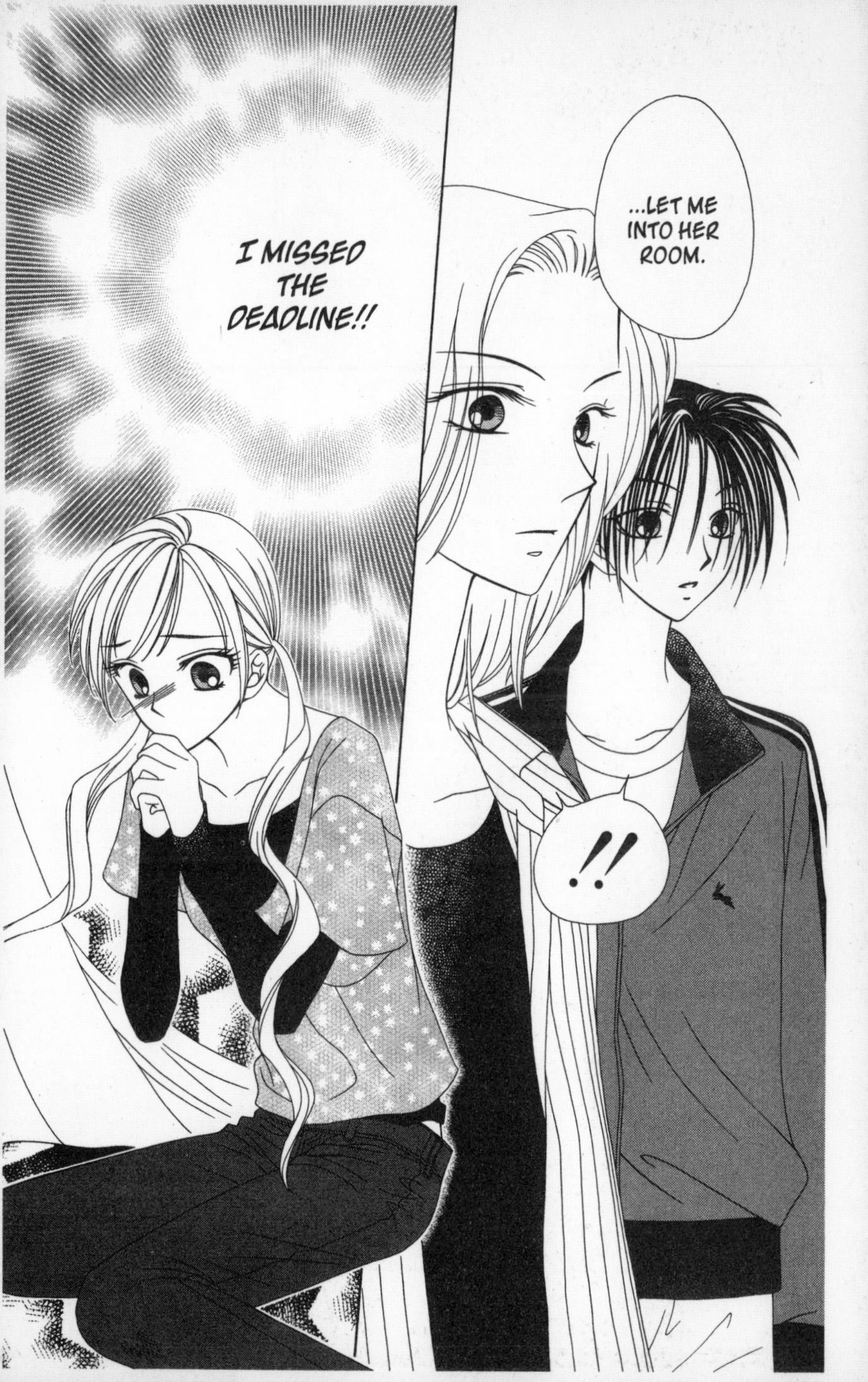
...LET ME INTO HER ROOM.
!!
I MISSED THE DEADLINE!!

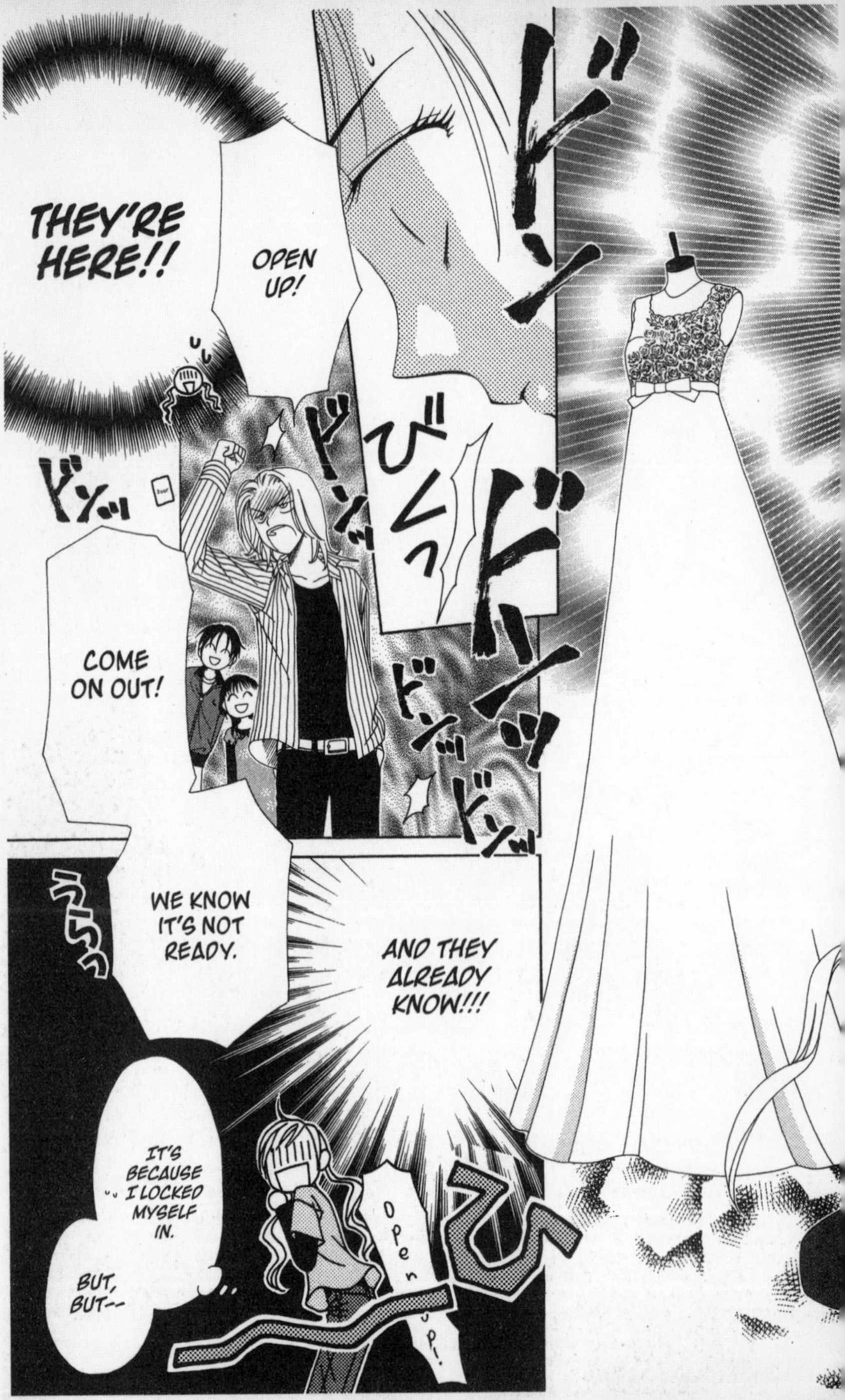
ドーンッ
THEY'RE HERE!!
OPEN UP!
ドンッ
びくっ
ドンッ
ドンッ
ドンッ
ドンッ
COME ON OUT!
WE KNOW IT'S NOT READY.
AND THEY ALREADY KNOW!!!
IT'S BECAUSE I LOCKED MYSELF IN.
BUT, BUT--
Open up!

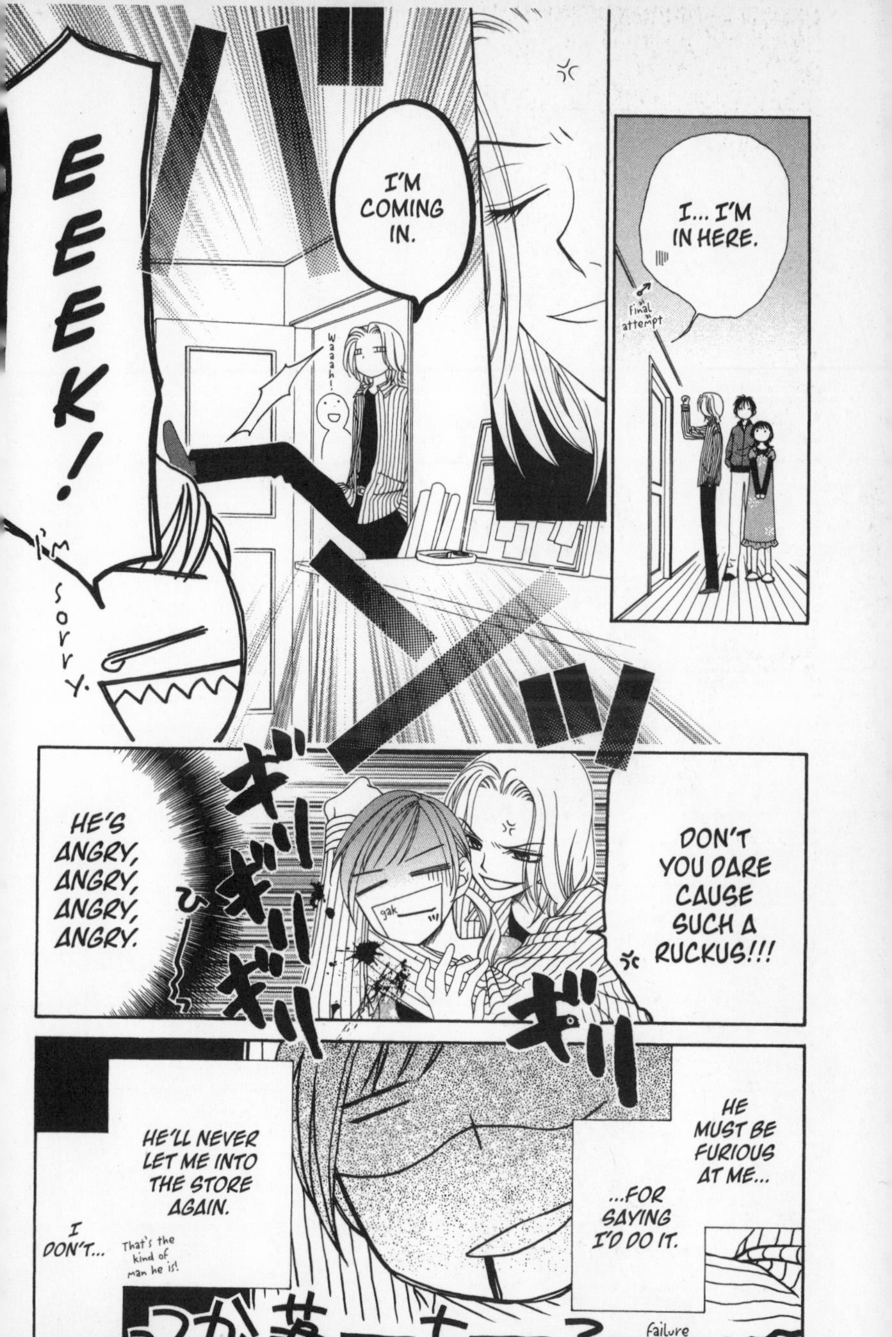
I... I'M IN HERE.
Final attempt
I'M COMING IN.
Waaah!
EEEEK!
I'm sorry.
DON'T YOU DARE CAUSE SUCH A RUCKUS!!!
gak
HE'S ANGRY, ANGRY, ANGRY, ANGRY.
HE MUST BE FURIOUS AT ME...
...FOR SAYING I'D DO IT.
HE'LL NEVER LET ME INTO THE STORE AGAIN.
I DON'T...
That's the kind of man he is!
ってか落ーちーる
Failure

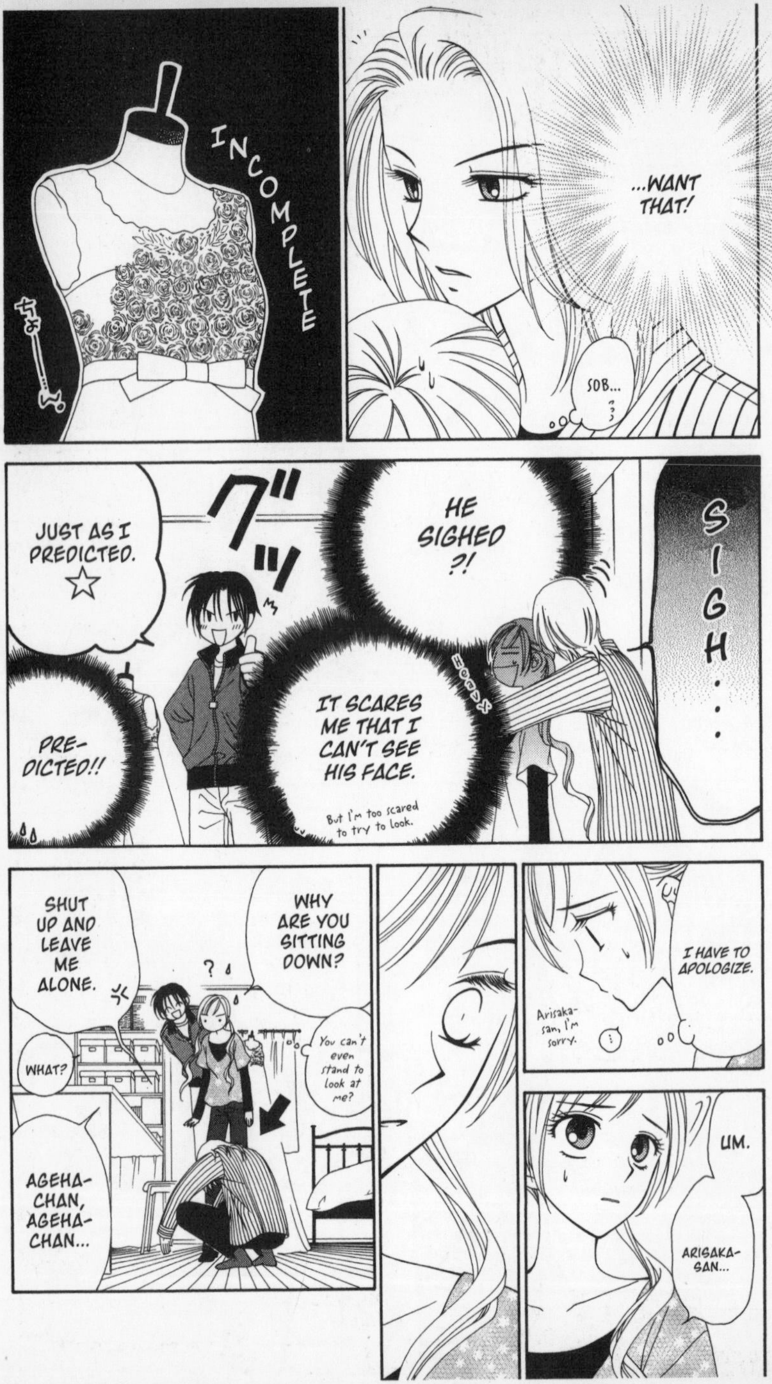
...WANT THAT!
SOB...
INCOMPLETE
SIGH...
Heavy
HE SIGHED ?!
IT SCARES ME THAT I CAN'T SEE HIS FACE.
But I'm too scared to try to look.
グッ
JUST AS I PREDICTED. ☆
PRE-DICTED!!
I HAVE TO APOLOGIZE.
Arisaka-san, I'm sorry.
...
UM.
ARISAKA-SAN...
WHY ARE YOU SITTING DOWN?
You can't even stand to look at me?
SHUT UP AND LEAVE ME ALONE.
WHAT?
AGEHA-CHAN, AGEHA-CHAN...

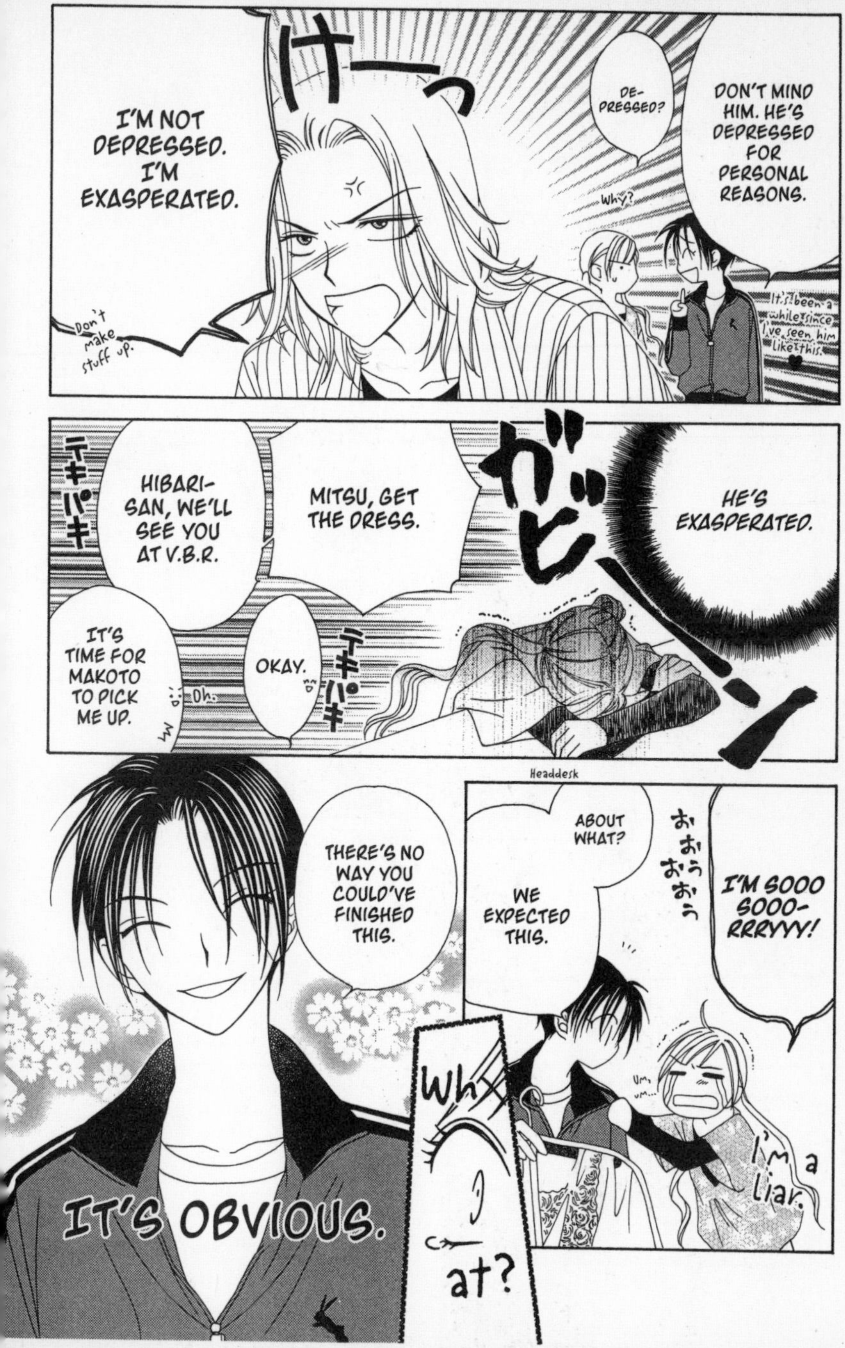
DON'T MIND HIM. HE'S DEPRESSED FOR PERSONAL REASONS.
DE-PRESSED?
Why?
It's been a while since I've seen him like this.
けーっ
I'M NOT DEPRESSED. I'M EXASPERATED.
Don't make stuff up.
ガビーン
HE'S EXASPERATED.
MITSU, GET THE DRESS.
HIBARI-SAN, WE'LL SEE YOU AT V.B.R.
テキパキ
OKAY.
テキパキ
IT'S TIME FOR MAKOTO TO PICK ME UP.
Oh.
Headdesk
I'M SOOO SOOO-RRRYYY!
おおうおおう
ABOUT WHAT?
WE EXPECTED THIS.
Um, um...
I'm a liar.
THERE'S NO WAY YOU COULD'VE FINISHED THIS.
IT'S OBVIOUS.
Wh at?

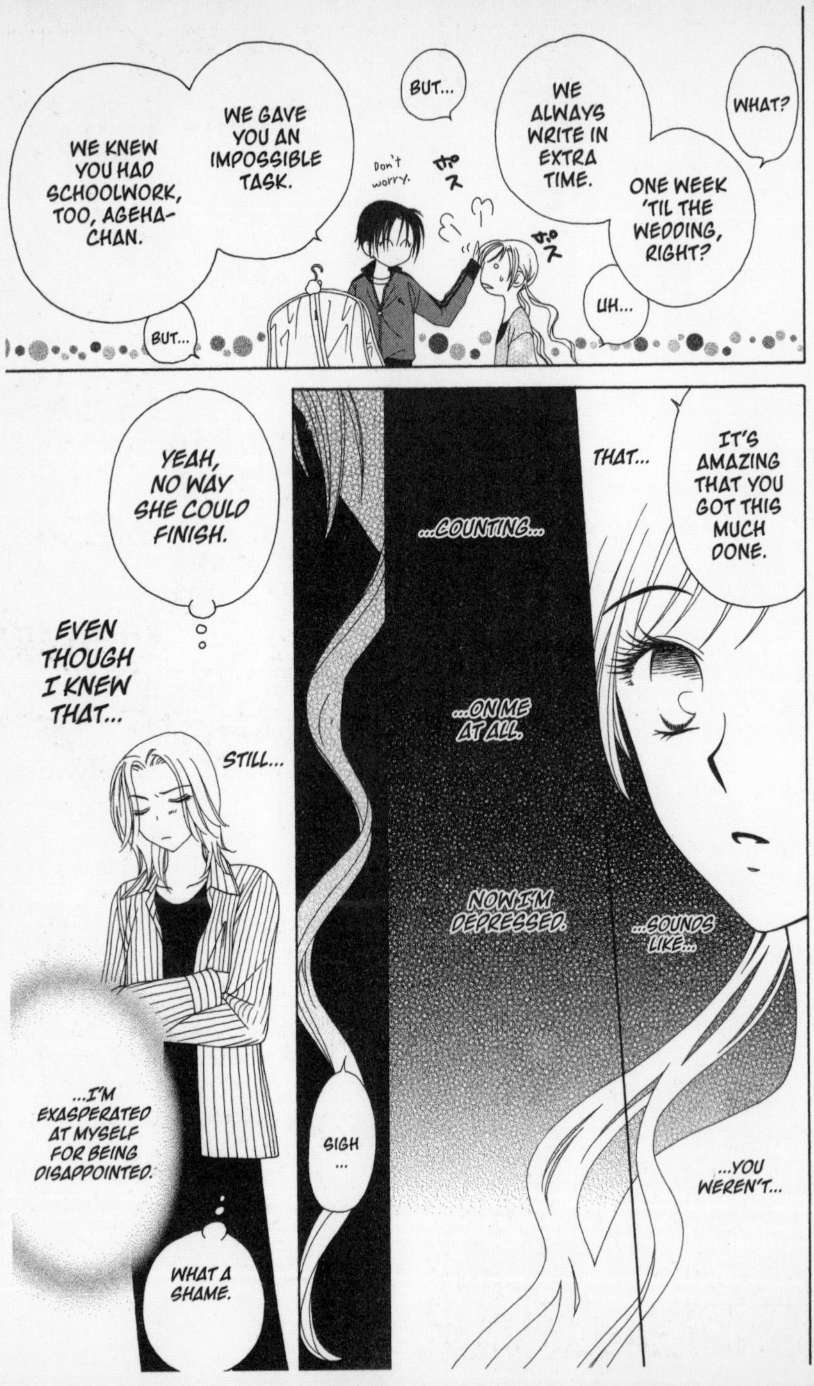
WHAT?
ONE WEEK 'TIL THE WEDDING, RIGHT?
UH...
WE ALWAYS WRITE IN EXTRA TIME.
ポス
BUT...
ポス
Don't worry.
WE GAVE YOU AN IMPOSSIBLE TASK.
WE KNEW YOU HAD SCHOOLWORK, TOO, AGEHA-CHAN.
BUT...
IT'S AMAZING THAT YOU GOT THIS MUCH DONE.
THAT...
...SOUNDS LIKE...
...YOU WEREN'T...
...COUNTING...
...ON ME AT ALL.
NOW I'M DEPRESSED.
SIGH...
YEAH, NO WAY SHE COULD FINISH.
EVEN THOUGH I KNEW THAT...
STILL...
...I'M EXASPERATED AT MYSELF FOR BEING DISAPPOINTED.
WHAT A SHAME.

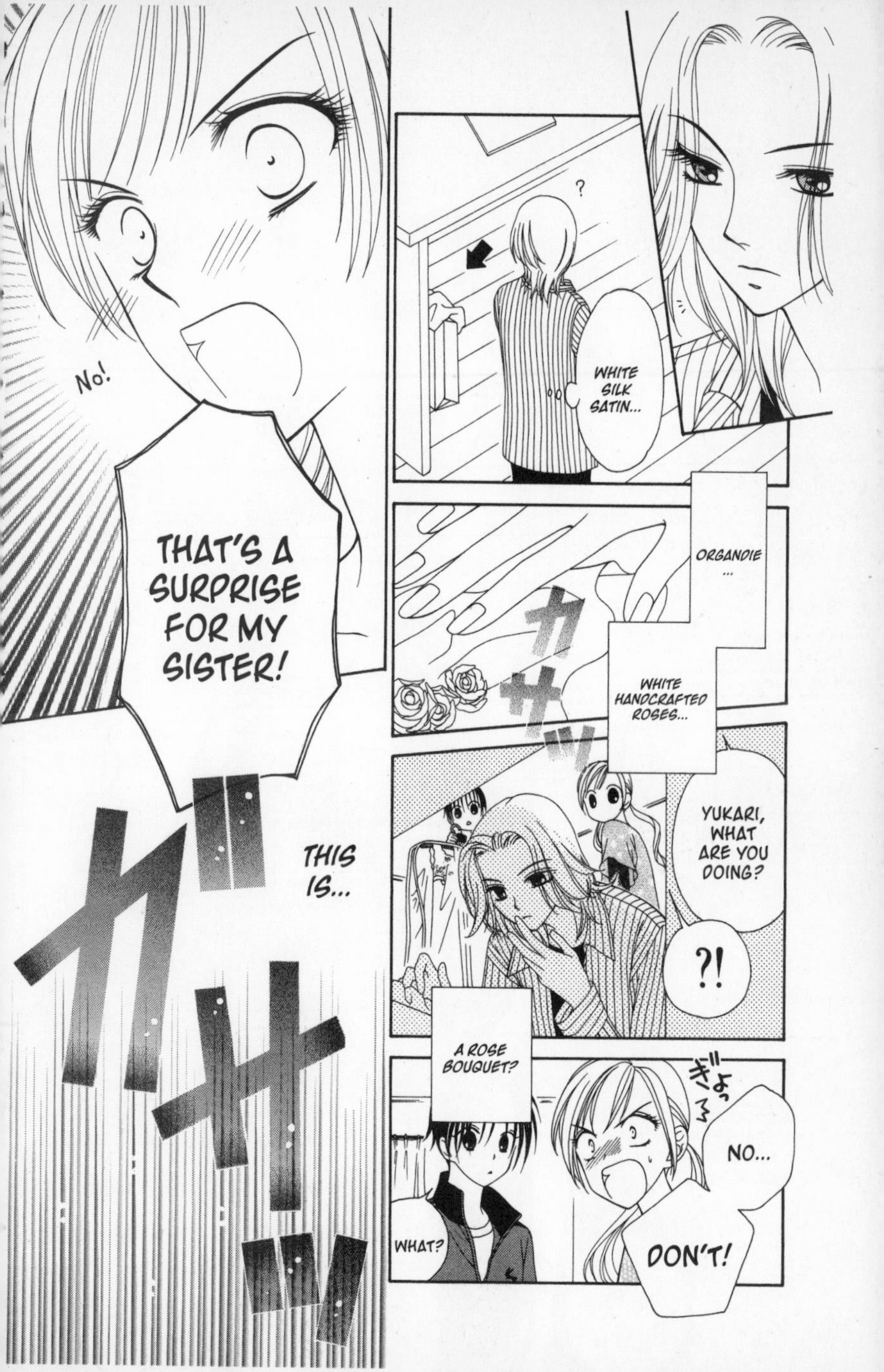
?
WHITE SILK SATIN...
ORGANDIE ...
カサッ
WHITE HANDCRAFTED ROSES...
YUKARI, WHAT ARE YOU DOING?
?!
A ROSE BOUQUET?
ぎょっ
NO...
DON'T!
WHAT?
No!
THAT'S A SURPRISE FOR MY SISTER!
THIS IS...
ガサッ

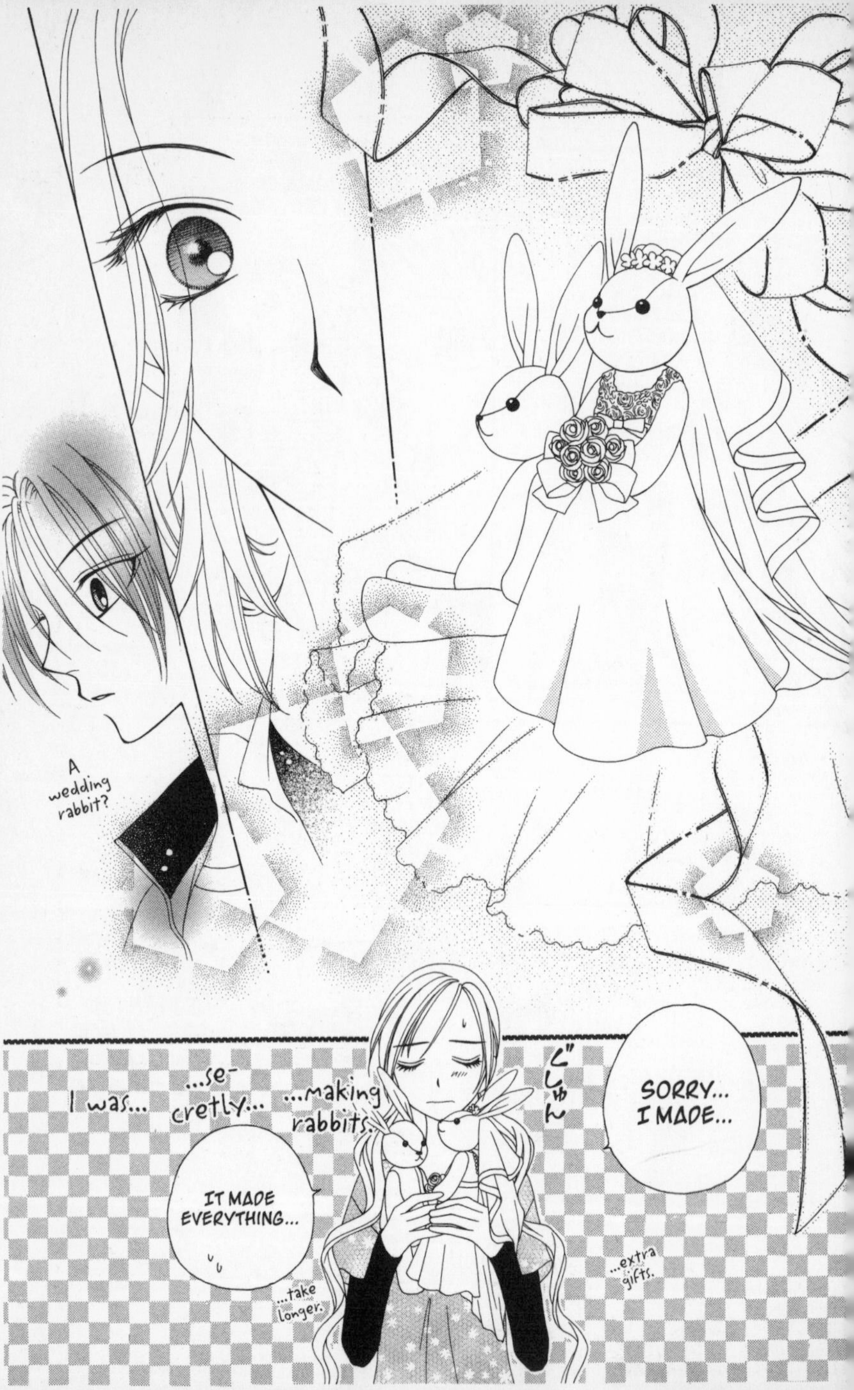
A wedding rabbit?
SORRY... I MADE...
ぐしゅん
...extra gifts.
I was... ...se-cretly... ...making rabbits.
IT MADE EVERYTHING...
...take longer.

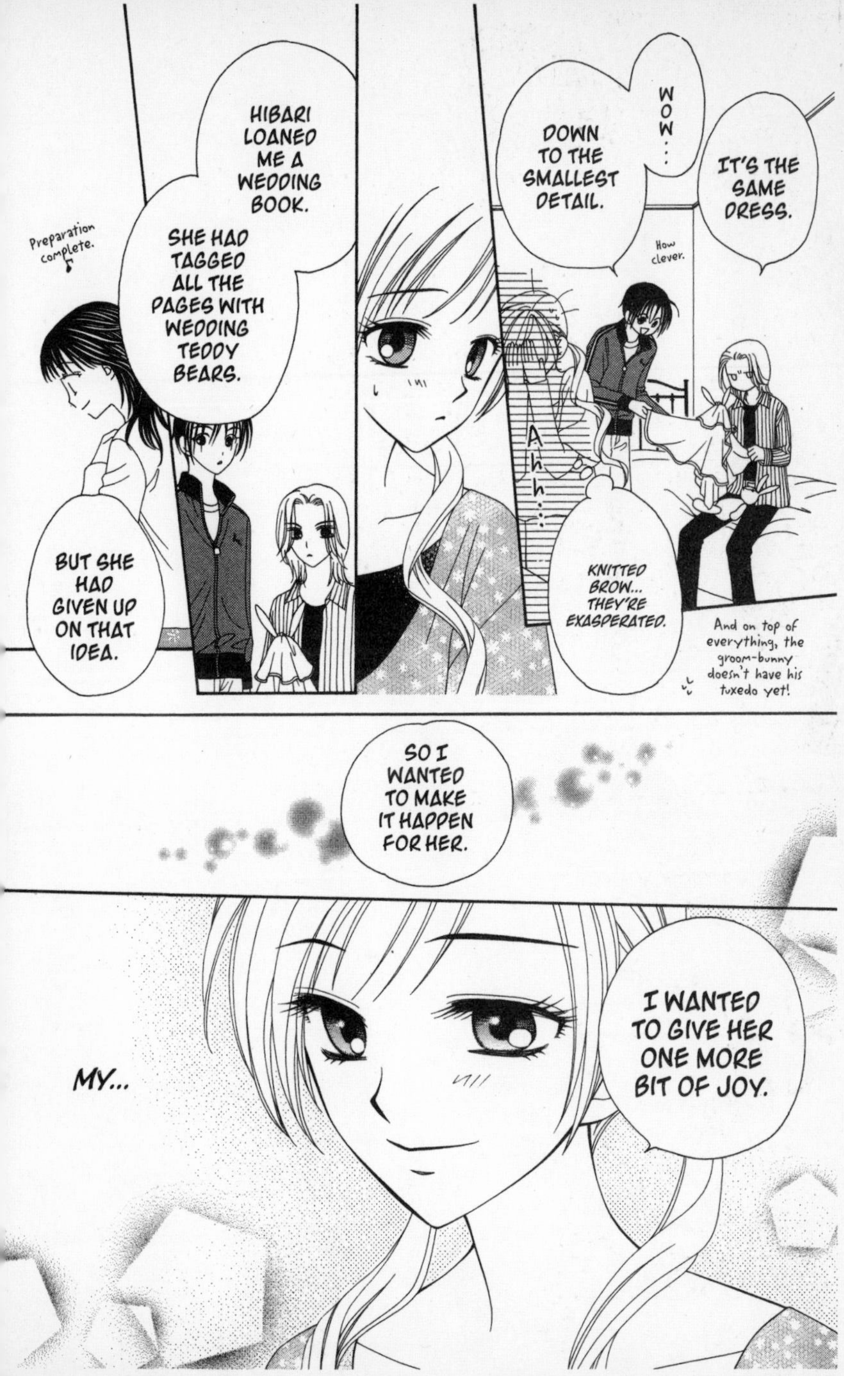
IT'S THE SAME DRESS.
WOW...
DOWN TO THE SMALLEST DETAIL.
How clever.
Ahh...
KNITTED BROW... THEY'RE EXASPERATED.
And on top of everything, the groom-bunny doesn't have his tuxedo yet!
HIBARI LOANED ME A WEDDING BOOK.
SHE HAD TAGGED ALL THE PAGES WITH WEDDING TEDDY BEARS.
Preparation complete.
BUT SHE HAD GIVEN UP ON THAT IDEA.
SO I WANTED TO MAKE IT HAPPEN FOR HER.
I WANTED TO GIVE HER ONE MORE BIT OF JOY.
MY...

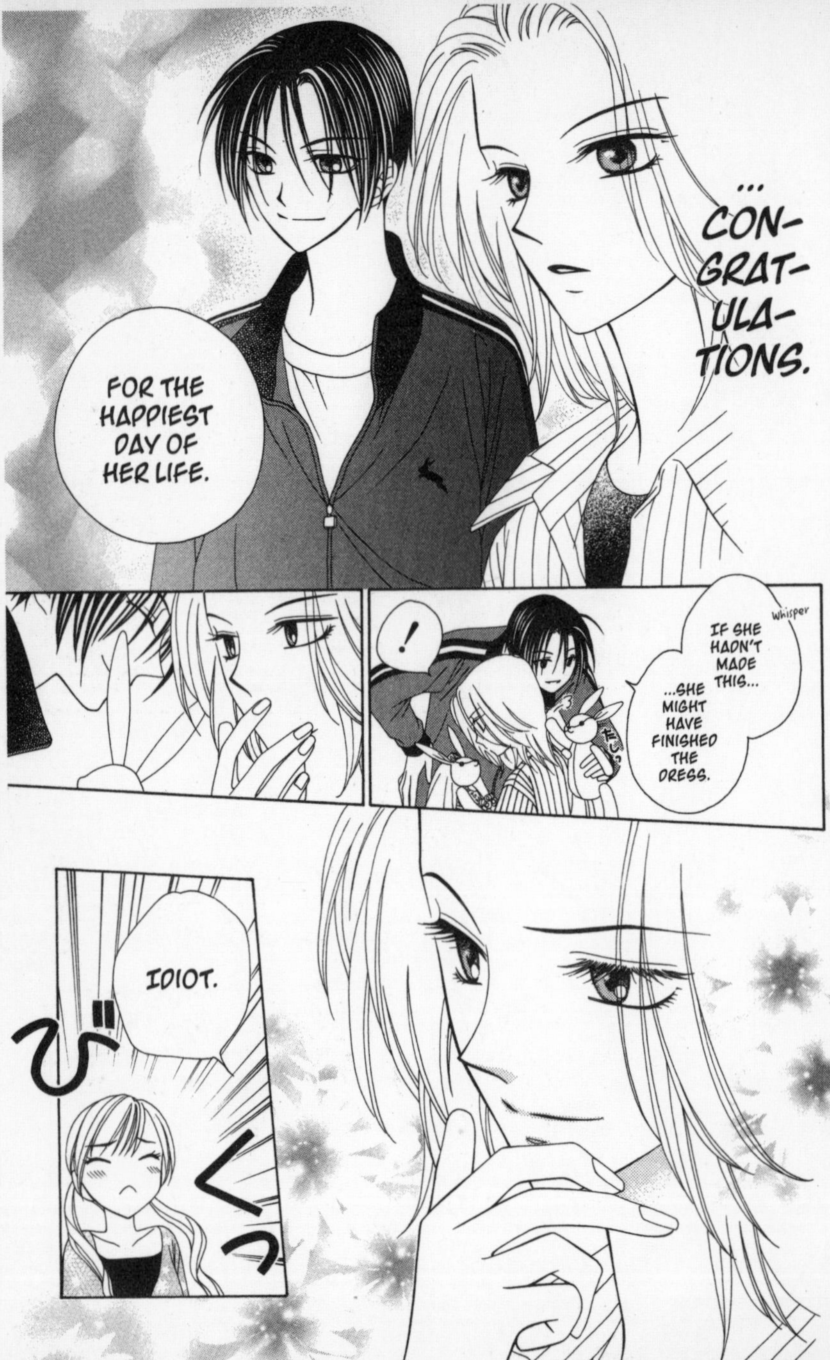
...CON-GRAT-ULA-TIONS.
FOR THE HAPPIEST DAY OF HER LIFE.
!
Whisper
IF SHE HADN'T MADE THIS...
...SHE MIGHT HAVE FINISHED THE DRESS.
IDIOT.
び
くっ

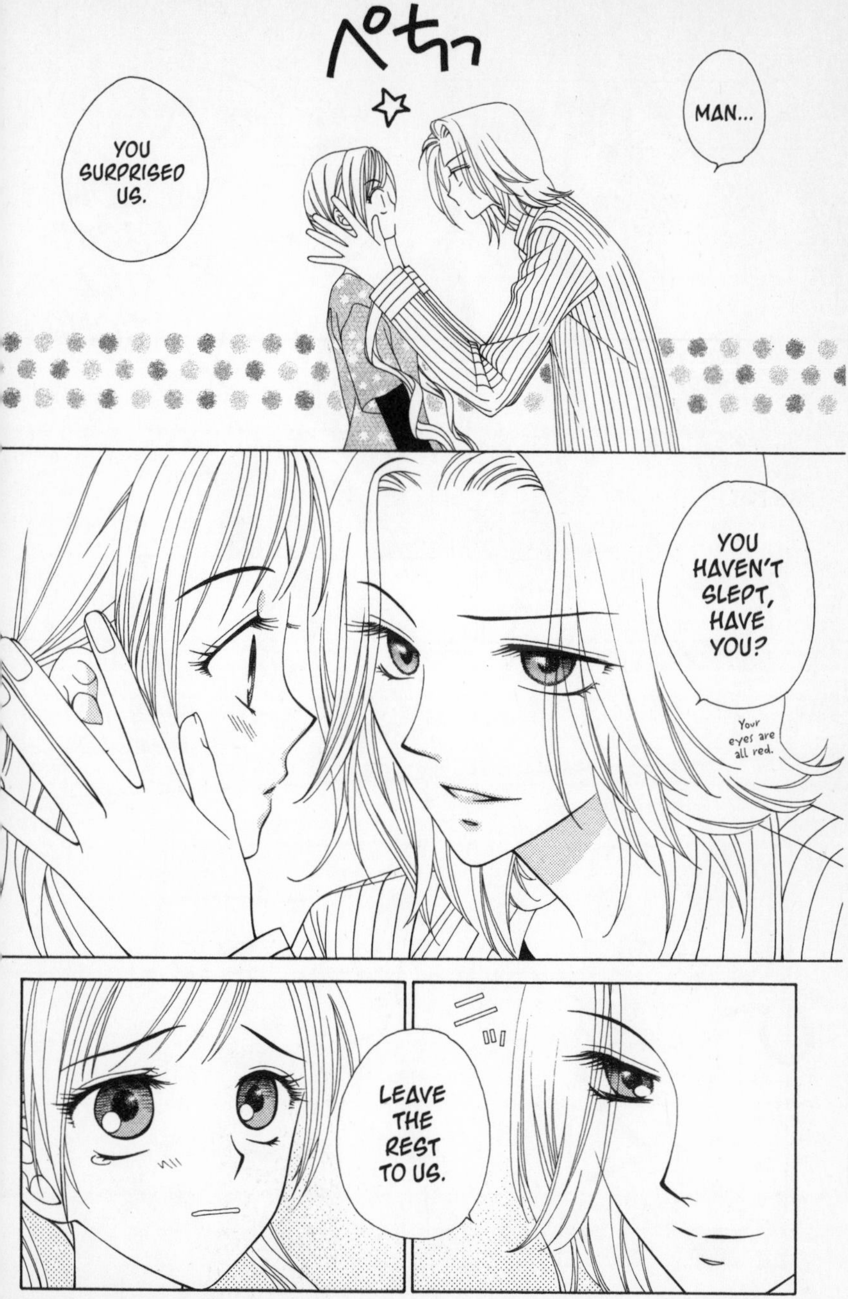
ぺちっ
MAN...
YOU SURPRISED US.
YOU HAVEN'T SLEPT, HAVE YOU?
Your eyes are all red.
LEAVE THE REST TO US.

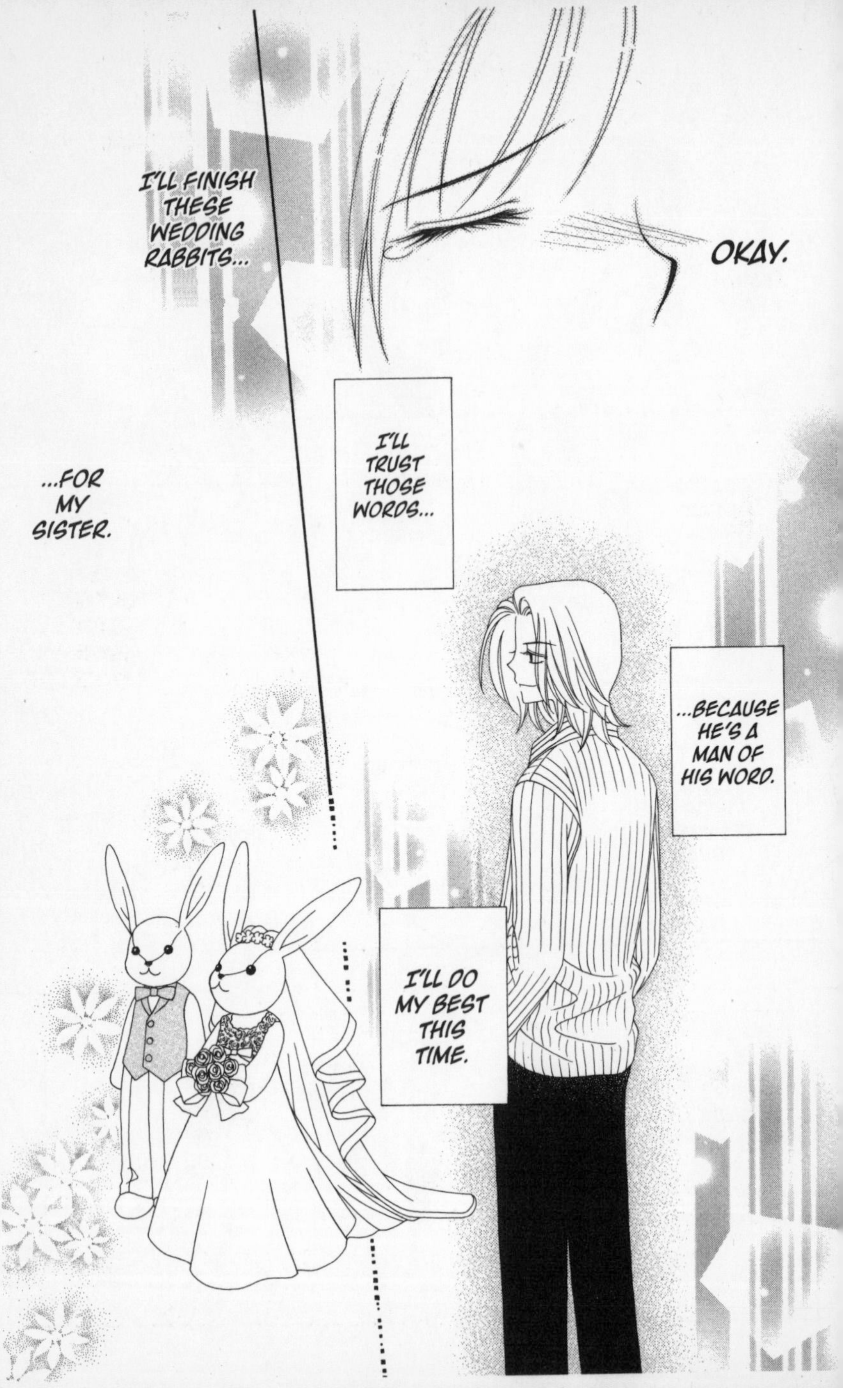
OKAY.
I'LL TRUST THOSE WORDS...
...BECAUSE HE'S A MAN OF HIS WORD.
I'LL DO MY BEST THIS TIME.
I'LL FINISH THESE WEDDING RABBITS...
...FOR MY SISTER.

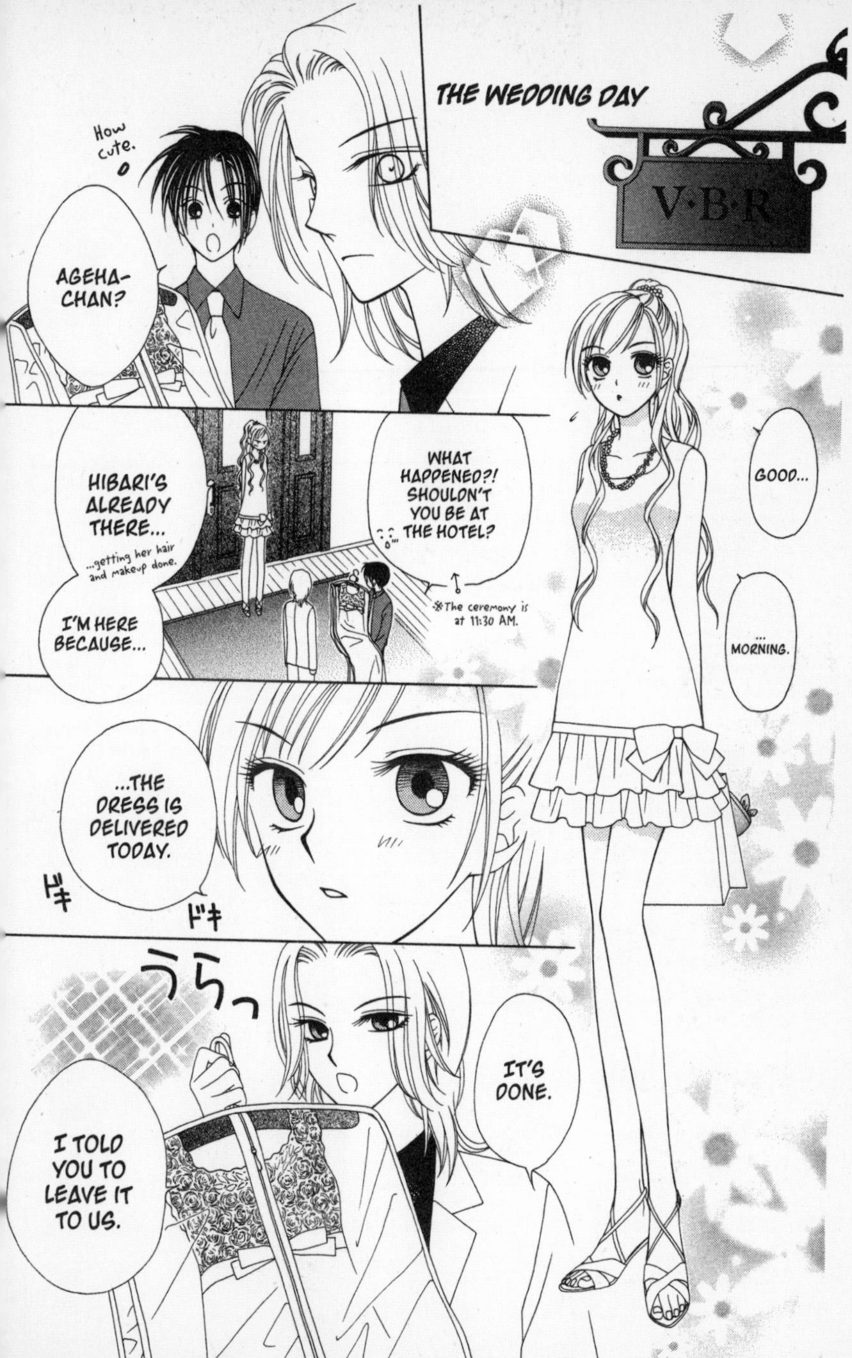
THE WEDDING DAY
V·B·R
GOOD...
...MORNING.
AGEHA-CHAN?
How cute.
WHAT HAPPENED?! SHOULDN'T YOU BE AT THE HOTEL?
※The ceremony is at 11:30 AM.
HIBARI'S ALREADY THERE...
...getting her hair and makeup done.
I'M HERE BECAUSE...
...THE DRESS IS DELIVERED TODAY.
ドキ
ドキ
うらっ
IT'S DONE.
I TOLD YOU TO LEAVE IT TO US.

This is the last sidebar. I hope you've enjoyed it along with the story.

Thank you to everyone who helped, and to all of you readers. Thank you very much! ♥

And thank you to Lotte Rose, a lovely custom-made wedding boutique, for allowing me to interview them.

I hope to continue doing my... ...best at Velvet.

It would make me happy to hear what you think.

Address:
Banri Hidaka
C/O TOKYOPOP
5900 Wilshire
Blvd. Suite 2000
Los Angeles, CA 90036

I await your letters! ♥

I jotted down some notes about our work.

Thank you.

To my best friend, Yoko, who works at a costume-rental store, thanks for helping me out. ♥

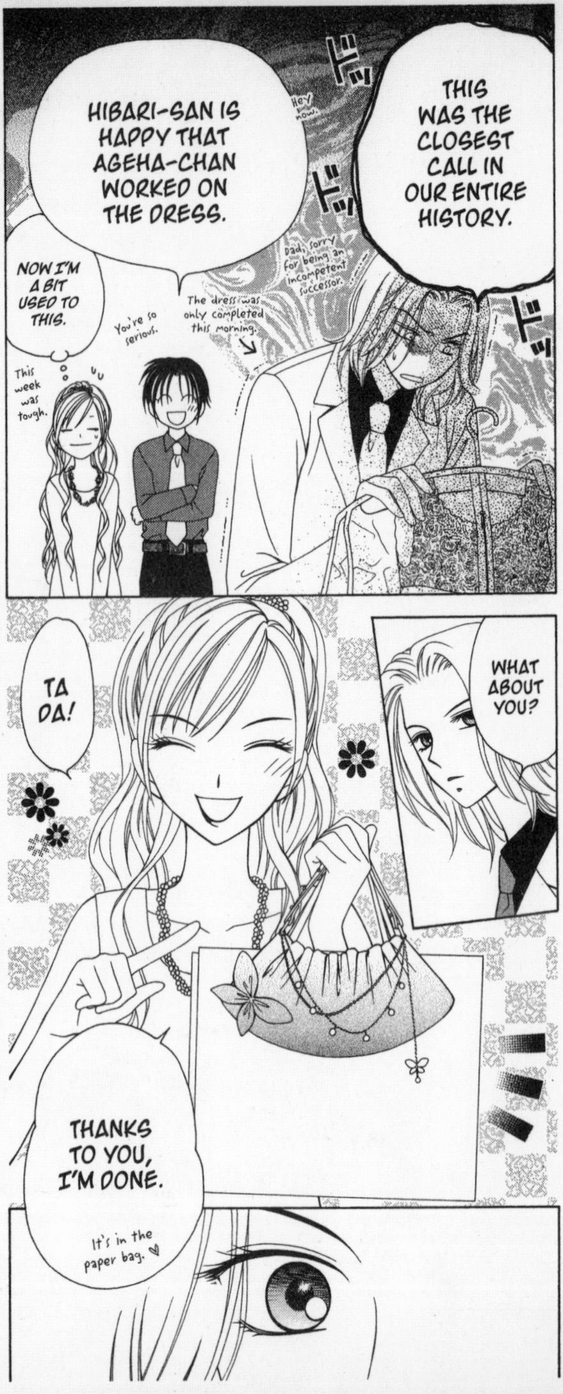
THIS WAS THE CLOSEST CALL IN OUR ENTIRE HISTORY.
Hey now.
Dad, sorry for being an incompetent successor.
HIBARI-SAN IS HAPPY THAT AGEHA-CHAN WORKED ON THE DRESS.
The dress was only completed this morning.
You're so serious.
NOW I'M A BIT USED TO THIS.
This week was tough.
WHAT ABOUT YOU?
TA DA!
THANKS TO YOU, I'M DONE.
It's in the paper bag. ♥

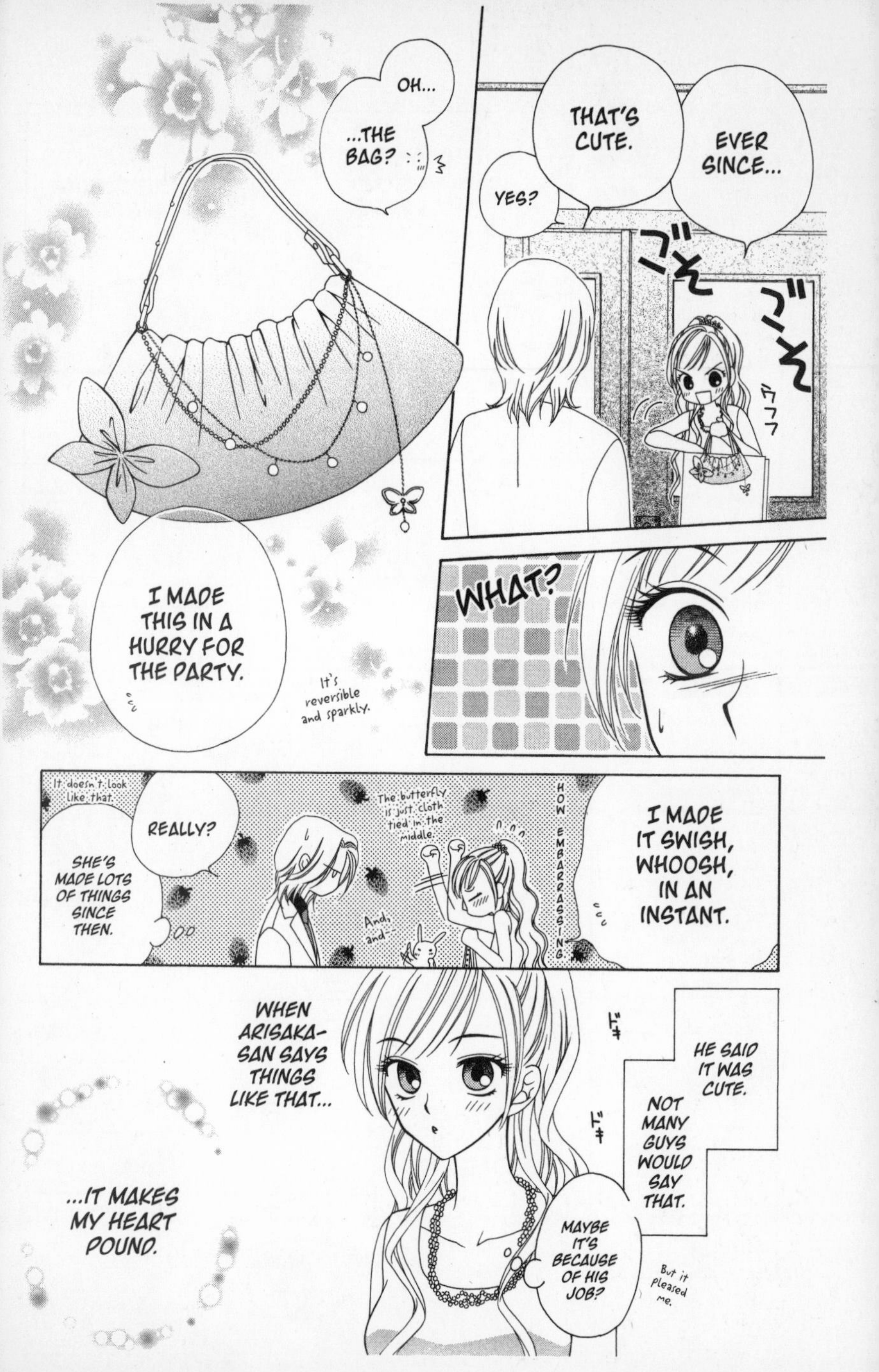
EVER SINCE...
THAT'S CUTE.
YES?
ごそ
ごそ
ウフフ
WHAT?
OH...
...THE BAG?
I MADE THIS IN A HURRY FOR THE PARTY.
It's reversible and sparkly.
I MADE IT SWISH, WHOOSH, IN AN INSTANT.
HOW EMBARRASSING
The butterfly is just cloth tied in the middle.
And, and--
REALLY?
It doesn't look like that.
SHE'S MADE LOTS OF THINGS SINCE THEN.
HE SAID IT WAS CUTE.
NOT MANY GUYS WOULD SAY THAT.
ドキ
ドキ
WHEN ARISAKA-SAN SAYS THINGS LIKE THAT...
MAYBE IT'S BECAUSE OF HIS JOB?
But it pleased me.
...IT MAKES MY HEART POUND.

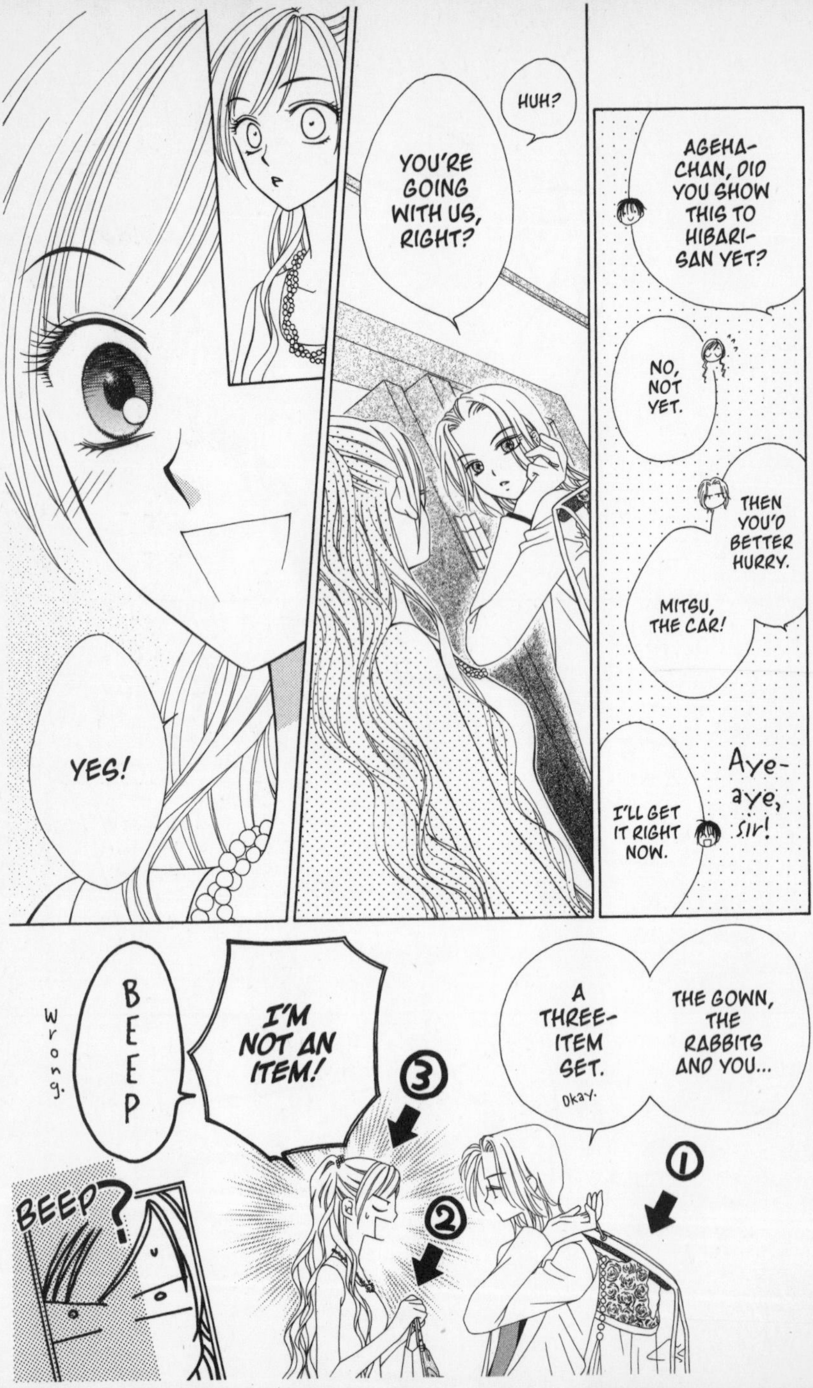
AGEHA-CHAN, DID YOU SHOW THIS TO HIBARI-SAN YET?
NO, NOT YET.
THEN YOU'D BETTER HURRY.
MITSU, THE CAR!
Aye-aye, sir!
I'LL GET IT RIGHT NOW.
HUH?
YOU'RE GOING WITH US, RIGHT?
YES!
THE GOWN, THE RABBITS AND YOU...
A THREE-ITEM SET.
Okay.
1
2
3
I'M NOT AN ITEM!
BEEP
Wrong.
BEEP?

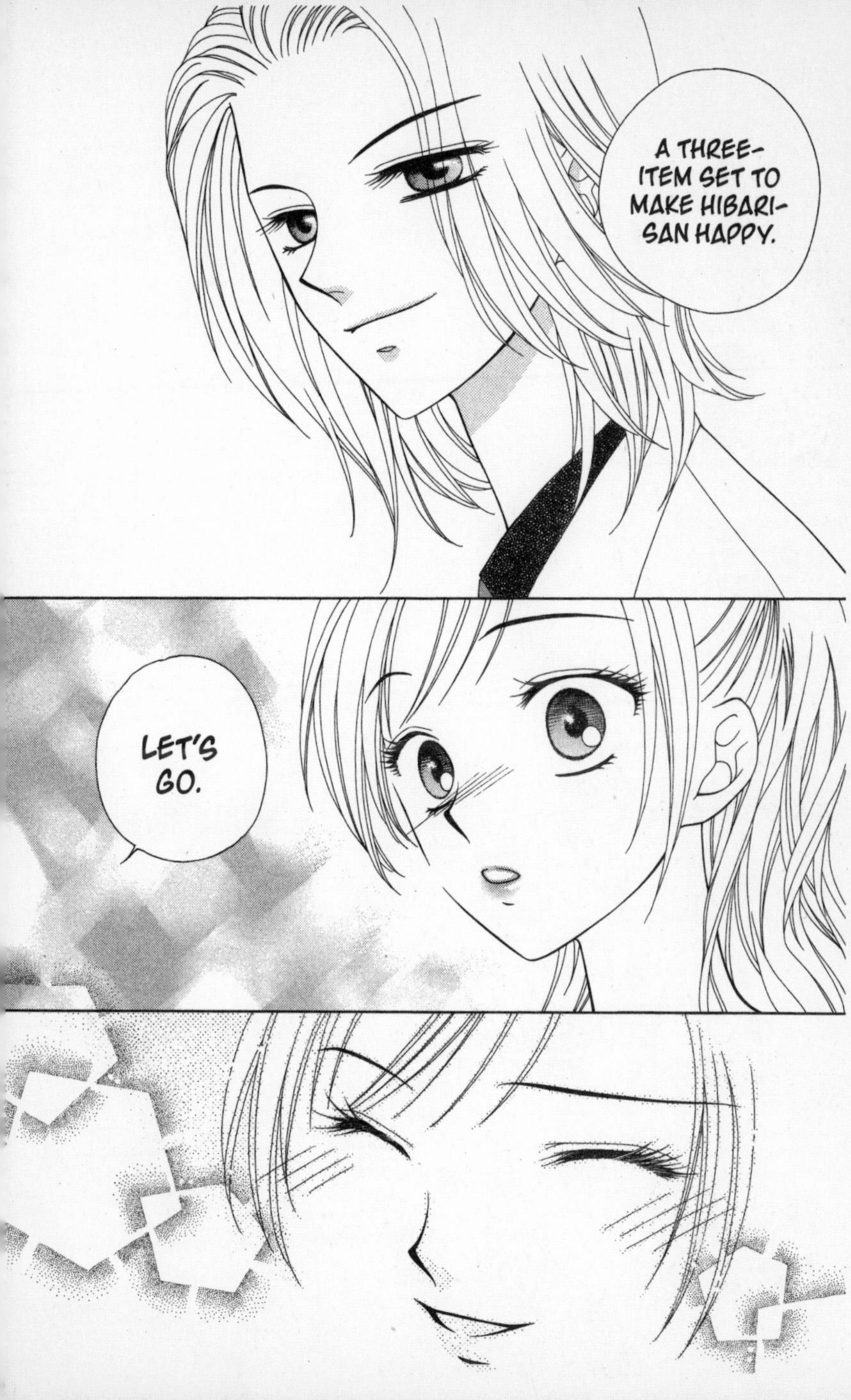
A THREE-ITEM SET TO MAKE HIBARI-SAN HAPPY.
LET'S GO.

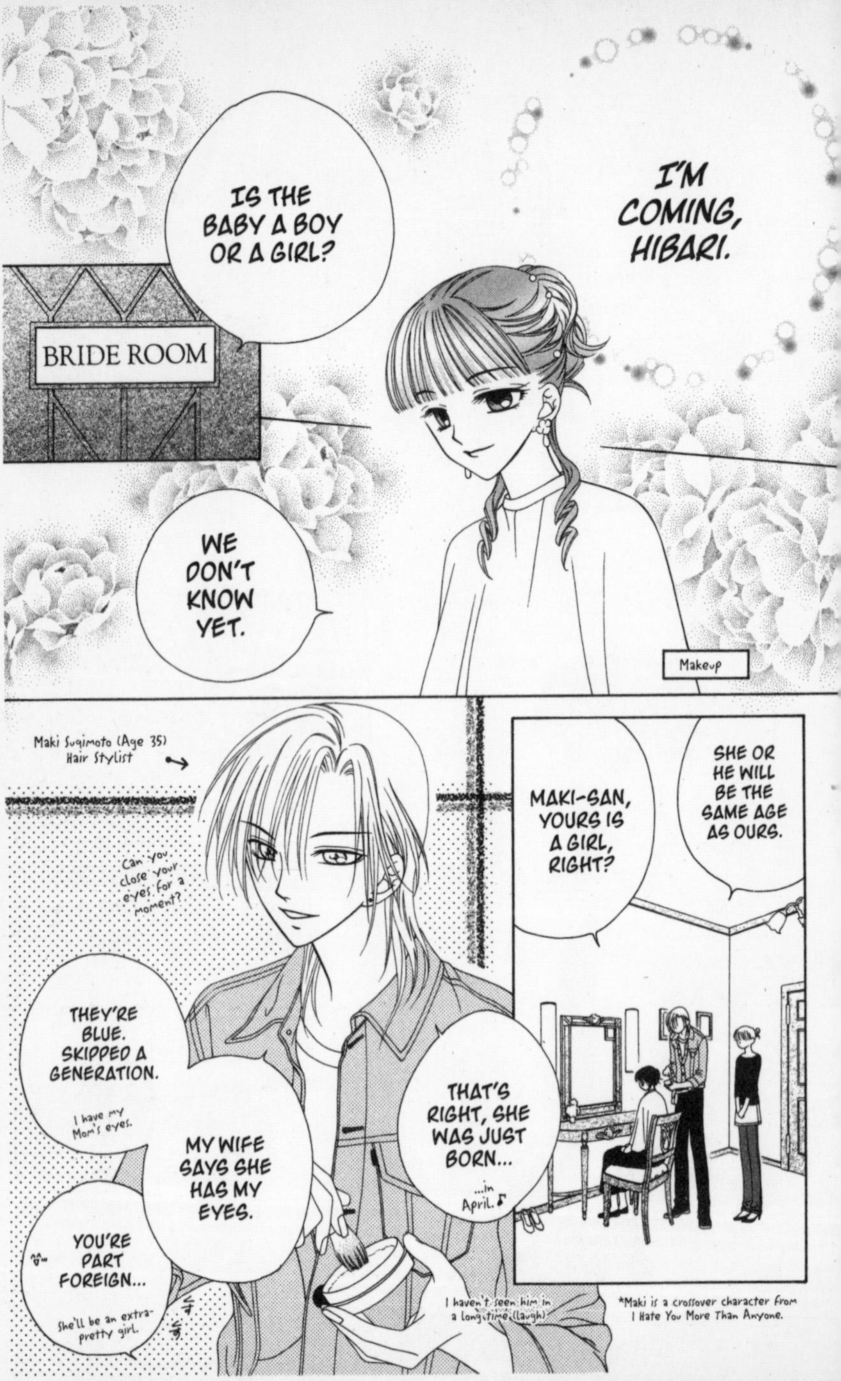
I'M COMING, HIBARI.
IS THE BABY A BOY OR A GIRL?
BRIDE ROOM
WE DON'T KNOW YET.
Makeup
SHE OR HE WILL BE THE SAME AGE AS OURS.
MAKI-SAN, YOURS IS A GIRL, RIGHT?
Maki Sugimoto (Age 35) Hair Stylist
Can you close your eyes for a moment?
THAT'S RIGHT, SHE WAS JUST BORN...
...in April. ♪
MY WIFE SAYS SHE HAS MY EYES.
THEY'RE BLUE. SKIPPED A GENERATION.
I have my Mom's eyes.
YOU'RE PART FOREIGN...
She'll be an extra-pretty girl.
I haven't seen him in a long time (laugh)

*Maki is a crossover character from I Hate You More Than Anyone.

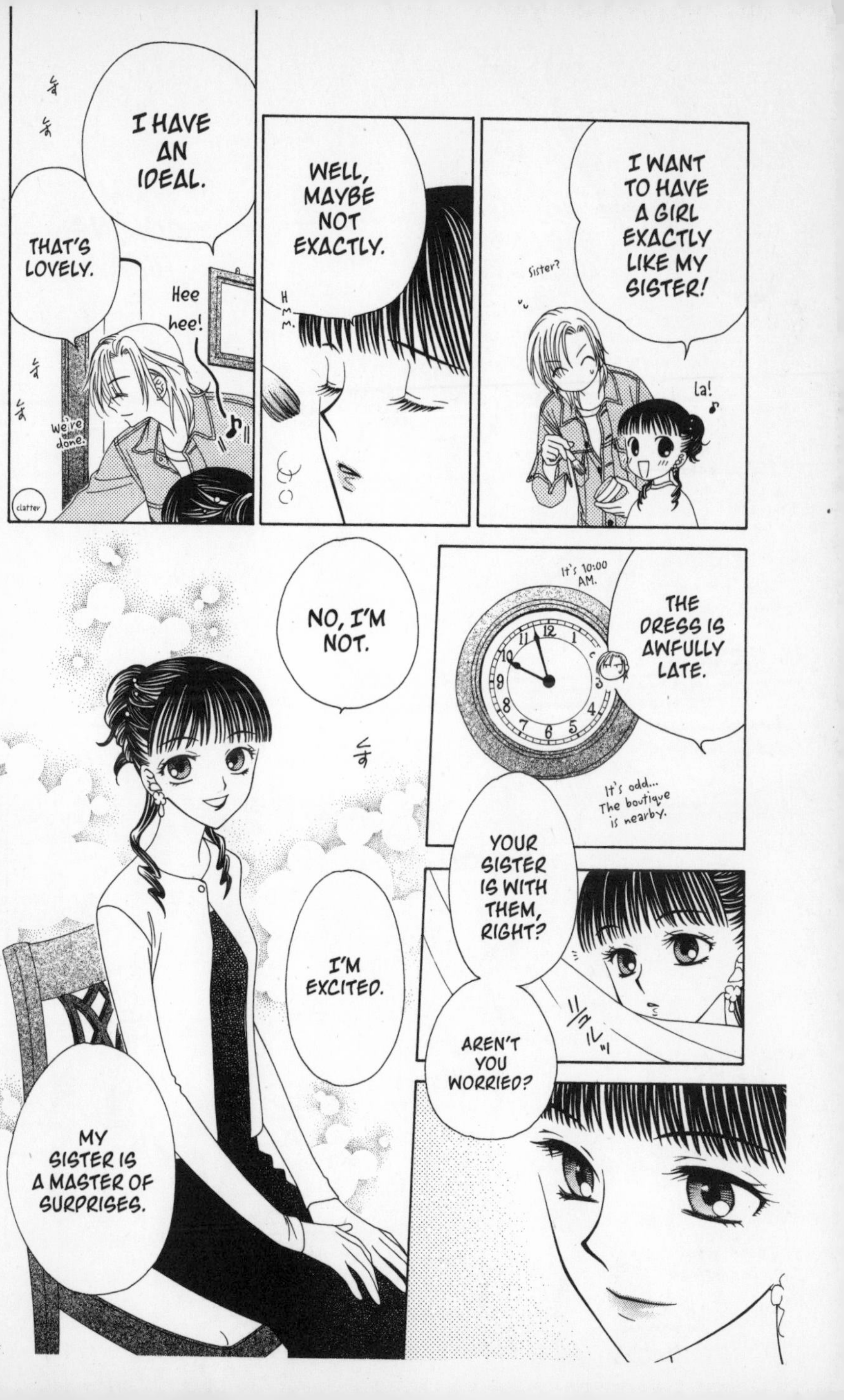
I WANT TO HAVE A GIRL EXACTLY LIKE MY SISTER!
Sister?
La!
WELL, MAYBE NOT EXACTLY.
HMM.
I HAVE AN IDEAL.
THAT'S LOVELY.
Hee hee!
We're done.
clatter
THE DRESS IS AWFULLY LATE.
It's 10:00 AM.
It's odd... The boutique is nearby.
YOUR SISTER IS WITH THEM, RIGHT?
AREN'T YOU WORRIED?
NO, I'M NOT.
I'M EXCITED.
MY SISTER IS A MASTER OF SURPRISES.

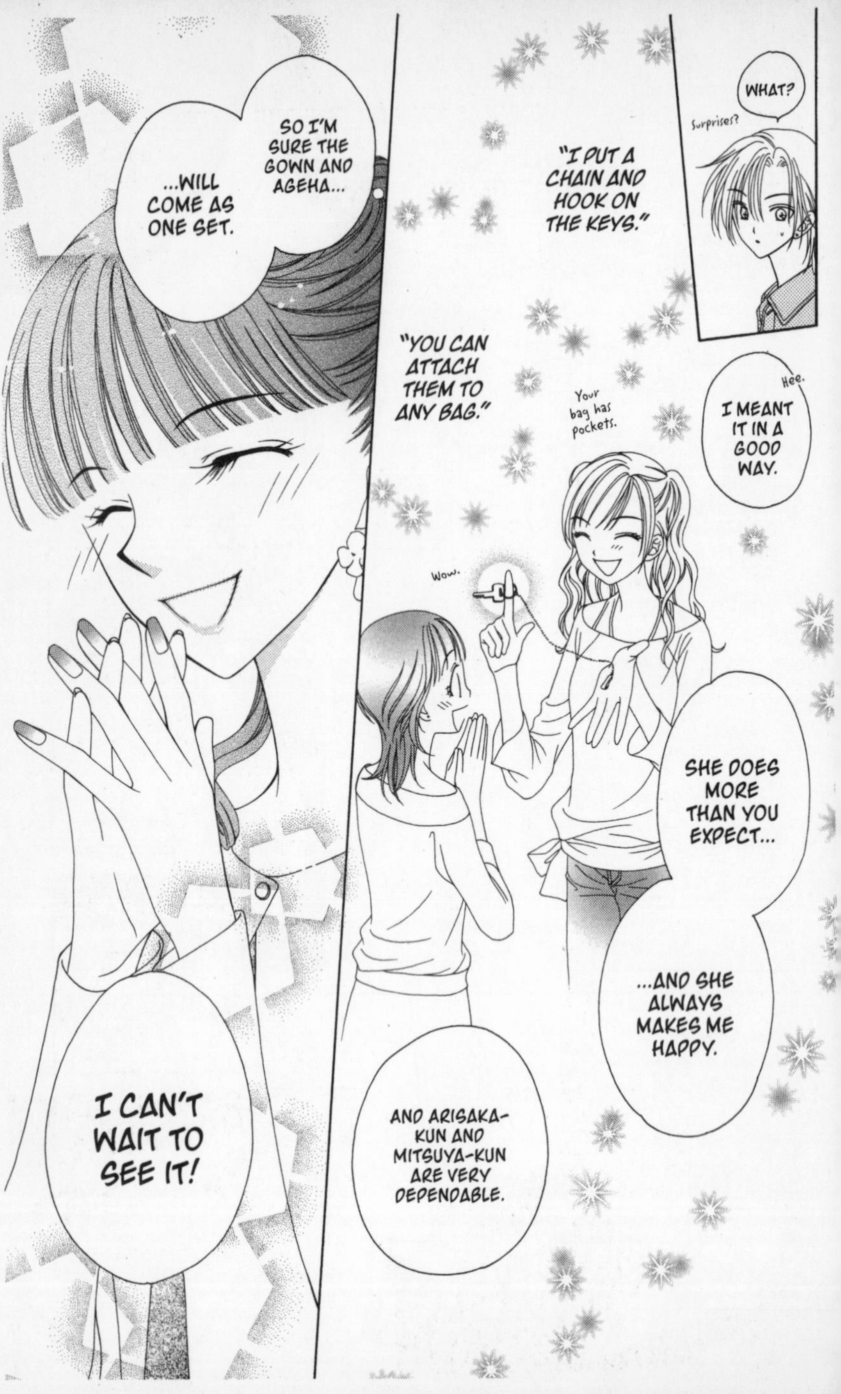
WHAT?
Surprises?
Hee.
I MEANT IT IN A GOOD WAY.
"I PUT A CHAIN AND HOOK ON THE KEYS."
"YOU CAN ATTACH THEM TO ANY BAG."
Your bag has pockets.
Wow.
SHE DOES MORE THAN YOU EXPECT...
...AND SHE ALWAYS MAKES ME HAPPY.
AND ARISAKA-KUN AND MITSUYA-KUN ARE VERY DEPENDABLE.
SO I'M SURE THE GOWN AND AGEHA...
...WILL COME AS ONE SET.
I CAN'T WAIT TO SEE IT!

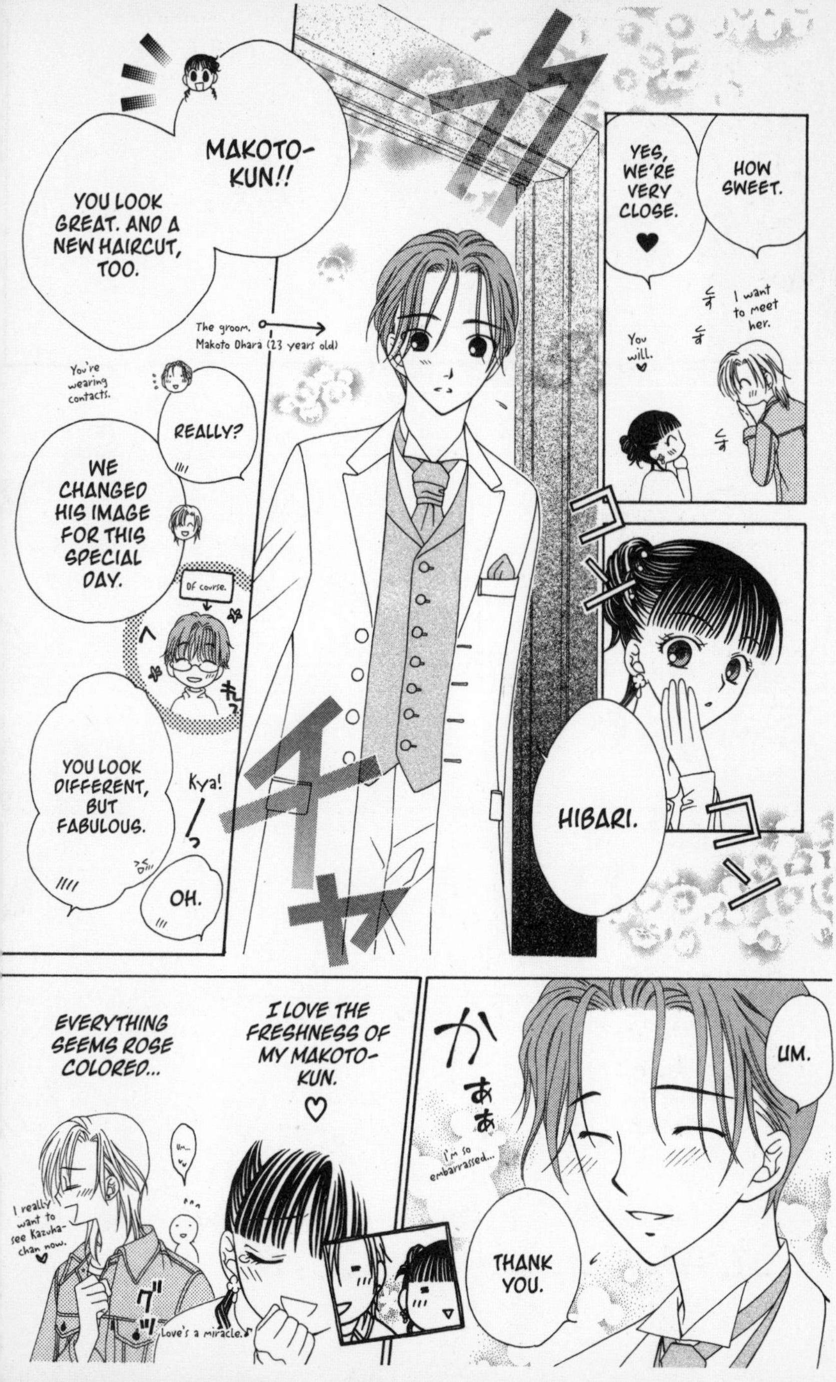

HOW SWEET.
YES, WE'RE VERY CLOSE.
I want to meet her.
You will.
HIBARI.
MAKOTO-KUN!!
YOU LOOK GREAT. AND A NEW HAIRCUT, TOO.
The groom. Makoto Ohara (23 years old)
You're wearing contacts.
REALLY?
WE CHANGED HIS IMAGE FOR THIS SPECIAL DAY.
Of course.
YOU LOOK DIFFERENT, BUT FABULOUS.
Kya!
OH.
UM.
THANK YOU.
I'm so embarrassed...
I LOVE THE FRESHNESS OF MY MAKOTO-KUN.
EVERYTHING SEEMS ROSE COLORED...
Um...
I really want to see Kazuha-chan now.
Love's a miracle.

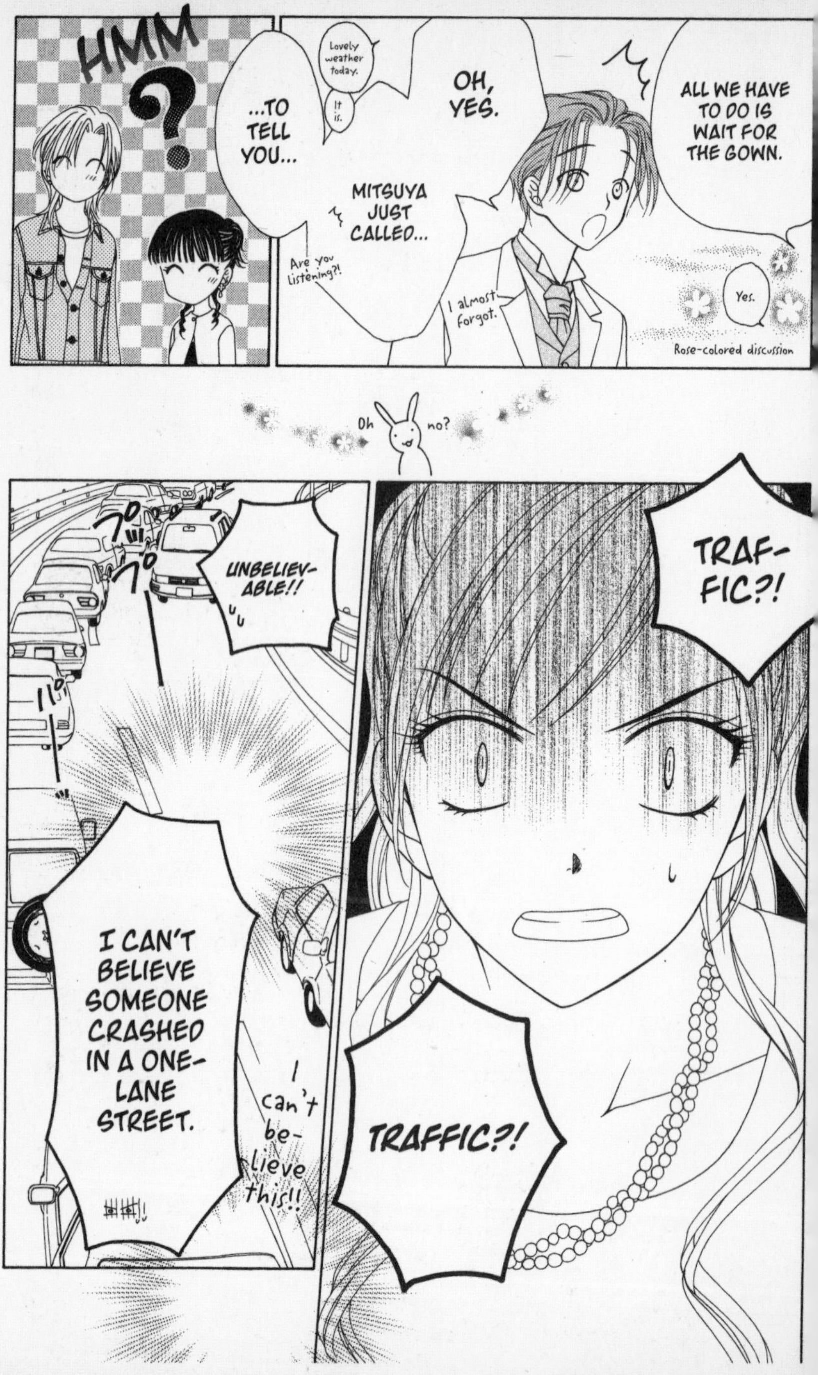
ALL WE HAVE TO DO IS WAIT FOR THE GOWN.
Yes.
Rose-colored discussion
OH, YES.
I almost forgot.
Lovely weather today.
It is.
...TO TELL YOU...
MITSUYA JUST CALLED...
Are you listening?!
HMM
?
Oh no?
TRAF-FIC?!
TRAFFIC?!
UNBELIEV-ABLE!!
I CAN'T BELIEVE SOMEONE CRASHED IN A ONE-LANE STREET.
I can't be-lieve this!!

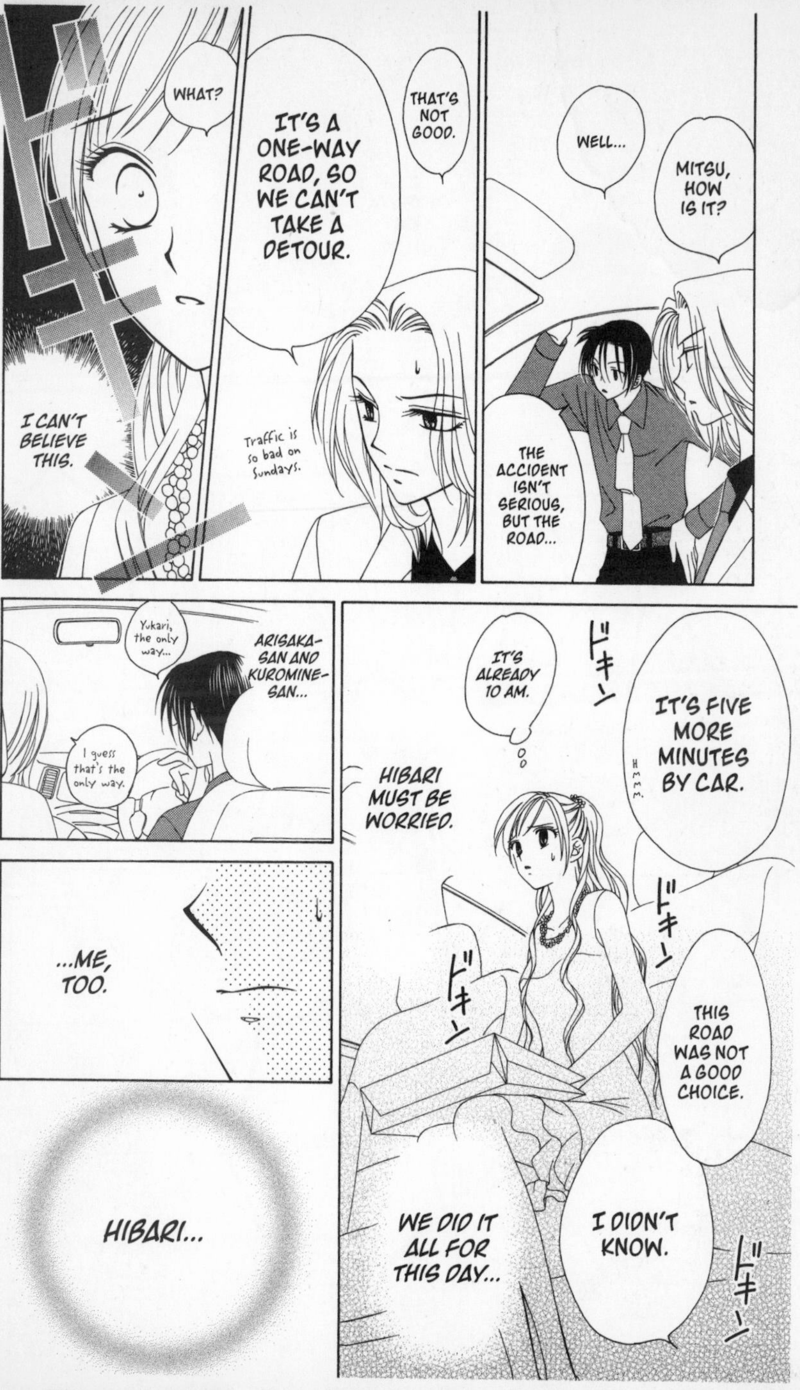
MITSU, HOW IS IT?
WELL...
THE ACCIDENT ISN'T SERIOUS, BUT THE ROAD...
THAT'S NOT GOOD.
IT'S A ONE-WAY ROAD, SO WE CAN'T TAKE A DETOUR.
Traffic is so bad on Sundays.
WHAT?
ドキ
I CAN'T BELIEVE THIS.
IT'S FIVE MORE MINUTES BY CAR.
ドキン
IT'S ALREADY 10 AM.
HMMM.
HIBARI MUST BE WORRIED.
ドキン
ドキン
THIS ROAD WAS NOT A GOOD CHOICE.
I DIDN'T KNOW.
ドキン
WE DID IT ALL FOR THIS DAY...
ARISAKA-SAN AND KUROMINE-SAN...
Yukari, the only way...
I guess that's the only way.
...ME, TOO.
HIBARI...

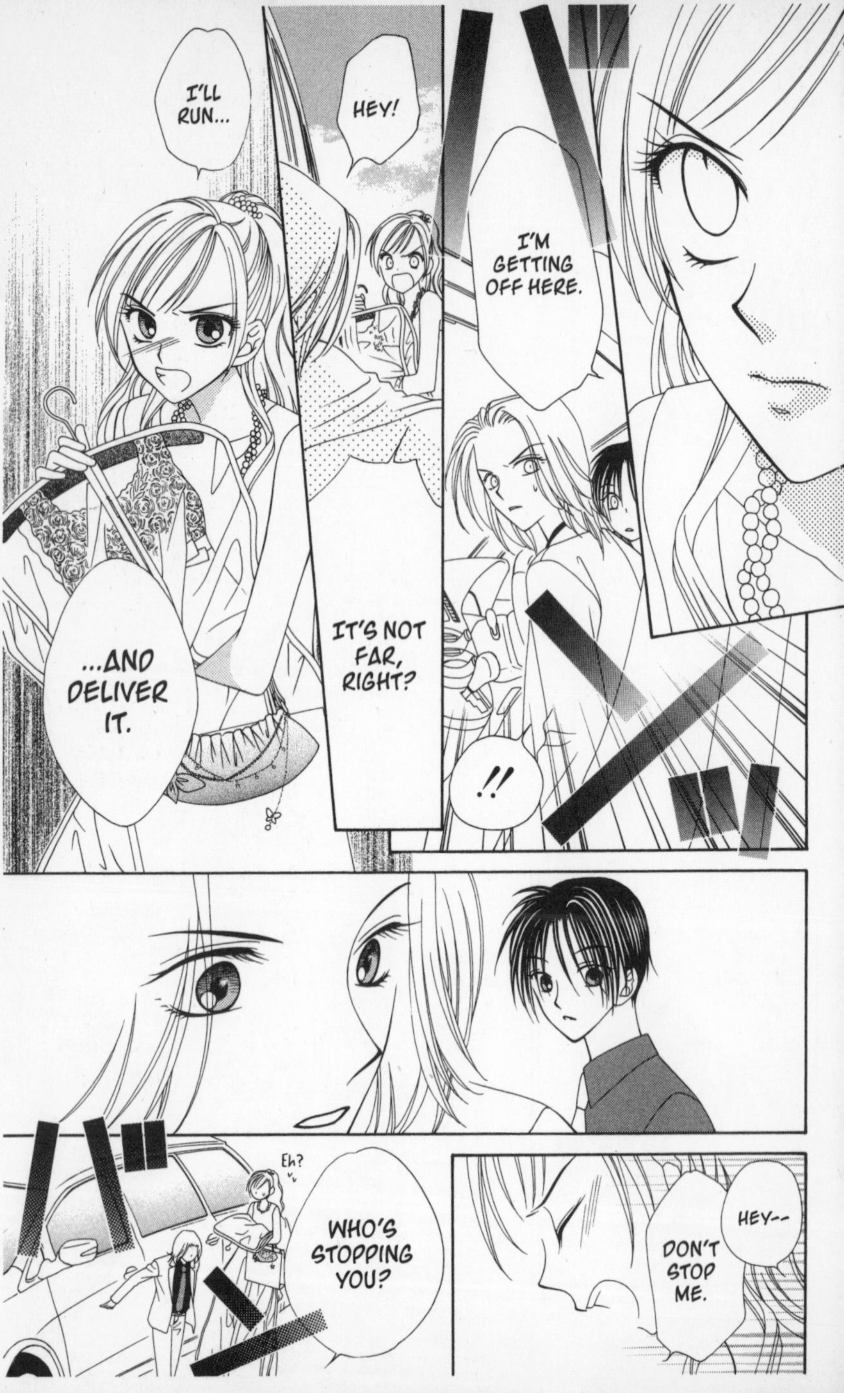
I'M GETTING OFF HERE.
!!
HEY!
IT'S NOT FAR, RIGHT?
I'LL RUN...
...AND DELIVER IT.
HEY--
DON'T STOP ME.
WHO'S STOPPING YOU?
Eh?

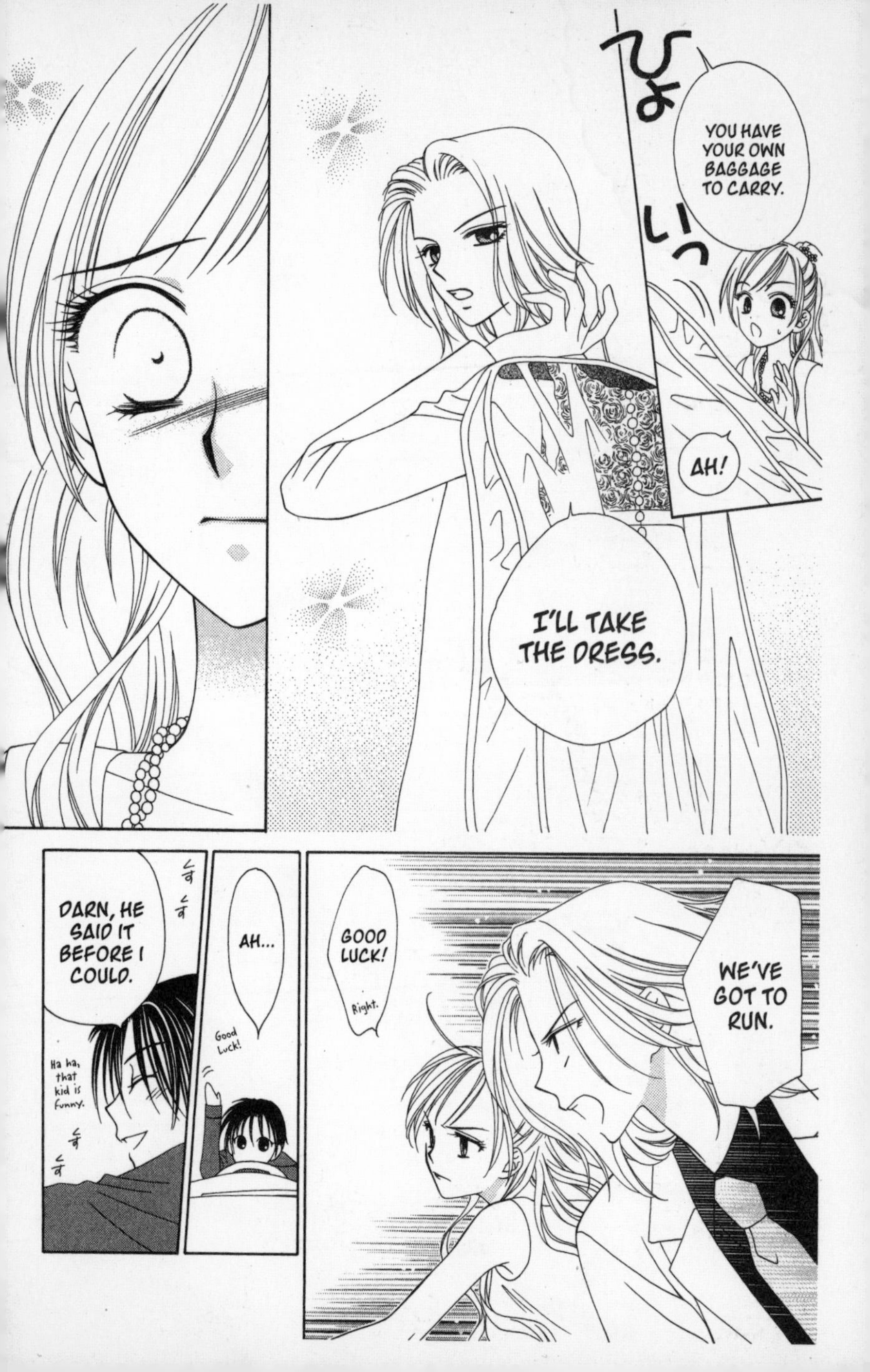

ひょいっ
YOU HAVE YOUR OWN BAGGAGE TO CARRY.
AH!
I'LL TAKE THE DRESS.
WE'VE GOT TO RUN.
GOOD LUCK!
Right.
AH...
Good Luck!
くすくす
DARN, HE SAID IT BEFORE I COULD.
Ha ha, that kid is funny.
くすくす

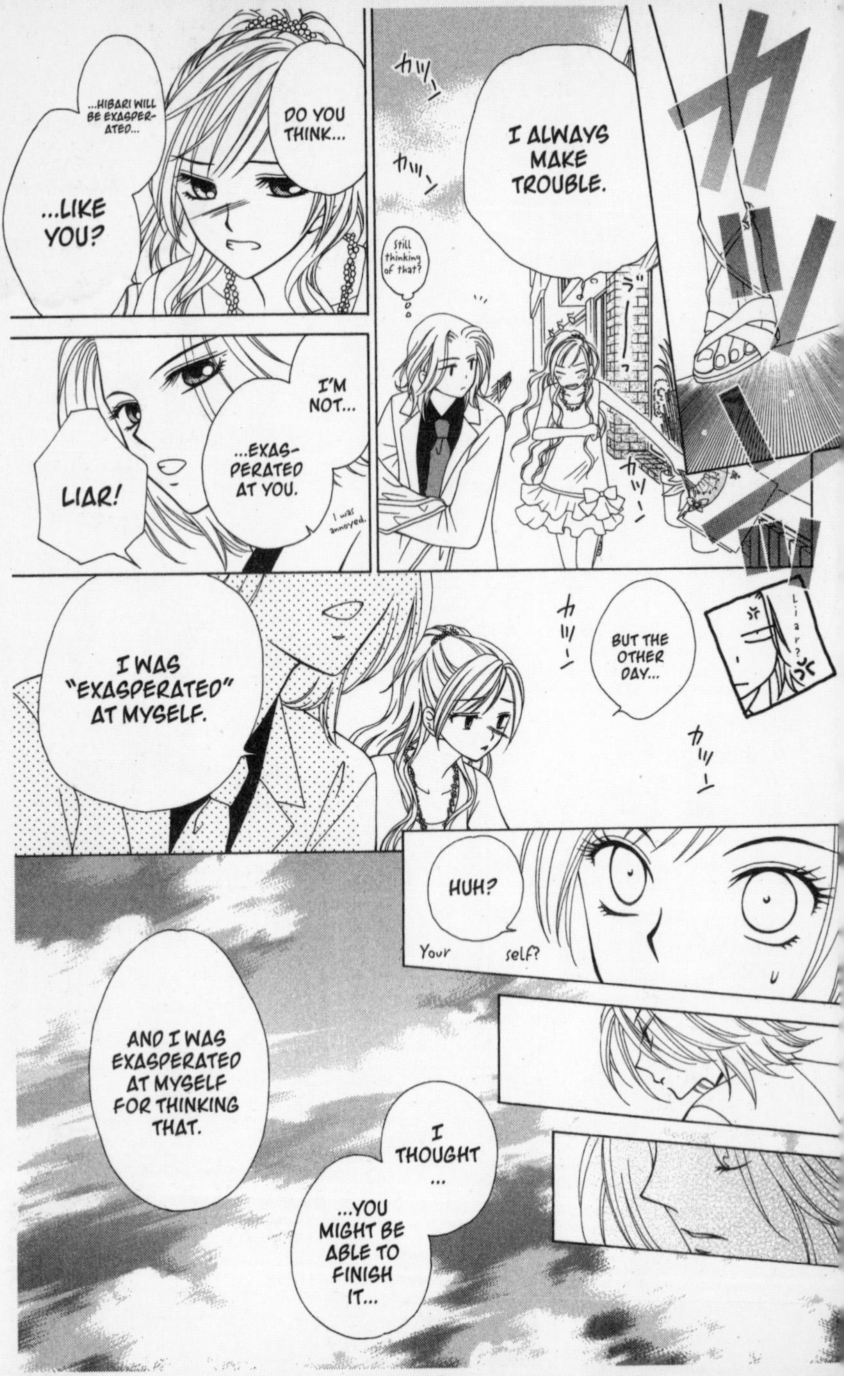
I ALWAYS MAKE TROUBLE.
Still thinking of that?
DO YOU THINK...
...HIBARI WILL BE EXASPERATED...
...LIKE YOU?
I'M NOT...
...EXASPERATED AT YOU.
I was annoyed.
LIAR!
BUT THE OTHER DAY...
Liar?
I WAS "EXASPERATED" AT MYSELF.
HUH?
Your self?
I THOUGHT ...
...YOU MIGHT BE ABLE TO FINISH IT...
AND I WAS EXASPERATED AT MYSELF FOR THINKING THAT.

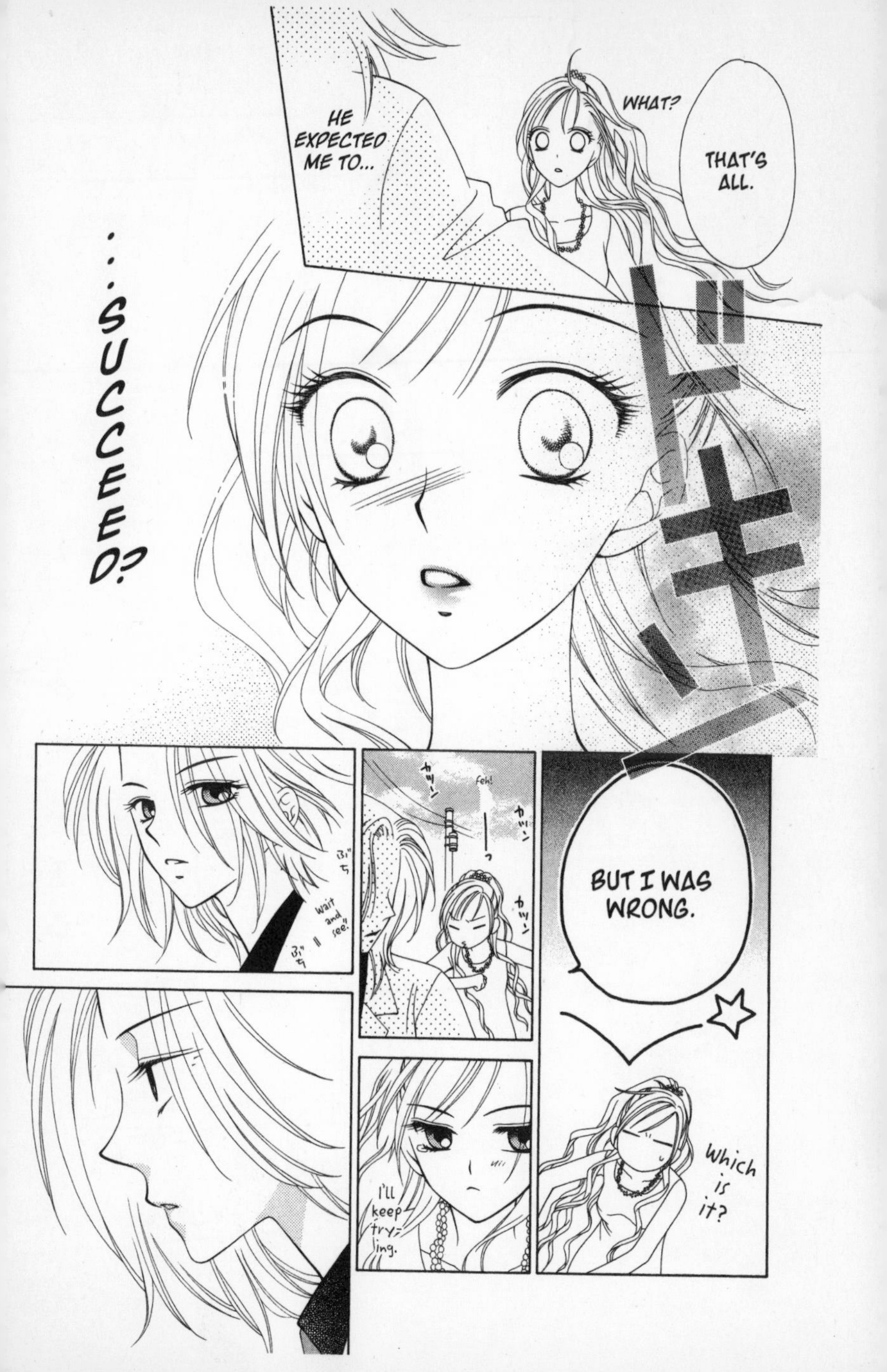
THAT'S ALL.
WHAT?
HE EXPECTED ME TO...
ドキン
...SUCCEED?
BUT I WAS WRONG.
Which is it?
カツン
feh!
カツン
I'll keep trying.
ぶち
Wait and see!!
ぶち

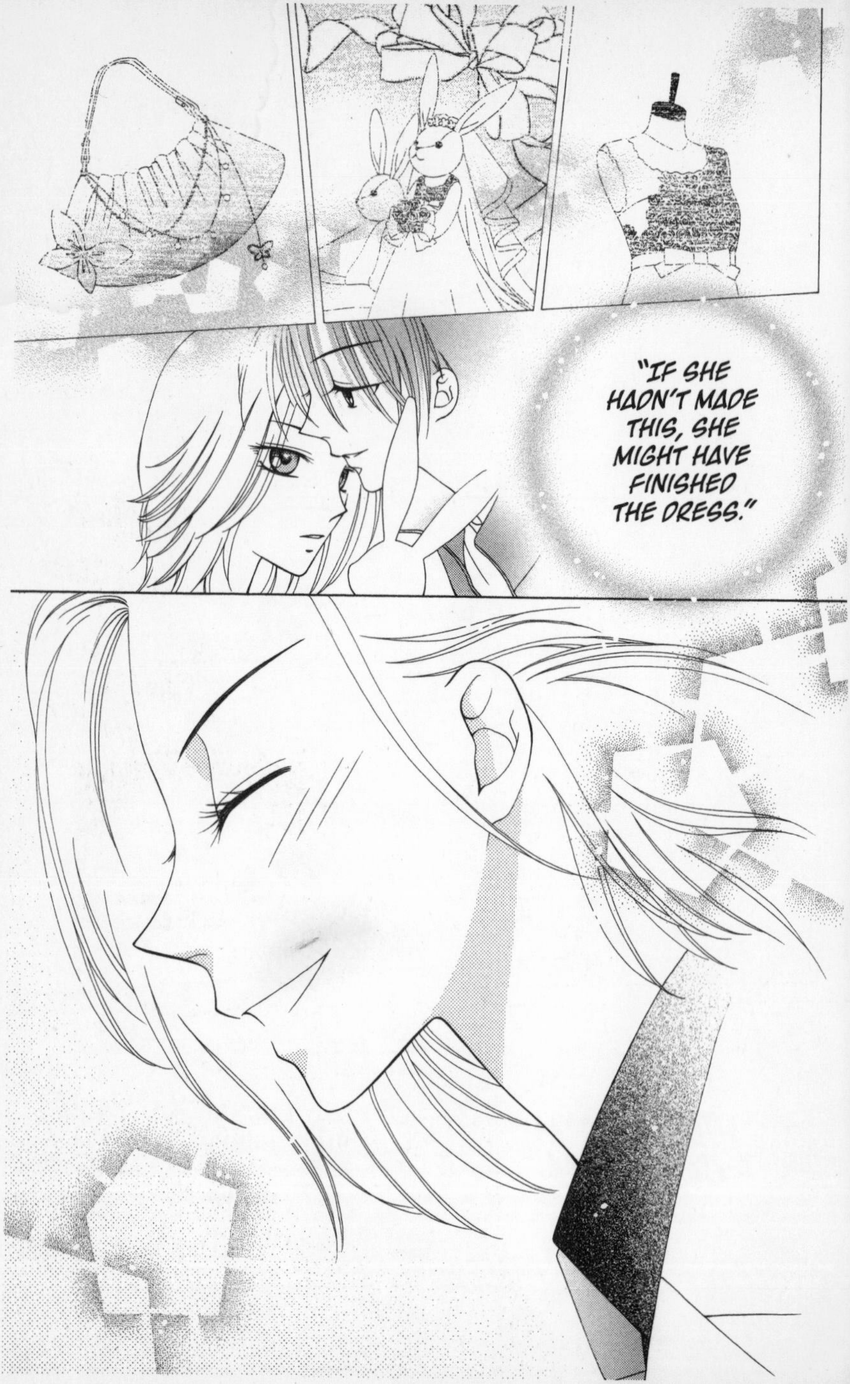
"IF SHE HADN'T MADE THIS, SHE MIGHT HAVE FINISHED THE DRESS."

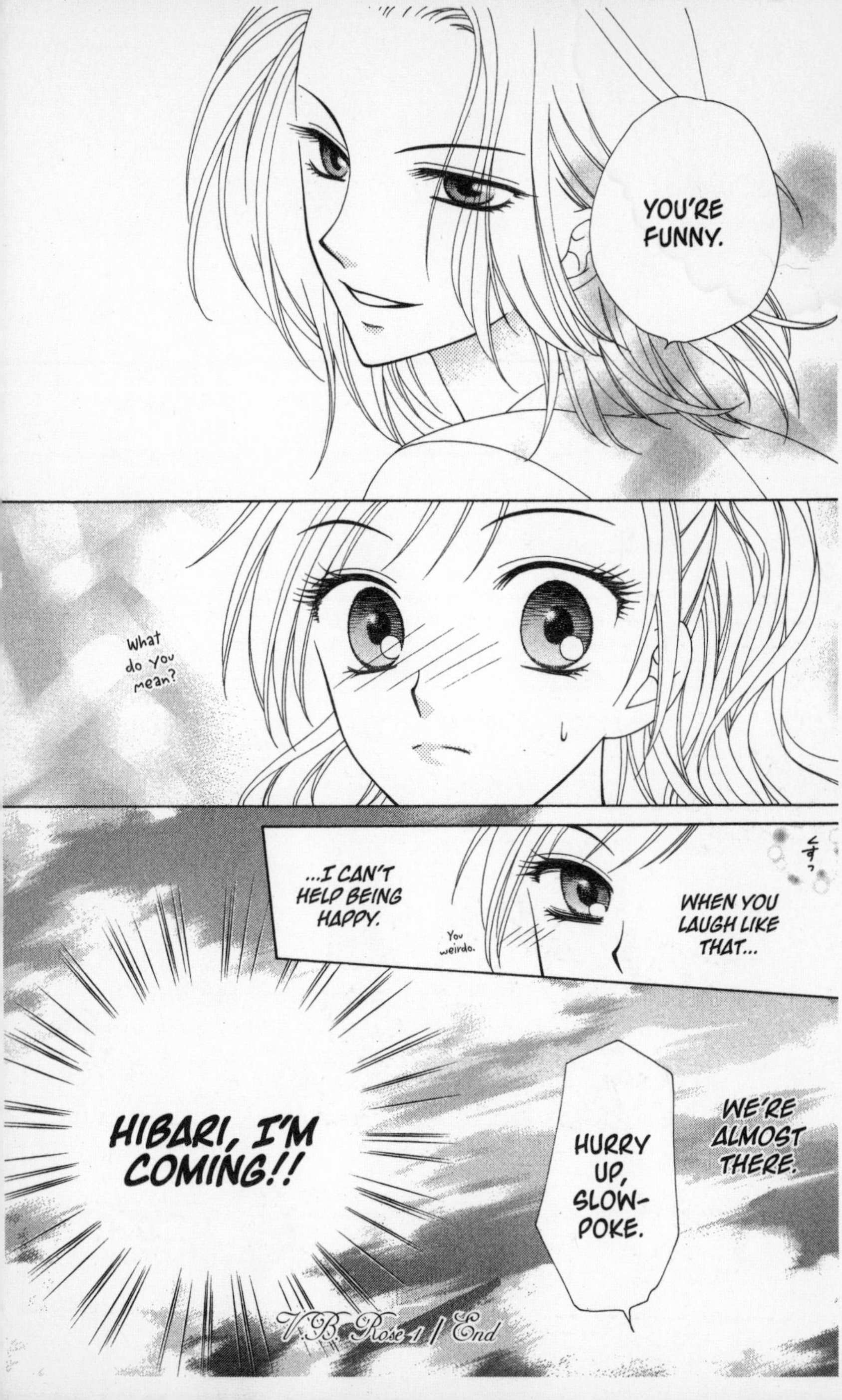
YOU'RE FUNNY.
What do you mean?
くすっ
WHEN YOU LAUGH LIKE THAT...
You weirdo.
...I CAN'T HELP BEING HAPPY.
WE'RE ALMOST THERE.
HURRY UP, SLOW-POKE.
HIBARI, I'M COMING!!
V.B. Rose 1 / End

Banri Hidaka's Everyday Heaven

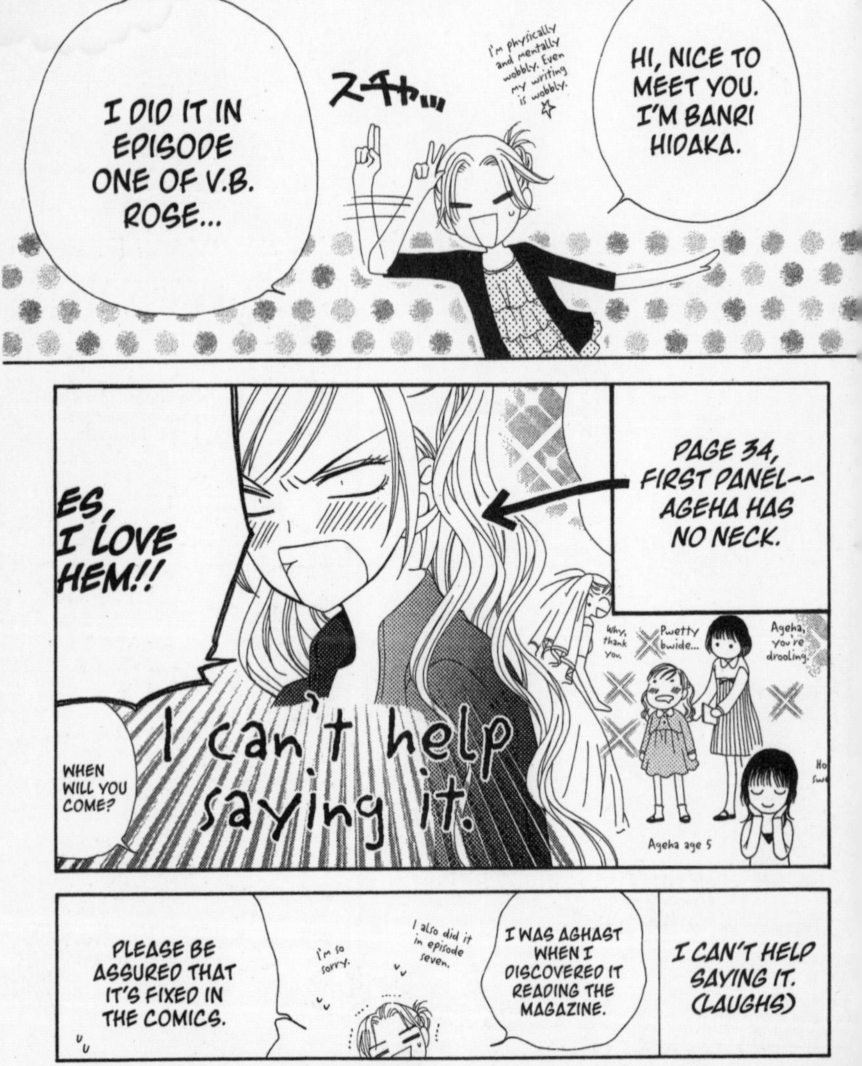
HI, NICE TO MEET YOU. I'M BANRI HIDAKA.
I'm physically and mentally wobbly. Even my writing is wobbly.
スチャッ
I DID IT IN EPISODE ONE OF V.B. ROSE...
PAGE 34, FIRST PANEL-- AGEHA HAS NO NECK.
Ageha, you're drooling.
Pwetty bwide...
Why, thank you.
Ageha age 5
ES, I LOVE HEM!!
I can't help saying it.
WHEN WILL YOU COME?
I CAN'T HELP SAYING IT. (LAUGHS)
I WAS AGHAST WHEN I DISCOVERED IT READING THE MAGAZINE.
I also did it in episode seven.
I'm so sorry.
PLEASE BE ASSURED THAT IT'S FIXED IN THE COMICS.
Too many forgotten drawings!

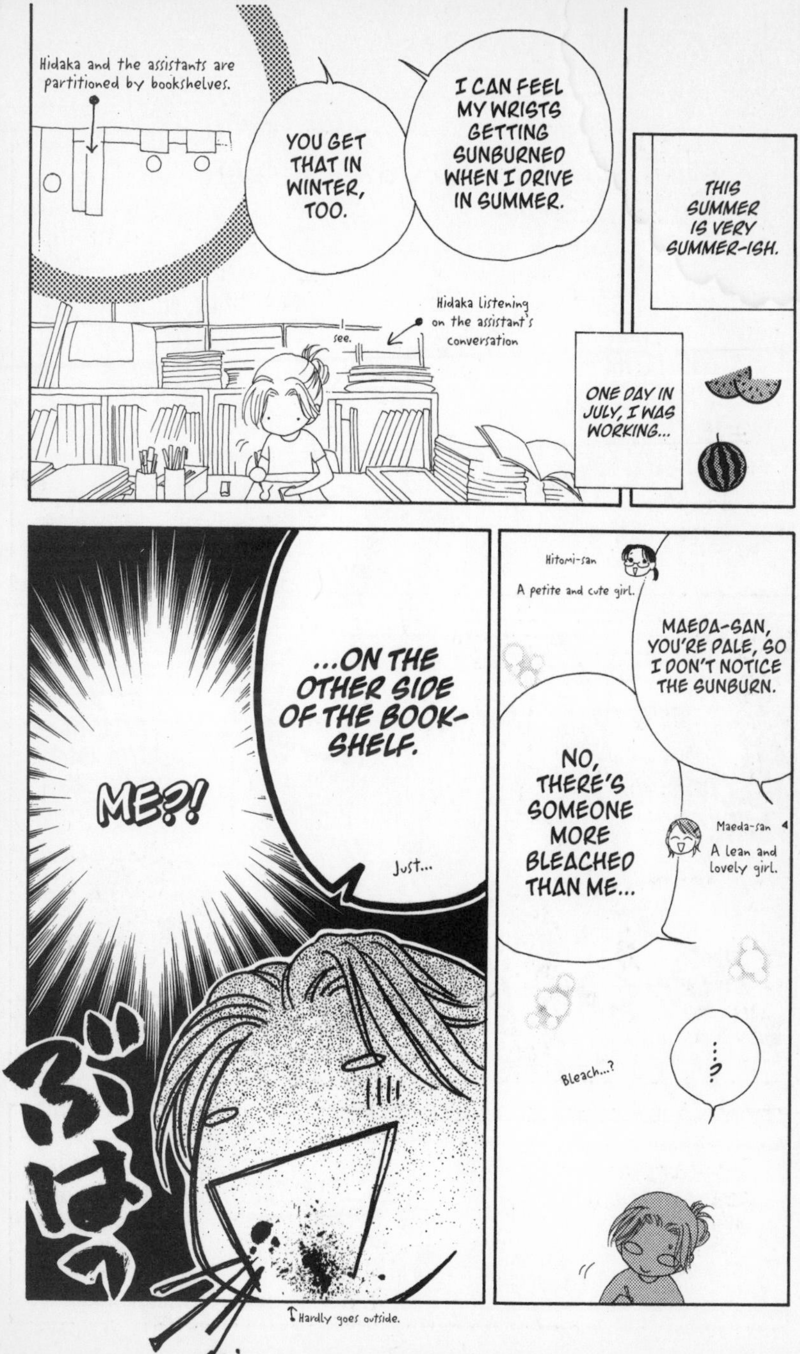
THIS SUMMER IS VERY SUMMER-ISH.
ONE DAY IN JULY, I WAS WORKING...
I CAN FEEL MY WRISTS GETTING SUNBURNED WHEN I DRIVE IN SUMMER.
YOU GET THAT IN WINTER, TOO.
Hidaka and the assistants are partitioned by bookshelves.
Hidaka listening on the assistant's conversation
I see.
Hitomi-san
A petite and cute girl.
MAEDA-SAN, YOU'RE PALE, SO I DON'T NOTICE THE SUNBURN.
NO, THERE'S SOMEONE MORE BLEACHED THAN ME...
Maeda-san
A lean and lovely girl.
Bleach...?
...?
...ON THE OTHER SIDE OF THE BOOK-SHELF.
Just...
ME?!
ぶはっ
Hardly goes outside.

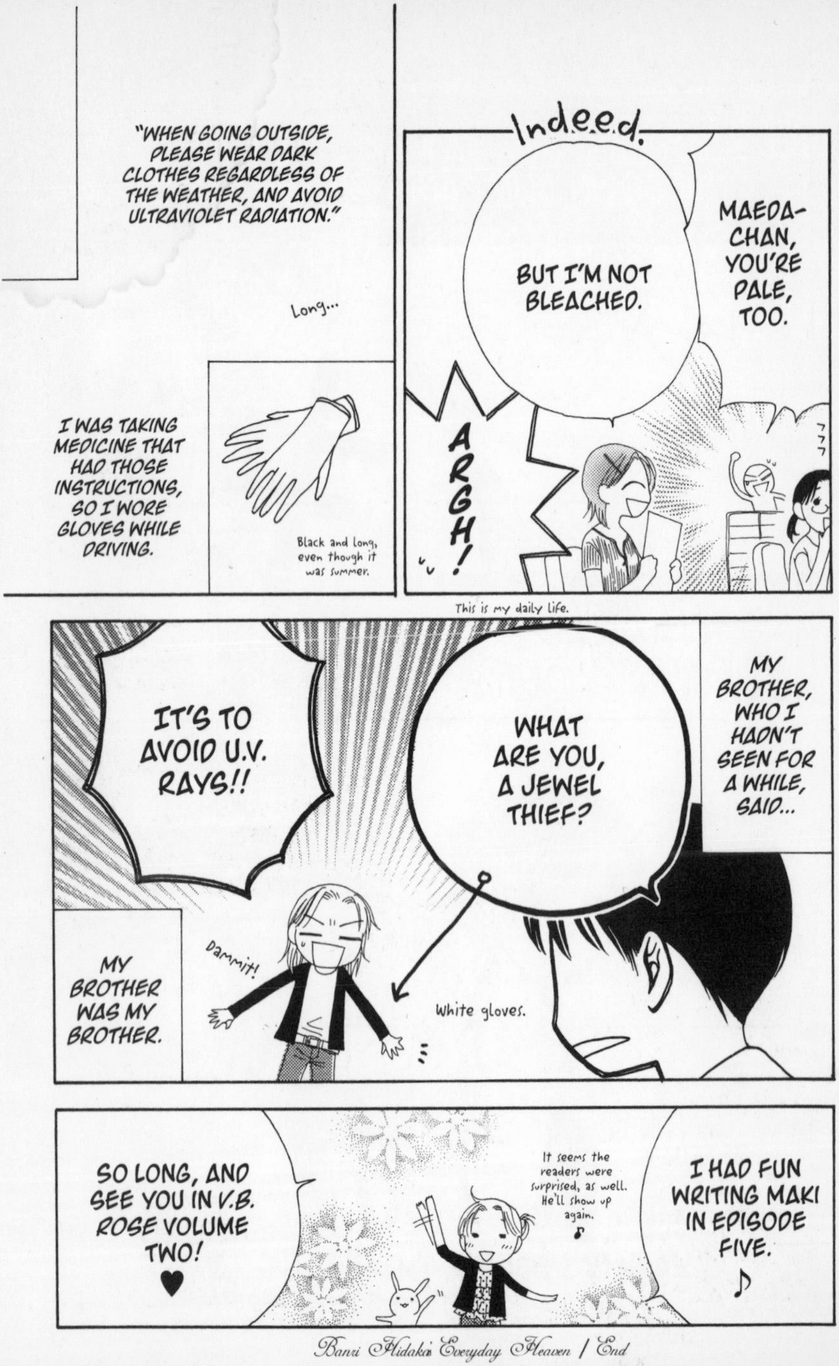
Indeed.
MAEDA-CHAN, YOU'RE PALE, TOO.
BUT I'M NOT BLEACHED.
ARGH!
"WHEN GOING OUTSIDE, PLEASE WEAR DARK CLOTHES REGARDLESS OF THE WEATHER, AND AVOID ULTRAVIOLET RADIATION."
Long...
I WAS TAKING MEDICINE THAT HAD THOSE INSTRUCTIONS, SO I WORE GLOVES WHILE DRIVING.
Black and long, even though it was summer.
This is my daily life.
MY BROTHER, WHO I HADN'T SEEN FOR A WHILE, SAID...
WHAT ARE YOU, A JEWEL THIEF?
White gloves.
IT'S TO AVOID U.V. RAYS!!
Dammit!
MY BROTHER WAS MY BROTHER.
I HAD FUN WRITING MAKI IN EPISODE FIVE. ♪
It seems the readers were surprised, as well. He'll show up again. ♪
SO LONG, AND SEE YOU IN V.B. ROSE VOLUME TWO! ♥

Banri Hidaka's Everyday Heaven / End

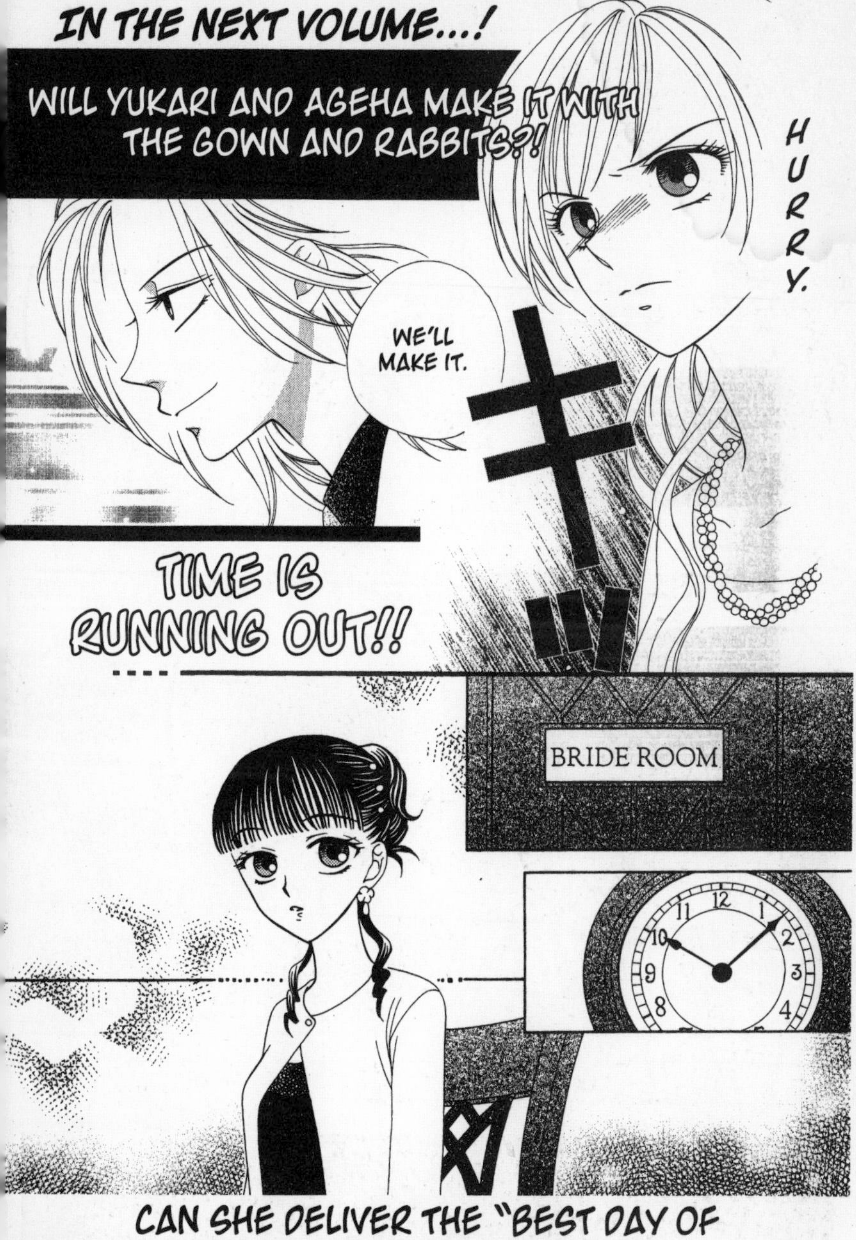
IN THE NEXT VOLUME...!
WILL YUKARI AND AGEHA MAKE IT WITH THE GOWN AND RABBITS?!
HURRY.
WE'LL MAKE IT.
TIME IS RUNNING OUT!!
BRIDE ROOM
CAN SHE DELIVER THE "BEST DAY OF HER LIFE" TO HER SISTER?!

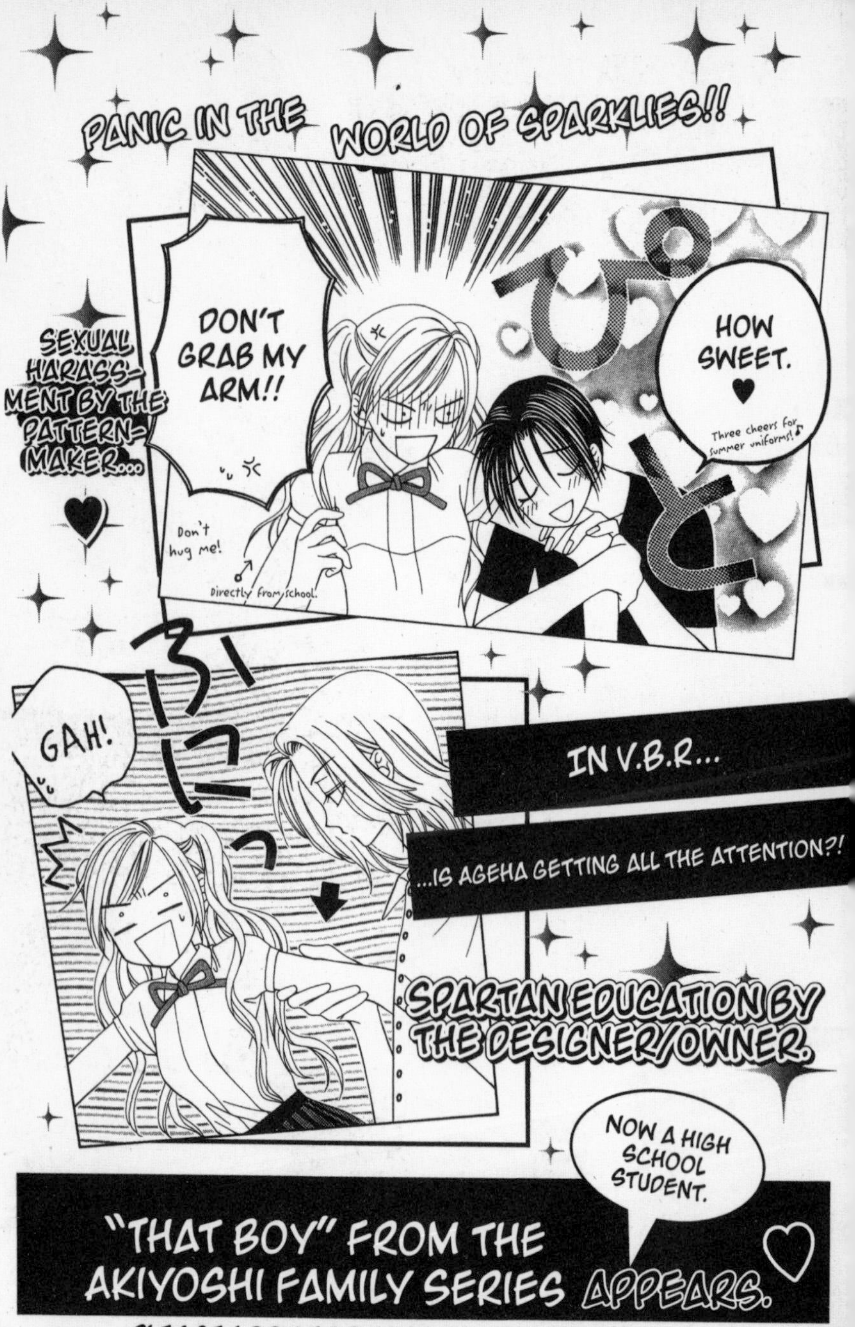
PANIC IN THE WORLD OF SPARKLIES!!
HOW SWEET. ♥
Three cheers for summer uniforms!♪
DON'T GRAB MY ARM!!
Don't hug me!
Directly from school.
SEXUAL HARASS-MENT BY THE PATTERN-MAKER... ♥
IN V.B.R...
...IS AGEHA GETTING ALL THE ATTENTION?!
GAH!
SPARTAN EDUCATION BY THE DESIGNER/OWNER.
NOW A HIGH SCHOOL STUDENT.
"THAT BOY" FROM THE AKIYOSHI FAMILY SERIES APPEARS. ♥

PLEASE LOOK FORWARD TO VOLUME 2!!

TOKYOPOP.com

WHERE MANGA LIVES!

JOIN the
TOKYOPOP community:
www.TOKYOPOP.com

COME AND PREVIEW THE
HOTTEST MANGA AROUND!

CREATE...
UPLOAD...
DOWNLOAD...
BLOG...
CHAT...
VOTE...
LIVE!!!!

WWW.TOKYOPOP.COM HAS:

- Exclusives
- News
- Contests
- Games
- Rising Stars of Manga
- iManga
- and more...

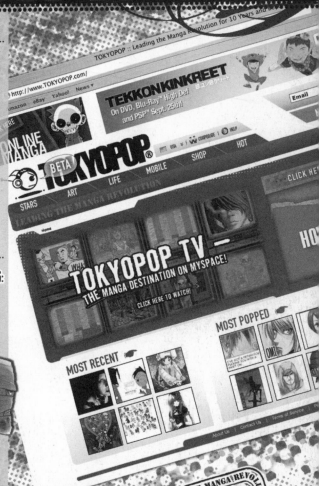

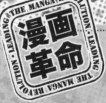

TOKYOPOP.COM 2.0
NOW LIVE!

Gyakushu! © Dan Hipp and TOKYOPOP Inc.

TOKYOPOP MANGA SUPPLEMENT

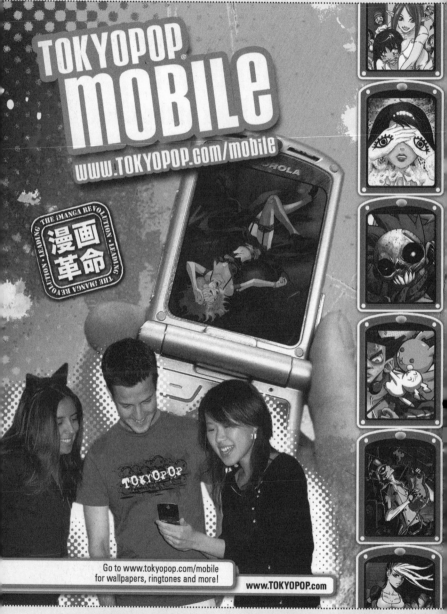

FOR MORE INFORMATION VISIT: WWW.TOKYOPOP.COM

STOP!

This is the back of the book.
You wouldn't want to spoil a great ending!

This book is printed "manga-style," in the authentic Japanese right-to-left format. Since none of the artwork has been flipped or altered, readers get to experience the story just as the creator intended. You've been asking for it, so TOKYOPOP® delivered: authentic, hot-off-the-press, and far more fun!

DIRECTIONS

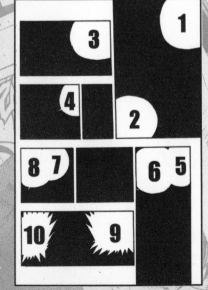

If this is your first time reading manga-style, here's a quick guide to help you understand how it works.

It's easy... just start in the top right panel and follow the numbers. Have fun, and look for more 100% authentic manga from TOKYOPOP®!

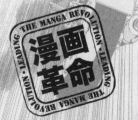

W9-CTF-700